# HAVE A GOOD WEEK... TILL NEXT WEEK

*British Wrestlers Of The TV Era*

John Lister

Copyright John Lister 2012-2018, All Rights Reserved
Cover image copyright PA Images, used under licence.

## Notes And Acknowledgements

In 2012, Fighting Spirit Magazine editor Brian Elliott suggested I write an out-of-the-ordinary piece looking at the career of Pat Roach, with a particular emphasis on his life and work outside the ring. Despite Roach being far from an obvious target for an audience of modern wrestling fans, the feedback proved so positive that Brian commissioned a regular series to be titled Greetings Grapple Fans, profiling wrestlers of the TV era.

Six years on, that series has finally come to an end and the time is right to present it as a standalone book that hopefully will serve as not only a series of profiles but a comprehensive account of a fondly-remembered period of history. By interviewing the subjects and their peers we aimed to get their insights into their careers and lives in the unique world of pro wrestling.

The text here is the copy that I submitted to the magazine rather than the published material. That means you will occasionally read content that had to be cut from the magazine for space reasons. On the other hand, it does mean the responsibility for typos and errors is entirely mine.

The content is for the most part unedited though I have corrected a few factual errors. I've chosen to present the pieces in alphabetical order rather than the order in which they were originally published, partly because the quality and style of the pieces improved as I became more comfortable and confident with the format.

In that vein, the piece on Big Daddy – the first official entry in the series – reads as overly negative in hindsight. This is largely because we were still feeling out the format and concentrated more on challenging myths than telling a life story. I trust the numerous mentions of him – both positive and negative – in the biographies of other wrestlers gives a more rounded picture.

There are a few obvious names who are not profiled in the book. For the most part, with living wrestlers at least, this is because they were either unable or unwilling to be interviewed. With Kendo Nagasaki being an obvious exception, this usually made it impractical to produce a piece with the depth for which we were aiming. I had profiled Dave Finlay before the series began but in hindsight the piece was not of the quality for which Greetings Grapple Fans strove.

As for the obvious question of why the book is not titled 'Greeting Grapple Fans', I used that title for a Kindle-exclusive compilation of articles long before I wrote for FSM and wanted to avoid any confusion. 'Have A Good Week...' seemed the most logical alternative and if anything is an appropriate way to mark the project's end.

This book would not have been possible without the help of numerous people, starting off with Brian Elliott who showed the dedication to running a series that would not necessarily have appealed to every reader or been a magazine-selling cover line, but trusted in my work to explore the subject in the depth it required.

Of course, I must also thank every wrestler, promoter and family member who took the time to speak to me, whether telling their own story or sharing their memories of former colleagues. I particularly appreciate those for whom opening up about this traditionally secretive business may not have been instinctive. I hope the finished product showed the respect that was intended.

Thanks also to Darren Ward for his efforts in raiding his extensive photo library to illustrate the original magazine articles, often finding images that even the article subjects had long since forgotten or even never seen.

I'd also like to acknowledge the help of Bradley Craig, Ron Harrison, David Franklin, Stephen Barker and the staff and members of the Wrestling Heritage website community, all of whom proved invaluable with research for specific articles. My apologies to anyone whose input I have overlooked here.

Finally, I must thank my wife Liz for many reasons, the most appropriate of which to mention here is three house moves in which she transported entire vanfuls of my wrestling-related detritus with minimal complaint. I hope this book goes someway to legitimising my claims that it was indeed vital for my work.

# CONTENTS

Adrian Street ..................................................................................... 1
Albert Wall, Gwyn Davies & The Heavyweight Title ..................... 10
Big Daddy ........................................................................................ 16
Billy Robinson ................................................................................. 22
Blackjack Mulligan .......................................................................... 31
Blondie Barratt ................................................................................ 37
Brian Dixon ..................................................................................... 43
Brian Maxine .................................................................................. 50
The British Bulldogs ...................................................................... 56
Catweazle ........................................................................................ 62
Chic Cullen ..................................................................................... 67
Chris Adams ................................................................................... 73
Colin Joynson ................................................................................. 79
Danny Collins ................................................................................. 85
Dave Taylor ..................................................................................... 91
Doc Dean ........................................................................................ 97
Drew McDonald ............................................................................ 103
George Kidd .................................................................................. 108
Giant Haystacks ............................................................................ 114
Jackie Pallo ................................................................................... 120
Jackie Turpin ................................................................................ 126
Jim Breaks .................................................................................... 132
John Cox ....................................................................................... 138
John Freemantle ........................................................................... 144
John Kenny ................................................................................... 150
John Naylor .................................................................................. 156
Johnny Kidd ................................................................................. 161
Johnny Kincaid ............................................................................. 167

| | |
|---|---|
| Johnny Saint | 173 |
| Kendo Nagasaki | 179 |
| Kid Chocolate | 186 |
| Klondyke Kate | 191 |
| Kung Fu | 197 |
| Len Ironside | 203 |
| Les Kellett | 208 |
| Mal Kirk | 214 |
| Mal Sanders | 220 |
| Mark Rocco | 226 |
| Marty Jones | 232 |
| Mel Stuart | 238 |
| Mick McManus | 244 |
| Mike Marino | 250 |
| Mitzi Mueller | 256 |
| Orig Williams | 261 |
| Pat Roach | 267 |
| Pete Roberts | 273 |
| Ray Robinson | 279 |
| Ricky Knight | 285 |
| Robbie Brookside | 291 |
| Scrubber Daly | 297 |
| Sheamus Dunleavy | 303 |
| Steve Grey | 308 |
| Tom Thumb | 314 |
| Tony St Clair | 319 |
| Tony Walsh | 326 |
| William Regal | 332 |
| FA Cup Final Day | 340 |
| The Holiday Camps | 346 |
| The Pre-TV Era | 354 |
| The Royal Albert Hall | 360 |
| The Home Nations | 366 |
| The Stampede Connection | 373 |
| Wembley Arena | 380 |
| Joint Promotions | 388 |

# ADRIAN STREET

Few people are lucky enough to have one of the most defining moments of their life captured perfectly on camera. But in the same way as Bobby Moore held the World Cup aloft, or Jimmy Snuka perched at the top of a steel cage at Madison Square Garden, Adrian Street will always have pictorial evidence of his triumphant return to the coal mine where his father worked.

The image of Street, in full make-up, glamorous robe and championship belt, contrasted with miners at the pit entrance, marked the moment he proved his father wrong, along with anyone else who doubted his potential. "They say a photo is worth a thousand words," Street told FSM. "That one was more like ten thousand, no, a million words... in fact it's still yapping today!"

Born in 1940, Street grew up in Brynmawr, a mining town of a few thousand in South Wales. His father spent most of his formative years fighting in the war and being held as a prisoner of the Japanese military. Upon his return, the paternal relationship proved troublesome, with the youngster frequently rebelling against his father's devotion to traditional religion or his expectation that Adrian would join him working in the mines.

Street showed an aptitude for physical combat from an early age, taking on everyone from classmates to fairground labourers and even a ram. In the human contests at least, he soon discovered that wrestling throws were often the key to success, despite occasionally being told by tutting adults that such tactics were unsporting in a fight.

His destiny was set the day a friend showed him a copy of a boxing and wrestling magazine, filled with images of US stars such as Don Leo Jonathan and Buddy Rogers, who soon became his idols. As he approached his 15th birthday he announced his intentions to leave school, move to London and become a professional wrestler, claims that earned him nothing but mockery given his slight stature.

Street soon began attending shows in Newport and Cardiff, once seeing lightweight George Kidd in a bout that would prove significant to his own career many years later. "He could make a cocoon out of your own body. But he wasn't everyone's cup of tea and some hecklers kept shouting 'When's the wrestling going to start.' George wouldn't respond to the chants and clearly decided he wouldn't fight, jump about or scream just because the crowd told him to. Eventually he walked out of the match."

A change in the law meant that Street would have been forced to stay on at school until the age of 16 unless he had a guaranteed job to go to. That forced him to follow his father into the pits, a job he found both miserable and recklessly dangerous. With his relationship with his father having descended into physical conflict, he gave his notice at the mine and made the move to London.

Whatever the challenges they brought, Street's early years proved formative. Having written five volumes of his autobiography to date, Street devotes the entire initial instalment, My Pink Gas Mask, to describing his time in Wales. It was a deliberate choice not to skip straight to the more marketable material.

"I figured that as an autobiography, the books are about me: I just happened to be a pro wrestler. What happens in book one is what made me. I may have made some strange choices, but the beginnings of my life is the foundation, just like you can't have a strong building without solid foundations. I was constantly told I was too young or too small to succeed, but I've come to learn that I thrive on negativity."

His early years in London were a cycle of entry level jobs, fruitless visits to the Dale Martin promotion's offices asking for a tryout, and visits to local gyms where, slowly and painfully, he improved his amateur skills. He also visited a boxing booth at a local fairground and, after successfully answering the challenge to survive three rounds with a resident boxer on several occasions, was eventually invited to join the regular crew. Here he learned how to pull his punches when boxing his colleagues, putting him in the unusual position of believing boxing could be fixed while pro wrestling was an entirely legitimate affair.

Eventually his gym time paid off and a pro wrestler got him a date on an independent show. Debuting under the name Kid Tarzan Jonathan as a tribute to Don Leo Jonathan, Street was booked to wrestle 'Gentleman' Geoff Moran. Unfortunately promoter Johnny Childs was unaware that Street had not been smartened up to the way professional wrestling operated. When Moran announced he would be taking the first fall in the third round and then taking a winning submission in the seventh, Street did not comprehend it was a booking instruction and instead assumed he was making an arrogant Muhammad Ali-style prediction of the outcome.

The bout began with several confusing minutes during which Street struggled to understand why his opponent was rolling around the ring before even receiving any punishment. Street then took a submission with a flying armbar, doing so much damage the official result was a first round stoppage win.

An angry promoter explained that the fans required at least half an hour's entertainment from a feature bout, but still the message didn't quite get through. Street was then sent to a local pro gym and told to inform trainer Johnny Kilroy that he should "teach me to die." Even with more explicit education in the ways of the professional business, it was still a slow adjustment process.

"I was a very poor learner and thick as two short planks. I had my own concept of what wrestling was about and had been dreaming about competing in it since I was 11 or 12. People told me different things about wrestling and it was very hard to get the ideas of out of my mind."

Indeed, Street maintained a physical style even as he slowly got to grips with the idea of co-operating in the ring. "I was told I was too rough by opponents who'd been wrestling for 20 years. I was so young and arrogant I'd say things like 'Take it like a man or get out of the business.'"

While it took some time to sink in, Street's debut performance taught him another valuable lesson. With Moran out for several weeks with a separated shoulder, Street was asked to take over his bookings, thus gaining financially from actions most would describe as unprofessional.

That isn't to say that Street, once fully adjusted to the realities of pro wrestling, would deliberately set out to injure an opponent (except as part of a personal dispute.) But he soon realised that for all the co-operation, the need to get yourself over meant there was a very real element of competition in matches, something his legitimate grappling skills let him take full advantage of.

"Selfishness is all important in our business. There's plenty of jealously but I don't hold personal grudges because if you did, you'd have to hold one against everyone. Yes, it takes two good wrestlers to have a good match, but there's no rule to say people have to be looking at my opponent more than me. Whatever it takes, I will get their attention!"

As he continued to pick up dates on the independent circuit, Street finally had the chance to work alongside one of his favourites from his time as a spectator. It proved a disastrous occasion.

"It was the first time I'd ever been on the same bill as George Kidd. I was working with Leon Fortuna, who was called Young Sullivan at the time, and we were so excited that after our match we ran to somewhere we could watch Kidd without even stopping to shower.

"The hall had private bath booths and after the show I was in the bath, talking loudly to Leon who was in the booth next door. I told him about the show in Cardiff where the crowd were heckling Kidd and I was having a go at them, asking 'Can you imagine how stupid some people are?'"

Street ended the discussion by explaining how the crowd had kept up their chants of "boring" to the point that they drove Kidd from the ring. Unfortunately

Street didn't know that Kidd was bathing in the booth on his other side, or that he had arrived only in time to hear the very end of the story, giving the impression Street was gleefully recalling the lack of crowd interest.

Kidd didn't bring up the issue but instead simply blanked Street upon future meetings, much to his dismay. To make things worse, Kidd eventually went so far as to refuse to appear on the same show as Street. That proved no dilemma for promoters, who simply dropped Street from the line-up on what would usually be among the most high-profile shows they ran. "I had no idea why it was happening, but that incident cost me a lot of money over the years."

Fortunately Street was able to find plenty of sideline work over the years, as diverse as posing for muscle magazines, dealing in what would now be referred to as adult toys, and even accepting commissions from other wrestlers to make metal miniature figurines of them. Later in his career he made a series of records and stumbled onto a moneyspinner when an opponent "riled him up" by breaking a disc before a match. Street made sure that at the next show a merchandise table had plenty of copies for fans to buy and break themselves, failing to realise that in attempting to anger him they were simply lining his pocket.

In 1961 his persistence finally paid off with a tryout for Dale Martin. He was asked to wrestle a man named Alan in a legitimate grappling contest and passed with flying colours. Promoter Jack Dale revealed the opponent was recent Olympian Alan Butts and raved about Street's "Lancashire turns" during the workout. Street opted to keep quiet about the fact he had no idea what such a move was and that everything he had done on the mat was "a product of pure blind panic."

Street initially found the big time world of Dale Martin and Joint Promotions confusing, particularly when he was assigned a manager, Mike Dmitri, who took 10 percent of his wages but didn't seem to offer much in return. (Dimitri, who had trained George Kidd, did eventually offer Street training in legitimate submission holds.) He was also told the Kid Tarzan Jonathan name which he'd established on the independent circuit and in muscle magazines was inadequate and that he would now be known as Adrian Stuart. As a proud Welshman that proved unappetising and he negotiated a compromise of using his real name.

As well as gathering more experience thanks to wrestling almost every night, Street began to pick up more insight into making it as a star. An encounter with Alan Colbeck taught him that he would get over by making matches competitive, regardless of his spot in the pecking order. Meanwhile a conversation with Joe Cornelius revealed that the sheer number of moves a wrestler knew was no guarantee of success. According to Cornelius, a wrestler telling a story was like a great writer who didn't need to use every word in the dictionary.

In March 1964, Street made his TV debut against Cliff Beaumont, a wrestler he'd privately dubbed "Stiff Cliff" because of the difficulty of working with him in the ring. There was little time to get frustrated however: the match came to an unscheduled end when an errant knee split Street's lip open and, with the broadcast being live, the referee was forced to stop the bout to avoid upsetting TV regulators. A philosophical Street reasoned the outcome was to his benefit as viewers would simply consider him unlucky rather than outclassed.

It wasn't the only TV bout of Street's with an unexpected outcome. In another match he was booked to lose to the little-known Idra Musa. Street suspected the booking, at Croydon, was an attempt by Dale Martin bookers to harm his standing before he returned to touring in the North for Norman Morrell. He simply informed Musa that the booking instructions had been a mistake, took a 2-1 victory, then pleaded ignorance after the affair.

As he established his name, Street began styling himself after the Buddy Rogers 'Nature Boy' gimmick, wearing increasingly distinctive coloured ring jackets and bleaching his hair. With audiences interpreting this as a sign of effeminacy rather than style, Street decided to play up to the image. Over the years his outfits morphed into a sea of rhinestones, sequins, furs, full make-up and a sexually ambiguous persona.

He also used some other creative tactics to build his standing. Dale Martin produced its own promotional posters in-house using a series of blocks, each bearing the image of a wrestler. Street discovered tight-fisted management would continue using the same blocks for years, even after wrestlers had visibly aged or changed their look, rather than pay out to make new blocks. He not only paid for a new block of himself, knowing management would be happy to use it, but intentionally used the largest available size. As a result, the matchmaker's intentions stopped being so important: sheer physical logistics meant Street would always receive prime billing on posters.

With his TV exposure, Street began working more dates for some of the Northern members of Joint Promotions. He found himself on a show in Hamilton alongside George Kidd, who was refusing to wrestle his planned opponent, a little know Belgian wrestler. Street proved the only viable replacement and made sure to take as much of the match as possible before the inevitable defeat to the national hero, sending the crowd on an emotional rollercoaster.

Kidd was not only impressed, but offered to book Street as a regular opponent, setting off a lengthy feud in which Street received some rare victories over the Scot, albeit in non-title affairs. It also led to the pair discussing their original falling out and discovering the misunderstanding.

Street also found himself part of an explosion of the tag team scene in the late 60s and early 70s. Initially wrestling with Tony Charles as the Welsh Wizards, he found greater success with Bobby Barnes as the Hell's Angels, earning main event slots in the UK and on the continent. The pairing frequently found themselves pushing the crowd heat a step too far, though Street was rarely intimidated by the threat of crowd violence.

"I was too dumb to be frightened, which was good in some respects. But I always wondered if bravery was commendable or stupid: I just don't know. Brave dogs usually end up dead. Brave soldiers usually end up dead too. But I always had such faith in myself, I'd do ridiculous things.

"The worst was probably at Liverpool Stadium. Whenever we stayed in the ring after the match, we knew that the longer we waited, the braver the crowd got. I'd usually just run out into them and open up a path like Moses parting the sea of reeds! I was not the brightest tool in the cutlery drawer..."

His life outside the ring remained just as colourful, encountering many of London's less law-abiding characters including Peter Rachmann, a notorious slum landlord who feuded with the Kray Twins. Street's personal life also had its own excitement: he returned home early one day to find his wife in bed with fellow wrestler Johnny Kincaid. Street took the opportunity to confirm that he was having his own affair with a younger woman named Linda and the foursome revised their living arrangements in a straightforward, if not exactly amicable manner.

Although Street had steadily increased his earnings as he worked his way up the cards, by 1974 he was informed there would be no further payrises. He chose to follow the example of Jackie Pallo and move back to the independent circuit where he correctly assessed he could earn bigger payoffs with fewer superstar names splitting the wage bill. Leaving Joint also made it possible for Linda to begin wrestling, working as "Native American" Blackfoot Sioux.

As part of his jump, Street even turned his hand to promoting and began working with notorious "outlaw" Orig Williams -- a man he'd previously taken to court after hearing he had been falsely advertising an Adrian Street impersonator. As partners the two had some financial successes as well as some memorable scrapes working with the likes of Dave Finlay Sr and Eddie Hamill in Belfast where it was hard to tell which was worse: the threat of sectarian violence outside the ring, or the very real need to dodge homemade knives and potatoes filled with razor blades and thrown into the ring by baying fans.

Although he eventually decided the stresses of promoting were too great compared to the pleasures of promoting, Street did gain a fresh insight from the experience. "I'd always been very anti-promoter, pro-wrestler. I was a wrestler and never wanted to be anything else. But I began to understand why promoters were the way they were. Wrestling was meant to be a man's world, but as a promoter, wrestlers often came across as back-biting, gossiping, snivelling bitches. It probably didn't help that I still acted as just the same as them, whereas most promoters were very aloof and kept guys at arm's length."

It was during his independent days that Street won the European middleweight title. Asked by a newspaper for an interview and photograph, he insisted on the shot being taken outside his hometown mine at the moment his father and colleagues returned to the surface.

"A Welsh artist later turned the photo into a painting but completely misunderstood the context. It was part of a series of mine scenes and he called it 'That's My Boy' thinking my father was looking on at me proudly. In fact he was probably looking at me and thinking 'What the hell?!'"

The photo would resurface numerous times over the years, usually portrayed as an example of the post-war collision between declining industry and popular culture. In 1998 Street agreed to it being used for the front cover of a Black Box Recorder album, though he wasn't particularly impressed with its title, England Made Me. Conceptual artist Jeremy Deller, the 2004 Turner Prize winner, saw the photograph and used it for the basis of a 30 minute documentary about Street which continues touring film festivals today.

Being a true independent contractor rather than tied to the booking calendar of Joint Promotions, Street was able to take on more overseas dates, one highlight being a Zambian tour where he dodged crocodiles in a foolhardy attempt to wade across the Victoria Falls. In 1981 he took a series of bookings in the Stampede promotion in Canada and, with the Big Daddy push in full effect, left for North America with no immediate plans to return.

Street then spent a period working in Mexico where, although his persona may have fitted neatly in the home of the exotico, he was no fan of the in-ring style. "It was not wrestling. If you want to see 10 straight minutes of acrobats, you might as well go to the circus. It was the silliest style I ever came across. There were some good wrestlers, but in the majority of cases anything resembling wrestling was purely coincidental."

He spent the rest of his career working the American regional territories, most often in the Southeast of the country. As well as working in Memphis where his outlandish gimmick was highlighted in several music videos (a popular promotional tool in the territory at that time) he visited the gritty roughneck world of Mid South Wrestling.

It might have seemed an odd fit given the local promoter's preference for ex-footballers and no-nonsense brawlers, but Street found acceptance despite his effeminate character. "Bill Watts didn't really like the gimmick, but he did like my wrestling. It didn't worry me either way: I always said I'm happy to beat somebody with a kiss or a kick! If I just had the gimmick and couldn't wrestle, I would never have got so far."

Street never wrestled for the WWF despite it being filled with larger than life characters, including Adrian Adonis being repackaged in feminine clothing and makeup in a less nuanced version of the Street character. Street says he did get an offer from McMahon and company, but not to wrestle.

"They wanted me to come in as a manager for a new team of Johnny Smith and somebody else who'd be called the Skinheads. It would have been be a racial, white supremacist kind of thing. I said no because I hate anything like that."

Indeed, Street's interest in different cultures wound up influencing his US run in a positive manner. "As a kid I was always enthralled by different races and cultures when I read books around the world. I loved Red Indians and African warriors and learned about the way that painting their faces and putting feathers in their hair made them look bigger.

"I managed to use that in my costume. When I got to the States I was only 5'7" and twelve and a half stone. I was able to build my boots up by two or three inches, but the rest of my costumes were as much about giving me size as it was my gimmick -- it just happened to fit in." And as far as the crowd reaction to elaborate feathered capes and headdresses went, "you could take it any way you like, as long as you look at me!"

Street began winding down his career in the mid-80s, wrestling mainly in Alabama before retiring to Florida where he and Linda began running a business named Bizarre Bazzar, producing wrestling gear under the SkullKrushers brand name. He worked the occasional match for local promotions over the years and made a point of wrestling in 2010 so that he could truthfully say he had performed in seven decades.

Although Street didn't get to wrestle his childhood heroes, he was able to meet some of them after moving stateside. While showering after a show in Florida he was told Buddy Rogers was waiting outside and would like to meet him. "I didn't believe it and thought it was a rib, so I said something like, 'yeah, OK, tell him to stand in line next to the Queen Mother and the Pope.' You could have knocked me down when I came out and saw he was really there! We wound up becoming friends and we even went to a rock 'n' roll show together in Greensboro along with Lou Thesz of all people!"

In 2005 Street finally met Don Leo Jonathan, at the Cauliflower Alley Club reunion in Las Vegas. The two would meet up again the very next day under unusual circumstances. "Having been with Linda since 1969, I finally decided to propose in Vegas and we had the wedding the next day as part of the reunion events. Don Leo Jonathan agreed to be my best man, while the service was conducted by Father Jason Sanderson, who used to wrestle as the Wolfman.

The wedding also offered a chance to remember Houston's Paul Boesch, who was considered one of the most honourable wrestling promoters and had died in

1989. "Paul had always offered me a place to stay if I needed it. His son Joey, who was just a boy when I met Paul, was blind but had grown up to be a great pianist and had a regular show at the Barbary Coast hotel in Vegas. He agreed to play the wedding march and then my favourite song, As Time Goes By, for the first dance.

With so many of the wrestlers attending the reunion weekend making a point of going to the wedding service, it proved a record-setting occasion. "I was told later that as far as anyone could work out, it was the most professional wrestlers ever gathered in one room at the same time."

On March 9, 2013, Street finally called time on his in-ring career. "I've been retired a year now, though I think I'm technically still the champion of Alabama. I'd always dreaded retirement like I dreaded death itself, but now it's happened and I'm 73, I'm coping with it. Since getting out of the ring I'm down 61 pounds from my peak weight, which is good news for my knees.

"I could go on about I miss this and I miss that, but really I miss the attention in a nutshell. I like performing. I know that what I do, I do as well or better than anyone else in the world.

"I'm not perfect, but the only thing that's stopping me being perfect is my modesty!"

# ALBERT WALL, GWYN DAVIES & THE HEAVYWEIGHT TITLE

For over a decade Gwyn Davies and Albert 'Rocky' Wall battled atop Britain's heavyweight division. John Lister explores their intertwined careers and the wider title scene.

Although in theory each of Britain's eight wrestling weights divisions had (in ascending order of importance) British, European and World champions, in practice that wasn't always the case. This was partly because of promotional partnerships with overseas groups with semi-consistent title lineages, but was also likely a credibility issue. While it was plausible that the British mat style would dominate the lighter weights, it would be tough to portray wrestling as a legitimate sport in which UK grapplers held every available world title.

In the heavyweight division, no serious claim to a world champion was made in Britain for much of the TV era. Meanwhile any tracking of the European crown was hazy at best and tended to be a promotional tool used more on the independent circuit. As a result, the British champion was top dog in the heavyweight division and, the likes of Mick McManus and Jackie Pallo aside, the heavy brigade generally received top billing. Colin Joynson recalls that "The heavyweights were most important and I learned my trade off them by watching them closely, particularly their timing."

Meanwhile Jon Cox recalls that banter between the weight divisions sometimes hid some real resentment about the respective payoffs. "We did one show in Trowell where the showers had a rubber button on the floor that you had to stand on to turn the water on. Albert Wall was just going out to the ring when Jimmy Breaks says, for everyone to hear, 'Don't you get embarrassed taking so long to get to the ring and then doing nothing?' Albert replied, 'Don't you get embarrassed when you stand on that button and nothing happens?"

For much of the first decade of the TV era, the British heavyweight title was dominated by Bob Robinson, better known as Billy Joyce. One of the true greats of the Wigan 'Snake Pit' and its catch-as-catch-can scene, when it came to the shows he was surprisingly something of a villain. Rather than outright rulebreaking, he took a leaf from the playbook of Dory Funk Jr by being a little too slow to break holds upon a referee's instruction, but a little too fast to attack after a break.

Joyce first beat Gordon Nelson in 1958 to capture the vacant title that had been stripped from Bert Assirati after his failing out with Joint Promotions. He is recorded as having quick exchanges with Ernie Baldwin, Dennis Mitchell and Geoff Portz over the next few years before dropping the title to Albert Wall on 20 January 1966 and kicking off a particularly eventful period for the title.

Wall had trained in his hometown of Doncaster under Johnny King before adopting a three-fold strategy to advancing his career: training in judo, lifting heavy weights (giving him a notable physique for the day) and learning the pro style at a gym run by former welterweight and middleweight title claimant Les Stent.

Despite his muscular bulk, Wall had a reputation for combining athleticism with aggression in a "no-nonsense" package and was compared by some to a larger Jon Cortez – something that's a significant compliment for many behind the scenes. Wall's signature move was particularly unlikely for a heavyweight: a diving headbutt that he did off the ropes and even at time from the top of the cornerpost.

During his career Wall took on several wrestlers who would become international names including Al Hayes, Kendo Nagasaki (who he defeated before the masked man first appeared on TV), Jean Ferre (later known as Andre the Giant), and his personal favourite opponent, the former heavyweight boxing champion Primo Carnera.

Having won the title at Nottingham, Wall returned four weeks only to drop it to Gwyn Davies on 20 February. In what became something of a pattern with the heavyweight title, it was far from a clean finish. Wall had already scored one submission and was in the process of applying an armbar to clinch the match when he "lost his footing" and fell from the ring, losing the title when he was ruled unable to continue through injury.

Davies – real name James McTiffin -- was born in 1935, only a few months removed from Wall. Although born in (and billed from) Wales, he moved to Yorkshire while still a baby as his father had been signed to play rugby league for Dewsbury. He was a third-generation wrestler with his grandfather having wrestled under a mask using names such as The Legionnaire and the African Conga, while his father worked as 'Killer' Ken Davies.

Albert Wall, Gwyn Davies & The Heavyweight Title

McTiffin originally explored a sporting career in both rugby and football, but decided to follow in the family trade. His father taught him the basics, memorably binding his hands and legs together so that he learned to take break falls (back bumps) intuitively, while further training came from the Taylor family.

With the usual practice being that sons would take a different ring name from fathers (to avoid emphasising the father's age if they were still active), McTiffin originally wrestled under his real name. However, this led to expectations, particularly in France, that he would naturally portray a Scottish character, complete with kilt. That not being to his taste, he eventually returned to the "family" name as Gwyn Davies.

Billed at 6'5", he could portray a heroic role, but also had the ability to act as a subtle villain, for example slipping from a legitimate chinlock into an illegal choke. His speciality move was "suspended fingerlock and lift": after applying a hammerlock (today's MMA Kimura) he would lift his opponent so that they appeared to be carrying their own bodyweight on the compromised limb.

Davies' initial title reign was an exact replica of Wall's: 28 days after winning, he too returned to Nottingham and lost the championship to Joyce on 17 March. Contemporary reports suggest this was carefully crafted booking that meant not only had Wall not been comprehensively defeated for the title, but had already proven he could beat the new champion.

The hot potato booking continued with Joyce holding the title for just two months before losing it on 4 May in Perth to Ian Campbell, a Scottish giant whose most high-profile bout was actually against soap opera character Stan Ogden in a 1964 edition of Coronation Street. In fact, not only is it almost certainly the most seen "wrestling match" in ITV history, but was at the time the most watched episode of Coronation Street ever, viewed in 9.44 million homes by an estimated 20.8 million viewers.

It was just a matter of weeks until the fifth and final title change of 1966 when Joyce regained the title in Edinburgh on 28 June. He then lost it for a final time to his Wigan protégé Billy Robinson on 18 January 1967, the last time a real contest determined the championship – in a manner of speaking. Robinson later wrote that Joyce (who may have known his time as heavyweight champion was drawing to a close) was only willing to lose it to him in a professional ring once Robinson could out-wrestle Joyce in a private gym contest. It's worth nothing Robinson was quick to stress said victory was more to do with Joyce's age than the pair's respective natural abilities.

While the title had bounced around and created a host of contenders, it was clear the plan was for Robinson to be the dominant figure and most debates today among fans of the era are simply about who should be ranked number two behind him. The problem was that he wasn't always around to defend the title. In particular he became one of the top stars in IWE, the number two promotion in Japan, where he was the top-billed foreigner.

He was by no means alone in IWE, which used several British heavyweights in the era including Wall, Joyce, Campbell, Jon Cox and Colin Joynson, who recalls Wall in particular adapted to the local scene well. "It was a very different style and a bit more crash, bang, wallop. Lots of Brits didn't like working with them, but they brought Albert back and we both educated the British guys as to what was expected there."

Having been as good as absent from British rings throughout 1969, Robinson's arrival in the AWA for an extended run the following year was the breaking point for Joint Promotions. "The promoters wanted the world champion regularly," explains Joynson, "so you basically had to spend most of your time here."

Recollections of fan reaction to the news of Robinson being stripped of the title are mixed, with some noting that however logical it was from both a real and storyline perspective, there was also a feeling that he had never been defeated in the ring. Others argue the subsequent decision to fill the vacancy with a single match – back in Nottingham – was the real problem. It wasn't that anyone doubted Wall's eligibility for the status, but rather than Davies would have been the 'fairest' opponent given his previous title run and victory over Wall.

Instead Wall took on Steve Veidor (a name likely taken from stevedore, a job title for a person who unloaded ships in a dock), another impressively-physiqued grappler who was well-established but arguably not yet at the very top level. In any case, Wall regained his crown with the diving headbutt and began establishing himself as the titleholder. This got off to a curious start with Wall taking several weeks away to compete in the Hamburg tournament, as well as losing to Georges Gordienko at the Royal Albert Hall in what was of course a non-title match given Gordienko's Canadian nationality. Wall later told his family that Gordienko was the greatest shooter he ever faced.

1971 was a banner year for the championship with Wall appearing on television more times than any other wrestler, taking on a who's who of the heavyweight division in Mal Kirk, Ian Campbell, Gwyn Davies, Mike Marino, Barry Douglas, Pat Roach, Steve Veidor, Count Bartelli, Tony St Clair, Bruno Elrington and Roy St Clair.

His reign was interrupted for four months, likely because he was departing for an extended tour of South Africa. Davies took temporary control of the championship, beating Wall on 18 January in Loughborough, though again it was a controversial decision. Davies engaged in rulebending tactics throughout, only for Wall to lose the match and the title by disqualification when he finally retaliated in kind. Shortly after his return he regained the belt from Davies at Belle Vue, Manchester on 5 May.

Wall made headlines of a less desirable kind the following year when the News of the World ran an expose after bugging a dressing room and recording he and Marino running through plans for the evening's match in considerably more detail than might have been expected for the style and era. Fans of the era recall the story being particularly impactful given not only Wall's air of legitimacy, but the underlying impression that even if wrestling itself might be shady, title matches were surely on the level.

Over the next few years Wall's appearances both on and off-screen gradually reduced and his last televised bout was in April 1974 against Pat Roach. The 'official' records show that he vacated the title after a temporary retirement through injury. In fact, he had decided to ply his trade on the independent circuit, including working for upstart promoter Brian Dixon, who took full advantage of his status. "I certainly billed him as British champion because nobody had beaten him. He came over the same time as Kendo Nagasaki, so they carried on their existing feud." Other promoters upgraded him to 'European champion', a more nebulous honour in that period.

Dixon believes that, money aside, Wall's main reason for making the jump was that he saw the writing on the wall with Max Crabtree taking more control of Joint Promotions in 1975 and beginning what would become the Big Daddy mega-push.

Wall retired completely several years later, which Dixon accredits to taking on work as a bailiff. "That job took over as got more involved in it. He was paid on commission and started doing very well and could work locally. He didn't go much on travelling: he was very much a family man."

Logically enough Joint Promotions decided Davies should fill what they saw as a title vacancy. This time it was a more conclusive ascendancy, beating Tibor Szakacs in the final of an eight-man tournament at Belle Vue on 15 February 1975. The highlight of his title reign was undoubtedly a televised defence the following year against Steve Veidor at the Royal Albert Hall. One of the few heavyweight title bouts of the era to survive on tape, it's a classic example of the effect of the sporting context of the presentation. What starts as an athletic contest saw a frustrated Davies turned to sneaky tactics before the bout turns into a heated brawl.

Davies's abilities notwithstanding, the days of the British heavyweight title's premier positioning were on the decline. While champions losing non-title matches to establish contenders was hardly unknown (Veidor in particular was established this way), Davies had high-profile TV defeats to Kendo Nagasaki that seemed more about building up an opponent for Big Daddy and company. He also had two bouts with Giant Haystacks, with a double disqualification followed by a DQ win for Davies that came across as a lucky escape.

On 28 May 1977, the era of Davies and his peers finally ended when he lost the title on a disqualification to Tony St Clair, a considerably smaller grappler who Max Crabtree had intentionally elevated to title to play an underdog role. While it was undeniably a serious attempt to create a new star, with St Clair up to the role, the title itself took a step down in 1979 when Joint Promotions began billing Spiros Arion as world champion to set up Wayne Bridges and John Quinn as the true heavyweight headliners. After St Clair jumped to the independents in 1982, it took three years for Joint to crown a replacement, leaving the title as good as non-existent for ITV viewers.

Davies continued wrestling until 1980 when he said farewell in a televised rematch with Veidor from Belle Vue. After retirement he worked on a family recycling business specialising in turning cardboard and paper waste into bedding for animals. He was a horse enthusiast and spent a decade as chairman of the British Show Pony Society, serving as a judge for the Horse of the Year Show.

In October 2017 he attended the Northern wrestling reunion in Leeds where he not only received a special honour but met St Clair for the first time since the night he dropped the title. Davies died two months after the event.

Following his own retirement, Albert Wall owned a bookmaker's office and a transport café. He largely left the business behind, talking little about it even to his family, never attending reunions, and only keeping in touch with a couple of former colleagues including John Cox. Wall died on New Year's Day, only a matter of days after Davies.

# BIG DADDY

As most pub quiz devotees know, Big Daddy's real name was Shirley Crabtree, leading to a common story that bullying at school toughened him up. What many don't realise is that until the mid 19th century, Shirley was a male name in the United Kingdom. In 1849 Charlotte Bronte wrote a novel of that title in which a man who hoped for a son and was so disappointed to have a daughter that he called her Shirley anyway. The book's popularity meant that Shirley became more common as a girl's name.

Ironically, Crabtree's grandmother was so fond of the book that she set her heart upon using the name, sticking to it when she had a son. Shirley Crabtree senior, whether proud of the name or simply wanting to share the embarrassment chose to pass it on to his son, who was born in Halifax on 14 November 1930,

Crabtree junior left school at 14 -- not unusual at the time for those from a non-academic background -- and began working at a mill where his job was to change bobbins of cotton. A keen swimmer and weightlifter, he followed his father by playing rugby league for Bradford Northern, though never made a first team appearance. The folklore has it that this was because his poor discipline meant there was too much risk of him being sent off. Fortunately the same can't be said of his nephew Eorl, now an England international.

Shirley also began attending a local gym alongside brother Max, and he took up wrestling, a sport that his father had also been a professional in. Crabtree junior was trained by former Bradford and Wakefield player Edwin "Sandy" Orford, who later had three bouts against perennial NWA World champion Lou Thesz during his UK tour. Crabtree debuted on 14 June 1952 at Newcastle's St James' Hall, losing to Orford by two falls to one.

Among Crabtree's initial gimmicks was "the Battling Guardsman", taken from his legitimate experience doing national service for the Coldstream Guards, the oldest army regiment still in service and best known today as part the Buckingham Palace changing of the guard ceremony. Publicity photos of the time show the unlikely sight of Crabtree wearing a wrestling leotard and a tall bearskin hat.

Other ring names used by Crabtree included "The Blonde Adonis" and "Mr Universe." Both may seem hard to believe for fans who saw his later work, but at the time Crabtree was a muscular figure who kept up his fitness working as a lifeguard on Blackpool beach.

At first Crabtree worked for various groups in the Joint Promotions alliance that dominated the business at the time and would soon tighten its stranglehold by gaining coverage on ITV. By the end of the 1950s, though, he began wrestling for brother Max's rival Twentieth Century Promotions.

The new decade brought the only titles of Crabtree's career: a British heavyweight reign and two European heavyweight titles. Neither of these championships were the "official" Mountevans championships that had been set up by a Parliamentary committee and generally controlled by Joint Promotions. Instead they were recognised by the British Wrestling Federation, in effect a fictional entity created by independent promoters to allow notorious hardman Bert Assirati to continue claiming the crown after his tough in-ring style and refusal to lose to "lesser" opponents saw him leave Joint rings. Similar problems on the independent scene saw the BWF title vacated (with promoters claiming an injury to Assirati) and the title wound up around Crabtree's waist.

What happened next has been grossly oversimplified and misreported, particularly in Crabtree's obituaries. The story goes that Assirati chased Crabtree out of the business and he was then unemployed for anywhere between seven and 15 years before brother Max brought him back as Big Daddy.

It's certainly appears true that a disgruntled Assirati stepped out of the crowd and challenged Daddy at least one show, something he'd previously attempted to do to Thesz at the Royal Albert Hall. Whether this really did turn into a sustained campaign of harassment is more questionable and may well be the type of exaggeration common in wrestling folklore.

What is certain is that Crabtree's absence from the business was nowhere near as significant as claimed. He returned to Joint Promotions in 1962 (after Max began working in co-operation with the group and sharing talent) and wrestled regularly until at least 1968. Now aged 38, he wound down his schedule, but appears to have made occasional appearances in Blackpool where the family reportedly promoted wrestling in discos and nightclubs, the shows often opened by musical performers such as Donovan.

Crabtree returned to the national stage in 1972, though it was under his own name and for Norman Morrell of Joint Promotions rather than for Max. He debuted on television in September and was booked on a win streak, defeating most opponents by knockout within a couple of rounds. The push concluded in a battle with fellow leading heavyweight villain Kendo Nagasaki in January 1973, with the masked man winning by knockout.

1975 saw Max Crabtree asked to take over the work of Joint's northern promoters as they eased into retirement. Around this time Crabtree began using the Big Daddy name on television, taking it from a character in the play Cat on a Hot Tin Roof. The Daddy character initially debuted on TV as the partner of Giant Haystacks and was officially a ring villain for the next couple of years.

Despite this heel status, Crabtree continued feuding with Nagasaki, including a December 1975 TV match in which he tore off his mask mid-match, though his celebration left him prey to what would be his last ever televised pinfall loss. Somewhat amazingly now that Daddy was being billed at an increasingly flabby 336 pounds (24 stone), the pair even engaged on a series of ladder matches around the country.

In 1977 Max took control of Dale Martin, the southern arm of Joint Promotions, making him clearly the most powerful man in the business. Perhaps not coincidentally, this was the year the Daddy character as we know it was born. At venues around the country he gradually switched from fighting heroes to battling villains, with the Haystacks split becoming official at the end of the year when the pair were scheduled to meet in a tournament final, but Haystacks simply walked out for the countout loss.

Daddy now took on a full-fledged hero image. Though there's an oft-cited story that his initial leotard was made by wife Eunice from a chintz sofa cover, he soon switched to a red, white and blue combo, along with a glitter-covered top hat. It's no coincidence that this resembled John Bull, a fictional character dating back to 18th century illustrations and designed to be the personification of Britishness. Daddy also became among the first British wrestlers to have his own ring music, the American folk song We Shall Not Be Moved.

Speaking in 1988, Daddy explained the thinking behind the character, and his brand of wrestling in particular: "There's a magic to it, it's very, very basic. It goes back to even the youngest childhood of Cowboys and Indians, and in our lives we never grow out of that. As long as there's a good baddy and a good goodie, there'll always be business."

Despite his portrayal as the ultimate blue eye and a friend to children everywhere, there are many accounts of Crabtree being less beloved backstage. A typical comment comes in Tommy "Dynamite Kid" Billington's autobiography where he recalls "You'd walk in the dressing room, he'd shake your hand and smile and say 'Eeee, Dynamite, it's good to see you.' And then, as soon as you'd walk out, he'd turn round to the other wrestlers and say 'Nothin' but a bastard.' I know, because I saw him say the same to everybody."

Of course, it's hardly unknown for somebody in the wrestling business to snipe about other's behind their back, but the two-faced allegations even spread to Daddy's supposed love of children. Several long-time fans back up the account given by Tony Walsh in his book "Minding My Own Business":

"I can't count how many times he made speedy exists from venues, leaving us to explain to hundreds of fans waiting outside for promised autographs and meetings that he'd had to leave and was sorry. More than once I've been faced with a little kid holding a poster and sobbing his heart out as his dad had told me Big Daddy had promised to sign it later."

On television however, Daddy remained a firm favourite, feuding first with Haystacks and then with Canadian "Mighty" John Quinn, who had marked an early TV appearance by grabbing the microphone and accusing the British of cowardice during the second world war. Such promos were rare enough in televised British wrestling, but the content firmly established Quinn as the leading villain, leading to what appeared to be a sellout crowd at Wembley Arena in 1979, with prices double that charged at the regular Royal Albert Hall shows. (This may have been a British attendance record, though there are unconfirmed reports of a 16,000 crowd at White Hart Lane in the post-war period.)

Such an event was a rarity, with promoters historically having concentrated on running regular events at smaller halls around the country, with virtually every town of any size getting a visit at least once a month and dozens of venues getting weekly shows. The idea of building to a single major event had seemed as unlikely as building the business around one performer -- two unwritten rules that were now being broken.

It's lucky the show had a strong supporting bill with matches including Steve Grey vs Jim Breaks and Marty Jones vs Pete Roberts, because the main event certainly wasn't value for money: contested under what Americans would call last man standing rules, it consisted of nothing but bodychecks, forearms and bodyslams, before Daddy took the win in a mere one minute and forty seconds with a back-body drop.

Despite his brief destruction, Quinn had a renewed push the following year, taking the "world heavyweight title" from Wayne Bridges via blood stoppage on the traditional FA Cup Final day show. Daddy crashed the celebration to set up a tag match at Wembley Arena where he and Bridges faced Quinn and Masa Fuji. Despite the villains losing in straight falls, it appears the plan was for Quinn and Daddy to have a rematch at the same venue on the August bank holiday; this was scuppered when Quinn jumped to rival promotion All Star Wrestling, complete with the title.

In 1981 it was Haystacks' turn to challenge Daddy in what would be the last of the Wembley Arena bouts. Again a knockout-to-win affair, the action was equally unimpressive, with Daddy getting the predictable KO at the 2:50 mark.

By this stage Daddy -- now turning 50 -- was almost exclusively a tag team wrestler, with his partner usually doing most of the work. This athletically-demanding role was performed by dozens of young grapplers including Davey Boy

Smith, Dynamite Kid, Bret Hart, Sammy Lee (later Tiger Mask) and Kwik Kick Lee (Akira Maeda.) It's hard to overstate just how pitiful Daddy's in-ring contributions became as the 80s rolled on, eventually reaching the stage where he would barely move during his brief spells in the ring, with opponents literally running towards him and bouncing off his belly.

This didn't stop Daddy becoming a genuine cultural icon thanks to his TV exposure. He was the subject of a weekly strip in the Buster comic, got a natural gig endorsing Daddies Ketchup and Brown sauce, and was a regular on Saturday morning show TISWAS. He was even lined up for his own spin-off, "The Big Daddy Saturday Morning Show" with co-host Isla St Clair, scheduled to start in October 1982.

Why the show never went ahead depends which story you believe: either Daddy withdrew through ill-health, his schedule made committing to a regular timeslot impossible, or he proved too nervous in front the camera during the shooting of a pilot. When it went on air, the show was simply renamed "The Saturday Show", with hastily rejigged opening titles, and Daddy's slot taken by future wrestling radio show host Tommy Boyd.

While Haystacks is remembered as Daddy's most frequent opponent, that honour actually belongs to Tony Walsh, who remembered in his autobiography that: "I was more than prepared to allow Big Daddy and his 24 stones of blubber to flop on me five nights a week. I'd let him do things to me in the ring that were not so much dangerous as bloody lethal. I know for a fact that no other wrestler would or could have done what I did. I made that man look like a million dollars."

Walsh performed this miracle at least 637 times in singles and tag matches according to an extensive record collecting by the British Wrestling Archive website. And whereas Haystacks eked out the occasional disqualification win, Walsh tasted 637 defeats. However, he was to gain revenge in a very real sense in 1985.

After the death of his younger sister in a road accident, Walsh was enraged to receive no messages of support from the Crabtree family, with the only communication being a phone call from Max enquiring as to when he would return to the Daddy roadshow. It was the last straw for a bitter Walsh, who took part in a tell-all series with the Sun, revealing that his matches with Daddy had been a sham. Crabtree convinced few with his retort that "This man's allegations are total nonsense. None of my fights are fixed. I've spent a lifetime helping kids and they love me." Walsh recalls Daddy even issued a public challenge to fight him for real at Crystal Palace, though perhaps wisely Crabtree quietly withdrew from the bout.

Another death two years later saw Daddy's public image take a hit. During a match at Great Yarmouth, Daddy hit his trademark splash to pin Malcolm "King

Kong" Kirk, but this time Kirk didn't get up from the fall: he was carried unconscious from the ring by eight men and declared dead from a heart attack in hospital.

The incident attracted worldwide attention, with the British Medical Association suggesting there might be a need for an upper age limit for wrestlers (Kirk was 51 when he died.) Daddy not only stuck to the line that wrestling was a legitimate contest, leading to police enquiries (though no further action was taken), but he wrestled the next night claiming that it was what Kirk would have wanted.

That view was challenged by Kirk's widow Ilona, who told newspapers of her husband's pitiful payoffs and insisted: "Big Daddy has only one thing in mind: himself. He's using my husband's death for publicity stunts. I don't blame him for Malcolm's death, but what he did was all publicity."

Crabtree's own obituaries claimed he was so distraught at the death that he retired from the ring. In fact, he continued wrestling for another six years, long after wrestling was taken off ITV. His career wound down after suffering stroke-like symptoms and his last recorded match came on 29 December 1993 in Margate teaming with Tony Stewart against the masked Undertakers. After several years of ill health, Crabtree died on 2 December 1997 after suffering a stroke.

# BILLY ROBINSON

When the British wrestling community met near Leeds on March 9th this year for its latest reunion, the plan was for retired and veteran wrestlers to elect the first three members of a new Hall of Fame in association with FSM.

Instead those on hand unanimously agreed that one man should earn the honour of being the initial inductee: Billy Robinson, whose death at the age of 75 had been announced just six days earlier.

Robinson was a man whose reputation straddled the worlds of amateur and professional wrestling and mixed martial arts. It would be hard to find anyone who has grappled for sport or a living that knew Robinson and did not respect him. The source of that respect varied from person to person, stemming from fear, admiration and gratitude, but it was respect nonetheless.

Born in 1938, Robinson grew up in Failsworth, Manchester in a fighting family. His great-great-grandfather had been a bare-knuckle fighter, while both his father and uncle had been involved in boxing and wrestling. Billy had begun training in boxing, only to suffer a torn retina when hit by a flying Coca-Cola sign thrown by a child. The injury put paid to his hopes of being licensed to turn pro and instead he turned to the grappling game.

Billy had already learned some basic moves from his father after being bullied by older children, but now decided he wanted to wrestle for a living. His father, a former wrestling promoter himself, advised him that although he could get an amateur grounding at a local YMCA (where he spent four years) there was only one place to go to complete his training: Riley's Gym in Wigan.

"Spartan" and "ramshackle" are terms often mentioned in descriptions of the gym and surviving video footage shows they are, if anything, an understatement. Riley had built the gym on small piece of land behind some terraced houses and every expense was spared. The building was nothing more than timber and corrugated iron, with the facilities consisting of a mat with little padding, a few chairs and nothing else. There was no toilet or shower and the primitive heating was more likely to bring scalding than comfort.

With children and women barred, the gym was no leisure destination. Instead it was a place for men to learn a very particular style of competitive wrestling, known as catch-as-catch can or Lancashire catch. Developed partly through Lancashire sailors travelling the world and picking up local combat techniques, it had emerged as a pastime for miners in the area to engage in competition and provide something for people to wager on.

The precise rules of each catch wrestling bout would be negotiated by the participants before the contest, but the basic principles were remarkably similar to those portrayed in pro wrestling. Competing usually for the best of three falls over a one-hour time limit, wrestlers could not use a closed fist but could use most grappling techniques to win by pinfall (for a three count) or submission.

While the two goals might seem contradictory in a genuine combat situation, Robinson discovered that allowing the possibility of a pinfall actually increased the likelihood of a submission. A man trying to lift his shoulders from the mat would usually either turn or bridge, leaving multiple limbs and joints exposed for a "hook" that would risk a submission.

According to Robinson, who wound up spending several years training in Wigan, Riley's most important lesson was the ability to learn. The key was not just how to do a hold, but why it worked, paying particular attention to the human anatomy's strengths and weaknesses and the way to get maximum efficiency from every movement.

While Riley, who would attend training sessions in a three-piece suit and trilby hat, was the undisputed master of the gym, Robinson had others to learn from in Wigan. His trainers included future pro wrestlers Bob Robinson (no relation) and John Foley, who would later wind up in Calgary as heel manager JR Foley. According to Robinson, Foley had the highest pain threshold of any wrestler he ever faced.

Robinson also caught the tail end of a lengthy residency by Karl Gotch, a Belgian who had wrestled in the 1948 Olympics. Quickly beaten by most on hand on his first visit to Wigan, Gotch had stayed for several years, becoming almost obsessed with learning every element of the style in the gym that he dubbed "the Snake Pit." By the mid-50s he'd developed to the point that one sparring session left Robinson unable to work for three days.

Despite the emphasis on submissions, Robinson still learned valuable skills in amateur wrestling where such dangerous holds were barred. He won the British championship in the light-heavyweight division in April 1957 at the Royal Albert Hall and also performed well in European championships.

It led to a memorable moment when Riley suggested Robinson take him out for a steak dinner, something that proved impossible thanks to Robinson's lack of funds. As Robinson noted in his autobiography Physical Chess, Riley replied "It just goes to show you, kid. You can't buy steaks with medals. It's time you turned pro."

Initially using the name Bill Kenton, Robinson made his debut in professional wrestling against Francis Sullivan on 14 October 1957. His legitimate skills appealed to promoters and within three years he had begun to appear on television. A year after that he returned to the Royal Albert Hall win the venue's annual heavyweight tournament (a British forerunner to WWE's King of the Ring event).

The building also played host to two more memorable outings for Robinson. In May 1963 he drew with Ian Campbell on a show attended by Prince Philip, while in June 1967 he beat Tibor Szakacs in a co-main event alongside Mick McManus and Jackie Pallo in what Dale Martin billed as "Wrestling's Night of the Year."

During this time Robinson had begun training amateur wrestlers. Of these three later turned pro themselves: his cousin Jack Robinson, Marty Jones and Johnny Saint. It's these three men who formally accepted Robinson's award for being inducted into the Leeds Reunion/FSM Hall of Fame.

Jones recalls that nothing he learned in Robinson's gym related to showbusiness. "He's never teach pro wrestling in an amateur gym. You'd never even talk the pro game in an amateur gym or you'd get your head screwed off! Even when pros like George Gordienko or John Cox came to visit, it was purely for amateur stuff."

Saint met Robinson by chance after Billy's mother opened a hairdresser in his street and began talking to Saint's mother. Saint originally planned to train as a boxer and sparred with Robinson, earning his respect for giving his best despite being a lightweight. "Billy was 6'2" and 15 stone and pretty much reeled me off the walls. But because I tried, he'd praise me and say, 'You caught me a good one there, John.'"

It was a similar story when Saint turned to wrestling training. "If you cowered, he wouldn't respect you. But if you got stuck in and tried, he respected you. When you got to the gym, you knew what you were there for, to be in their spirit, to be competitive. Billy always had a knack for moves. He said there was only two ways to do a move: the right way or the wrong way, to make it easier or harder for yourself."

Jones also noted that Robinson practiced the same commitment he expected from his students. "One time he broke his leg and came to the gym with it in a cast. But he was still skipping when we did skipping training: now that's dedicated!"

Both men point out that Robinson helped their pro careers in ways that went beyond simply learning to grappler. "I owe him everything," says Jones. "In Japan you just had to mention his name and you were in straight away."

Saint concurs. "When you went into the pro job, you'd notice all these big outlandish guys with long hair. But an average-looking, ordinary guy like myself could walk into any hall and say, 'I'm from Billy Robinson's gym" and you instantly had pedigree and people knew you could look after yourself."

Robinson was now firmly established on the small screen. In 1967 he had 11 televised matches, as many as top star (and booker) McManus, including an appearance on the prestigious FA Cup Final Day show.

Among his most frequent opponents were good friends Geoff Portz (who became godfather to Billy's son Spencer) and Dennis Mitchell, along with Albert 'Rocky' Wall. As Adrian Street told FSM, on one occasion at least Robinson and Wall were certainly not on friendly terms.

"Albert was a great performer, a hell of a performer, but as far as a shooter goes he was not at the same standard as Billy Robinson. A green MC who didn't know what else to say got carried away with himself and turned round and said 'In this corner, Rocky Albert Wall, the number one British contender.' They would have had a good match if he hadn't have said that.

"But Billy went after poor Albert because he was going to show the world who the number one contender was. It was a massacre, it was awful. Then back in the dressing room, Albert said 'Billy, what the hell was all that about?' So Billy smacked him right across the face, knocking him across the dressing room. There was a lot of bad language involved. That's the way Billy was."

Jim Breaks recalls that Robinson had a severe reputation behind the scenes. "He always looked well, put a good show on, and he could do the job. But he was not right easy to get on with and was a bit nasty out of the ring.

"The big lads who went on with him had to be careful. If they did 'owt wrong, he'd probably give them a good hiding. People who were billed against Billy, they did what Billy said."

Jake Shannon, who worked with Robinson over the past seven years to revive the catch wrestling style under the brand name Scientific Wrestling, believes that although Robinson didn't particularly love the idea of working with an opponent to produce an entertaining bout, neither did he resent it. "It wasn't his preference, not his cup of tea, but there was no other venue for his skills. He believed that if you are a wrestler, probably at a minimum -- even if it's a work -- you should know how to wrestle. Some people who came into wrestling as performers were scared of the guy."

Saint notes that Robinson was able to successfully adapt because, even though pro wrestlers worked together, "he was certainly controlling the matches. The business is about bums on seats. Unless people understand or are fans of it, the amateur style can be boring."

Indeed, while Robinson was frequently praised for his tight, believable ring style, he was willing to modify legitimate holds to make them more visually appealing to viewers watching on television or from the back of a hall. Among his signature moves were an over-the-knee backbreaker, a reverse neckbreaker which would later become Rick Rude's Rude Awakening, and a move also used by Jackie Pallo which was officially known as the "over the shoulder belly-to-belly piledriver." Japanese commentators opted for the catchier name "tombstone" which is why Mark Callaway adopted the move upon being rebranded as the Undertaker.

Robinson eventually took the European heavyweight title from Bob Robinson (who now used the ring name Billy Joyce) in 1965, beating him again for the British crown two years later. The latter may have been the nearest thing to a legitimate championship change in the World of Sport era. While the match itself had a pre-determined outcome as usual, Robinson would later maintain that Joyce was only prepared to drop the title after Robinson beat him for real behind closed doors.

That's not to say Robinson was under any illusion that the win proved he was inherently more skilled than Joyce. He readily admitted that the age difference between the two proved the deciding factor, just as it did when he eventually began getting the better of Karl Gotch in the gym. "I don't know how it would have been if Gotch or Joyce were at their best and I was at my best."

Robinson was already in demand on the continent, winning tournaments in Germany and working in Spain where he met Sophia Loren and dined with Ernest Hemingway. But his big international break came in Japan where the main JWA promotion, reeling from the death of founder and cultural icon Rikidozan, had begun using Gotch as its top foreign star. Gotch, who would later main event the first New Japan Pro Wrestling show, earned such fan appreciation he would become known as "the God of wrestling" in the country.

Rival promotion IWE then hired Robinson as its top foreigner, an intentional attempt to use a fellow Snake Pit alumnus to give credibility. It led to some amusing antics as the pair, unable being seen together publicly in the midst of a wrestling war, snuck around to meet up for secretive sparring sessions in Tokyo.

Robinson would go on to play important roles for two more promotional rivals who both emerged from the collapse of JWA. In 1975 he worked a famous 60-minute draw with New Japan's Antonio Inoki. He moved to All Japan the following year and had a high-profile bout with Giant Baba, sticking with the promotion for several years.

It was during an early trip to Japan that Robinson met Calgary regular Dave Rulh and accepted an offer to visit Stampede Wrestling. Here his initial performances impressed so much he was built up as the top babyface and booked to put over long-time lead villain the Mongolian Stomper to set up NWA title challenges against Dory Funk Jr during Stampede week, the biggest series of shows in the promotion's calendar.

That was the idea anyway. Unfortunately, the Stomper, whether fearing that Robinson was trying to take an unscheduled victory or simply believing he was dishing out too much legitimate punishment, simply walked out of the match before the finish. As the unexpected winner Robinson was put in several title bouts against Funk Jr and, after a series of fast-paced 60-minute draws, was a made man on the North American scene.

Robinson relinquished both his European and British titles, the latter ironically being picked up in a tournament final by Albert Wall. Save for a brief visit to the UK in 1978, Robinson spent the rest of his in-ring career overseas. He worked in several US territories but made his home in the AWA where his ring style particularly appealed to promoter Verne Gagne, a former national amateur champion in the college ranks.

While he took part in many televised bouts, the best remembered footage of Robinson at this time came in the 1974 film The Wrestler where he effectively played himself under the name Billy Taylor, taking on Mike Bollar, played by Gagne in the concluding scene.

Behind the scenes, Robinson not only acted in a policeman role (taking on and deterring those who had the gall to challenge the legitimacy of the business) but was a major player in training AWA wrestlers. Unlike in his British gym he was training people specifically for pro wrestling, but with a twist. While wrestlers were encouraged to "go with moves" during training for demonstration purposes, the trainees were never specifically told they were being trained in performance rather than competition until the time of their public debut or even later.

It was in these training camps that Robinson's fearsome reputation developed, most notably in an incident when he responded badly to a claim by skilled amateur the Iron Sheik that he could not beat him at grappling. Whether or not Robinson made clear he intended to answer the challenge under catch rather than Olympic rules is up for debate, but either way a well-placed knee to the hip brought the challenge to a painful end. Such stories even led Billy Graham, who believed that as a bodybuilder with no amateur background he would be a particular target risk, to tape razor blades to his fingers before a match with Robinson, a deterrence that appears to have been effective.

Many of the most infamous stories about Robinson during his globetrotting days happened away from the ring of the training mat. During a tour of Australia he spent several hours in a hotel room in a lengthy impromptu grappling session with Jack Brisco to test their respective skills. Brisco later remarked that although he had encountered numerous wrestlers claiming to have inescapable submission holds, Robinson was the only one who could put them on from any position in the middle of a scuffle.

A less sportsmanlike encounter came in Japan where a heated exchange between Robinson and Peter Maivia (the grandfather of The Rock) escalated to a full-blown brawl. While the wrestling rumour mill somehow turned the outcome into Maivia gouging out Robinson's eye, a fanciful story that presumably stemmed from the damage caused by the childhood accident, the only thing that is agreed by both participants and spectators alike is that Maivia's final move was to bite clean through Robinson's cheek.

Only one man claimed a decisive victory over Robinson in a street fight. Ed White, who held the WWF tag titles as Moondog King, not only knocked Robinson to the floor and kicked him into a helpless state, but reportedly even urinated on him. It should be noted that White had attempted to get Robinson intoxicated, then suckerpunched him from behind rather than issue a challenge. It seems White was neither proud of the attack not confident of repeating it: he no-showed the following night's wrestling show (perhaps correctly guessing he was now booked against Robinson), and the incident was never mentioned in White's authorised biography.

Robinson began winding down his career in his late 40s and his last recorded US match was a draw against Tom Zenk on February 4th, 1988. He then began working as a security guard and training colleagues until receiving a call from Japan.

By this time, several wrestlers trained in submission by Karl Gotch had broken away from New Japan and formed the Universal Wrestling Federation, a promotion which placed even more emphasis than the major Japanese groups on a realistic-looking ring style. Although the initial version of the group faltered, a relaunch in 1988 had proven so successful that it regularly sold out buildings in a matter of minutes despite having no television coverage and attracted a reported 50,000 fans to the Tokyo Dome.

The UWF splintered after a management fallout, with one of the resulting promotions being the UWFi with top star Nobuhiko Takada. While still doing worked matches, the promotion was presented as a "real" alternative to mainstream pro wrestling. Wrestlers had to have genuine skills to be able to perform in the bouts and there was often minimal cooperation before the planned finishes.

Robinson accepted a role as UWFi trainer, initially working with American grapplers such as James Maritato (later Little Guido/Nunzio.) Later Robinson moved to Japan full-time to train the native roster and even had an exhibition match in 1992, a 10-minute draw with Nick Bockwinkel.

After the promotion closed in 1995, he acted as head of a gym known as the UWF Snake Pit. The gym slowly changed its emphasis to genuine mixed martial arts competition with the emergence of Pride Fighting Championships, initially built around Takada. Perhaps Robinson's biggest success came with former UWFi performer Kazushi Sakuraba who replaced Takada as the main native star with a series of wins over the seemingly invincible Gracie clan, including a win over Royce Gracie after 90 gruelling minutes.

Later Robinson returned to the US where he continued running training seminars. His colleague Jake Shannon tells FSM that "He had a real passion for catch wrestling, he lived and breathed it; it was his life. He was old school, not soft: he didn't give a crap about telling you how awesome you were. That wasn't his job, his job was to get excellence, so he pushed you very, very hard. He had a reputation for being severe, but he also had a knack for pushing you in a way that drove you and made you excel. He had a particular way of seeing holds, like a sixth sense, and could spot ways where moving a few degrees or a couple of inches could make the move more effective."

The catch training wrestling wasn't just appreciated by pure martial artists. Barnett worked pro wrestling matches in New Japan, while British wrestler Jack Gallagher turned to Robinson for inspiration after deciding to ditch his original "Jack Toxic" gimmick. He began training in legitimate wrestling at the Aspull Wrestling Club in Wigan, which was the successor to the now defunct Snake Pit and was run by Roy Wood, one of the last men trained by Billy Riley.

Gallagher noted that "before I'd stepped a foot in Aspull, I happened across a video on YouTube of an old pro wrestler (Billy) torturing two poor MMA fighters with what he called "the double wrist lock." He broke every part of the move down into such detail, knowing what to do and what not to do, as well as why. I was amazed. It all started with Billy Robinson and that double wrist lock."

So taken was Gallagher with the video that he flew out to the US for a two-day seminar with Robinson. "We were spending the last hour or so focusing on the double wrist lock. The first catch wrestling move I ever saw and the signature hold of my hero Kazushi Sakuraba. At one point Billy used me as a dummy to explain the finer points in the application and it was only as I was getting back to my feet I realised that a few years ago I was watching Billy Robinson teach that hold and mention how his 'boy Sakuraba beat the Gracies with it,' and now here I was having the same man apply that hold to me."

After returning to professional wrestling and establishing himself as one of the most respected grapplers on the British scene, Gallagher found it wasn't just the knowledge of how legitimate holds looked -- and felt -- that could benefit his professional work. Speaking on the Taylor Made Talks podcast, he explained that catch wrestling instincts lent themselves to a visually appealing, fluid performance style. "I'd naturally move from hold to hold because Billy taught me that if you put a hold on for six seconds and don't get any result, it's time to try something different. If you've got a hold on right, you'll get a submission within six seconds."

Shannon noted that catch wrestling skills can indeed cross the line between performance and competition. "I remember Chris Benoit vs Kurt Angle as a modern-day example of using chain wrestling but not trying to really go for it. Meanwhile UFC had a similar bout with Randy Couture vs Mike Van Arsdale that also had lots of chain wrestling, but a more violent version.

"What we taught is legitimate competitive style, while pro wrestling is doing a performance version of that. We got invited to Couture's gym and did a seminar attended by Daniel Bryan of WWE as well as MMA guys."

Bryan himself told WWE.com of his admiration. " My favourite guy to watch who you don't hear a lot about, who to me is a legend, is Billy Robinson. In Japan, he was considered a legend, and he trained a lot of the original shoot fighters, but his pro wrestling was amazing. He was probably one of the most technically gifted guys you'll ever see. As far as doing cool, legitimate stuff on the mat, there's nobody better."

Robinson returned to the UK on several occasions in recent years for seminars, on one occasion training MMA fighter Danny Mitchell -- the nephew of none other than Albert Wall. By this time Robinson was walking with a cane after a string of surgeries including having both knees replaced and the removal of part of his spine. Shannon recalls that "It was hard to stop him getting on the mat. He would get so frustrated because he had in his mind what he wanted and he would go through torture with those knees and that hip to get down and show us. I always said that the day he could no longer get on the mat would be the day he passed away."

When news of Robinson's death broke, three words were recalled by everyone who trained with him, three words he'd picked up from Billy Riley. It was a phrase wrestlers would hear repeatedly as they tried to learn a move and, sometimes frustratingly, even once they thought they'd mastered it: "Do it again!"

"We joked about putting it on a t-shirt," Shannon recalled, explaining that pro wrestler Harry Smith was among those who heard it regularly. "Billy held Harry to such a high standard and would shout at him 'Do it again! Harry, do it again!' He was brutal on him."

"But then Harry won his first ever grappling tournament despite being much less experienced than the competition. I was copied in on an e-mail where Billy congratulated him. It simply read 'Do it again!'"

# BLACKJACK MULLIGAN

American wrestlers once used the insider term "carpenter" to describe a wrestler who usually lost his matches but had a reputation for reliably making his opponents look good. It was a term of respect, reflecting the idea that while the stars might draw a good house, the carpenter is key to building that house.

If there were a similar term in the United Kingdom, it would surely have been "floor layer." That's not only because it was literally Blackjack Mulligan's day job, but also because among his peers at least, he was widely acknowledged as being among the best at making somebody a star while still retaining his own crowd appeal.

One of the bigger men of his era, it was actually his small size that indirectly led him to the grappling game. "My dad got a television in the 1950s and wrestling was on when I was about 12. I said 'Ooh, I'm going to be a wrestler.' Of course, they looked at me and said, 'Don't be silly.'

"Eventually I started bodybuilding when I was 18 and only weighed about nine and a half stone. I went to competitions and won a show. I started wrestling because the gym I used had a wrestling part as well and I went in early on Sunday morning waiting for my partner to come training. There was a wrestler waiting for the same thing, so he said, 'It's freezing cold, let's get in the ring, pull around and get warmed up.' I thought 'I'll kill this bugger' because he wasn't training like I was: I was twelve and a half stone by then. He sat me on my backside and threw me all over and I thought 'I'll have some of that!'"

Mulligan took his new skills to an annual fair at Newcastle that included a boxing and wrestling booth where professionals would take on challengers from the audience. His first attempts didn't go too well -- "I got my backside kicked" -- but he returned the following year and became a regular part of the crew, wearing a mask to protect his identity. "God, that was rough up there. You'd be black and blue when you came off, but the money was silly. One week I came off with £120 when my [regular day job] wage was about four or five pounds."

While there was always the fear of a trained professional slipping through the vetting of would-be challengers, Mulligan recalls that unskilled fighters could be just as dangerous. "They were full of beer and bravado, but they'd get in the ring and you'd see the fear in their eyes. When you go for them, they've got arms and legs swinging so you'd just got to drop them or put a submission or sleeper on, just a quick thing that makes them pass out in a few seconds. It's not something that hurts them, you're not cutting the wind off because they'd panic and be kicking and screaming. Instead you put a sleeper on, they can't move, they pass out for a few seconds, and nobody's hurt."

The experience also gave him some valuable insight to some of the holds which the uninitiated might dismiss as 'show' moves from the pro game. "These submission moves, they work if you can get them on. It's like if you've got a killer punch: if you hit me, I'm down, you know it and I know it. But if you can't hit me with that punch it's no bloody good is it. If I can kick your balls up your throat before you hit me, it doesn't matter how good it is. Submissions, if you get them on, that's it."

On the odd occasion, however, flight was better than fight. "You always had an escape route because sometimes the crowd went for you. It was really packed in there and if they pulled you outside you were dead because everybody had a kick at you like a mob." Fortunately, Mulligan had a tried and tested strategy. "You run up the corner and jump off the top rope to the floor in one of the corners [of the marquee]. When you jumped, everybody cleared, so you'd have time to get under the tent, into the caravan and get changed. Then I'd come back in the front without the mask and tell them 'He's run for the car park, you'll find him there.'"

He then translated his booth experience into a pro career in the early 1960s, with his original ring name coming as a surprise. "It was a spelling mistake: they put Larry Coulton instead of [real name] Coulson and it just stuck. It was in their books and they'd printed off all the posters, so I just left it."

He also underwent an unexpected change of persona after his debut. "The crowd will typecast you. I came off after my first bout and the promoter said, 'They don't like you,' and it was like a dagger in the heart. I really wanted everyone to like me, but he said, 'The crowd will say what you are,' so I thought 'Well, there you are.'"

In hindsight, Mulligan believes it was better for his career longevity. "If you're a young lad and you're top of the tree and they love you, when you're up there there's only one place you can go and that's down. They'll get sick of you after a while and you lose your top spot. But the villains, you're always there. So, I think I picked the right one: they need the villain. You get Johnny Saint and someone of that calibre and it's a really good technical match, very clever, but then you get the rabid grannies and they want someone to shout at."

Sometimes it went beyond verbal abuse. "I've had some injuries off them as well. At Derby I was coming out of the ring and this woman swung a handbag at me and bust my ear. I said to take a look in her bag and she had a whole brick wrapped in a towel. They kicked her out, but she was such a character they let her back in after a while: you see them on the front row and they add to the atmosphere. But they started checking her bag!

"I've had hat pins stuck in me, cigarettes put out on my back, been hit with a chair and my head split, my back scratched, spat on... if you're a villain and they saw you in your car, they'd scrap it if they could. It was terrible."

After making his TV debut against Ray Steele in 1971, Coulton decided to enhance his villain status by repackaging himself: "I changed my style and everything. I had big suede boots like pirate boots, the black cape, my hair was long, my beard was long." He also agreed with a promoter on a change of name to Mulligan, joining several other Brits in adopting ring names of American wrestlers, most notably Greg Valentine and John 'Killer' Kowalski. In this era at least, it was simply a case of borrowing a name rather than an attempt to mislead fans, most of whom would never have heard of the American star anyway.

Unlike in the US, British wrestlers were usually on a fixed fee rather than a percentage of the takings. However, it was far from a transparent pay scale. "You made your own price for the promoter: you got what you thought you could and he give you what you thought you were worth. Nobody knew what anyone else got. but everybody tried to get as much as they could. It depends how the crowd took you and if they could use you regularly, if the crowd come to see you."

Mulligan was certainly valuable to promoters, often being the opponent for high profile television appearances by featured performers. In 1975 he took on George Kidd in what was both Kidd's last TV match and the only one where footage is widely available today. Despite Mulligan being very much a heavyweight and Kidd a lightweight, the match still worked. "He were like a little whippet. Have you ever tried to catch a chicken? You cannae catch it, can you? You get hold of it and it gets out: he was like that."

Another notable opponent was Sammy Lee, better known as Satoru 'Tiger Mask' Sayama: "He wasn't here very long. I could work with his style. He was quick, he was really well trained and fit as a butcher's dog."

Mulligan even took on a non-wrestler in the form of showjumper Harvey Smith, making his only TV appearance. "He had a farm up here and another lad, [pro wrestler] Tally Ho Kaye was mates with him from the horses. He used to come up and train with him and two amateur lads. He was a strong fellow: when you ride the horses, you need your knees and your shoulders to hold them, so he was bloody strong. It was in all in the newspapers and the promoter liked it because he'd bring all the horse people in. He was no slouch: he could do the job."

With his natural strength and limited experience, wrestling Smith was a physical experience, something that was certainly not uncommon for Mulligan. He uses another combat analogy to explain how some bouts took more of a toll than others. "Suppose you're a boxer and doing all these exhibition bouts, the after-dinner things where people get dressed up. When you're boxing there, you get a fat lip, you get a bust nose, you get a black eye, but you're not fighting for anything big, so it's like a rough workout. But sometimes you get in and you think 'He's gonna try and hurt me, he's going to drop us' and then you've got a fight.

"If you get in the [wrestling] ring and they thought they could throw you around, some of them would do it. They'd slap you round and hurt you. If you wanted a fight you could have one, a right go -- but other than that it was more like a stiff workout. It were up to you how far you wanted to take it."

Across more than 30 TV matches, Mulligan only scored the victory on two occasions. One was when he replaced Lucky Gordon to team with Scrubber Daly as the Masked Marauders, defeating Colin Bennett and Eddie Riley to set up an unsuccessful challenge to Big Daddy and Kid Chocolate on the 1983 Cup Final Day show. The other was in a six-man tag match, though Mulligan was eliminated before his team took the victory. (The match is best remembered for the appearance of Nigerian wrestler Samson Ubo who didn't quite seem to grasp what was going on.)

Away from the cameras, Mulligan's most memorable match didn't actually have a finish, taking place at the infamous Eldorado Ballroom in Edinburgh, known for the audience's hostility to English grapplers challenging local heroes. "Up there, if they cannae get you, they'll get your car, so we parked up in a big lay-by and took a taxi. It was a tag match against two young lads – not any good, but they were local and the crowd was there to see them. Plus [local legend] Andy Robbin had been on earlier and he was mentoring them in the corner, and they even had marching pipers and drummers come into the arena for their entrance."

That might have provided enough heat in itself, but Mulligan decided to use memories of the Battle of Culloden to further enrage the audience. "I brought a red coat and jacket: it was too small for me so the lad I was tagging with put it on. All the Scots there went berserk. I'd phoned up a taxi half an hour before we got in the ring and told it to wait outside and we had all our gear packed.

"I banged one of the [opponents] in the nose, made them bleed and threw them into the crowd. While they were worrying about the kid, we got out of the ring, through the doors, picked up our bags, in the taxi and off. I'm shouting to get away and the crowd comes bursting out and a dustbin went through the back window. The driver shot up the road, straight over a roundabout flattening all the flowers, and he's screaming. They chased us up the road and saw us get out on and switch cars in the layby and then two cars chased us on to the motorway!"

Fortunately, there were lighter occasions in the ring. "This lad came in and he'd done a bit of wrestling. He dressed like RIcki Starr, the ballet dancer, and wanted to be like him, but he was useless, he couldn't do it. I'd switched my trade for a while because my knee was a bit bad for crawling round floors, so I had a part time job checking boilers. I'd gone to this one and there was a breakdown. I did fix it, but I was black like coal and all scruffy.

"I turned up and said to the promoter 'I'll just get a quick shower,' but he said not to bother. This lad was all in his white ballet gear and didn't know who he was on with. The place went crazy: he'd slap me and there was soot coming off me, my face was black, everything was black.

"You should have seen the look on this lad's face: I chased him round the ring, had him on the deck, got a hold on him, really playing it with the crowd. The referee got a bucket of water and chucked it on us and it was like mud. I got a hold of this kid and he was screaming: he got out of the ring and he was all black... he never come back!"

Mulligan wound down his career after the end of the TV era, though his final match was not planned to be a retirement. "I hadn't been doing any for a while, but there was a show five minutes from where I was living, and I took a sub job. I turned up and was on with this lad and the promoter said, 'He used to watch you on television when he was a kid,' and I went 'Oh, bloody hell.'"

"He was 20 years younger, fit as a butcher's dog, and knew a little [wrestling]. I was throwing him around at 20 miles an hour and he was coming back at 30 miles an hour. By the end of the second or third round I was breathing through my backside, he was just that fit. It felt like when a little dog's attacking you all the time and you push it away, but it keeps coming back. Giant Haystacks was in the back pissing himself laughing and said, 'I think you've wound him up.'

"Somebody had told him to get stuck in and he was coming at me like a steam train. I'd been throwing him around and he'd done almost nothing to me, so imagine how I looked [to the crowd]. That were that! I was too busy to do any more matches. A couple of years after that I started falling to bits."

Mulligan had his hip replaced 20 years ago (with the artificial joint now due to be replaced itself) and recalls the physical toll wrestling took upon him. "I had my collar bone smashed, both my ankles fractured, major back operation, arm smashed up, nose smashed, teeth pulled out, bruised ribs, fractured ribs, bruised kidneys, the lot!"

Perhaps the worst injury came in a bout with Mohammed 'Little Prince' Alam. "He was really, really stiff. You knew getting in you'd have to have a go... he was trying all the time. I'd thrown him to the ropes and he's come off and I was going to hook him and throw him over the top, but he slapped us hard on the side of the head and it was like the trick where you hit the top of a milk bottle and it blows the bottom out. It just went 'pop' and started bleeding and now I've got no eardrum, just a hole."

Blackjack Mulligan

While he says "I'd have looked after myself a bit more," Mulligan would change little about his life either as a wrestler or as a floor layer. "I worked all over on big jobs like hotels and the QE2. I really liked it and it wasn't like some people who are making good money but would rather do something else. I'd still go into flooring and I'd still wrestle."

And looking back on his in-ring career, Mulligan shares the attitude of his peers who note that wins and losses aren't the only sign of a job well done: "If you can make everybody look good, you're a star."

# BLONDIE BARRATT

"Falling on my arse was my spot," Blondie Barratt readily recalls. "I have no delusions of grandeur!" It's a humble statement from a man who's earned a reputation as one of the most reliable performers still active today after four decades in the job.

Born Bob Nickerson, he was a fan from an early age, growing up in Rushden, the home of wrestler and promoter Ken Joyce and his brother Doug. "The earliest show I can remember was at a local football club carnival with Joe Cornelius against Bruno Elrington. After that I used to go to the Northampton Drill Hall with my dad and brother every week, plus there was a monthly show at the Windmill Club in Rushden."

While the East Midlands may not be remembered as one of the great wrestling regions of the UK, Barratt recalls that "there were a lot of good wrestlers from the area like the Wensor Brothers, Tony Rowney, Gypsy Smith and Pete LaPaque, plus the promoters usually brought a car-load of wrestlers down from the north for each show, so you had good line-ups. I was right into it as a kid: I wanted to be somebody famous."

Like many fans, Barratt ignored warnings not to try what he saw in the ring. "Me and my pal would have a pull around and copy what we'd see." But unlike many young fans, he took it a stage further and began performing in front of a crowd. "I joined the Northants Area Wrestling Club in Burton Latimer, run by Norman Baish."

It was a curious set-up at which the regulars learned and trained in the basics of amateur wrestling but then used the moves to put together low-level shows in the pro style at venues such as clubs and fetes.

Here Barratt met a fellow young enthusiast named John Lowing, who would later become his regular opponent Johnny Kidd. The pair hit it off from the start. "We always worked well together: it was partly the sheer amount of time we spent working, but we did just sort of gel from the start. We know each other so well that we could do the matches just as good even today, albeit it a bit slower!"

Kidd and Barratt adopted their respective hero and villain roles almost as soon as they started training together, a typecasting Barratt has never regretted. "I used to love the baddies as a kid. They are the ones people always remembered, whether it was because they got their arses kicked, or because they cheated to win."

It was a combination of this rudimentary early experience and old-fashioned networking that got Barratt into the more established professional ranks. "You used to chat to the wrestlers and meet them after shows to get autographs, so they started to remember you. I'd often see Ken Joyce around town and get chatting to him, and eventually he decided to give me a show."

That show was at the Lings Forum in Northampton, against Jackie Robinson, the cousin (and trainee) of shoot-wrestling legend Billy Robinson. The basics that Barratt had already picked up were enough to survive the experience, though it was a performance without a crowd present that took him to the next step.

"I went to Bletchley Leisure Centre in the afternoon before a show and had a pull-around with Jackie Turpin. I don't know who, but somebody must have been watching and thought I had an idea what I was doing. I got booked for a Joint Promotions show in Digbeth against Lucky Gordon and then the next thing I knew, I got a date sheet with something like 29 or 30 jobs in the 31 days of the month!"

While the work was welcome, the logistics were a challenge. "You'd be bouncing round the country like being on a pinball machine. One night you'd be in Carlisle, the next in Southampton." Barratt believes this wasn't simply a case of office-bound bookers doing a poor job of scheduling. "It almost felt like a test to see if you stuck at it. You'd end up so tired, you didn't know your arse from your elbow."

At this stage Barratt, like many British wrestlers, still held down a full-time job. "I was working as an engineer servicing moulding machines. It wasn't a really big firm, so they'd sometimes let me leave early to make a date. It was very hard, but I wanted to make the sacrifice."

Once he had made it to the venue, Barratt would often be in for a long night's work. "Sometimes Max Crabtree would tell you to go out and deliberately try to get the bird [a negative reaction]. You'd try to get the slow handclap so that everything was ready for the crowd to come up with the next match. When you got to a show and saw you were on right before Big Daddy, you knew you'd be doing seven or eight rounds."

"I got some great advice back then, which was that if you wanted to be a success as a wrestler, you had to be able to do four things: wrestle, be a villain, be a babyface, and do comedy." Barratt refined his skills with the last of these by working regularly with comedy performer Catweazle in the last match of the evening. "We called it the 'send them home happy' slot."

Barratt recalls several opponents from this era who he considers historically underrated. "I always look on Ken Joyce as an all-time great. Even though he was knocking on a bit in the matches from TV that you can see today, I thought he was equal to or better than Johnny Saint and Steve Grey.

"Johnny South was very good too. And Kashmir Singh wasn't a big name, but I always liked working with him. I never had to talk to him or Johnny Kidd before a match because they were so smooth, and you always knew where their arm or leg was going to be. With some of the newer guys today you aren't sure, and you've got to watch out or you'll get a boot in the face!"

Barratt's television debut was originally scheduled in 1982 when he lost to Johnny Kidd in what should have been Kidd's first televised victory in six attempts; in the event, the match was cut for time reasons. Instead Barratt first appeared in 1985, teaming with Peter Kaye in a losing effort against Danny Collins and Greg Valentine. His next small screen appearances came in a different setting after he turned crisis into opportunity.

"I was working for a new company by now and fitting in the wrestling was getting hard. My new hours were 6am to 6pm, which really didn't work for the travel. Even if I could get off early, I'd rush off to shows and be home around three in the morning and then have to get up for work at five. On nights I wasn't wrestling, I'd fall asleep as soon as I got home.

"I was working as a chargehand [supervisor] and the company told me they needed to make a redundancy and asked who to lay off. I volunteered to take redundancy, which went against everything I'd been told: wrestling was a hobby, and the rule was that you shouldn't put your hobby before a job. But it definitely worked out!"

Around the point he went full-time, Barratt began working for Joint Promotions' main rival, Brian Dixon's All Star Wrestling. "My first match was at Kings Lynn against Johnny Saint, which was a high profile main event and a real baptism of fire. I wasn't always in the main event with Brian, but I was getting my share of big matches."

Kings Lynn was notorious among wrestlers as a distant venue with poor road links, but Barratt recalls it as memorable for another reason. "It was a right old dump. There was a crowd of gypsies there and you'd always have one of them pay to get in and then he'd open the fire doors out the back and let 30 others in.

"One night we had a riot with Dave Finlay and Tony St Clair. One fan jumped in the ring and Finlay broke his jaw, and the next thing you knew it was like a John Wayne film with him fighting through the crowd. In the end we had to sneak Finlay out the building and have him change cars down the road."

Barratt's next TV appearance came on cable channel Screensport where he teamed with Rocky Moran in a tag tournament, wrestling Clive Myers and Fuji Yamada (the future Jushin Liger) in the final. Barratt would regularly wrestle New Japan performers who'd been sent to the UK as part of their education process.

Blondie Barratt

"I was their bump man. The communication was hard as you couldn't talk the match through, so you had to watch out for the flying kicks they liked to do because you weren't sure about where they were coming from! The only negative I had about those matches were that if a Brit went over to Japan, they'd probably get beat. They always won here and then went home, leaving us here to plod on."

Tag teaming was becoming a speciality for Barratt at this point, with his first All Star match on TV coming with Bobby Barnes against Robbie Brookside and Wayne Martin. "We were billed as the Hells Angels, which were originally Barnes and Adrian Street. I always looked up to Street as a fan because he was so different and such a star, so it was a dream come true to emulate that."

Barratt's best-known role was as the tag partner of Kendo Nagasaki, including a notorious TV tag bout that ended with a "hypnotised" Brookside turning on partner Steve [William] Regal. Barratt is carefully diplomatic about such events. "Let's just say it was the Nagasaki show, to get him over. It was always him as the star and then three others in the match.

"But I would never knock it. Teaming with Kendo really raised my profile and we were always top of the bill -- even though mine was the little name on the poster! We teamed for four years and went on with everybody, both babyfaces and heels."

Barratt likens his role, working much of the match before tagging the veteran Nagasaki in, to being a heel equivalent of the youngster teaming with Big Daddy. "It was bloody hard work, with a lot of blood spilt, but we were the top of the tree. I remember that the fans really hated us. Normally I'd be pleasant with fans after the show, despite my image in the ring, but Nagasaki would never speak to anyone. He kept the job proper. Him and guys like Mick McManus were real personalities, out of the ordinary. They were genuine celebrities, not like the reality show rubbish you get today."

By this time Barratt was known as "the Rock 'n' Roll Express", though with US wrestling coverage minimal in Britain at the time, it wasn't a case of false advertising. "How I got the name is somewhat lost in the mists of time. I was teaming with Steve Peacock at the time and we both had long blond hair, so Brian Dixon may have pinched the name."

Over the years, Barratt would work under not just different names, but different personas. These included "the Grim Reaper", "Dunk" and "Happy Humphrey", the latter two being takeoffs of WWE wrestling clown Doink. It led to a busy but lucrative schedule.

"I'd wrestle twice on shows, which at that time meant double money. I enjoyed doing the clown gimmick with the comedy and custard pies just because it was the total opposite of my usual role. In fact, I got so used to it that one night I was wrestling for [tribute show promoter] Klondyke Jake and worked against his son, who was doing the clown gimmick instead of me. It was an odd experience, a bit like working in reverse gear. I knew the clown role so well I was almost doing it for him, putting myself into position.

"The clown stuff would probably go down like a lead balloon today, but it worked particularly well on the holiday camps. It wasn't a normal wrestling crowd there, so all they really wanted was a bit of movement and lots of entertainment."

The ability to work several roles made Barratt particularly valuable to promoters, who sometimes went to extremes. At one camp show he and Johnny Kidd used masks to put on a three-match show by themselves. Barratt also remembers a particularly gruelling night where he wrestled four times in the same elimination tournament. The biggest challenge came when the Royal Rumble format became popular in the UK.

"It always meant I'd get eliminated right away and then have a rapid change of clothes before coming out again. Unlike in America which was two minutes, we often only had about 30 seconds between entrants because the show had to be done in time for people to get the last bus. I used to be rushing in and out, and I always remember looking back at the entrance to the dressing room where Mal Sanders would be stood smiling because he always did the deal where he got disqualified in his match and was barred from the Rumble!"

Barratt's career highlight as a singles wrestle came in December 1991 when he beat Doc Dean for the British welterweight title, holding it for seven months before dropping it back in a return bout. "Even though the TV heyday was over, I was quite proud of the title reign. Now there's five thousand promotions, all of them with their own champion, but back them you were still recognised as the only British champion. I'd never knock holding the title: it was definitely prestigious to be listed as champion on the posters."

After moving to Sheffield at the turn of the century, Barratt became involved in a training school at the 393 club in Hillsborough, eventually taking it over and promoting shows under the Rebel Pro Wrestling banner. Training has proved a mixed experience.

"It definitely helps keep me fit. Some guys listen and want to learn the job, and others don't. You do get too many people these day who think all they have to do is buy a pair of boots and they'll be on a show the next week, or they just want to learn 57 highspots and never touch the floor.

"What they do now is fabulous, and I don't think the style of a four-match show over two hours would work today. The job has changed ten million percent: it used to be a special occasion where you'd see a middle-aged man dressed up in suit and tie with his wife, and few kids. Now you've got so many children in the crowd, they want to see people fly about, so you need action right from the beginning, a bit of crash, bang, wallop.

Blondie Barratt

"But I do miss how we used to tell a story in the ring, put a hold on, work a bodypart. We used to tell a story in a match which was 25 minutes, the same as an episode of Coronation Street. A match without a story can be like watching a kettle boil: the two best wrestlers in the world could have a match, but if they don't involve the audience it will be rubbish."

While his 60th birthday may be approaching, and he readily refers to himself as "an old hand", Barratt firmly expects his career will gradually wind down rather than he ever set a firm retirement date. Even with a reduced schedule, his mind is still very much in the business.

"I still referee on shows and I'll often be in there with two lads working and catch myself thinking 'Oh, you shouldn't have done that, I'd have done this instead.'"

And while most of his trainees have the goal of making it to WWE, Barratt is more than satisfied with his own career. "I tell them to never stop dreaming, but to realise that's a very big dream and they'll be very lucky to get it. But I had my dream of being a wrestler and achieved it.

"I had fun matches, and it was never a chore."

# BRIAN DIXON

Last September Brian Dixon's All Star Wrestling -- already the third oldest active promotion in the world -- passed the landmark of having run longer than Joint Promotions and its successors. Yet Dixon cannot remember for certain how he got interested in professional wrestling in the first place.

"As a child I used to go to live entertainment shows with singers like Brenda Lee and Wee Willy Harris on my own as a child and try to get autographs. But I can't really recollect my first experience with wrestling. It may have been when I was helping out in a shop and the couple there used to tell me about going to Liverpool Stadium."

Whatever the spark, as he approached his teenage years Dixon took it upon himself to try to get to the venue, only to be thwarted at the first attempt. "I'd phone the Stadium every Friday to try to book ringside seats, but they were always booked up permanently by regulars. What I didn't realise is that the other thousands of seats were unreserved!"

"After a couple of months of this I missed the match I really wanted to see, Jack Pye vs the Zebra Kid. I heard afterwards that Pye had unmasked him and I decided that was it, I had to find a different way in. I asked the couple at the shop to take me to my first show, where I realised all you had to do was pay two shillings on the door!"

With that logistical hurdle overcome, Dixon soon became a regular at the venue, making friends with a teenage boy named Mark, the son of wrestler Jim Hussey. Dixon expanded his schedule to make regular stops at weekly shows in Manchester's Belle Vue and the Preston Guildhall. His first steps beyond merely sitting in the crowd was with the launch of a fan club for Jim Breaks, and then the A-Z fan club which covered all wrestlers.

Dixon expanded into writing, publishing his own magazine named WrestleSport and writing about British wrestling for the American magazine Wrestling Revue where he shared column space with Lia Maivia, future grandmother of the Rock. He also began seconding wrestlers at local venues, leading to a big break. "Kent Walton mentioned me being in the corner at a televised show and mentioned the fan club. I got no end of letters coming through after that."

There was still a big barrier to the inner workings of the business at this time, an approach Dixon continues to appreciate. "I was a bit naïve at the time about wrestling, but in some ways, I still like to think I'm a bit naïve. As a second, I was travelling round and Quasimodo and Billy Hayes were working Monday in Altrincham, Tuesday in Warrington, Wednesday in Buxton, Thursday somewhere else, Friday in Liverpool, Saturday in Belle Vue and Sunday in Blackpool.

"Still, I didn't really think through the reasons behind them being on together every night. My thinking was more that if they were knocking seven kinds of shit out of each other every night, I couldn't wait to see what the fight was going to be like on Sunday when they were beaten down!

"Even today, I still see wrestling as an industry where the fans and wrestlers should be two different identities. I'll never talk about results or finishes with fans. It appals me when magazines talk about finishes and what's going to happen. Fans and wrestlers should be two different things, but too often today the wrestlers are fans. I keep the two sides separate myself. It's an old-fashioned way perhaps, but it's the way I intend to carry on, the way I know, and the way I was able to survive."

Although Dixon attended a gym in Crosby with friend and wrestler Kevin Conneely, becoming a wrestler himself didn't really appeal. Instead he turned his attention to refereeing and picked up work for independent promoter Orig Williams, working full time for several years in the UK and abroad.

One of Williams' main attractions was using female wrestlers (who were not used by Joint Promotions or featured on television) with Mitzi Mueller the top star. "I accidentally stood on her hair while refereeing and she really let me have it in the dressing room afterwards, calling me a clumsy oaf and all sorts. But then we fell in love and we're still together 45 years later."

While it was the start of one partnership, it marked the end of another. "Orig didn't like his lads mixing with the public, and he didn't like the men mixing with the girls, so we fell out once Mitzi and I became heavily involved. I knew the women were a novelty and I had a chance to make it promoting myself using them as a main attraction."

Working with the assistance of wrestlers Monty Swann and Bob Bell, Dixon's first event as a promoter came in October 1970 when he was a few weeks short of his 23rd birthday. While the show at Marple Baths drew an encouraging crowd, it was an unprofitable evening thanks to the night's takings being stolen when he made the mistake of leaving them in his car overnight.

Dixon stuck to the promoting game nonetheless and credits his early successes to quality matchmaking. "Dale Martin had become so big by then that it became what I called a sausage factory. They were running three or four shows at a time in London and for each one they'd just stick eight names on a bit of paper, send it out and that was the show. There was no real imagination and it lacked excitement. We had a new look and knew we could offer an equal or better presentation, so the sky was the limit."

Ironically, though, Dixon believes he fell into a similar trap at times. "We were soon running 10 shows a week: we got carried away, there's no two ways about it. It was a headache to come up with [line-ups]. Some were good, some bad." Even with such mixed results, Dixon developed an unbreakable rule in promoting, one he wishes others shared. "Once you book a venue, you must never cancel the show, even if you only sell 50 tickets. The show must go on, no matter how much you lose. If you think of how excited a kid is when they are going to see the wrestling, cancelling on them is the biggest disgrace to the industry you can do."

During his early years, Dixon had what he calls his most embarrassing experience as a promoter. "We were running the Town Hall in New Mills and our van broke down, so we got there about six o'clock, which is very late to be putting up the ring. There was already a crowd building up and by about 6.45 it was raining so we decided we had to let them in, even though we were still working on the ring. As they were sitting down we had the shell of the ring together and had just put the boards in. I decided I'd better check the support bars underneath were in the right position before we put the padding and canvas on.

"With 400 people watching, I started jumping on the boards. It turned out the bars weren't in place and as I jumped, one board went flying up in the air, while I dropped out of sight through the gap it left behind. All I could do was crawl under the ring to the dressing room: there was no way I could compere the show after the fans had seen that!"

There were certainly plenty of happier times however. "I ended up running the Liverpool Stadium for about five years. Given I'd started out selling programs there, I really felt I'd made it as a promoter."

One of Dixon's less successful venues had an unexpected benefit. "We'd put on shows regularly at lunchtime a pub called the Wellington in Shepherd's Bush. We started a couple of times a week but eventually the guy there had us running five times a week: I don't know why, because there were often only 20 or so people in the crowd! But a lot of the Dale Martin wrestlers were based locally and would come along to the shows. They'd noticed us running here, there and everywhere, but now they could see we ran a good show and had quite good performers."

Giving the opposition a glimpse of his increasingly professional set-up made things easier once Dixon began the slow process of persuading top-line talent to join his promotion. He says three wrestlers coming on board were particularly significant, the first being old Liverpool Stadium friend Mark Hussey, now known as Rollerball Rocco.

"Mitzi was the best box office star I ever had, on every occasion, but Rocco was my most important acquisition. He took me along to an entertainment events exhibition in Bournemouth and introduced me to all the top venue managers. They all recognised him but were surprised to find out he was still wrestling because Dale Martin had told them he'd retired! That was a big deal because the managers gave us a chance and we were able to sell out some of the traditional Dale Martin venues, which was a real scoop.

The second of the important jumps was John Quinn, who joined All Star just a few months after beating Wayne Bridges on television to win Joint Promotions' recently-created world heavyweight title, coming over to Dixon with belt in hand. "He'd made his name with microphone work and was hot property. He was big, big business."

Kendo Nagasaki also came out of retirement to wrestle for Dixon. "We did a deal where we were working in partnership and he showed me such a lot, about not just promotion, but the business side of it, like book-keeping and VAT. He was a great mentor and I owe him a great deal of my success. He also had a lot of great ideas for presentation like the lumberjack match gimmick: he picked up a lot of ideas from working in Canada and brought a fresh approach."

Having originally promoted as Wrestling Enterprises of Liverpool, Dixon now had a talent roster to justify his new name of All Star Wrestling and believed he was ready for television exposure. "It took us many years to get on, and a lot of it was down to the help of John Harris, our master of ceremonies, who was the best letter writer in the business and would write letters on my behalf to the TV companies.

"Things really changed when LWT got a new producer called Mike Archer who was interested in what we had to offer. Out of the blue I got a letter inviting me to dinner with him at Simpsons in the Strand in London. There was nothing concrete and it took six to nine months for anything to happen, partly because the ITV sport management team were so tied up with the [1986] World Cup. They kept saying they'd look into it, but eventually I got the word that it was definitely going to happen; it was just a case of figuring out the contract situation with Joint."

Dixon can now reveal that it was only the knowledge that a television slot was on the way that allowed him to survive those last few months. "We were running too many shows, which meant some of them didn't get the personal touch they deserved and some of them were losing money. It got to the point where I was writing cheques for bills without the money in the account and praying there'd be money come in from a show in time to cover it.

Brian Dixon

"At one stage the bank manager wrote to me and said he didn't want my business any more. Thankfully I managed to persuade him to give me two more months because the TV contract was coming, and he stood by me. It was one of my real low, low times and having been at real rock bottom, I really do appreciate the good times."

All Star did indeed get a total of 19 televised slots across 1987 and 1988 in a new format shared between Dixon, Joint Promotions and the WWF. With Dixon believing that "everybody involved in the TV had got lazy after being on for so long," he tried a fresh look with the return of Rocco and Nagasaki to the TV screens, the first televised outing for Fuji Yamada (the future Jushin Liger) and unconventional match formats such as a Disco Ladder bout.

Surprisingly, given Rocco's past run-ins with broadcasting regulators, Dixon got no advance warnings about any restrictions he faced on content. That was until an angle in which Kendo Nagasaki "hypnotised" Rob Brookside to turn against tag partner Steve (now William) Regal, something that didn't just upset wrestling purists.

"We didn't realise how controversial it would be. LWT had lots of complaints and it was a learning curve for us. I learned that we're guests in the viewer's home, so we have a duty not to do anything to offend them."

During this time, Dixon finally ran a live event in Joint Promotions' former flagship venue, the Royal Albert Hall. It followed the lifting of a London council ban on female wrestlers thanks to a long-running campaign by Mitzi Mueller, assisted again by the penmanship of John Harris. The show drew a disappointing crowd, something Dixon attributes to a misguided decision to run on a Friday rather than the venue's traditional midweek slot but was memorable for being Mueller's first -- and last -- headline slot in central London.

"Mitzi had ended up in hospital and a specialist said the bones in her spine were rubbing together; if she carried on they'd wear away and she'd be in a wheelchair. We booked the Albert Hall and I made a last minute decision that she'd announce her retirement after the match. It took a long time for her to get used to being out of wrestling. I'd go off to a show at lunchtime and leave her behind, and it was like a dagger in her side. But she realises now that if she'd carried on, I'd be pushing her around in a wheelchair today."

All Star's TV run was cut short when ITV chief Greg Dyke dropped the wrestling slot in 1988, with Dixon subscribing to the theory that Dyke intentionally moved the timeslot around repeatedly to damage viewing figures and justify the cancellation. At first it appeared All Star, which used a combination of action packed matches and long-running rivalries to persuade fans to return to venues, might be better placed to survive going dark than would Joint Promotions with its Big Daddy roadshow.

Brian Dixon

That proved the case at first, but Dixon notes that a couple of years of strong business were followed by an inevitable decline as wrestlers were no longer household names. It led to a slump throughout the 1990s, with Dixon at one point cutting his schedule down to just a few regular venues such as Croydon, Norwich and Hanley.

He moved into other areas of promoting, starting with music shows featuring the likes of Hawkwind and The Commitments; in both cases, Dixon decided he couldn't deal with the headaches that came with their off-stage activities. He found more success putting together package shows with Slade, Sweet and Mud, which did well as Christmas tours but didn't lend themselves to year-round schedules. At one stage, he even got into promoting male strip shows, getting a major boost from the success of The Full Monty. "That was one of my biggest eye-openers in life. If men behaved the way the women in the audience behaved at those shows, they'd be in jail!"

As the new millennium began, Dixon got a consistent barrage of calls from venues interested in wrestling, at which point he realised the revived interest in WWE programming could help British business. Initially this involved using British performers in gimmicks remarkably familiar to those seen on Sky and Channel 4. "Orig Williams was having success with those shows and we decided to work together as he had the gimmicks and I still had the venue contracts, which was great as it mended the fences between us. They weren't meant to be a con show: we billed them as tributes. They were good lookalikes and they could do the job [wrestle] well anyway. But WWE lawyers heard about them and issued writs, so that was the end of it."

He then discovered that wrestling was still popular, even without such an explicit WWE influence. "I got the contract to run Butlins, which really informed me about what shows would work. The market is always changing: when I started, parents would go to wrestling and drag along kids. Today it's the kids that want to go and their parents come along to look after them. It's purely a kids' show with no extreme stuff, no bad taste, or bloodshed."

That's not simply a personal preference on Dixon's part. It's a necessity for keeping the valuable contracts at venues such as theatres which bring a major benefit: such venues have their own in-house advertising departments which bring attention to all their shows.

Dixon notes that the Butlins shows remain the best crowds for people to learn from. "It's a captive market, particularly if it's raining, and then it's up to the wrestlers to entertain them, keep their interest, and hopefully get them to come along to theatres in their town."

The camp shows are perhaps the clearest example of Dixon's oft-cited advice to wrestlers to "show out" more -- that is, to engage with the audience rather than concentrate solely on the athleticism. He uses the country's regional divide as an example to wrestlers.

"I tell them how in the North, you can go out, say hello to people in the street and start to recognise them, but in the South, particularly London, people walk about with their heads down. Or imagine if you went to a service station for dinner every night: you'd soon feel bad because even after a week, the staff wouldn't recognise or acknowledge you.

"When you go out to the ring and smile and shake hands with the crowd, you're making a connection: you're making a semi-friend. The kids feel like you're their best mate and they care what happens to you in the match."

Perhaps the best example of that is Dean Allmark, who commonly takes the lead blue-eye (babyface) role on shows and is none other than Dixon's son-in-law. That's not to say he had an easy route into Dixon's admiration. "He'd come from the same little promotion as guys like Robbie Dynamite, Kid Cool and Mikey Whiplash, who'd really surprised me with how good they were. But Dean introduced himself as a kickboxer and said, 'I don't really need to learn much, I'm a natural.' I thought 'you big-headed little sod!'"

Thankfully Allmark went off to get further education from Klondyke Kate -- in both wrestling skills and attitude -- and returned with a more suitable outlook. That made things easier when he began a relationship with Dixon's daughter Letitia, who had followed up a successful spell as one of the few female car salespersons to become All-Star's resident ring announcer.

If this sounds reminiscent of the Vince McMahon/Stephanie McMahon/Triple H dynamic, the succession process may wind up in a similar manner. "I'd like to retire," Dixon reveals, "but right now there's nobody to hand it over to. Dean is the best son-in-law you could hope to have, but right now he has no interest in the business side. His whole life is wrestling and -- quite understandably -- he's often blinkered and can only think about his own match."

That leaves a more likely long term plan of Letitia taking over the business side, with Dean taking charge of the in-ring operations, though with the couple having two young children, this is still some time away. In the meantime, Dixon remains busy, noting that after years of encountering wrestlers from smaller promotions who lack polish, "there's so many good wrestlers now and to give them an opportunity is great."

And more than four decades on, he remains as much a fan of wrestling as the teenager who first began hanging round the Liverpool Stadium. "If I spent the amount of time I devote to wrestling on any other business, I'd be a millionaire. I love this job I'm doing, and I never dream going to a show. I may get despondent if we draw a bad crowd, but I never get fed up with wrestling."

Brian Dixon

# BRIAN MAXINE

Many wrestling fans would have relished the opportunity to punch Brian Maxine in the face during his career. Had they come across him in the years before he got into the grapple game, they'd have been able to do just that -- or at least give it a try.

"I worked on the fairground booths, usually as a boxer alongside two wrestlers," Maxine told FSM. "We'd usually take on challengers late at night who'd come from the pub, full of vigour and wanting to take out their frustrations. They'd get a fiver if they stood the distance -- three two-minute rounds."

As did several other pro wrestlers, Maxine learnt both performance and combat skills on the booths, with his task being to win without necessarily destroying an opponent in quick fashion. "There was [showmanship] to an extent: it was to the booth owner's benefit that we kept getting challengers. But I'd be fighting guys who were six foot tall and 20 stone, so if you had the capability to take a knockout any time you wanted like I did, then if you saw a chance you'd usually take it. Lose too often and you wouldn't be employed! I usually liked to go for a second round knockout, and the owner could rely on that."

Maxine's next round of physical training was neither for profit nor entertainment. "I was in the last intake for National Service [a compulsory military posting]. I was in the Cheshire regiment with a guy called Monty Swann, though he managed to get a medical discharge. He went to the sick bay every day with some excuse and after the three months training, when we got posted abroad, he managed to get out of it. He was fit as a fiddle, the fittest man you'd ever see!"

Upon returning from his overseas tour, Maxine began learning professional wrestling with his brother, who performed under the name Buddy Ward. (Ward made headlines in 2010 when he made a return to the ring at the age of 75.) To his surprise, he found that Monty Swann had also begun a successful career in the pro ranks. Ward and Swann encouraged him to join them and began training him for the ring.

"I found it quite easy to transfer the skills from the booths," recalled Maxine of his time boxing, and occasionally wrestling, the public. "My brother phoned me up and asked if I would do a match in Morecambe. I wasn't really sure I was ready, but he said, 'You'll be OK, you'll sort it out, and if you get stuck just knock them out!'"

Fortunately, such a conclusion didn't prove necessary and Maxine impressed promoter Jimmy Lewis, at the time a claimant to the world welterweight championship. "He asked if I had my datebook with me, and of course I didn't have one, so he told me 'get a diary, send it to me, and I'll fill it up.'"

Like most wrestlers who stuck to a particular region of the country, Maxine initially combined his ring career with a full-time job. But where most wrestlers counted down the hours till they could clock off and head to a show, Maxine had the reverse experience.

"I was working in Ellesmere Port at the Stanlow refinery as a pipe fitter and welder, while wrestling mainly around the Manchester area. I worked the night shift, so I'd get my mate Sam to clock me in and then drive there after a show, sneak in and pretend like I'd been working the whole time. It was definitely a bit of a comedown to go from a show to work."

As he became more established on the wrestling circuit, Maxine eventually packed in the night job. His initial momentum was halted by an injury, though not one suffered during a show. "It was the first time at Chester Town Hall, where my brother worked for the local promoter. We went down in the late afternoon and he introduced me to the promoter and we did a little demonstration in the ring for him. I managed to break both my tibia and fibula trying out a hold and was out for six months."

Early in his career, Maxine faced a tough decision when invited to meet Norman Morrell, who promoted a large region across Yorkshire and Northern England. "He was the main man, the instigator of Joint Promotions. He told me 'I'll fill your diary: you'll work seven days a week if you want to. I can't give you a pay rise, but every night you want to work, you'll be on.' I asked him about the pay and he said I'd have to take £2 less than what I was on, so I decided not to take the job."

Maxine managed to keep his datebook filled nonetheless, and it only took a few years before he made his television debut in 1965. The booking couldn't have been much more high-profile: he lost by two falls to one to Mick McManus. The pair would go on to have several notable bouts over the years including a Royal Albert Hall clash. In 1978 McManus beat Maxine on TV in a tournament bout, only for Maxine to beat McManus in a middleweight title defence a few weeks later. It was only the third time that somebody pinned McManus to win a TV match and would prove to be the final such occasion.

Over the following years, Maxine became a regular on television, establishing himself with some serious self-promotion. He began wearing a crown and declaring himself 'King of the Ring', also handing out promotional flyers and even business cards to ringsiders to make sure he was remembered.

"I got a reaction: either fans enjoyed it, or they hated it. The other wrestlers never said so to my face, but they didn't like me getting so much attention. I'd call myself the greatest ever, which is an easy thing to say when you're talking about yourself!"

Maxine recalls taking a deliberate approach to wrestling on television. "I found the best way to handle the cameras is to almost forget they are there, unless you are doing something specific to acknowledge them. Sometimes I'd shout at [commentator] Kent Walton, either for publicity or my own amusement."

The combination of a colourful character and his legitimate grappling skills made Maxine an ideal candidate for a championship given the philosophy of promoters in that era. That came to pass in September 1969 when he beat Alan Sargeant for the British welterweight title. In June 1971 he took the British middleweight title, making him the first man to be British champion in two weight divisions at the same time during the Mountevans rules era.

That achievement was later matched by the Dynamite Kid, who held both the welterweight and lightweight belts in 1978. But while both men quickly vacated the lighter of their two titles, for Maxine it was just the start of his record setting. He continued to hold the middleweight crown for the remaining 17 years that wrestling was on TV, and beyond. "It was my intention to go on a long time. I had no intention of being a flash in the pan."

Indeed, Maxine never lost the middleweight title in the ring and it wasn't until 2000 that promoters began billing other performers as defending the British title in the weight division. While some reports of bouts in the later years of his career involved promoters billing Maxine's matches as being for his title belt only (and not the championship itself), Maxine maintains that he continued to claim the title until his retirement.

"I was still billed as the middleweight champion, I was still having title defences as the middleweight champion, so that makes me the middleweight champion!"

Whatever the correct cut-off point for his title reign, Maxine was the undisputed champion for at least the best part of three decades, a record that beats even the 26-year run as world lightweight champion of George Kidd and will presumably never be beaten.

The said title belt was another of the ways Maxine stood out from his peers. While most British title belts were modest affairs, he had an ostentatious creation that earned him the nickname "Gold Belt", with some wrestling folklore putting its value at £5,000. However, the belt Maxine continues to own today is not the "original" model.

Brian Maxine

"The belt was stolen when I was wrestling at Wembley Town Hall. I was in the third match on the show. I remember Mick McManus was on second and he came in to get changed, and then I went out after the interval. When I came back, the belt wasn't there. The second swore he took it to the dressing room and left it in my bag. At first, I thought it was just a prank and that one of the other wrestlers had hidden it. In the end I reported it to the police and it wound up being reported on the show Police 5 with Shaw Taylor [a forerunner to Crimewatch.] What really happened to the belt never came to light."

Maxine was no stranger to television outside of wrestling. He appeared in skits on shows with both Les Dawson and Kenny Everett, the latter of whom apparently had the power to throw him around the ring using just the power of his fingertip. Maxine also appeared as a regular character playing a heavy in the sitcom Bowler (a spin-off of The Fenn Street Gang) and had a minor part in The Bill.

Having earned membership of Equity, his main acting work came in the theatre, however, with the debut of Clare Luckham's play Trafford Tanzi about an oppressed housewife who becomes a wrestler. On the recommendation of Brian Glover, who wrestled as Leon Arras, Maxine was hired to train the actors in performing the wrestling moves.

"I had to take out the dangerous stuff. It was athletic, but actors are not of the same breed as wrestlers, so I had to calm it down a lot. I had to be very specific about what they would do, particularly as a lot of it had a man wrestling a woman."

The theatre set-up, with the ring in the middle of the audience rather than facing one way from the stage, was another aspect in which Maxine could lend his experience. "It was a bit like stepping back in time to days gone by for them, back to the way theatre was in the round in Shakespeare's time. But if an actor is any good, they'll be very adaptable."

Maxine toured with the play for some time, at times appearing in front of the audience playing the role of referee. He even appeared in the West End's Mermaid Theatre for a while before being replaced. "New management came in and brought in their own people. Once Toyah Wilcox took over the lead role, they decided it was easier for her to learn more judo moves than wrestling, so I was surplus to requirements. I saw the show after they changed the moves and I felt a lot was lost in transformation."

The play's enduring popularity meant Maxine was able to take trips to Norway and Israel in the role of fight director. He was then hired to work in New York on a Broadway production of what had been renamed Teaneck Tanzi, starring Debbie Harry of Blondie in the lead role, and comedian and renowned wrestling devotee Andy Kaufman as the referee.

"I saw a lot of Debbie Harry: my hotel was on one side of Central Park and she lived on the opposite side, so I'd quite often go over to have something to eat or watch TV."

Unfortunately, the play made history when, after a series of previews, it officially opened with a matinee performance only to close with an evening performance the same day. "There was a bit of anti-British feeling at the time. Showbiz is a weird place and a lot of plays there were British, so some of the Americans were up in arms asking why they didn't have American plays. The critics knocked it badly."

Even with his theatre experience cut short, Maxine had remained busy outside the ring by following his love of country music. He recorded three albums with EMI: the first two, King of The Ring Sings and Ribbon of Stainless Steel were mainly made up of covers, while I'm Your Man contained original material.

Although Maxine promoted and sold records at wrestling shows, sometimes giving performances during the interval, he was no gimmick musician. In 1974, the Country Music Association voted him Britain's most promising performer. He was joined on his albums by various members of folk band Fairport Convention including Sandy Denny and film still exists of him performing with the group at its annual festival Cropredy.

"I recorded my first album at Abbey Road studios in Studio 2, which was the same studio and even the same microphone that the Beatles had used. Coming from the Liverpool area, that really was quite a thrill."

At one stage Maxine was touring with a band while still wrestling. "It was a bit difficult when I went on tour, but I'd try to do both in one night. As long as the music venue was within say 30 to 50 miles of the wrestling venue, I could do my match, drive straight to the gig, and come in right on time to go on stage. Luckily, I was big enough in wrestling that I could persuade promoters to let me go on early to do that. If I couldn't, I'd just take the night off from wrestling for the music. It was fantastic, a different way of life."

According to Maxine, it was music rather than wrestling that would lead to his biggest career regret. "After Teaneck Tanzi I went down to Nashville for a couple of weeks and was offered a contract with Harlan Howard. He was a songwriter who'd had some massive hits with big stars. They wanted me to go and stay on his farm in Tennessee and experiment with different writers.

"My style was very straight to the point, nothing fancy, it was right there on a plate. His stuff was more poppy with lots of strings. The idea was that he'd take some of my rough edges off and make it smoother, while I'd help make some of his songs a bit more down to earth.

"Unfortunately, I had mortgages to pay and the like, so I flew back home with the plan to go back out there in three months. However, I got into a divorce that wound up going through the High Court and took a year to settle. It meant I lost ground and it really was a chance that was in the moment. That's my biggest regret: I should have just packed another bag and flown straight back to the US."

Maxine continued wrestling in the post television era, working for All Star Promotions for several years before taking on a veteran role for groups that favoured the traditional British style such as Premier Promotions and LDN. He also worked in a non-televised match at the WWF's 1991 "Battle Royale at the Albert Hall" show, though it proved a more significant bout for his opponent Steve Regal who impressed management and eventually earned a job, albeit after a six-year detour via WCW. Recalled Regal in his autobiography: "The night was a complete sellout and I was very nervous, but Brian made me look like a million dollars, and I've always thanked him for that."

It appears Maxine's final match may have come against Johnny Kidd in 2008, though Maxine notes he never had a formal retirement. "To be honest, I don't know when and where my last match was. I reduced the time I wanted to wrestle because I was busy writing my own songs and enjoying life in general. I didn't intentionally decide to end wrestling, it just came about that the breaks between matches got longer and longer!"

# THE BRITISH BULLDOGS

"They were two of the best wrestlers ever to put on wrestling boots: the only thing that let them down was their size." That's the memory of Tony 'Banger' Walsh of two cousins who made their name on the worldwide scene but started their wrestling careers in their native land.

Like so many grapplers, Tom Billington's life in professional wrestling began by chance. Although he had trained in boxing as a child, he never considered wrestling until accompanying his father, a builder, to a job on the home of Ted Betley in Warrington. A former pro himself, Betley had opened a gymnasium where he taught legitimate grappling skills to local wrestlers as well being closely linked to the rugby league fitness scene.

Marty Jones recalls that Betley's gym "had lots of amateur lads like John Naylor, Alan Woods, Jack Fallon, and Steve and Bernie Wright. Anyone in that gym was a bit special. It was full of hard men and a serious, straight wrestling gym." Billington accepted an invitation to begin training at the gym, where Jones recalls his first impression being that of a "snotty kid." It was shortly after this that Mark Rocco had an unusual, if telling, first encounter with Billington, who occasionally hung around pro shows.

"I was booked to work at Wigan, a small show, and it was Christmas time. I got there a bit late and there were decorations up all over the place and hiding in this Christmas tree was the face of this cheeky young lad about 13, 14 and he was looking through the Christmas tree. And I said to him "Watch yourself you don't knock that tree over." And the first thing he said to me was "Go on, fuck off!"

Fortunately, Billington was more respectful at Betley's gym, also learning at a facility run by Fallon and visiting the notorious Riley's Gym in Wigan, better known as the Snake Pit. He was determined to turn professional and did so in 1975, recalling his first match as being against Bobby Hems in Malvern Wells.

Now using the name Dynamite Kid, Billington made what was billed his television debut in a match from Lincoln airing on 30 October 1976. (He was advertised against Pete Meredith in the TV Times for a show that aired three weeks earlier, but it doesn't appear this bout aired.) Not only was the newcomer allowed to display a surprising level of offense against veteran Alan Dennison, but

Dynamite was booked to avoid the seemingly inevitable loss. The match ended with Dynamite unable to continue after landing throat-first on the top rope.

Custom had it that the opposing wrestler in such a situation would be offered the opportunity to be declared the winner by a referee stoppage. Given Dennison was known for a rulebending style, fans might have expected him to follow the likes of Jim Breaks in gleefully accepting the win. Instead he delivered a rare in-ring promo that served as both a babyface turn of sorts and a ringing endorsement of the newcomer:

"Ladies and gentlemen, this had been an experience for me like I have never ever known before. This boy, by the way, is 17 years of age. And he may to you, as he does to me, look a little bit amateurish but by God these moves. I've never ever seen one man in the world do the double arms up the back and handspring out of it so personally, with the referee's permission, I would like him to make it a no contest because I do not want this [win]."

Dynamite was an instant hit and was by far the most successful of the generation of newcomers given a concerted push as matchmaking duties passed from Mick McManus to Mike Marino and then Max Crabtree. In 1977 alone, he appeared on television a dozen times, only one match fewer than Big Daddy, who was in the first full-year of his push as top babyface.

The youngster also began mopping up championships, first beating Jim Breaks for the British lightweight title at Belle Vue on 23 April 1977. He then defeated Breaks (who had moved up a weight division) for the British welterweight title in a televised match from Preston on 25 January 1978, making him a double-weight title holder at the age of just 19. British wrestling custom meant he surrendered the lightweight crown, but within three months was again a double champion after adding the European welterweight title to his collection.

During this period, he also made his Royal Albert Hall debut on a show attended by the Queen's cousin, the Duke of Kent. His opponent on that night was Steve Grey, who remembers Dynamite as being "incredibly athletic: he could really move around. He had a great engine as well. I was fit and could get most of my opponent breathing heavy, but he could keep up. He had an incredible move where you threw him down and he did a handspring and popped up, but it looked like he'd bounced off his head."

Shortly after winning the European title, Dynamite made a trip to the Stampede promotion in Canada, having been recruited by Bruce Hart on a European tour. It was a move made against the wishes of Max Crabtree who warned him that he would have to surrender both titles and would not be in the championship picture if and when he returned.

Writing in his autobiography Pure Dynamite, he recalls initially deciding against the trip, only to change his mind when a promised pay rise turned out to be just an extra one pound a match over the £12 he was already earning. While Billington's recollection that he didn't return to England for another 13 years was most definitely faulty, it was indeed the case that Crabtree did not trust him with titleholder status again.

Belts aside, Dynamite made several return visits to the UK over the next five years, often fighting headliners such as Marty Jones and Mark Rocco. The latter -- no stranger to an aggressive, fast-paced style himself -- recalls that fighting was often the operative word.

"He was an amazing wrestler, and absolutely fearless. He wasn't very friendly to any other wrestlers: not everybody liked going on with him, a lot of people got damaged by him. Whenever you'd put me and Dynamite on a show, if you put the match on again next time the hall would be full. But we always ended up either in hospital or should have gone to hospital!

"When we had a match, I used to say to my missus 'I might come home in an ambulance, I'm on with Dynamite.' On one occasion, in a previous bout I'd hit the corner post and my foot missed the corner post at high speed and a sharp hook behind it ripped into my thigh and I needed 15 stitches. We patched it up as best we could and we had a show that I had to do. It was a big thing for [Dynamite] and Max said to just take it easy. I just said 'Do whatever you want, just watch you don't rip my leg open again.' The first thing he did was rip my leg open!"

Bret Hart, who wrestled Dynamite in both Stampede and the UK before their WWF days, told FSM that physicality was an issue from the start. "We weren't good friends at first -- there were a few potatoes flying about -- but eventually we respected each other. He was a great innovator, so agile and built like a bullet. When he did the diving headbutt it was like watching a missile."

Tony Walsh believes Dynamite's aggression was as much about making the match as good as possible as anything else. "Tommy took no prisoners. If somebody was not pulling their weight, he'd sharpen them up."

No sooner had Dynamite made his first overseas voyage than his first cousin David Smith, four years his younger, had turned pro himself after also going through Ted Betley's ranks. While he was later known as Davey 'Boy' Smith (the story going that his father had mixed up the spaces for middle name and gender on his birth registration form), he started out as simply 'Young David', an appropriate name given he made his TV debut aged 15. As with Dynamite he avoided defeat on his first appearance before the cameras, drawing one fall apiece with Bernie Wright.

According to Rocco, the timing of his debut may have hurt Smith in the early years. "He started too early and didn't have enough background before he started wrestling [pro]. The older guys who don't like the new young lads jumping about, they restricted him physically by holding him down and not letting him do his stuff. He was very young for his years so didn't get going straight away."

The youngster's inexperience also showed outside of wrestling, as Rocco remembers. "He was very shy back then. I used to introduce him to girls outside the dressing room and he'd turn red, purple and blue."

Mal Sanders recalls an incident when Smith demonstrated a memorable lack of focus. "When he was just starting to make his name, he was teaming with Pete Roberts in a two-on-one handicap match against Giant Haystacks. As always Roberts was very well turned out and his hair looked good and smart. They came to the ring first and Davey was just stood there looking at Pete. The lights went out and the spotlight came on for Haystacks and Davey never took his eyes off Pete the whole time. This went on for about five minutes -- that's how long it took Haystacks to get in after doing all the stalling and arguing with the crowd -- and finally the bell goes for the match. Davey's still staring, and Pete looks at him as if to ask what's going on. That's when Davey just pipes up, in his Northern accent, "'Ere, have you got lacquer in your 'air?"

Smith would gain much-needed experience in the role of Big Daddy's partner where he would take a pounding for much of the match before making the hot tag. Frequent opponent Tony Walsh remembers that David's youthful looks -- a literal baby face -- were perfect for the role. "He was cannon fodder. It would get the crowd going with me doing my villain stuff and Giant Haystacks using his weight. It worked and would get an enormous amount of heat."

Eventually Smith was judged old enough for a singles push and, as so often with lighter babyfaces of the era, Jim Breaks was the man to make him. Their onscreen rivalry began in a match from Aylesbury that aired on 8 December 1979. With Breaks the British welterweight champion and Smith still in his teens, it was announced that Breaks would not only give Smith a one-fall head start but would hand over £100 of his own cash (around £500 in today's prices) if he managed to score a fall.

That's exactly what happened, the finish meaning that although Breaks was only pinned once, Smith not only got the money but was also technically a two-falls-to-one winner of the bout. That inevitably led to Breaks demanding a rematch and agreeing to put up the title in a bout airing three weeks later.

Smith again prevailed by two-falls-to-one, this time earning both falls in the ring, and briefly appeared to be the new titleholder. However, Breaks successfully challenged the decision on the grounds that Alan Dennison -- now established as a supporter of younger talent and billed as Smith's mentor -- had unfairly distracted him leading to the finish.

The third match in the trilogy aired on 23 February 1980 from Southend, with Dennison banned from ringside. It was a genuine classic, going one fall apiece to a

12 round draw. Although he didn't capture the title, Smith was portrayed as having pulled off a great achievement: one fall down going into the final round, he successfully played Breaks at his own game by feigning injury to lure him in to a pinfall. Dennison came out to celebrate, setting up a feud that saw him capture the title himself later in the year.

Such success not only led to confidence in the ring, but also behind the scenes. The pair would eventually be known on a worldwide stage for their fondness for practical jokes: Davey Boy's being largely playful and Dynamite's not so much. Tony St Clair recalls Dynamite living up to his name. "He was always good for a laugh, great to be with, but horrible to drive with. He'd go at 100 miles per hour on small country lanes, driving on the left hand side, then the right hand side, then down the middle, putting you in precarious positions."

Marty Jones admits that "they learned to play pranks from us, though John Foley used to do the biggest tricks. They shared his attitude that if you don't like it, tough shit." Tony Walsh is straight to the point with his recollection. "They were typical northern pisstakers. Funny, funny, funny, but caused havoc wherever they went."

Meanwhile Mark Rocco says they did "all sorts of stuff. They did stuff which was just crazy and dangerous. They were both fearless and they wanted to outdo each other by how amazing they could do things." He's more diplomatic about assigning blame though. "Put it this way: I've seen all sorts of stuff happen where I can't actually blame them for it happening, but they were there, and I don't think it would have happened if they weren't!"

That reputation was enhanced on the pair's international travels, with both men working in Canada. Tony Walsh says they were determined to make it on a worldwide stage: "If they wanted to go somewhere, they'd go. Wild horses wouldn't stop them."

Smith joined Dynamite in Calgary in 1981, feuding on and off for two years with Dynamite in a heel role. They then formed a tag team in Japan (where Dynamite had helped revolutionise junior-heavyweight wrestling with Tiger Mask) and took the pairing back to Calgary in 1983, the same year both made their final appearances on World of Sport. They then took the act to the WWF where they were renamed the British Bulldogs and held the tag titles during the post-territory boom period. The pair's family tree became more complicated in this era with Davey Boy marrying Bret Hart' sister, while Dynamite married Bret's wife's sister.

During this time, they made another couple of ITV appearances when WWF programming made an occasional appearance in the Saturday afternoon slot. However, although they toured continental Europe in 1987 with the WWF, the pair never actually teamed as the Bulldogs in the United Kingdom. Dynamite suffered a serious back injury in 1986 before the pair left the promotion in 1988. They continued teaming in Japan but broke off personal relations after Davey Boy was rehired by WWF in 1990 without Dynamite's knowledge.

Both would wind up working in the UK, albeit under different circumstances. Dynamite returned home after the team's split and picked up several dates with All Star and Orig Williams' shows but was struggling physically. Tony St Clair recalls that Dynamite found it a tough adjustment to make. "It really hurt him to have to do tags with three other guys carrying the action because he couldn't put his full act together."

The only time the two were in close proximity after their split in 1990 came, according to Dynamite, in 1994. Davey Boy, having headlined Wembley Stadium as SummerSlam 1992 and then had a run with WCW, spent several months working for Max Crabtree, ironically in the role previously held by Big Daddy. Dynamite recalled seeing him advertised for a local show and going to the venue to confront him only to be removed from the building.

Dynamite retired in 1996 after a final bout in Japan for Michinoku Pro. The following year he became confined to a wheelchair through back injuries that were judged inoperable thanks to complications from the 1986 incident. He has continued to suffer poor health since and has been relatively reclusive, though famously appeared at the Revival show in Crystal Palace in 2002 where he endorsed tournament winner Jodie Fleisch.

Davey continued to bounce back and forth between WWF and WCW, suffering a serious back injury when landing on a trapdoor under the ring that had been set up to allow a surprise entrance. That led to a spinal infection that resulted in several months in hospital and in turn serious painkiller addiction problems. Smith died in 2002 from a heart attack which the autopsy revealed may have been the result of steroid abuse. His son Harry later had a WWF run and is currently a New Japan roster member out on loan to Pro Wrestling NOAH.

# CATWEAZLE

"You didn't usually know who you'd be wrestling at a show till you got there. When you saw your name next to Catweazle's, you knew you were really in for a nice night."

That's how Mel Stuart remembers a wrestler who never held titles and rarely main-evented, yet is one of the most fondly remembered characters of the World of Sport era, particularly by the more casual viewing audience. Indeed, so well is Catweazle remembered that there's even an outlandish urban myth that he once beat Mick McManus by two submissions via tickling, a story about as accurate as the idea Kendo Nagasaki was never seen on TV without his mask.

Catweazle began life as Gary Cooper, a name shared with a film star of the era to the delight of trivia fans. He came to wrestling relatively late, working until his late 20s at the Doncaster locomotive works, a job that gave him the right to free train travel, which proved a major financial advantage at the start of his career.

After a spell boxing at a local club, he began training in wrestling in Leeds at a gym owned by independent promoter and former middleweight champion Cyril Knowles. Initially wrestling under his real name, frequently in a villain role, he continued his training in Barnsley under Charlie Glover, the father of actor and wrestler Brian 'Leon Arras' Glover.

His big break came alongside fellow trainee Al Marshall, who tells FSM that he had been offered trials with leading northern promoters De Relwyskow and Green. "Gary came along for the trials as well: he was [already] good at the time, really, really good. I had family and a full-time job so couldn't travel far and George De Relwyskow said, 'If you're not going to work in Scotland, we're not going to use you.'

"Because he could get about with the trains, Gary jumped at the chance and went working up at the Eldorado Stadium in Edinburgh. It had a very ferocious reputation and anyone who was English was tore apart by the crowd."

It was this hostile response spilling over into mockery that would spark Cooper's change of character thanks to his resemblance to a children's television character played by Geoffrey Bayldon. "People in the crowd at the Eldorado started to call him 'Catweazle' because of his appearance. George DeRelwyskow got wind of this and decided to see if there was any copyright on the name, which there wasn't. So they called him Catweazle and of course he went on telly and became an instant success."

Cooper debuted on the small screen in August 1971 with a draw against Dane Curtis, with Kent Walton mentioning his real name during early appearances but also using the new moniker. The debut came four months after the conclusion of the Catweazle TV show, which featured Bayldon as a time-travelling wizard.

Other than the name, the only thing Cooper took directly from the show was to bring a plastic toad to place on the turnbuckle pads in his corner, aping the TV wizard's "animal guide" Touchwood. While Cooper came to the ring in a sackcloth-style robe similar to that worn by the TV character, he would initially wrestle the bout in striped trunks, later switching to a unique one-piece affair that resembled a Victorian bathing costume.

Cooper would eventually meet Bayldon when the actor was performing in a London play and there were no problems over the shared character. Indeed, it's arguable Cooper's Catweazle had become as or more famous than the original.

Cooper's daughter Cyndi recalls that fame had its pros and cons. "He couldn't have a meal uninterrupted without somebody coming over asking for an autograph: it used to drive us mad actually. Sometimes when you're out with a family, you just want to have a family meal, you don't want people coming over, but it's all part of the job I suppose. And when we were in pubs and people were coming up trying to buy us drinks, that bit was good!"

Indeed, she remembers her father had a real love of life. "He spent most of his time in the pub: that's most of my childhood memories actually. There was a family room in the back where we used to sit with the other kids until goodness knows what time and there was always a lock-in. What you saw was what you got with him: he was really funny, a joking around chap."

Cooper's love of performing certainly extended beyond his job. "We had an amateur dramatics society down the road and he used to go along. He didn't do any plays [in public] or anything, but in the room he'd be acting around with the other members and really enjoyed it."

Cyndi also remembers that her home life had some unusual elements. "Everyone came round our house. Giant Haystacks would always give us each a pound for pocket money to buy sweet, so to us he was good! And we used to have massive collection of Touchwoods because the public used to send us loads of frogs and we had hundreds of them, which he really used to enjoy."

It seems the success of the Catweazle character was at least partly due to its authenticity, with Cooper being equally upbeat in and out of the ring according to Al Marshall. "The comedy bit was so natural for him. He was a naturally happy-go-lucky guy. Whatever he said, he made you laugh: anything he did was so comical."

"He didn't give a shit about anything. He had the nickname 'Chuffer' because he wouldn't swear: it was always 'chuffing this' and 'chuffing that' in his right broad Yorkshire accent."

Alongside the likes of Les Kellett, Catweazle was among the leading comedic performers of his era. Much of his antics involved his mouth, whether it be elaborate sequences spraying water at hapless opponents, burping, or making the most of his false teeth whether by design or accident.

"I had to stop myself laughing during some matches," Mel Stuart recalls. "One time he had me down on my knees in a Japanese stranglehold and I was acting all serious when he took his teeth out and put them on my head! In another match, he had me in a straight armlock and was bending down when his teeth fell out and slowly rolled perfectly down my arm!"

Neil "Tom Thumb" Evans, who teamed with Catweazle early in his career, had a similar experience. "It was almost difficult to wrestle him because you'd catch yourself laughing. He was superb at what he did."

At live events, Catweazle would frequently fill a uniquely British position known as the "happy match", a closing contest so-named because it was designed to send the crowd home happy, often calming them down after a heated reaction to main event villainy. Evans recalls it as "like signing off at the end of the night," while promoter Brian Dixon has previously used the analogy of dessert following a main course.

While best known for his comedy, Catweazle's peers testify to his versatility. Evans remembers he would sometimes open up the show to get the crowd going, while Stuart recalls working with him in "villain" matches (a more traditional babyface vs heel contest) and even a more traditional babyface vs babyface pure wrestling performance.

"We worked at Margate and worked straight all the way through. The crowd weren't laughing, but instead clapped at the end of each round. Even in the happy matches, his comedy wasn't over the top. He wouldn't be funny all the way through the match: he knew how to fit it all in."

Al Marshall concurs that Catweazle was technically solid underneath the comedy. "To do the clowning around, you've got to be able to do the job in the first place."

That said, the comedy did restrict Catweazle from achieving some of the more traditional measures of success for major stars. He was never in the championship picture, made no appearances on FA Cup Final Day specials, appeared only on the lower-profile 1980 edition of the Wembley Arena shows, and rarely appeared at the Royal Albert Hall more than once a year.

Yet despite this he remained a perennial favourite on television as well as becoming a trusted regular opponent of Mick McManus in his final years. Indeed in 1982 he was picked as the opponent for McManus's final television appearance. Further evidence of his importance in his role came when he provided light relief against Shane Stevens at the first All Star Wrestling event taped for television, a match that lived on as a clip in the fondly-remembered opening sequence of the standalone wrestling show that followed World of Sport's departure.

Tragically Cooper was diagnosed with cancer in the early 90s, battling the disease for well over a year. Steve Grey recalls that, publicly at least, he faced it with a characteristically upbeat approach. "He never made the cancer a big secret; he was always open about it. He'd say, 'I'm still here... it's just one of those things.'"

Eventually the disease was to claim Cooper's life, though not before he'd had a chance to leave some instructions for his funeral. It became one of the most legendary stories in the British wrestling community: per his orders, as the service came to the committal stage and his coffin began to be rolled out of view ready for cremation, the room was filled with the sound of Jerry Lee Lewis's "Great Balls of Fire." Cyndi Cooper recalls that now "Every time I hear that, it reminds me of him and I have to laugh!"

As Frank Rimer explains, Cooper's death would indirectly spark a process that helped keep the memories of his career and those of his colleagues very much alive. "He left a thousand pounds in his will for the boys to have a drink, which of course they did! While they were there, Joe D'Orazio spoke up and said it would be a good idea for people in the wrestling business to meet up socially without waiting for somebody to die.

"That led to the idea of a reunion, and referee Mal Mason agreed to hold the first one in his back garden in Kent. As Mal was working only for Brian Dixon at the time, he wasn't in touch with a lot of the Joint boys, so the first reunion had only six people: Mal, Joe, Pat Roach, Johnny Kwango, Tony Scarlo and John Hall. Joe said they should try again and a couple of weeks later they got 13 people in.

"From there they moved to holding it at Joe Cornelius's pub in the West End of London, which was easier for people to get to and the event was more successful. When Cornelius moved abroad, it went to Wayne Bridge's pub in Greenwich and then followed him to Kent where it's still held every August to this day."

The reunion has truly gone from strength to strength, growing from around 150 wrestlers in the early days at Greenwich to an event also attended by relatives and fans of the business. Rimer notes that this year's reunion attracted a record 480 guests.

Among those was Cyndi Cooper, making her second visit after spending more than decades completely unaware of her father's legacy. "I didn't know anything about it until three years ago. When my dad died, I was only about 24 and I lost touch with all of it and never really kept up with anybody in wrestling.

"I'd been completely out of the loop and still would be if it wasn't for Facebook. I had a friend on there, somebody I knew for reasons nothing to do with wrestling, but he kept posting about wrestling all the time. So I inboxed him and said, 'I don't know if you're interested, but my dad's Catweazle.' He put me in touch with Ken Sowden at the reunion, and I went along a couple of years ago and then again this year.

"I'm quite a shy person and with such a big group of people and it having been such a long time, I wasn't sure if I'd recognise anybody. But I went along and everybody was very friendly and lovely and I made some really good friends. Meeting Clive Myers again was a big thing because he played such a pivotal role in organizing my dad's funeral, so it was really nice to go up and say thank you for that.

"This year I got an award that I accepted on my dad's behalf, which was really nice. It really meant a lot to me that he was remembered after all this time."

# CHIC CULLEN

It's not unusual for two wrestlers to hail from the same town, or even to have attended the same school. But Frank Cullen explains to FSM that Raploch Road in Stirling had an unusual claim to fame as home to two future World of Sport stars: "Andy Robin lived at number 1 and I lived at number 41!"

This piece of trivia wasn't the source of Cullen's entry into the business however: instead that came from a medical issue that for many people would be a deterrence from an athletic life. "I've had asthma all my life and, in those days, we used to go to youth clubs in Stirling. All my buddies were playing five-a-side football or were playing rugby at school and I couldn't really join in because I couldn't breathe good enough to run. I used to sit on the wall and watch and one day when I was 10 discovered in another part of the building there was Olympic wrestling and I joined in."

After seven years of attending classes, Cullen received some career advice from trainer Brian McInally. "He had done a little pro wrestling and said I'd probably enjoy it so give it a try. I was a big fan of pro wrestling and really enjoyed it."

Getting a break was easier said than done however. An invite to a show in Glasgow run by Joint Promotions and boxer Peter Keenan didn't lead anywhere. Instead Cullen began regularly attending show in Stirling run by independent promoter Orig Williams, who dismissed him several times until eventually giving him a try-out in what proved to be his pro debut against Carl 'Jason' McGrath in 1976.

"I went on the last week of the tour with Orig in Scotland and they were showing me stuff every day and at the end of the week I expected to be sent home, but he said 'No, would you like to come and live in North Wales?' He even came to see my parents in Scotland at the end of the week and I went with him and never looked back."

Despite being just 17, Cullen moved to Rhyl and quickly found himself overseas. "I went from living in a pretty grim area of Stirling to touring Spain and wrestling in bullrings. Except the fans didn't know we were coming so quite often there was nobody there. It was a dreadful tour but a good experience."

While the payoffs weren't always up to scratch, the need to eat on a budget led to a fond memory. The wrestlers parked the ring van in the middle of Madrid and, passers-by saw an exterior covered in posters billing the vicious and dastardly "Dragon Chino." What they didn't know was that Crusher Mason -- the man behind the gimmick -- was inside rigging up a camping stove to feed the crew with hot dogs.

"Within a year I was flying because there were no wrestling schools then, so you had to rely on somebody to take you under your wing and show you. With Orig we were lucky that we had Crusher at the time, known here as the Mighty Chang. He and Orig and other guys were training me every day, sometimes twice a day, so that was invaluable. My job was travelling around, putting the ring up, wrestling in the afternoon with people who were willing to train me, and wrestling at night on the shows, so I got a lot of experience very quickly."

Cullen's career progressed when he moved to Merseyside and began making his name wrestling for Brian Dixon. After three years, he took another step. "Even when you were working for the opposition in those days, [Joint Promotions boss] Max Crabtree knew who was who on the other side of the fence. They kept tabs on you, When I was still working for Brian, I had a falling out with him and he said why don't you try Joint Promotions. I called Max and he said "Yes, I'll be happy to have you" and next thing I knew a date sheet came through the door."

Within a matter of weeks, Cullen was on television in a losing effort against John Elijah. Crabtree rebranded his new star as "Chic" Cullen, with the alliterative name coming from the fact that he reminded the promoter of fellow Scottish grappler Chic Purvey. It was a name that stuck and certainly more successful than an alias Cullen used when inviting challengers from the audience at Blackpool Pleasure Beach. Rather than the intended moniker of the Aztec Warrior, promoter Bobby Barron mistakenly introduced him as the "Artex Warrior", prompting several long-running jokes about Cullen being a "highly decorated wrestler."

Another new name came when Cullen made his way over to Stampede Wrestling in Calgary and was rebranded as Robbie Stewart. He was one of several British wrestlers to visit the territory during the era. "Bruce Hart was a big mark for the British style of wrestling. He also was bringing in people who were roughly the same size as him: he had method in his madness there. He wanted people who were perfect foil for the Hart Brothers to knock them off. My recommendation came from Big John Quinn: he put in a word for me."

Cullen made several visits to Calgary over the next five years, wrestling the likes of Adrian Street, Dynamite Kid, Cuban Assassin and Chris Benoit as well as teaming with Eddie 'Kung Fu' Hamill. Unlike the haphazard schedule of British wrestling in this era, Cullen enjoyed the weekly loop, despite the lengthy drives. "You're well established in these places. Stampede used to film the show in

Calgary every Friday night and overnight they would edit it in studio and then show it on Saturday afternoon. That was your promo for the week: it was great, it was like your own shop window. It was free advertising. This would continue week after week, they had a good system."

While Bruce Hart was booking, family patriarch Stu Hart was still in charge upon Cullen's arrival and he found him to share common traits with British promoters. "They're all very cheap: none of them wanted to pay you. It was kind of hard to get money out of them, you thought you were worth a bit more. Some guys couldn't even afford to exist: they expected you to have a good reliable car to go up and down the motorway and you couldn't even afford a car sometimes. They all had that general negative about them. As people they were all decent people, you could chat to them in the car on the way down or chat to them quietly. They always appreciated what you did.

"Stu Hart was a great old guy. You could sit and chat with him for hours. But he'd call you and after half an hour he'd say, 'Who's paying for this call?' I'd say 'Oh, you are Stu' and immediately he'd go 'Oh, I've got to go now, bye.' They were cheap, but they were interesting characters too."

Back in the UK, Cullen entered the championship picture, first taking the British Heavy-Middleweight title from Alan Kilby at the Royal Albert Hall in 1984, the first of three runs with the title. He also achieved world champion status at the same weight, taking the title from Mark Rocco, albeit only for a month. "Titles meant something then: it was considered a privilege to be asked to take one of these belts. Not so nowadays: people can't even have a photograph without a belt over their shoulder. They've lost all respect for belts and the meaning of them.

"Even if you turned up with [another promotion's] belt back in those days, the promoter would say "Where'd you get that, what are you doing with that, put it back in your bag, don't let me see it again.' Nowadays everybody's got one, so it means nothing."

While Cullen travelled the world, particularly with Orig Williams, he struggled to get into some of the most lucrative markets for a touring Brit. "In those days the ones who were successful in Japan and Germany made it harder for the people who wanted to go there. You would say to one of the established guys 'Can you take my promo package with you?' and they'd go 'Yeah, yeah' but you'd know it never got there." While he eventually got a break, getting booked for the shoot-style UWF promotion through Pete Roberts, the group folded before he could make the tour.

Towards the end of 1985, Cullen decided to return to work for Dixon's All Star Promotions. Unlike many colleagues who made the jump, he says money wasn't the primary factor. "Joint insisted I live in London and I couldn't settle in London on my own. I was comfortable on the Wirral where Brian was based, I had roots there almost. By that time, I was about to be married and my wife lived there. Probably it was my comfort zone. I could sleep in my own bed every night rather than a guest house in London or a bedsit. I'd come from a little town in the country in Scotland and trying to live in Brixton in London, it's a huge, huge change and I was too young to cope with it."

The timing of the move meant Cullen was only off ITV for around a year (during which he appeared on cable channel Screensport) and was on the first All Star show after the ITV slot was shared at the start of 1987. He wrestled Mark Rocco at the London Hippodrome and recalls being invited by owner Peter Stringfellow to come back to the venue later that evening when it returned to its usual purpose as a nightclub. Such generosity proved short-lived when the wrestlers placed a drinks order and discovered a single beer would cost them the equivalent £13 in today's money.

Cullen continued wrestling in the post-TV era and into the 90s when he took advantage of changing tastes and began taking bookings on the Germany and Austria circuits. Once the home of the British heavyweights it was now open to lighter, faster-paced talent. Here he worked many times with a favourite colleague. "Danny Collins was very underrated around the world, he could have done more travelling. I regret very much that when I used to have these amazing wrestling matches with Danny that we weren't on TV.

"We went to Germany as tag team, but [promoter] Rene Lassertesse would rather have us wrestling each other, so we spent three or four nights a week as a tag team and the other three or four nights against each other. It was a very special, unique wrestling match where all the guys used to come out to watch it. We were very proud of the matches we did and if anybody out there has those matches on film, I'd love to own one!"

By 2002, Cullen was ready to take on a new challenge. "I'd had a bit of a gap, time out of the business, then Brian Dixon asked me to work some shows. I was in my mid-to-late 40s and still wrestling, still enjoying it. But something happened one day where Brian said, 'I don't even like going backstage any more, it's just all squabbling, people being stupid and stuff. Could you take care of that for me?'"

I said I could see what needed to be done, I could take these young guys and say, 'Here's what needs to be done, here's what you're doing tonight, and this is how you're doing it.' That kind of developed and Brian said, 'Why don't you step out of the ring and just do that.' And I was ready to step out of the ring, I was having hip and knee issues, so I did that. I was kind of running things backstage, I started matchmaking and bringing in other guys from different places to try and compliment the British talent."

Cullen did indeed hang up his boots after what was planned to be a final bout against Drew McDonald. As part of his matchmaking period, he vacated the world heavy-middleweight title that he had won from Robbie Brookside a decade earlier and had technically never lost. The new titleholder, capturing the crown in a tournament, was a young masked visitor in the form of Brian 'American Dragon' Danielson.

As well as booking, Cullen also turned his hand to a new-found passion as a trainer. "It was easy because I found out that by that time I was enjoying that more than I was wrestling. I still coach wrestling now and I enjoy it very much: it's definitely my calling." He was particularly involved in helping newcomers from other fields including World's Strongest Man competitor Jamie Reeves, bodybuilder Ian Harrison, and Mike Ahearne, better known as 'Warrior' from the TV show Gladiators. They weren't the most unconventional trainees he worked with however.

"The day of a show at Hanley, Brian said, 'Could you go down this afternoon, the ring's going to be up early and there's some American female wants to learn how to wrestle. It's all above board and she'll pay you.' So I went down, and this little midget came in. She was very nice, and I called one of the wrestling midgets from Birmingham and asked him to help -- it was easier to teach two little people than it was one. So we had a couple of hours in the ring and she put on a little demonstration match that night. I never saw her again.

"10 years later I found out she was a porn star, Bridget 'The Midget' Powers. I wish she had told me that at the time: that would have been an interesting conversation! I think she was genuinely trying to get into wrestling as a breakaway from her porn."

After creative differences with Dixon, Cullen returned to Scotland where he made a brief comeback for the local WILD promotion, with his final match coming almost exactly 30 years after his debut. He went to a time limit draw with Allan Grogan on a show which featured early appearances from current ICW stars Drew Galloway, Red Lightning and Liam Thomson.

Cullen then returned to British Columbia in Canada where he worked as an emergency first aid attendant in oilfields, briefly ran a sports bar, and continues to train wrestlers today. "Now what I do is I don't just throw open the doors and let anyone in, I kind of hand pick who I want. I do advanced stuff so you're teaching people who already have a foot in the door and they know a little bit already and you can take them up that extra gear or two.

"They're all very polite and respectful, probably more so now than ever, but almost over the top 'Yes sir, no sir' and I think 'Don't call me sir, my name's Frank, you're here to learn, I'm here to teach you, let's get on with it.'"

He recently visited the UK and acted as an agent at the World Association of Wrestling TV pilot tapings where he was pleased with the ring style. "Nowadays, especially under Ricky Knight's watch, it's what I've always thought there should be: a fusion type of wrestling. I was never keen on it to go from British to American overnight and that was something I instilled in Brian Dixon when I was running there. I talked about that philosophy with Ricky: British wrestling with a modern twist."

Looking back on his career, Cullen differs from many stars of the 1980s and 1990s who wish they could have been born a decade earlier and enjoyed more time in the TV and mainstream spotlight. "I'd rather have been born about 15 to 20 years later because there are far more opportunities for wrestlers now than there was back then. They might have been household names 10 years before I was born, but it's never been easier than it is now for wrestlers to make it in WWE or Japan because the door is open now.

"The world's a smaller place and with social media they quickly know who's who and they've probably been watching you for a while. These talent departments, they're always on the lookout for something new, the next big thing. Little Jimmy Suzuki, the photographer, he goes round the world and comments on people when he goes back [to Japan]. And with contacts in WWE like Darren [William Regal], if I have a wrestler who I think is worth a try-out, I'll phone them straight away and they'll set it up.

"Today if you're worth your salt and you're good and you look the part, you're the total package, now's the time when you're going to make it [in the major promotions]. We never had that opportunity."

# CHRIS ADAMS

For such a physical activity, personality and drive are two of the most important factors in professional wrestling. For all his physical gifts it was that personality and drive that brought Chris Adams to a successful wrestling career, but that same personality arguably led to his untimely demise.

As with many of his peers, Adams came to the grappling game from a legitimate combat sports background but it was judo rather than amateur wrestling where he made his name. His father Cyril trained both Chris and brother Neil, who remembers one highlight of their early success came when both won national championships on the same day.

While Chris was said to be in the running for a trip to the 1976 Olympics, it never panned out. Instead it was Neil who rose to glory, not only capturing the world championship, but also taking a silver medal at both the 1980 and 1984 games. Speaking to FSM in 2011, Neil said that "I think [Chris] realised that he was never going to reach the very top with his judo, so he decided to go into something else entirely. He was a very determined guy and he was a very strong independent person who didn't want to fall into my shadow "

Jeanie Clark, Chris's long-term partner, tells FSM "Chris always knew that he was never going to be as good as Neil although they had a brilliant relationship and Neil supported Chris."

While he had trained in architecture and had the makings of a stable if unexciting career working for local government, Adams still had the drive to succeed in athletic endeavours. While only a casual fan of TV wrestling as a child, he had been captivated by the new generation of talent, most notably Tom 'Dynamite Kid' Billington.

Fate was on Adam's side as he was able to break into the business thanks to time training at Nelson's Gym in Warwick, the former home of boxing great Randy Turpin. Here he met Turpin's son Jackie and Tony 'Banger' Walsh, both established pro stars. The connections were made, and Adams was quickly brought into the business.

While it's a stretch to say Adams never had any training, his education was both brief and informal. Walsh gave him a crash-course in the basic holds and he also received some tips from Peter "Tally-Ho" Kaye, but much of his training was of the on-the-job nature and Turpin recalls that "he had to learn the ropes and it took a while for him to learn the trade."

Of all combat sports, judo was arguably the most useful for adjusting to pro wrestling. As much as amateur wrestling is a valuable base, Jim Breaks has previously spoken of the challenge of retraining the body to fight the instincts of seeking a dominant position and keeping your back off the mat. Turpin has also recalled the adjustment involved in learning to pull punches and taking physical abuse on a nightly basis rather than the intense but sporadic punishment from a fight. As Doug Williams recently told FSM however, judo not only has several holds and throws that can easily be tweaked for pro wrestling, but it also makes landing as safely as possible on your back a matter of instinct.

Promoter Max Crabtree appeared to be particularly taken by Adams and he became one of the success stories from a programme of pushing new talent into the limelight to overcome the impression of 1960s stars hanging on past their prime. While in many cases this was most definitely "too much, too soon", Crabtree stuck with Adams thanks in part to the credibility he brought with his legitimate athletic background. Not only was Adams' black belt status frequently stressed, but he wrestled barefoot as wrestling historian Bradley Walsh explains.

"He didn't really particularly enjoy doing that, but it was done to reinforce the image. This was coming off the heels of the film Enter The Dragon, so there was a real martial arts craze over the UK. The wrestling fraternity were trying to capitalise on that, so you had the likes of 'Iron Fist' Clive Myers and 'Kung Fu' Eddie Hamill."

So eager were promoters to build the new star, Adams may well have had the quickest ever route to the small screen. His debut appears to have been against Kaye in Digbeth on June 8, 1978 and it was just 34 days later when the pair wrestled again in Adams' first televised match. Indeed, in his first 12 months as a TV star, Adams appeared on 12 shows -- seemingly sparse in a US context, but a rate far in excess of even the bigger stars in British wrestling, let alone a rookie.

Arguably the only wrestler Crabtree was pushing to the same extent at this time was his brother Big Daddy, who teamed with Adams on several occasions. Jeanie Clark recalls that Adams wasn't seen as a threat to Daddy, who was targeted at more of a family audience, while the good-looking youthful Adams drew the attention of women.

"He always had a lot of charisma and charm with the girls: he had a ladies man image. He was good looking and had his own following and fanbase. I don't think it crossed with Big Daddy: he had a different appeal."

Not long into his career, Adams met Clark after a show in her hometown of Southend and the pair began a relationship. This would eventually lead to Clark working as a second in his corner, enhancing his image, and joining him on the road where he would usually be accompanied by Walsh, Turpin and another local wrestler, Ringo Rigby.

Clark's good looks being, to say the least, a drastic change from the traditional British wrestling second, she was soon making the headlines herself, with photo stories in both the local and national press. It wasn't until shortly after Clark's first television appearance in October of 1980 that the pair let it be public knowledge that they were in a relationship.

That wasn't a personal issue, but rather a business one as Clark was -- unbeknownst to the many young female members -- running Adams' fan club. There was a certain irony in her being the one preparing and sending out a signed photograph and a welcome letter that, at the very least, allowed the recipient to infer Adams was single and available.

Inside the ring, Adams continued to thrive. While he didn't lift any titles, he did make it to a final of a televised tournament for the vacant British heavy-middleweight title, losing out to Mark Rocco. This tournament featured a couple of career developments, one coming in the semi-final where he achieved a disqualification win over Mick McManus. Despite the nature of the finish, a win over such a legendary figure was still a rarity at this stage, let alone for somebody barely six months into their career.

Adams' quarter-final bout against Rigby also had a first. Following Adams' winning the first fall in traditional fashion, the pair donned judo jackets and engaged in a special contest where the first man to throw his opponent to the floor three times was the winner. Both the ring announcer and commentator Kent Walton appeared confused about whether this constituted a second fall or was simply extra-curricular activity.

However, the throws format (which Adams had been doing at several non-televised matches) popped up on television several times in subsequent years, both as a tiebreaker in drawn tournament matches and as a standalone match. For the most part Adams would be victorious, though he was defeated 10-9 by Alan Kilby in the semi-final of a tournament to celebrate 25 years of televised wrestling.

The martial arts element was highly stressed, albeit with the occasional liberty taken. While striking is barred in competitive judo, Adams's signature move in the UK was a reverse "thrust" kick dubbed the "mule kick" by Walton. Later in his career Adams would refine this to a high side kick that he dubbed the "superkick", a move later used by the likes of Shawn Michaels. Adams would also form several tag teams with the likes of Clive Myers (as the "Martial Arts Fighters") and Rigby, as well as teaming with fellow judo player Pat Patton at the 1979 Wembley Arena spectacular.

Chris Adams

Although Adams surprisingly didn't make the cut for the follow up Wembley show the next summer, one the main eventers that night would change his career. Yasu Fuji, a Japanese wrestler who'd made a career in territories such as Portland and California, was himself a martial artist. He suggested Adams would be a good fit in Los Angeles where wrestling was run by the LeBell family, including the legendary 'Judo Gene' who had a natural affinity for grapplers with a legitimate background.

Adams indeed received an offer and jumped at it. While many British wrestlers were content with their life at home, he was still hungry for both money and fame and several of those close to him say he had concluded he had gone as far as was going to be possible in his home country.

Clark recalls that Adams wasn't fazed by the way the stateside move meant being asked to do promos for the first time. "I think Chris really adapted well to that. He was just a natural: he has a good sense of humour and was quick-witted. He just kind of fell into it. Everybody loved his British accent and his little dimples and found him charming."

Los Angeles brought the expected glamour for Adams and Clark, including being among the audience for the filming of the Thunderlips (aka Hulk Hogan) scene in Rocky III. Adams also made some trips to Mexico City where he beat Perro Aguayo to kick off a two-month reign with what was then billed as the WWF light-heavyweight title, a championship licensed to the local UWA promotion.

After a brief return to the UK so that Clark could give birth to the couple's daughter, the pair returned to LA where they hooked up with fellow visitor Rigby. Adams also had a spell in Portland before really making his name in World Class. Here he initially played the English gentleman babyface, a role that would always limit him to second-fiddle given the domination of the local hero Von Erich brothers.

After a long feud with Jimmy Garvin, in which he battled for the affections of valet Sunshine, Adams took on villainous manager Gary Hart and began teaming with Gino Hernandez. Adams turned against the Von Erichs, setting off a year-long feud that culminated in a match at the Cotton Bowl where Adams and Hernandez lost the bout and, as a result, their hair. That led to a split between the two and a return to babyface status for Adams, but the planned feud was interrupted by reality when Hernandez died from a cocaine overdose.

Adams went on to take the promotion's heavyweight title, billed as the World championship thanks to a recent split from the NWA. While such status was questionable at best, it marked the first occasion a British grappler had held what was promoted as a world heavyweight championship by a major promotion in the US.

It was a title Adams would never lose in the ring, with the reign ending with another dose of reality. He spent several months in prison after assaulting a pilot when airline staff refused to serve him any more alcohol because he was intoxicated.

By this stage of living the wrestler lifestyle, it was clear that drinking caused a significant change in Adams' usual charming demeanour. Speaking in the documentary Gentleman's Choice, promoter Tom Lane described Adams as "the closest thing to Jekyll and Hyde I ever saw. When Chris was sober his name fit him perfectly: he was a gentleman. When he was drinking or on several other substances. he was Hyde." Neil Adams confirmed that to FSM, noting that "He could be quite aggressive in a lot of ways, which I think was added to by the alcohol and other substances."

After leaving prison, Adams spent time in Mid-South before returning to Dallas, a territory now known as the USWA and controlled by Memphis's Jerry Jarett. Here Adams would finally bring to reality an angle he had been pitching for five years: the ex-wife storyline.

The idea had first come about after Adams and Clarke had split up in 1984 over his having affairs. After an initially painful period, the pair had returned to having an amicable relationship once they were living apart. Both had married: Adams to a new girlfriend named Toni and Clark to wrestler Billy Jack Haynes in what was designed as a marriage of convenience for immigration purposes but blossomed into a brief relationship before a divorce.

Adams' original idea was for Clark to be billed as his ex-wife (the pair never married in reality) and begin managing Hernandez, bringing Toni into the feud. While Clark repeatedly rejected the idea over the years, she was finally talked into it when Adams identified a hot prospect in his training class by the name of Steve Austin.

"Chris was the director [of the angle]," Clark recalls. "He would give me very specific directions, saying I should act like Joan Collins from Dynasty and to go out there and be the bitch. He was extremely creative and fell into putting the angles together really naturally."

Adams believes the feud worked so well because of the unique blend of trust between the participants and the edge of reality. "When I first came to talk to Chris about doing the angle, Toni burst into tears knowing we were a true ex-boyfriend and girlfriend. But Toni and I became such good friends and all four of us had good chemistry."

To extend the lengthy feud, which ran for most of 1990 and featured a host of stipulation matches, the women were brought into several mixed tag and even singles matches. Clarke explains that their portrayal as non-athletes with little technical grappling was itself very real. "I never got any training whatsoever:

Chris brought us girls in and just said 'go out there.' We were just meant to catfight. In one match Chris told me to pick up the bell ringer, an iron bar, and to hit him in the neck, but to watch how I hit it. Somehow I actually broke my hand!"

The feud, which picked up business in a slowly-dying territory, came to a natural end when Austin picked up a spot in WCW. Ironically the storyline had turned even more real with Clark and Austin starting a behind-the-scenes relationship and eventually marrying before divorcing in 1999.

Adams continued to bump around the declining Dallas scene for the rest of the 1990s before spending a couple of years on WCW's legendarily immense roster where he mainly worked in an enhancement role or on bottom-tier TV shows.

By this stage his clearly addictive personality had brought him down an even darker path, with recreational use of GHB a particular problem. He and a new girlfriend both overdosed in 2000, leading to her death. Adams was charged with manslaughter, but the case would never come to trial. On 7 October 2001, Adams was fatally shot during a brawl with drunken close friend William Brent Parnell, who successfully argued it had been a case of self-defence.

Writing in her recently-published autobiography Through The Shattered Glass, Clark summed up her take on Adams' wasted life. "When I met Chris Adams, he was such a charming and funny guy with unlimited potential. He was a caring and sensitive individual who just wanted to be loved.

"By the end, Chris lost all the qualities he once possessed, alienating almost everyone who cared for him. He became a violent man and he died a violent death."

# COLIN JOYNSON

"People don't realise some of the guys that are underrated are the best workers in the business. Without them, some of the superstars would draw nothing." That's the view of Colin Joynson, one of the most dependable wrestlers on the British circuit for much of the TV era.

His father was a plumber by trade but also a keen amateur wrestler who had trained TV star 'Jumping' Jim Hussey on the mat. (Ironically Joynson himself would go on to train Hussey's son Mark, who became Rollerball Rocco.) With the Joynson family regulars at the Kings Hall in Manchester's Belle Vue, it was natural that he should follow in his father's footsteps. "When I was 16, my father wouldn't have me hanging round the streets with all the deadheads. He sent me to the YMCA and wrestling had just started on the television, so he said, 'You've got an interest; go and learn to be an amateur.'"

While he learned the amateur style, Joynson was keen to extend his wrestling repertoire. "I'd watch and watch and watch the pro moves at Belle Vue and then when I was at the YMCA there was another amateur wrestler called Jimmy Hart: we used to go into the judo room on the quiet and practice doing what we'd seen at the shows."

Within six months he had turned pro and had just a handful of matches for independent promoters in 1960s before taking it upon himself to walk into the dressing room at Belle Vue and ask for work. As was common, he had to undergo a gym try-out, wrestling referee and former pro Martin Conroy "for about three quarters of an hour." He passed the audition and four days later was travelling to Neath as the latest member of the Joint roster. At times it proved overwhelming.

"I wrestled Tony Charles and I thought I was on with God because I had seen him at shows so many times. He used to throw a dropkick and he seemed to hover in mid-air. He threw me to the ropes, I went flying off the ropes, and he was hovering there in front of me like a bleeding sparrow! I was so shocked to see him there, instead of turning my head away to try to ride it, I turned my head into it in shock. Bang, I was down on the floor, I was out. I wasn't unconscious, but I just couldn't get up. The referee was counting me out and Tony Charles looked down at me and said, "You turned your head the wrong way you bloody stupid bugger!"

It took around a year for Joynson to start feeling comfortable in the ring, only to find his career rudely interrupted in a bout against the notoriously hard-hitting Keith Martinelli. "We were on last. Billy Hargreaves was the referee and when we came in the ring, he said 'Make it quick lads, I've got to take the ring down when we've finished and then I'm going on my holidays.' Three minutes into the first round Keith broke my leg and turned around to Billy and said, 'Was that quick enough?'

"I went to hospital at Stafford, but they had no X-ray facilities at night, so they gave me paracetamol and told me to drive home. I managed to drive on the leg by just barely pressing the accelerator rather than pushing it. The next morning, I went to hospital in Manchester and they confirmed it was a fracture and put me in plaster. The doctor who did it said 'You're a wrestler aren't you?' I said 'Yeah' and he said, 'But it's all playacting isn't it?' I said, 'This is the best bit of playacting you've ever seen!'"

Injuries were a common occurrence, and later in his career Joynson regularly sought medical help from Manchester City football physio Freddie Griffiths. "He used to treat me and say 'Right, I'm going to put a dressing on it and support, and I want you to have two or three weeks off.' I'd say, 'No Fred, I'm wrestling tonight, I'm at Wolverhampton.' He'd say 'But I've just got your knee right' or my ankle or elbow or whatever and I'd say 'Fred, if I don't go, I don't get paid. I'm not like these footballers who can have three or four weeks off and be paid every day.' He said, 'With you, we're going three steps forward and nine steps back every day.' But he used to keep me fit, keep me in the job."

Indeed, even the broken leg only led to a six week absence. "I used to wrestle 3-4 times a week as a part timer while I was an apprentice toolmaker and wanted to give up my trade to go full time at age of 18. [Promoter] Arthur Wright wanted me to go full time, but my father said 'No, carry on as a part timer till 21, get your trade, then make your mind up what you're going to be.' When I turned 21, I went to the chargehand said 'I'm going full time as a wrestler' and they said, 'Just serve a couple of weeks as a tradesman to get your indentures, then if you ever need to come back, you've always got a job here.'"

He soon began making his name nationally, making his TV debut in 1963 against his old gym pal Hart, now known as Terry Downs. While a heavyweight, Joynson had impressive agility, which almost paid off on one occasion. "I used to take a big backdrop: I was well known in the business for taking bumps. At one show, [promoter] Jack Atherton says to me 'Now then, young Joynson, if thee can touch the lights with a backdrop, I'll give you extra money' So I had Roy St Clair backdrop me about four times. When I came to Jack Atherton afterwards he gave me my wages and my petrol money and that was it. I said 'Jack, what about my bonus.' 'No lad,' he said, 'I can't pay you any bonus: you've broke my fucking ring!'"

Joynson also began working overseas with several trips to Africa and Israel, though Europe proved his favourite destination. "In Germany you could go to the World Cup in Hannover in September and you'd be in the same hall every night for two months. I saw what the German wrestlers did, and I bought a caravan and took my wife. I had my son was only a baby at the time and took him as well. I used to be in Germany three months in the spring and three months in the autumn just touring round with the caravan. We did that for about seven years until my son went to school."

He also made several trips to Japan's IWE promotion. "I went to Bill Robinson's gym in Failsworth to train in shoot moves because we didn't know what we was going to get in Japan: we didn't know what they were like. And a lot of lads didn't like Japan because the wrestlers were hard and [the match] was all for them." Still, his initial trip was a success and he was asked to stay on a further six weeks to show the ropes to the next group of Brits to tour the country.

While in Japan, Joynson saw some very diverse American talent. "We were there with the McGuire twins. They were about 60 stone apiece, but they weren't wrestlers, they were just a gimmick. They used to ride to the ring on these little minibikes and then when they got to the they'd stand on boxes so all the young Japanese wrestlers could roll them in the ring. They used to just stand in the ring and waddle their bleeding bellies and that was it. Just a gimmick. But then there was Brute Bernard, an American guy: he was a fantastic grafter."

After Europe, Africa and Asia, Joynson almost made it four continents. "There was a guy called Cliff Irons who worked in the building trade with my dad. He's gone to America after the war, and he knew a guy called Willie Gilzenburg, who was involved with the New York wrestling. My dad wrote to Cliff, sent him some photographs of me and said I wanted to get into America and go to New York. He passed this through to Willie Gilzenberg who got in touch with Vince McMahon senior.

"McMahon wrote me a letter and said, 'You're not really big enough Colin: you're 15 stone but you're only five foot seven and in New York we like the giants.' He said 'What I can do is bring you in as a carpenter' which was like a job man. 'It'll be good experience for you and an introduction to the States.' So I was booked to go in May 1971.

"In January I went to Sweden and while I was away there was a post strike in Britain that lasted about eight weeks. I came home just before the post strike ended and then two weeks later all the mail started coming through and my work permit and visa to go into New York arrived. So I phoned Vince McMahon senior in Washington and I said 'I'm very sorry I've not replied to your correspondence. I've only just got my work permit and visa now to sign: am I still coming in to New York?'

"And Vince McMahon Sr said 'Joynson, the boat sails once and you've goddamned missed it.'"

With dreams of Madison Square Garden dashed, Joynson turned his attention to duos action. "It was at a time when all the tag teams were coming of age, with Bert Royal and Vic Faulkner, Roy & Tony St Clair, Abe Ginsberg and John Foley." After a couple of impressive singles matches against one another, he and Steve Haggerty formed a tag team named The Dangermen, taken from a 1960s Patrick McGoohan TV show.

"We were at Pontins at Prestatyn. In the dressing room there were some Christmas party hats and on the hats was a skull and crossbones. I said to Steve that would be an ideal motif on our leotards, so we took the skull and crossbones off a hat to use as a template, cut out some leather, and had them fitted on our leotards. We wrestled as The Dangermen for about three or four years but once again I fell out with Mick McManus over money. I got the sack, but was reinstated four or five months later and in the meantime, Steve teamed with Mel Stuart. When I came back we still used to travel the country together but never wrestled as a tag team again."

Back in singles action, Joynson had a couple of memorable matches for unconventional reasons. "At Cliftonville, we used to wrestle outdoors in a bandstand. It was raining this night and you can imagine they're all there sat waiting for Big Daddy with overcoats and rain macs over their heads. The ring was undercover, but you still got wet and there was no atmosphere because they were all piss-wet through and cold.

"I'm on with Wayne Bridges and we're working away, grafting, trying to get some heat and nothing was happening. All of a sudden, I stopped the match because there was a guy climbing over the fence. I said, 'Well that's about it' and Bridges said to me 'What's the matter?' and I said 'I've heard about them sneaking in, but look at him: he's sneaking out. The fellow's on top the fence climbing out of the place!"

Another unconventional show took place at a home for people with what would today be called developmental disabilities. "I watched the first match from the dressing room door and I thought 'I can't work in front of all these people.' I'm not being awful, but they were crackers. So, I'm on with Tony St Clair and as the match started, I can't watch because they were all, just... not all there really.

"I've got Tony down in a wristlock and he said to me 'Have you noticed, all the daftest ones have got pointed heads?' so me, like a fool, I'm looking out the ring and the next thing I know he's got his hand on my head. I said, 'What are you doing?' and he said, 'Come to think of it, your head's a bit fucking pointed." So we both got the giggles.

"The referee was Joe D'Orazio, who used to do a lot of work with disabled people and I threw Tony off the ropes and he did a one-handed handstand and landed on his feet. Joe said, 'Oh that's torn it,' so I asked why, and he said 'They'll all be practicing that on the lawn tomorrow. Can you imagine?'"

When Max Crabtree took over at Joint Promotions, it led to an unexpected repackaging for Joynson. "I went in to see Max and I said, 'I need more money, I need to put my money up in London because I'm paying for my accommodation and food down here and when I've done six jobs I'm worse off than if I'd only done three jobs up the north.'

"Max was a cynical bastard: he said to me, 'Keeeeed, look at you, look at your name... Colin Joynson. You sound like the man from the fucking Pru.' He said 'Shave your hair off, and grow a big beard and I'll give you whatever you want. Look at Mal Kirk: he couldn't lace your boots up, but when he shoves that big ugly head out that dressing room door [the crowd react].'

"Well he was right, but I said, 'Yes Max, but with all your gimmicks, you're still going to need wrestlers in this business.' But that's why in 1977 I changed my name to Bulldog Joynson. I always wrestled abroad so I used to have the Union Jack on my tracksuit and leotard. There used to be a Bulldog Bill Garnon, but he was long since retired so I wasn't treading on his toes."

Like many wrestlers, Joynson began winding down his career by moving into the pub trade, though finding premises was a problem. "We'd knocked a few pubs back that we didn't like the area. When you're taking a pub as an ex-wrestler, you're [potentially] taking all your customers on. If you're taking a pub as an ex-toolmaker or an ex-reporter from the newspapers, then that's OK. But if you're an ex-sportsman you're a target for the numpties."

Eventually he settled on the New Inn in Bolton, around 100 yards from the site of the old Wryton Stadium, the town's main wrestling venue. While he initially retired in 1980, Joynson returned to the ring on several occasions because "you can't get the urge out of your body. I came back and did a few more jobs basically just for publicity for the pub: If you're on telly Saturday afternoon you'd see the people coming to the pub on a Saturday night to see you and have a look."

One such occasion came after a high-profile bout with Spiros Arion, who was being pushed as the first recognised World Heavyweight Champion on British screens. Joynson took a beating to put over the newcomer. "It was blood, snot and shite. It only lasted about six minutes and we had a riot on our hands. In fact, they threatened to take the wrestling off the television: they said to Max Crabtree 'We treat professional wrestling as good family entertainment and that was nothing but sheer utter violence.' When it was shown on TV I was in the pub, people were looking at me and there was blood and everything in the match. This one guy looking at me said to his girlfriend, so I could hear, 'What did I tell you, not a mark on him.' So I said to the guy 'The match was three weeks ago mate!'"

Joynson's final bout came in 1988, capping off a 25-year run on television. "I'd not done a job for about four years. Marty Jones came one Christmas to see me because we're good old friends and we started talking shop. I said I saw the matches at the weekend on television and they were crap and if I couldn't do better than that, I'd give up.

"Three days later Marty phoned me up and said, 'You'd better get yourself fit, Colin.' I asked why, and he said, 'You're on TV with me January 19 from Burnley.' The match came over quite good, but I knew when I came out that there were certain bits of timing that weren't right. I suffered with trapped nerves from neck and was partially paralysed down one side. When Freddie Griffiths spent 12 months getting me fit again and said, 'What will you do now?' I said I might just do the odd match. He said 'No, one more knock on your neck and you're paralysed for the rest of your life', so that was the end of it. 30 years and I wouldn't have changed it for anything."

Although he suffered the effects of diabetes, losing a leg in 2002, Joynson remains upbeat: "I'm 74 but I'm a fit 74." He's a regular on the reunion circuit, including having taken over the late Pat Roach's role at The Bridges pub in Kent each August where he reads out the list of wrestlers who have passed away in the previous 12 months. It's a role he took for good reason. "I always like to say something about every one of them, and almost everyone I speak about, I've worked with."

And it was at one reunion that Joynson received a plaque that summed up his reputation among his peers. "It says 'one of the most underrated workers in the business, bump taker to the stars, Bulldog Colin Joynson.'"

# DANNY COLLINS

For most wrestlers FSM has profiled in its Greeting Grapple Fans series, getting into pro wrestling involved a chance meeting or other quirk of fate. Danny Collins is most definitely an exception to that pattern.

"I started going regularly to watch wrestling with my parents from the age of seven and immediately thought 'I want to do that.' It completely snowballed from there and took over my life. By the time I was nine I'd started amateur wrestling."

Whether it was times changing or the youngster's particularly eager attitude, Collins didn't follow the traditional route of building up experience as an amateur and only then trying to break into the professional game. "I was doing the amateur training in Bristol but twice a week I'd travel up to Gloucester to train pro. It was definitely difficult to learn the two styles at the same time because they have so many differences. The amateur wrestlers certainly weren't much impressed that I was off doing the pro stuff, but they knew that was my dream, so they lived with it."

Collins spent several years training with Steve Speed, a local grappler who would go on to make several TV appearances, including partnering Collins in a tag bout. That training concluded in an unusually seamless transition to the professional business in 1983.

"I literally finished school [aged 16] and turned pro. My debut was against Adrian Finch and it was quite surreal as it was at the Colston Hall, the same venue I used to go and watch wrestling."

Collins was quickly taken on full-time by Joint Promotions and moved to Leeds where he lodged with relatives of the famed De Relwyskow/Green promotional pairing that had once ruled Northern rings. That's not to say Collins had it easy.

"I was beaten up badly every night just to see if I had what it took. I'd go back to Leeds every night and the grandma I lodged with would patch me up and send me back out the next day. At that time people used to talk about the pro game having a seven year apprenticeship to see if you were good enough. Even though I had a good push, it really took about 10 years before I felt completely comfortable and accepted."

It wasn't just a case of physical punishment: Collins recalls the mental challenge as well. "Because it was so fast, it was hard to suddenly adjust from being a fan to being thrown in at the deep end. It really was a case of going from a boy to having to be a man, working the job full-time."

Even if proving his dedication to his fellow pros was a long-term project, the combination of Collins's natural talent and his distinctive youthful good looks was enough for promoters to put him on the fast track. "I had something unique: a real baby face. It fitted the slot they had for me perfectly because it was so easy for me to get sympathy and I showed a lot of spirit."

Barely a couple of months after turning pro, he made his television debut as a late replacement for John Naylor against Jim Breaks, even picking up a fall in a 2-1 defeat.

The pair would become regular rivals on TV in what, by World of Sport standards, was an intricate storyline in the early months of 1984. After picking up his first televised win, against Peter Kaye in January, Collins took part in an eight-man tournament in February. Here he defeated Sid Cooper and Pete LaPaque before scoring a shock disqualification win in the final over Breaks, who by now was the reigning British Welterweight champion.

That led to a challenge match in March in which Breaks offered to pay £500 to Collins if he managed to score a fall over him, something that did indeed happen, albeit it in a non-title match. As a result, Collins earned a title match in April which went to a no contest after both men had earned a fall. While Collins would take the championship from Breaks in a non-televised affair at the Royal Albert Hall -- which had actually happened before his first televised title shot aired -- he settled any confusion with a successful defence against Breaks on TV in May.

"He was a great old pro," Collins remembers of Breaks. "He had amazing timing. I probably learned the most from working with him, just from interacting in the ring and working on timing. He was such a great teacher, you couldn't help but learn."

Collins would go on to exchange the title with the likes of Steve Grey and Sid Cooper, winding up as the final British welterweight titleholder of the TV era. In 1985 he captured the European welterweight crown from Jorg Chenok in the feature bout on the high-profile FA Cup Final day broadcast.

The title was something of a genuine European championship, booked by French promoter Roger Delaporte. The victory led to tours of France and Spain, the former of which was a particular challenge. "It wasn't just that I was going there at 17, not speaking a word of French. They also wrestled the other way round from us, linking up and working from the right rather than left, which was difficult to adjust to because it just felt arse-backwards." Foreign travel would become a regular part of Collins's schedule. "I worked in Dubai, Kuwait... I was lucky enough to get to wrestle pretty much everywhere I wanted to go."

During 1985, despite not yet having reached adulthood, Collins made a brief tour of the United States. Here he worked for Bob Geigel's Central States Wrestling, a Kansas-based NWA promotion. "It was a great experience because some real legends passed through like Harley Race and Ric Flair. I was also on shows with guys who were just starting out but went on to be big stars like Razor Ramon and Shawn Michaels."

He then moved on to an independent promotion run by Killer Kowalski where he recalls accidentally breaking the arm of a headliner. As so often happens in the bizarre business of pro wrestling, Collins almost benefitted from the misfortune. "Kowalski asked me to extend my run to take over the guy's bookings. I kind of wish I'd stayed longer, but I already had dates back home and said I couldn't miss them."

Collins's return to UK rings was abruptly halted later in the year when he began showing signs of serious kidney damage, seemingly exacerbated by his in-ring activity. "It turned out to be a form of birth defect that meant the kidney was enlarged. In fact, I was told it was actually lucky I'd been wrestling and that brought attention to the problem. Had I not wrestled, there's a good chance it would never have been discovered and it would have turned cancerous and killed me."

The kidney had to be removed, leaving Collins on the shelf for around six months. "They told me I would never wrestle again, but there was no way I was having that."

Although Collins was soon back on the box regularly, doing everything from challenging much heavier opponents such as Dave Finlay to teaming with Big Daddy, his career faced another obstacle in 1988 when ITV cancelled the wrestling slot. "It definitely hurt: there was still plenty of work about, but a lot of the older names saw things were going to slow down and decided to call it a day, so the pool of experience dwindled off."

Only 21 years old when ITV pulled the plug, Collins had just five years to make his name on the small screen. "In hindsight, it would have been good to have come along ten years earlier, so I could have worked with some of the older stars like Mick McManus or Vic Faulkner. But I have no real regrets about my career and wouldn't change a thing."

Less than a year later Collins was working for the WWF on its first live UK show: the only problem was that he wasn't on the Sky broadcast. He would wind up working several dates on UK tours, including dark matches before TV shows in 1989 and 1991 and Sheffield in 1992.

Danny Collins

"They had to book some British guys because of the visa and work permit situation. At the time the government classed professional wrestling as a sport, so legally the shows were classed as a tournament and it was supposedly unfair to have a tournament over here where all the participants were Americans. A few years later they changed the status to entertainment, so they didn't need to use Brits anymore."

While some involved in those early bouts have complained about being treated almost as second class citizens, shoved off into their own subpar changing facility and sent out early in front of a largely unfamiliar audience still filing into their seats, Collins has a philosophical view of his WWF bookings. "It was no big deal to me: I didn't have a big ego, and just saw it as a good payday."

As he continued to grow, Collins moved up the weight divisions. In 1991 he captured the vacant world middleweight title in Bath, defeating Owen Hart in a genuine classic, bringing together international styles and fast-paced reversals four years before Dean Malenko and Eddie Guerrero made their names with a similar recipe.

"That was a real career highlight, my absolute favourite match. Owen was the nicest bloke and what happened to him was tragic. That match was the result of two real pros coming together, which is when something special happens. I tell trainees that it's like the chemistry of a ballroom dance. You can bring together a dancer from Sweden and a dancer from Canada and without talking they can do a perfect tango. But it only works if both of them have it, otherwise one of them can't follow. It's hard to put how a real one-off match like that works into words, but I guess it would be 'professionalism'."

Collins went on to win the British heavy-middleweight title. This led to a controversial bout at Croydon where, after receiving a blow to the head, he erupted in a furious rage and attacked the referee, causing a title loss via disqualification. While this was merely a one-off to heighten interest in his rivalry with Richie Brooks, as the 1990s rolled on Collins eventually began working as a heel ("Dirty Dan Collins") in some venues. He recalls that the change was as much about logistics as it was storyline drama.

"In most matches the villain leads the bout. The problem was that a lot of the veteran villains had moved on, so it became very difficult for me to work with more inexperienced guys. They were not strong enough to lead and it made the matches awkward.

"It was a great experience working as a villain: I felt very confident and I enjoyed doing it a lot. Of course, the age thing helped it work: I guess I didn't have the same appeal of when I looked younger! Nowadays the younger generation guys do such great stuff it's easy for me to switch back and forth."

The villain role was particularly pronounced in Germany and Austria where Collins became a regular in the annual autumn and winter tournaments. "It was a real privilege because it was a place for big men: they never normally took anyone under six foot. But they brought me over to be Finlay's tag partner just because of my ability, which was a great compliment."

The tournament format meant the same crew of wrestlers worked in the same venue every night for six weeks or more. Like many visitors, Collins found it an artistic challenge, with no opportunity to simply repeat signature routines. That said, it was a challenge he relished. "If you can't do your business, people see through you very quickly. Some fans would save up all year so they could go to those shows every night, so it really was the same people watching you. A lot of wrestlers would leave within a couple of weeks because they found that too stressful."

In 1996, Collins finally had an opportunity to tour Japan after putting on an impressive performance against a visiting Great Sasuke for All Star Promotions in Portsmouth. Collins made two trips for Michinoku and had a brief run with the British Commonwealth Junior Heavyweight championship, a Japanese title that later became part of the "J-Crown", a collection of eight championships unified in a high-profile New Japan tournament.

While Michinoku was known for its mix of high-flying and comedy, Collins found the style physically relentless. He once recalled being in so much pain during the trip that he was unable to move for more than a day and even feared for his life at one stage. Despite that, "I had a great time. It was almost a different business over there: you had to really get stuck in."

That physical style finally caught up with Collins as the new century arrived and he took several years away from the business. "I still have a crushed disc in the base of my spine and one in my neck, plus a separated shoulder and an undiagnosed lump about the size of a golf ball. I was taught to ignore pain, but I felt I needed a break because the business was changing so much. I wanted to take time to concentrate on training and get my strength up. I just didn't take into account how strong a hold the business had on me!"

"I've never had any really serious injuries, which I put down to my training. Some of the guys now are getting things like broken backs or broken necks that we never used to see."

When he came back to action in the mid-2000s, Collins immediately noticed a difference in the industry and, unlike some of his former colleagues, viewed this largely a positive. "The style had become more technical, more skilful, more athletic. There's also more of an American influence, with high-flying. I just had to adapt: things just wouldn't work the same today as 30 years ago. But it shouldn't be a surprise: you can see that kind of change in any combat sport."

As well as returning to the ring, Collins has started his own training business, running a weekend-long camp once a month. "It's really going well and I'm getting good feedback. People are travelling a long way: we just had five guys drive through the night to get here from Brussels and there's another come over from Ireland where he works out at Dave Finlay Sr's gym. It reminds me of my own training: I would have crawled to the end of the world over broken glass to get into the business.

"I'm getting a new lease of life from the training, getting the same buzz as when I started out. I want to teach the guys the right way and most of them I only have to show them once; they are very teachable. I limit it to around 24 or 25 guys on a camp to make sure everyone gets enough time to learn: I don't want to turn it into a factory line.

"I try to help guys be different, so they can stand out. I can also help to get their first bookings because promoters know I can be trusted when I say somebody is ready. Usually I'll be booked on the show alongside my guys, so they know they have to perform!"

While he's still yet to hit 50, Collins is content with the fact that his career will one day wind down. "I don't think I'll ever set a formal date as my official retirement match. I'll continue until I can't switch off the pain and do the job, or if I feel I'm no longer giving value for money. I don't want to be at the point where people say, 'He used to be amazing.'

"But wrestling's been good to me. I've still got all my own body parts. Apart from doing a little property renovation, I've only ever been a full-time professional wrestler, but it's put my kids through private school and put a Merc in my driveway. I've worked with lots of one offs, real characters: villains, rogues and comedians.

"The whole time has been amazing."

# DAVE TAYLOR

"When I were amateur, I hated professional [wrestling]" Dave Taylor tells FSM. " I just thought it were all pathetic because I were like a real wrestler. But after my dad had beat the shit out of me a dozen times and my grandad had beat the shit out of me, I began to realise that it's a lot harder than what I thought it were!"

To say Dave Taylor hailed from a wrestling family would be a spectacular understatement. His grandfather Joe won the British amateur featherweight championship four years and placed fourth in the 1932 Olympics. His father Eric took his skills to the pro ring and was the first British Heavy-Middleweight champion of the Mountevans era, holding the title for 13 years before becoming an independent promoter. Eric's cousin Jack competed in the 1956 Olympics. Dave's brother Steve was a regular pro on television. And Dave's daughter Donna had a brief pro career, becoming a fourth generation competitor.

But it was grandpa Joe who gave Dave Taylor, already a keen amateur, his toughest wrestling lesson. "I'd just come from the British championships in Edinburgh, and I'd got third place and I thought I were the bees knees. We had a wrestling mat on the farm where I lived, and my grandad came over, I think he were about 65, and he said 'Go on, we'll have a pull.'

"I'm thinking, I'm a lot bigger than him, a lot younger than him, I'm thinking 'Shit, I don't want to hurt him.' Well he beat the shit out of me. I could not believe it, a little skinny old man dragged me all over the mat. I could not believe how good he was at that age. And I thought I were the man!"

Taylor continued to improve in the amateur ranks, reaching second place in a later British amateur championship for those in-between the junior and senior divisions, and even harbouring thoughts of going to the Commonwealth or Olympic Games himself. "I don't know if I would have been good enough or not; maybe if I would have stuck with it."

That ended when he joined his father Eric on a tour of Sweden where "I got more per day than I got per week working at a brick factory." He chose to follow his father's career path rather than that of his grandfather. " My grandad weren't a fan of professional... He didn't particularly like it, but he knew we had to make a living. Plus he were a real small guy, he only weighed nine stone, so it wouldn't have been a lot of good for him in then days. He was smaller than Jim Breaks, who was like one of the smallest wrestlers there was."

For the first two years of his pro career, Dave mainly wrestled his father, who would appear under a mask as La Masque Argent or the Exorcist. "Every show that he promoted I normally wrestled my dad. He promoted a lot in those days because he'd just got Les Kellett, so they promoted four or five times a week. Eventually I had to say to my dad, 'Look, I need to wrestle somebody else, cause I'm not learning anything' [new]."

From there Taylor continued his grappling education against the likes of Lee Sharron and Bobby Graham. "It were best to wrestle the old-timers because it were them that learned you what to do. They stopped you from doing stupid things, when you thought 'I'm going to do this', they'd just hold you down, tell you 'Calm down, you'll get your shit it, don't worry about it, stay here.' And that's how you learned to work. That's what's wrong with today: nobody's wrestling older guys, they're all wrestling guys the same age as them and both of them know nothing."

Taylor's first international experience came with a trip to Mexico where he came to like the style despite a tough first experience, wrestling in Arena Mexico the same day he arrived in the country. "Trying to keep up with the speed that they were going and not knowing anything they were doing, with the altitude, I nearly died. I could feel my lungs bleeding, I was sucking air up my arse!"

Despite the promoters leaving Taylor to get to shows around a strange country by himself, he enjoyed his run and would have stayed longer had it not been for a leg injury. "The money were good there: I was living like a millionaire. Of course, when you changed the money back into English, it weren't worth nothing!"

Another adventure came when fellow Brit Chic Cullen invited him to Canada's Stampede promotion. Dave's older brother Steve had been wrestling there for around a month, suffering at the hands of villains, with the plan for Dave to come to the rescue. That's not quite how things worked out.

"Cullen picked me up at the airport and says the plan had been dropped and 'They're going to call you Tim Shea, the sheep farmer from Australia.' Everyone's asking me why me and Steve looked alike. Plus there were a picture of us in the programs with 'Steve Taylor and Dave Taylor' written underneath it!"

Despite the unusual billing and the payoffs being too low to extend his stay, Taylor gained from the experience. "The work was excellent, everybody were good. When you work with good people you learn, and I learned a lot there."

Taylor retained his new-found Australian heritage, under his own name this time, on a trip to South Africa. He made a spectacular debut, albeit behind closed doors. "You had to have a wrestling license. You had to go in front of the Board of

Control and wrestle, which I couldn't believe. I thought it were real and you had to wrestle real. They put me in the ring with this guy and I'm thinking it's straight, so I beat him in about 20 seconds: I flattened him. The promoter Johan Hefer runs over and says 'Come here, come here, what you doing? It's a work!' So I got my license in a few seconds!"

The situation was somewhat reversed when Taylor found himself in a misunderstanding during a Middle Eastern tour. "Wrestling Indians was the closest it got to being real, without being real. This Indian came into the dressing room and he had a turban, cauliflower ears and a flat nose. I didn't know that if Indian wrestlers have seen you wrestle and respect you, they bow down to you and kiss your feet. So when he did that I jumped up and did what the sand wrestlers do: I hit myself in the thighs and stared right at him.

"This guy ripped his turban off and wanted to go at me quickly. He said, 'You insult me, I'm Asian games gold medallist.' So I said 'OK, me British champion, Olympic Games. Go on then.' I were bullshitting on my side, but he weren't bullshitting! He went 'Sorry, sorry, sorry' and shook my hands, and I thought 'that were near, that were very near.'

Of all his foreign destinations, Germany became Taylor's home-from-home. It had been a long time coming as he'd visited as a child with his father and been told to come over if and when he grew up and turned pro. When he took up this opportunity, Taylor was invited for a three-day try-out: "I were full of piss and vinegar. I thought I knew everything."

Such over-confidence proved problematic to say the least. "I worked with Mal Kirk and he said to me 'Can you throw an elbow?' I said 'Yeah, no problem, I can throw elbows.' He said 'Ok, hit me with three or four, do this and that.'

"In the ring I went to hit him with an elbow and smashed him right in the mouth, bust his mouth open. I couldn't do an elbow! Kids todays are like 'I can do everything!' and I were just the same. He didn't do anything about it, which was a good job as he could have killed me! He came out the ring and he said 'Look, when you can't do something, just say you can't do it.' Mick McMichael took me into the arena the next afternoon and showed me how to do it right, and I've been throwing uppercuts ever since.

Taylor's initiation didn't get any smoother. "Three days in to the tournament, I worked with Dave Morgan. I'd heard that he'd mess you around. He did something at the end of the round and I back-kicked him -- it could have been a little stiff... He looked at me and went 'Oh! Funny bastard, huh? You want to go?' My asshole dropped out!

"I asked Mick McMichael, who was refereeing, 'What's he talking about, he wants to go?' He said 'Take no notice of him, he's a bullshitter. He's trying you out.' I said 'Well, it's fucking worked!'

Dave Taylor

"I'd always been told by my dad 'Don't back down, you can do the job straight.' I thought, well, the only thing I can do is kick him in the balls. But I went to link up with him and everything were fine. Back in the dressing room, he walked in front of me and stopped and I thought 'Uh oh, here we go.' He looked at me and said 'Hmm, you wanted to have a go at me, right?' and I said 'Yeah, I did, yeah.'

'OK' he said, and he put his hand out and said, 'You'll do me.' He were just trying me out to see if I would have a go, and when he saw I would he respected me. After that we travelled together, worked out together; I were one of his only friends for 10 years."

Taylor would eventually begin working as long as nine months a year in Germany and Austria: "If you did your job right, it were the best place to be."

While his visits to the UK became increasingly rare, Taylor did win the British heavyweight title in King's Lynn in 1991, following in his father's footsteps. "I'd been working with [champion Dave] Finlay for a couple of years. We'd do him over, a draw, stuff like that, but I never won. It were the most heat I've ever seen in England at any show: people couldn't believe it would happen, it had escalated up to this. It established me more and I enjoyed it. And Fit couldn't wait to get rid of the belt: he was sick of carrying it around!"

Opportunity knocked in 1995 when WCW was looking for bodies to fill out a 60-man, three-ring battle royale on the initial World War III pay-per-view and Steve [now William] Regal suggested Taylor's name. He made an unintentionally solid first impression.

"I were down to the last 10 in one ring, and then you had to all get into the main ring. There's Hogan, Macho Man, all the big stars. I go to climb in the ring and Paul Orndorff got hold of me, so I punched him. But it connected and smashed his mouth open. And he went 'Whoa!'

"And then Hogan goes to get hold of me, so I turned round and gave him an uppercut and he goes 'Whoa!' and I could see on his face he's thinking 'Fuck that!' I thought 'Shiiit, I just hit two of the top guys here', and Orndorff could have kicked my brains in because he's a genuine tough guy. Ever since that, whenever I see Hogan he goes 'Here he comes, Mr Uppercut!'"

Despite the mishaps, Taylor was offered a full-time contract and became a 'Squire' to join 'Lord Steven Regal' and 'Earl Robert Eaton' in the Blue Bloods. He also took part in an infamous "junkyard battle royale" for the WCW hardcore title and was one of the few participants who enjoyed the experience. "I loved it! I thought it were the funniest thing I've ever seen in my life because I just kept running up and hitting Knobbs of the Nasty Boys with a hubcap. I just kept rolling about in tyres."

It didn't go so well for everyone however. "It were a genuine junkyard out of town. We went there during the day to look at it and we had to plan escape routes for the finish when explosions went off. I'm looking at all these cars and I said 'Look, don't anybody slam anyone through these windscreens because it's laminated glass and when it breaks it's like a bunch of knives sticking straight up.' When the match starts, first thing that happens, one of the Mexicans backdropped somebody into the windscreen. He couldn't get off the windscreen because he was pinned to it."

Following WCW's closure, Taylor spent time working as a trainer in several of WWE's developmental territories before making an unexpected comeback to the ring around the age of 50. Spotting an extra payday he volunteered to work as a stunt double in the motion capture studio for a WWE video game. After Taylor spending an entire day replicating the moves of most of the performers on the main roster, stunned agent Tommy Dreamer asked if he'd be interested in joining the roster of the planned ECW touring revival.

"I said yes, and they asked me to make a vignette aligning myself with Regal and Finlay. I got 50 of the trainees sat in the room watching the TV and it were Finlay and Regal wrestling each other. One of the guys shouts 'Dave, come to the back, your pals are wrestling.' So I go 'This is wrong this, they shouldn't be fighting each other, they should be fighting Americans. If I were there with them we'd be the strongest team they'd ever seen.' Then I kick them out of the dressing rooms, and go a little crazy. I sent the tape, they got it Friday morning, then Friday afternoon they call me and tell me they want me on TV on Monday. Straight in, no dark matches, nothing!"

During a two-year in-ring run for WWE, Taylor's most notable match was a four-way tag team ladder match, though initially road agents suggested it would be an easy night for he and partner Regal. "They kept saying to me 'We don't want you to go up that ladder' cause I were like 50 years old. I said 'Do you think I can't climb the bastard ladder?! I can climb straight to the top of that ladder with no hands!' They were like 'Bullshit' so I went straight to the top of the fucking ladder and said 'Look, can anyone else do it?'

In the event, Taylor wound up following the suggestion, to great effect. "The thing that stuck out most to anybody were not Joey Mercury's eye getting poked out, not the winners going over and winning the belts, but me and Regal arguing about going up the ladder because we were scared of heights. JBL put it over like we had vertigo! It wasn't planned, it was just when we in there that we did it."

After Regal was drafted from Smackdown to Raw, Taylor drifted into teams with Paul Birchall and Drew McIntrye before being released in 2008. Since then he's made several independent appearances but after a lengthy break following a hip replacement, has found it hard not wrestling regularly.

"I love being on the road, just everything about it. My dad finished wrestling about 55 because he'd had both his hips done and the doctor told him must never wrestle again. It's not like today: my doctors told me, yeah, wrestle again, no problem. He went downhill that quick, he got a bit of dementia. You imagine, you've spent all your life travelling, going to different places in the world -- even if you were in England you were going to some place every day, five, six times a week. And then all of a sudden nothing? Ooh, it's bad.

"I go berserk sometimes here. I go to England at least four times a year to get out. I have to do, otherwise I'm just a gardener! You climb the walls. I talk to Regal now and he's telling me he's going to India, England and Brazil inside a week. And I tell him 'I know it's hard, but I wish I were doing it.'"

That said, Taylor is clear the end is in sight. "I don't think I'll be doing any more wrestling in the states. In Europe they're more respectful of older wrestlers. In America they look at you and they're like 'You old fart, you stink, you're useless.' I'll never wrestle here again. I'd like to go to Germany and do a retirement match or a legends match, maybe somewhere like Hannover where I worked half my life. I've got a couple of matches left in me."

And while he didn't think of himself as a veteran until working in the US, Taylor's attitude to a potential final bout mirrors back to that of his original teachers. "I don't want to be wrestling some young guy and having to slap them or fight them because they want to get their shit in. I want to wrestle somebody who can work."

# DOC DEAN

Ian 'Doc Dean' Brown, who retired in 1998, has now spent more time as an ex-wrestler than he spent in the business. But the memories remain fond to this day. "There's nothing bad I can say about that job. Not one thing. I loved every minute of it and it was the best job I ever had in my life."

While many wrestlers get into the business through a family connection, Dean's was a little more distant than most. "My stepdad's sister was married to [referee] Frank Casey. When I was 13 or 14 he asked me if I wanted to help him out. I started by going to help him put the ring up. One time I went to Scotland and helped him put the ring up there and they were short of several wrestlers and asked me if I'd get in and have a go. From that day onwards, I just continued doing the job."

Although the experience kickstarted his career, the show was so low-scale that Dean can no longer remember the name of the promoter. "It was just some oddbod in Scotland, not a major promoter who does it all the time. Just some odd guy with a couple of clubs, a couple of halls to do. I never went back there for the same person."

Having been bitten by the bug, the 14-year-old Dean began working regularly and, like many in the Greetings Grapple Fans series, gained a lot of experience from the holiday camp circuit. "It was definitely on the job, that's how I learned, going out doing shows every day. I had no one-on-one training in the gym when I first started. There was no such thing as that back then.

"It took a while to properly feel comfortable and know exactly what you were doing and feel OK. I think it was a couple of years. It wasn't something you could just learn in the space of a few weeks. That was where being on the camps helped, wrestling different people, being taught by different people."

Despite his youth, Dean had to learn to integrate with the existing crew of wrestlers. "There wasn't a [brutal] apprenticeship like the other boys, but I still had to go through one. It's a very tight kind of club and once you're in, you're in. To get into that, it's not so simple, it's not so easy, it's not for your everyday Joe."

And although he came in for his fair share of ribbing, Dean took it as a good sign. "If they're not pushing your buttons and doing things to you, or if they're not talking to you, [that means] they don't like you. I think at the beginning they kind of took to me, but it still takes a little while."

After establishing himself both behind the scenes and in the ring, Dean began working regularly for fellow Merseysider Brian Dixon's All Star Promotions. While still a teenager, he made his TV debut in 1988, making him one of the final new faces on the small screen. Alas it would be only a single appearance with ITV pulling the plug at the end of the year.

Instead Dean would mark his development with championship gold, taking the British welterweight title from Mal Sanders in 1990 and then exchanging it with Blondie Barrett before a second reign ended at the hands of Steve Prince. While the lack of television meant the title wins received comparatively little publicity, Dean still remembers the initial victory as a major milestone.

"It was brilliant: it was the best thing in the world, the best thing that ever happened to me. It was like an acknowledgement of being able to do what you do and do it OK. I kept that belt for quite some time and carried it round the country and whether it was on TV or not didn't really matter to me. Even to the public, when you went back to that hall or venue, they were still appreciative to you as a wrestler because of how well you worked and the people you worked with and the kind of matches you had. [A title was] always a big deal, a big thing -- just one big acknowledgement to say, 'Ok kid, you've passed your test here; let's see how you go from this point on.'"

Dean also began taking overseas bookings, particularly on the continent. He recalls that despite the language and style barrier, working with new opponents was well within his capabilities. "The French and the Germans pretty much wrestled like yourself and if they had any different stuff going on that you weren't used to, that's when it was down to you to be good, to be able to adjust and make that match look as good as it should do.

"Wrestling is wrestling if you know what you're doing. If you know what you're doing you can wrestle anybody. You've just got to get to that level. Somebody else's style didn't really matter: bite your bottom lip, get stuck in and make it happen. Work around other people's style. You really wanted to wrestle the way you wrestled, not the way somebody else's style was. You would kind of take that equation out and make it what you wanted it to be."

Arguably the most memorable part of Dean's career came in the early 90s when he formed the "Liverpool Lads" team with Robbie Brookside. With older wrestlers beginning to call it a day once they realised the TV era was truly over, Dean & Brookside's feuds with the likes of the Superflies (Ricky Knight and Jimmy Ocean) and Task Force One (Steve Prince & Vic Powers) became headline attractions and helped All Star establish its position as promotional top dog while Joint Promotions' Big Daddy roadshow began to run out of steam.

The pair even made a brief return to mainstream television when Brookside was the subject of a documentary in the BBC 2 series Video Diaries. Dean filmed the vast majority of the footage and even provided a bonus for the tape-trading community by shooting ringside as Vader regained the WCW title from Sting in Dublin. While the broadcast was good exposure, the audience was hit by the show being up against a much-hyped Nigel Benn vs Chris Eubank boxing match. Dean was philosophical about the subsequent lack of boost to business.

"It was great exposure and stuff, it was awesome being on TV. But I wasn't really expecting anything from it, just to carry on and do my job. I was hoping it would mean the wrestling business would be a little stronger and we could take it to different towns and get more people inside the theatre. But I'm not the kind of guy that expects things should be given to them."

With no national coverage, consistency in storylines and personas across the country was on the decline and that was certainly the case with Brookside and Dean in the mid-90s. In smaller venues visited for one-off shows, the pair continued to team up. In the remaining regular venues, the pair broke up and began a bitter rivalry. In Croydon, where Brookside had previously flirted with the dark side when "under the influence" of Kendo Nagasaki, Dean remained a crowd favourite. But elsewhere he took the villain role for the first time. It proved a career highlight and a memory that exhilarates him today.

"It was amazing. It was just amazing to be playing a babyface all those years and then be given the opportunity to play a villain. The sheer fun of being a good guy 10 or 12 years and then being a bad guy. People would go nuts. I'll never forget it: an old lady 50, 60 years of age trying to pull my clothes off while I was on the outside of the ring waiting to be tagged. She ripped my clothes off just because I'd turned from a nice guy to a horrible guy and she'd never seen that kind of thing before. She thought I was diabolical.

"It was real exciting time and real fun. It also made me feel better: being able to wrestle and do what you do and then be able to change from a nice guy to a bad guy and morph yourself into something else is not an easy thing so to be able to do that, the recognition in my head was awesome. The whole thing was great, I used to love it.

"They thought 'Look at this little fellow, he used to be a good little kid and now look at him.' They used to not take kindly to it. To get that response, getting people turning their back on you when you were a villain, that was what I didn't want to do, so to get people hating me and wanting to rip me down off the ring and climb in and get me, that was great. Best job in the world!"

It was an era of standout matches for Dean, including a bloody ladder match with Brookside in Croydon. A tag match in Bristol pitting Dean and Fit Finlay against Brookside and Dave Taylor went to a 30 minute draw that contemporary accounts described as an "all time classic." And in another Bristol bout, Dean's villain stature was so established he even took a win over the legendary Johnny Saint.

The rivalry, along with the pair's contacts from working in Europe, attracted international attention and Brookside and Dean were both booked for the 1997 incarnation of the Best of The Super Juniors tournament. Here Dean was conscious of avoiding the common mistake of trying to adopt the local style of wrestling.

"You might want to do their type of stuff, but they've already got two or three hundred people who do that and they're brilliant at it too. You just do what you do and once you become successful at something you just continue to do what's successful. You don't try to change that because someone else had a different style. You have to do what made you successful.

"That's what keeps the clock ticking. Once you go to start doing other people's stuff you don't really get anywhere in life. If you keep doing the stuff they've already got in their country, then it doesn't really work for them. You just have to keep doing your own style and be intelligent enough to work around other people and make not such a good match turn into a brilliant match depending on what you did and how you did it."

Although Dean wound up with a losing effort, he did have two victories. One was more notable in hindsight, beating future WWE performer Chavo Guerrero Jr. The other was most definitely notable at the time with Dean beating arguably the biggest star in the tournament, the then-reigning IWGP Junior-Heavyweight champion Jushin Liger. While the result may have been necessitated by the need to make the final group table work out as desired, Dean still took it as an honour.

"You go to anyone else's country and you go over on somebody with so much history, so well known, on TV... it was amazing. I even had people like Chris Jericho come up to me and say 'Damn, you went over on Liger, huh?' I think they were jealous! Really jealous because I think they wouldn't have mentioned it otherwise.

"It made me feel ecstatic, unbelievable. It's kind of like you're getting to the top of your career. You can't go any further once you get that high at the top of the ladder. I was completely shocked when that happened. I wasn't expecting it at all."

1997 was certainly a globetrotting year for Dean. A planned excursion to AAA in Mexico fell through but he and Brookside were hooked up with WCW where they became regulars at Orlando television tapings and the occasional live broadcast of Nitro. Dean recalls having mixed feelings of excitement at working for a big-time company but concern about being established in an enhancement talent role.

"You get worried about the way they're using you and you go on and just do a couple of little things and even when they show the footage on the TV it's not always the whole match. You get kind of worried but at the same time you're glad you're still working and you're kind of hoping that it's going to be a long-term career. At the beginning I felt 'You're put on with this guy, obviously they're going to make him look good now' and you start worrying you're going to be a knockoff guy."

While US wrestlers often had something of a reputation among British grapplers as being too much about showmanship and lacking in the fundamentals, Dean recalls being impressed by the legendarily deep WCW roster. "To be honest, most of them (could do the job). There was so much charisma and talent around, you just had to do what you had to do to make it right for you. There was a lot of foreigners; it wasn't just a room of Americans who all worked the same. It was quite a crazy crew out there from all over the place."

Even with limited career advancement, working with such a diverse range of opponents was a chance for Dean to use his experience. "I'm not one of those people to go out and blow my own trumpet and say I was brilliant, but I was OK, I was good at what I did. Because I was good at what I did I got to travel the world. If you end up being someone who's only half-decent at the job you're going to get a few matches in England and that's as far as you're going to go.

"Keep in mind too, we came to WCW at a time when WWF was kind of starting to fall down the hill a bit in terms of wrestlers, attendances, stuff like that. So a lot of people, good people, all ended up in WCW when we did. I [almost] think we got there at the wrong time because there were so many wrestlers, it didn't give you a chance to get much further."

While Brookside returned to the UK after a few months, Dean had good reason to stay and continued working for WCW until the summer of 1998. It was that same reason that then led him to hang up his boots aged just 28. "I came to retire because I was in America, I met a woman and I fell in love. So I figured 'What do I do?'

"Do I stop being in love and go back home and just stick to my normal job and my normal life, or do I change it. Especially living in America, I didn't want to go back in a car travelling 365 days a year. It was nice to be home and go out in the day and come back home. I just wanted to see what a change of life would be like, live in the normal world, the real world so to speak. I don't really regret it, I don't regret nothing. If you're going to do something you do it and you move on, you can't regret it."

While he would change nothing about the course of his career, Dean admits his timing wasn't ideal.

"I'm not jealous about it, but it would have been nice to be born earlier and it would have been nice to have been born later. In the earlier days you had all the TV and people like Dave Finlay and Rollerball Rocco. I wouldn't have wanted to be stuck with Big Daddy or that in the early days, that's not something I would have appreciated, that's not me, not my style, not my temperament, full stop. I would have looked to have been working with people like Kid McCoy, Danny Collins, people like that on TV, actually doing proper wrestling matches. Being able to do 6 x 5 minute rounds or a 30 minute match without repeating the same move twice. "

"Also, after my career, maybe in the last 10 years, a lot of English people have had more chance to come to America and work for the bigger companies and have [long-term] contracts and stuff."

Today Dean continues to work as a plumber in Orlando but, even nearly two decades, later, wrestling still holds a big place in his heart.

"Wrestling is the only thing I've ever missed in all my life. The only thing. With all my decisions I've made about life and moving on and leaving wrestling behind and getting a normal job and being a normal person, I don't regret none of it, but I've missed it. Every single day, for the rest of my life. Once you get that bug and you've been bitten by it, it just become a fever all over you and sticks into you for the rest of your life. It's something you can't get away from."

# DREW MCDONALD

Drew McDonald, who died last month aged 59, had a successful in-ring career. But it was his warmth and personality behind the scenes that his peers remember most vividly.

Born Charles Shaw, McDonald had trained in amateur wrestling and martial arts, but never had any intention of turning professional. That was until a friend put on a fundraiser show at a school for disadvantaged children in Perth and asked him to step in on short notice to replace a wrestler who had pulled out. McDonald survived the experience, said to be against Scottish legend Wild Angus, and took up the profession full-time.

His most high-profile match came early in his career and in surprising fashion. He appeared on the 1984 FA Cup Final day special as a valiant substitute wrestler teaming with Big Daddy against Giant Haystacks. His later TV appearances were in a more familiar villain role, working initially as the masked Spoiler, managed by his real-life partner Monika who was billed as Dr Monica Kaiser, one of the few valets/managers on television.

McDonald teamed with Rasputin in a short feud with Big Daddy and Kashmir Singh that saw him first unmasked after losing a bout by knockout, then finding himself on the wrong end of a hair vs hair bout. As he later put it: "I was stuck in the Big Daddy tag for what seemed like a lifetime: a good match for earning you a living as you were wrestling every night, [but] a bad match for learning anything."

McDonald would go on to wrestle around the world, most notably during a 1987 spell in the Stampede territory under the puntastic name Ben Doon McDonald. Back in the UK in the post-television era, McDonald rebranded himself as "The Ultimate Chippendale." While his physique hardly lent himself to the role (the irony was designed to irritate the crowd further), he certainly had a look suited to a classic ring villain. Greg Lambert, who managed McDonald in later years, recalled "He had that big bald head, the Fu Manchu moustache and a glare that could stop traffic. Without a doubt, he was the most convincing ring villain on the British scene of the past 20 years."

That appearance wasn't enough to stave off utter confusion in one incident McDonald recalled when writing on a British wrestling forum: "Giant Haystacks and myself [were] sitting outside a hall somewhere drinking coffee. Two old ladies came up to us and produced their autograph books to be signed by us. Haystacks signed their book then handed it to me while he asked them if they were having a good time or something like that. I signed the book and handed it back to the ladies: they looked at the signatures, then looked at the posters on the wall of the building behind us, then tore the page out of the book and said to us 'You're not Chas and Dave!"

McDonald would play an important role in the "new school" era of the late 90s and early 2000s, memorably destroying Jodie Fleisch as part of a tournament at the Revival show aired on Bravo. He also played a key, if underappreciated, role at the first FWA British Uprising show, as Alex Shane recalls.

"Dino Scarlo's strategy in the FWA was to use Drew and Robbie Brookside to bring the audience down before the highly anticipated match between Doug Williams and Jerry Lynn. The 'new school' fans were not the biggest fans of that decision, but as Dino explained to me 'You can bring them down with two professionals who look and act like wrestlers or you can do it with two untrained, flippy floppy backyarders. Which do you think it better for the overall show?' He was right, and I still believe to this day that Jerry Lynn and Doug's incredible reactions that night would be half of what they were had Drew not been called upon to know his role and do it perfectly.

Indeed, while McDonald was no fan of the 'new generation' style, something he wasn't shy to make clear backstage, Shane believed that "More than anyone else of his generation that I ever worked with, Drew had the spirit of innovation and intense wrestling passion of that someone 20 years his junior."

Writing in his first autobiography, Chris Jericho recalled a bout in Germany where McDonald took particular pride in having got a great reaction from the crowd despite having done absolutely nothing for the first 10 minutes. Dave Taylor tells FSM he had a similar experience. "We wrestled for 15 or 20 minutes in Hannover, did a little bit of comedy and a little bit of wrestling, but for most of it we hardly touched. But we brought the tent down and got a standing ovation! He could wrestle both ways, as a babyface or heel, and either way he was excellent at it."

Although McDonald was a proponent of the less is more philosophy, what he did do in the ring was supremely professional. Alex Shane recalls the first time he wrestled McDonald: "I was meant to be pushed off of a balcony by Dino Scarlo, after chasing him up there. For the chase and balcony climb to work, Drew needed something to 'take him out' for long enough for Dino and I to get up there. As I was pondering ideas, Drew calmly said 'Why not give me a tombstone on the concrete?' I was a little taken aback. I said to Drew 'I've never performed a tombstone in the ring, let alone on the floor and you're 20 stone plus.' He looked at me and said 'The worst you can do is break my neck and I've already done that before. It will be easy'.

"Now I was stunned. Part of me still thought that he was almost mocking the stunt based nature of what I was going to do, so I was totally confused if it was a 'rib'. He then said 'Try lifting me up for it. I was reluctant, but he kept asking, so against my better judgement I went to hold him. As if by magic, he was already up in the tombstone position before I even knew what happened. It was like dealing with a Jedi! I still didn't think he was serious, but sure enough when it came to the match he called for it and I did it. Drew showed me that night just how little I really knew."

That's echoed by Dean Ayass, who recalls flooring McDonald with a chair to end the Scotsman's run in the FWA. "I helped him up and was saying that I was sorry, but we both knew that, given the circumstances, we needed to do something more. He shook my hand, held on to it, and pulled me in for a short clothesline. We didn't say a word, but we just knew without speaking that we were going to do this. It was magic. I took a bump and eventually left the ring, holding my neck. Everyone, including some of the wrestlers watching from backstage, thought he'd taken my head off, but the truth of the matter was that he literally hadn't touched me, and I'd just sold it right. Drew was the safest wrestler I ever worked with and I could totally trust him to do anything in that ring."

In-ring skills aside, many wrestlers' memories of McDonald are of his antics backstage, only a small portion of which are suitable for publication. More than one wrestler has described McDonald as being like a family member, with Danny Collins noting "Drew made friends very easy. He was a proper man's man, a rogue in and out of the ring, always ducking and diving. He just seemed to fit in and it was as simple as that he was always nice to be around."

Dave Taylor recalls McDonald as being a memorably engaging storyteller. "We were driving back to Yorkshire from Great Yarmouth, which in them days would take five hours or so and normally all you cared about was getting home as soon as possible. I was meant to drop Drew off in Leeds where I'd dropped him plenty of times before. But even after five hours we're chatting away and suddenly we realised we'd arrived at the turning for Bradford, twenty minutes or so past Leeds. We just looked at each other and said, 'What the hell are we doing here?'"

McDonald was no stranger to crafting a story, as Klondyke Kate recalled. After a spectacularly unsuccessful attempt to keep up in a drinking session with the rest of the crew, she was violently ill. "Can't elaborate too much but Drew found a bottle top in my sick and then proceeded to tell the world I'd vomited up a bottle top. Not that funny you might say but Drew was a master storyteller and elaborated until it was a really funny story and that was the magic of Drew!"

McDonald famously had a stronger stomach himself. Speaking to Glasgow's STV, Jack Jester recalled a night in a Glasgow club in which a toilet attendant made the mistake of suggesting McDonald could benefit from a splash of overpriced aftershave. McDonald asked him to point out the most expensive brand, removed the bottle top, and downed the contents in one swig.

For all his bravado and outrageous behaviour, McDonald often showed loyalty in a more low-key way. Dean Ayass recalls "After my then wife left me in 2005, Drew would email me on a regular basis just to see how I was doing and to give me encouragement to keep my chin up during a low time. He always had that big warm smile on his face every time he greeted me."

Such warmth wasn't restricted to those inside the business. Dave Taylor remembers a trip to a Southampton hotel where McDonald had stayed around a year earlier. "Even though it was a year ago and he'd probably only spent 15 minutes in the lobby then, he knew and remembered every member of staff by name."

Perhaps McDonald's character is best summed up by Ricky Knight, who notes that it wasn't simply the common case of a ring villain being a nice guy outside the ring. "The real two sides to his character was that when he was in the ring or around the boys he was an outrageous character, always the entertainer. But when that was all done, there was nothing he liked more than to get home to his wife and his dogs, then go fishing and almost be a loner."

(Of course, even the fishing threw up a memorable McDonald story when, confronted by two youthful troublemakers, he calmly dispatched both into the river.)

The Knight family represents two generations of wrestlers with reason to remember McDonald warmly. In his later years he worked on a freelance basis as a talent scout for WWE and recommended the future Paige for a tryout. After she was rejected on an initial look as attempting to be "too divaish", McDonald took the time to sit down with her and encourage her to return to a future try-out with her more familiar and natural Goth-like character and showing more aggression rather than merely performing moves smoothly. It's advice that paid off, and advice that Paige remembered when she marked McDonald's death by writing his name on her arms for a RAW TV match, a move acknowledged on commentary by JBL who remembered McDonald from his time in Europe.

The universal respect and friendship McDonald had within the British wrestling community only made it more of a shock when news broke earlier this year that he had been diagnosed with terminal cancer. He passed away at home with Monika on February 9th.

"We'll all miss him to bits," noted Danny Collins. "It's such a big shock factor. He was such a big athletic guy, so full of life, it's just so hard to believe he could be gone so quickly."

Drew McDonald

# GEORGE KIDD

Debate England's biggest wrestling star and you can argue for the golden age of Pallo and McManus, the mainstream celebrity of Big Daddy, or the worldwide exposure of the British Bulldog and William Regal. But pose the same question for Scotland and there's only one answer: Dundee's George Kidd.

In what almost sounds like a comic book story, Kidd developed his interest in combat sports as an undersized child picked on at school. He discovered that grabbing a hold could be an effective way to defend himself against punches, including once using grappling to hold a considerably larger boy in place long enough to bite him before running away.

Kidd later went to a local boxing club which did not pay much heed to weight divisions, again leaving him vastly outsized. He recalled having to depart the facility after instinctively responding to a hard punch by legdiving his opponent and taking him to the ground.

The experience led Kidd to explore a wide variety of combat and fitness techniques, being one of the earlier proponents in Scotland of martial arts such as jiu-jitsu, as well as taking up hatha yoga. Len Ironside, a Scottish wrestler who regularly drove Kidd to shows, tells FSM that this led to a misconception. "He kept himself extremely supple. A lot of people used to think he was double-jointed. Well, there's no such thing! It's just that he was so supple and could move in and out of holds in a fantastic way."

Kidd then joined the Navy in 1943, working as a mechanic in the Fleet Air Arm, which offered his first opportunity to wrestle competitively. After the war ended he made his first appearance on a professional wrestling show, beating William Galloway on 2 October 1945 at the Caird Hall in Dundee in what was billed as a "novice competition." Later that month he defeated 'The Irish Boy' in a "local amateur competition."

It's not entirely clear how these bouts -- of which only three are on record -- were conducted and whether they were intended as a way to expose Kidd before his professional debut, or if they were instead legitimate amateur contests designed to add variety to the show.

In any case, Kidd was soon judged ready to appear in a more traditional pro wrestling role, making his debut against Murdo White at the Eldorado Stadium in Edinburgh suburb Leith on 7 January 1946 and then returning home to the Caird Hall to face Len Ring the following night.

While there's no record of Kidd having undergone formal professional training at this stage, it seems he picked up the business quickly, working for Joint Promotions member Norman Morrell in Newcastle later that year as well as picking up the Scottish lightweight title in 1947, beating Tony Lawrence in a tournament final.

With local promoter George De Relwyskow reportedly believing Kidd was too small to make it as a full-timer, Kidd took the step of spreading his wings to try to enhance his knowledge of both competitive grappling and professional performance style.

He began visited Morrell's gym in Bradford where he was initially rejected as too small, despite having already worked for Morrell. Again, the size jibe irritated Kidd and the story goes that he challenged Morrell to a legitimate grappling contest in which, although decisively beaten, he impressed with his refusal to give in to a submission hold. Kidd stayed for more than a year of training with both Morrell and former Olympic competitor and Empire Games medallist Joe Reid.

His training voyage continued with a trip to the infamous shoot wrestling home of the Snake Pit gym in Wigan, later telling the TV Times that "Three weeks there advanced my career by five years!" He then rounded out his education by visiting London to learn leg submissions from Dave Armstrong and even going over to France to learn from submission guru Mike Dmitri. Kidd also recalled getting an unorthodox piece of advice from Bert Assirati relating to diet rather than wrestling: "I used to go to the abattoir every morning with a pint jug, fill it with bull's blood, boil it on the stone and drink it."

In the same interview, Kidd discussed the finished product of his training. "People say there is a George Kidd style of wrestling. Well, it's flattering, but not true. I might have invented one or two tricks, like rolling up into a ball, but mostly I copied the best wrestlers, adapted their moves to suit me, and put it all together in a neat package."

That may have been modesty as the consensus of wrestling historians and those in the industry is that Kidd most definitely did develop a distinct style: a fast-paced blend of legitimate grappling, reversals and apparent trickery that influenced a generation of lightweights and became particularly synonymous with British wrestling among an international audience.

Len Ironside explains that "George had an unusual style because he was all about pulleys and levers and things like that, it was all based around that mechanical sort of thing. It was beautiful to watch and it's something you don't see today."

Writing in his series of autobiographies, regular Kidd opponent Adrian Street said simply "George Kidd was without a doubt the very best technical wrestler that I ever saw in all my years associated with the sport." He also revealed a secret of how Kidd developed his moves: "Always the innovator, George practiced everything he had learned in a way that made his style unique. He drew footprints with chalk on the floor of his gym that would correspond with the way he moved into an offensive or defensive position. It thrilled him every time he could rub out one more footprint"

Kidd was credited with inventing two trademark holds in particular. The former, the surfboard submission, had been done elsewhere by Mexican Rito Romero (who called it the Romero special or La Tapatia), though it's unknown if Kidd had seen the hold or developed the move independently.

Kidd also created the trick of rolling into a ball and waiting for his bemused opponent to take a proffered hand, at which point Kidd would unroll and take control. That was certainly a British original, taking advantage of the local rule that you could not attack a grounded opponent unless part of a continuous sequence of chain wrestling, meaning the seemingly obvious counter of kicking Kidd's back would be illegal.

Ironside recalls that the style was so influential that Kidd became protective. "He wasn't a great believer in taking other guys into the game. In fact, at one point he used to insist the promoters kept the doors to the dressing rooms closed until his bout had passed because he didn't like people copying him."

While some fans argue that later in his career Kidd's performances became more of an exhibition of his own abilities, Jackie Pallo noted in his autobiography that Kidd certainly wasn't selfish in the ring. "He was faster than a twinkle in the eye, and his escape moves were magic. But George always made me look good while I lost. In other words, like me, he felt it was best to arrange to beat someone without destroying or humiliating them."

Pallo also recalled an incident that illustrated Kidd's diversity. While he was best known for his fluid, sportsmanlike style, and generally favoured clean bouts in England and on television, in his native country he would often take on villainous invaders in more heated affairs, as happened one night against Pallo in Glasgow. "I'd just done something nasty to George when the referee shouted 'Quick Jackie. Get out!' I looked around, and there was this large lad climbing through the ropes, waving a huge bayonet, looking at me with bloodshot eyes as if I was dish of the day. Probably kebab."

Although Pallo and Mick McManus were arguably the first wrestlers among the lighter weight divisions to become automatic headliners anywhere in the country,

Kidd preceded them in overcoming the prejudice that a lightweight wrestler could never main event. As well as engaging the crowd with his style, Kidd was perfectly capable of putting in the time needed for such a position. Max Crabtree told The Wrestling author Simon Garfield that "he'd do an hour and get a standing ovation like Barbara Streisand." Meanwhile Bernard Hughes, a long-time fan at Newcastle's St James Hall, remember seeing Kidd wrestle to a draw in a match with an unusually epic duration of 15 five-minute rounds.

That was a championship match, something which would be a mainstay of Kidd's career. He followed his Scottish title with a win over Jack Dempsey in 1948 for the British crown. Some accounts have him taking a claim to the European title the following year, though this isn't confirmed by reliable records.

While British titles were in theory governed by the Mountevans committee (and in practice controlled by Joint Promotions) and European titles more loosely overseen in partnership with promoters on the continent, world title claims in the UK were rarer. Kidd, however, was the first Brit to be credibly billed as a world champion, listed as defeating Mexican Rudi Quarez for the lightweight title in 1950.

Kidd's championship status was confirmed later that year when he battled Rene Ben Chemoul. Several accounts had it that Kidd beat Chemoul in Dundee to win the crown. In fact it was Chemoul who took the title in Dundee, setting up a rematch where Kidd regained the crown in Paris, an unusual booking pattern that no doubt left audiences disappointed on both sides of the Channel. The Paris match set off an unprecedented 26-year reign as world champion for Kidd.

Despite his position as world champion and a firm favourite of commentator Kent Walton, Kidd's bouts were a relative rarity on the small screen. He only appeared around two dozen times, with just one match on the much-hyped FA Cup Final Day spectaculars, beating Leon Fortuna in 1969. This was partly down to the simple fact that the vast majority of shows were broadcast from English venues, but according to Len Ironside it was also a result of a deliberate policy by Kidd. "He always felt that if you wrestled on TV, you never got the fee from it that he should get. Working the halls, he got a percentage of the gate and it was always packed when George Kidd was wrestling. On television you just got this flat rate fee and he thought that's not fair."

That's not to say Kidd didn't make many appearances in England, or that he didn't hold his own in the prestige stakes. He had high-profile matches against McManus at the Royal Albert Hall and Jackie Pallo at Nottingham Ice Rink and, despite both men being superstars in a higher weight division, neither beat him decisively: McManus won on an injury stoppage while the Pallo match went to a draw. Kidd was also part of the famed 1963 Royal Albert Hall show attended by

Prince Phillip, staving off the title challenge of Spain's Modesto Aledo. One story even has it that the royal specifically asked for Kidd to be on the bill.

While Kidd may have been known mainly by wrestling aficionados in England, he was a genuine celebrity in Scotland. He regularly appeared on mainstream television shows and had such credibility that several news shows aired footage of him training for upcoming bouts, with one segment featuring him comparing techniques with a boxer.

Meanwhile Kidd's abilities to entertain with impressions of celebrities led to him fronting two TV shows on Grampian, the ITV broadcaster for the North and East of Scotland. The Wednesday Show was a magazine program similar to today's The One Show, while The George Kidd Show featured celebrity interviews and variety acts. In 1965 Kidd was voted Grampian TV's Personality Of The Year, and in the same year he was made a "First Citizen" of Dundee, roughly equivalent to being granted the freedom of the city.

While Kidd could be withdrawn, and firmly believed newcomers to the dressing room should know their place and keep quiet, Adrian Street recalled that he had a reputation for entertaining his colleagues with humour and impressions. "George could be extremely funny, but as with so many others in our business, it was only funny to George when he was telling the jokes, and it was not funny at all when he became the brunt of one."

That led to an infamous incident when fellow Scottish star Andy Robin made the mistake of sending up Kidd's in-ring routine when he was in the dressing room. "According to Andy, the moment the door had slammed behind them, George had stuck a handgun halfway up Andy's snout and threatened to blow his brains out if he ever saw him aping the Champion's repertoire again."

That wasn't typical of how Kidd treated people, as Len Ironside revealed. "Although he never showed himself to be very generous, he actually was very generous. When [boxer-turned-wrestler] Randy Turpin went through depression and committed suicide, George sent the family £600 to help them through a difficult period. Now that wasn't something he would boast about or say anything about, but I know he did it."

That generosity was in force when Kidd, having already spent some periods wrestling on the independent circuit, began promoting shows outside of the Joint Promotions stranglehold. Ironside likens his managerial style to that of fellow wrestler-turned-promoter Jackie Pallo. "He treated wrestlers the way he felt he should be treated. He paid them properly: there were no arguments about it, everything was done as it should be. He felt that's the way a show should be run. It should all be smooth, there should be no arguments about money in the dressing rooms and stuff like that. He wouldn't rip them off and the guys knew he wouldn't rip them off."

If Kidd did have any ego, he was able to put it aside for the sake of his shows. "He had plenty of variety. George always said that there's room for everything in wrestling, though he wasn't keen on comedy stuff, but he always accepted that there was room for a bit of anything in wrestling and it was a general all-round good package. He had people like Andy Robin topping his bills, because he knew that's what the crowd would want. He knew how to make a good match."

Despite his move to the independent circuit, Kidd was brought back for a final TV appearance in 1975 for a show with an England vs Scotland concept, defeating Blackjack Mulligan before teaming with Lee Thomas to beat Mulligan and Peter Kaye to complete a three-bout sweep for the Scots.

Kidd decided to hang up his boots in 1976, with his last recorded bout being on April 1 in Glasgow when he teamed with Thomas to beat the "Skinheads" team of Terry O'Neill & Roy Paul. He surrendered the world title as an undefeated champion, with Johnny Saint winning a tournament to win the vacant crown. While Saint maintains he did not intentionally use this opportunity to "claim" some of Kidd's old tricks, Len Ironside recalls that Saint and others were under pressure to maintain the style.

"Max Crabtree was very keen on that. He really wanted Johnny Saint to be the next George Kidd. Actually, Johnny had his own style and it was good to watch, but Max used to encourage a lot of the younger guys to try the George Kidd stuff. Crabtree knew that was a big loss to him. It was one of the bones of contention really with a lot of the English promoters, the fact that George, at the end of the 60s, he didn't really want to travel too much. Having the world title in Scotland where there was no access to it in England, was quite a difficult thing for promoters to accept. They made sure that the next champion that came after Kidd would be around the halls in England."

Following his wrestling days, Kidd owned and ran several pubs in Dundee before retiring to the coastal suburb of Broughty Ferry, perhaps best known as the home of sitcom character Bob Servant.

In August 2015, Kidd was inducted as the first member of the Scottish wrestling Hall of Fame. The ceremony took place at the first wrestling show at Caird Hall for 20 years and included Ironside, wrestling historian Bradley Craig and Dundee's Lord Provost (roughly equivalent to a mayor) Bob Duncan presenting a plaque which now hangs permanently in the hall's lobby.

Ironside says he was surprised to find that even younger members of the media who covered the event were aware of Kidd's status. "It's just one of those legends and I think any Scots wrestler that you know would know about George Kidd. They may not have seen him, they may not have been around when he was around, but they would know of him and certainly he was very much at the forefront of the fans minds. "

# GIANT HAYSTACKS

"When did I first realise my dad was different to other people?" Noel Ruane takes only a moment to ponder FSM's question before giving a definitive answer. "The day he picked a car up and flipped it over."

The dad in question was Martin Ruane, better known to wrestling fans as Giant Haystacks. The car in question belonged to the TV crew producing a sketch for the Little and Large show. "He was supposed to throw it down the road, but it ended up flipping over too many times. They asked him to do it again and after the effort he'd already made, he gave them what I can only describe as a very impolite response.

"I still didn't really grasp how unusual it was until we went back to school and were having the 'So what did you do during the holidays?' discussion. When nobody believed my story, I finally realised Dad was really something special."

Though of Irish heritage, Martin Ruane was born in London in 1946, reportedly weighing an eyewatering 14 lbs. His family moved to Salford when he was three. After leaving school he worked in a variety of labouring jobs and later became a nightclub doorman. (One story has it that he'd have preferred to be a concert pianist, but this was impossible given the size of his fingers.)

Ruane was spotted by a local wrestler, Billy Graham (no relation to the WWWF grappler or the evangelist.) Graham persuaded him to try wrestling, with his booking coming against Milton Reed, an actor who'd appeared in Dr No and wrestled as the Mighty Chang. It's not entirely clear whether that match actually went ahead, but Ruane was soon wrestling dates under the ring name Luke McMasters.

Graham then took him to meet Brian Dixon who had recently begun promoting a breakaway group in opposition to the main Joint Promotions cartel. "Just by looking at him I could see he had potential," Dixon recalls, "so I gave him a chance. He didn't really serve a long apprenticeship: in fact, just three months later he was off on a tour of India."

Dixon rebranded Ruane as Haystacks Calhoun, a name taken from an earlier gargantuan wrestler who'd been mentioned in American wrestling magazines Dixon had read. This wasn't an uncommon practice among UK promoters: names such as Skull Murphy, Blackjack Mulligan and Greg Valentine all featured on both sides of the Atlantic.

Later Dixon refined this to simply Giant Haystacks. Although some wrestlers knew him simply as "Stacks", even long-term friends in the business generally called him Luke rather than Martin. Indeed, many newspapers and books later erroneously "revealed" that Luke McMasters was his real name.

In 1975 Haystacks had built up enough of a reputation that Joint Promotions brought him in to team with Shirley Crabtree, now rebranded as Big Daddy and working as a villain. Haystacks' first appearance on TV came in a disqualification loss to Roy and Tony St Clair and the pair continued a path of destruction until late 1977 when Haystacks refused to wrestle Daddy in a tournament final.

The pair wrestled hundreds of times over the next decade. Although Haystacks suffered a quick defeat to Daddy at Wembley Arena in 1981, he did receive a big push in the build-up to the event, winning five straight singles matches by knockout. Unlike many of Daddy's victims, he was quickly rebuilt on TV afterwards, winning one contest in just 28 seconds while his losses mainly came via disqualification or by walking out of the match. In 1985 he even won a handicap match against Johnny and Peter Wilson, an unusual set-up in what was still nominally presented as a sports broadcast.

Haystacks also took part in an extremely rare in-ring interview at Croydon the month before the Wembley show. Not only was Walton interviewing a wrestler almost unheard of, but the nature of the television program meant that such a promo, specifically hyping up a particular match at a particular venue, was also very unusual. Haystacks certainly made the most of it: as well as vowing to add an extra four stone to his existing 39 stone bulk, he opted for show rather than tell. Asked what he would do to Daddy, he simply took hold of a horseshoe and stretched it straight.

Noel Ruane remembers just how heated crowds got over such actions and the contrast with the image of Daddy. "Our family went to a show at the Blackpool Tower where Dad was wrestling him. The jeers for Dad were absolutely thunderous. I remember thinking 'Oh my, we'd really best not cheer for him tonight!'"

Away from the ring, such danger wasn't a regular problem. "Dad was very good on keeping his family private and keeping us in the background. He tried not to involve us in publicity and we only appeared in a couple of newspaper photoshoots. Because of that, people very rarely made fun of us for who we were."

At times Daddy and Haystacks were in the ring together literally every night and once would have worked nine straight days were it not for one exception: the Sunday in the middle when Haystacks was replaced by another villain. The reason was his strong Catholic beliefs: wherever possible, he avoided wrestling on

Sundays and even frowned on his children doing anything that could be classed as industrious.

Sundays also meant a traditional roast dinner. While there have been several publicity shots purporting to show a typical breakfast or other meal for Giant Haystacks, Noel Ruane shared his father's actual dietary preferences with FSM. "It takes a lot of food to keep a body that big running, but he didn't eat any rubbish: you never saw dad at a burger van. He just liked good healthy food... with very healthy portions.

"On a Sunday he'd happily polish off a whole shoulder of lamb, along with a side dish of roast pork. Then he'd have a large apple pie and a cup of tea -- except his cup was actually a pint pot. After that he'd usually have room for some bread and jam or a big hunk of Battenberg cake."

It wasn't just food that had to be supersized however. "The whole house was upscaled, including the furniture. Whenever I go back to the family home, I see his huge chair. It's so large I get swallowed up in it and could happily sleep there."

Ironically sleep and seating were two of the bigger problems for Haystacks when he was driving to and from shows. Nobody disliked his company or being with him -- quite the opposite in fact as he was an engaging storyteller -- but there were some logistical issues that meant he found it difficult to keep travelling partners. "If you were in his car as a passenger, it was terrifying because he could fall asleep at the drop of a hat" recalls Dixon. "But if you gave him a lift in your car it was doubly bad. Not only were you worried about his bulk wrecking the car, but he'd sit asleep in the passenger seat and slowly tip over towards you. You'd be sat with one hand on the wheel and the other trying to hold him off from slumping onto you!"

Life on the road -- and further afield -- presented a bitter irony. "Dad absolutely loved travelling the world," Noel recalls. "He'd captivate you with tales of the characters he'd met, particularly fellow giants like Andre and the Big Show, and he was always talking about Hulk Hogan and wanting to wrestle him. When he talked, hours would pass during which you could have heard a pin drop because everyone was listening."

The problem was that the physical journey detracted from the personal one. The problems of cars were nothing in comparison to the discomfort and embarrassment that came with a man of such size on airplanes. Countless wrestlers have countless stories of Haystacks suffering misfortune on flights and while such tales should always be treated with a dose of scepticism, he did publicly recount at least one incident of squeezing into a plane toilet only to find himself without the elbow room to rotate and make his exit.

Such problems weren't enough to prevent him becoming a world traveller, particularly in the early 1980s when he wrestled in Canada, Hawaii, New Zealand,

Australia and Africa, after which he repeatedly shared his pride at being an honorary citizen of Zimbabwe. In Canada he wrestled for Stampede as part of English manager JR Foley's heel stable. Rebranded as the Loch Ness Monster he teamed with the Dynamite Kid to hold the promotion's North American tag titles, though it appears that outside the ring the pair didn't get on so well, with Haystack's no fan of Dynamite's often vindictive brand of prank-based humour.

In Australia he worked for the local World Championship Wrestling promotion in its final years, sometimes using the nickname "Mighty Goliath". Here he was photographed in the ring battling Andre the Giant. It doesn't appear the pair had a singles bout, instead clashing in tag matches and a series of Russian Roulettes, the local variant of a battle royale.

Closer to home, Haystacks made several appearances in the German and Austrian tournaments, winning the 1982 Bremen competition over the likes of Otto Wanz, John Quinn and All Japan's Masao Ito. (Generally his strong ring persona didn't require championships to boost his standing, though he did hold the British heavyweight title for four months at the end of 1978, exchanging the belt with Tony St Clair.) Though the format of several weeks based at the same venue made such trips a welcome relief, it appears Haystacks's favourite foreign venue was the Republic of Ireland.

Writing in his own autobiography, Orig Williams -- who promoted or organised many of Haystacks's foreign ventures -- remember that "As soon as we boarded the ferry for Holyhead to Dublin, his accent would change from Cockney to Irish." Williams also wrote of Haystacks's obsession with Irish bare-knuckle fighters, particularly the folklore that the toughest man in any village would wear a red scarf. Nobody else was permitted such apparel and the only way to take it was to successfully challenge and defeat the existing holder. Williams was eventually persuaded to find a red scarf for Haystacks to wear in local pubs during wrestling tours but whether the tales were pure myth, or he was simply so huge, nobody chose to take issue with him.

That's not to say Haystacks sought confrontation. Indeed, one story has it that a lout once threw a drink at his wife Rita in an attempt to provoke him into a fight, but Haystacks managed to keep his cool. Noel Ruane explains that attitude held true at home. "He never shouted at us or lost his cool when we misbehaved. He'd just address us calmly, which was much scarier! He'd just rationally explain why what we had done was wrong."

There was certainly no hiding place for Haystacks in public. Even putting his size aside, he had become a recognisable public figure, not just from wrestling but from a string of TV appearances. He guest-starred as himself (or a character very like it) on shows including Send In The Girls and Gone to Seed, occasionally appeared alongside Daddy on Tiswas, and most famously appeared in scenes alongside Paul McCartney in his musical film Give My Regards to Broad Street. In Northern Ireland he attracted attention by giving sports and chat show presenter Jackie Fullerton a particularly impactful bodyslam after the host questioned the legitimacy of the wrestling business.

Haystacks also appeared in a TV commercial for potato snack Skips, the punchline being that he admired their light and dainty build. He even released three songs (Baby I Need You, Big Splash and It's OK For Santa) under the billing of "The World's Biggest Recording Artist." The musical connection continued in the 21st century when a California punk band took his name, while last year a two man play "Big Daddy vs Giant Haystacks" toured the country, sometimes appearing in the same halls where the pair once wrestled.

He also took advantage of his fame on a more personal level. In later years he worked for a debt collection agency, the idea being not so much that his size would intimidate late payers, but rather that a visit to their office would attract so much attention that it would embarrass them into settling up.

Although he was best associated with Daddy, Haystacks wrestled a wider variety of opponents and was comfortable in singles matches. He took on opponents of a range of sizes and styles, from fellow heavyweights such as Ray Steele to the smaller Marty Jones, and even a series of bouts with Kwik Kick Lee and Flying Funaki, better known as Japanese shoot-style pioneers Akira Maeda and Masakatsu Funaki. He even once took on Wayne Bridges in a ladder match, though on his first attempt to retrieve the cash prize it took just two steps, a lot of shaking and a bit of a creak to confirm that he would not be reaching the top rung and claiming victory.

Following the removal of British wrestling from ITV in 1988, Haystacks capitalised on his name value by working for a wider range of promotions, including televised wrestling shows in Wales and Scotland. He also returned to wrestling for Brian Dixon, most notably feuding with Kendo Nagasaki including a bout televised as part of a BBC 2 arts documentary series Arena.

During the matches with Nagasaki (and later his imitator King Kendo), Haystacks heard the cheers of the crowd for the first time since his visits to Africa. Dixon believes this wasn't so much the way the feud was promoted or a sign of begrudging respect, but simply the numbers game. "Nagasaki always had somebody on his side like [managers] Gorgeous George or Lloyd Ryan, while Haystacks was on his own. British people always instinctively support the person at the disadvantage when it's a two-against-one situation because they see it as unfair, even if the one is a man the size of Haystacks."

Having worked a single date against Steve (later William) Regal on the first WCW tour of the UK, Haystacks finally began a US run in 1996. He debuted in the closing moments of the main event of SuperBrawl, going nose to nose with Hulk

Hogan. Now part of the Dungeon of Doom stable, he returned to the Loch Ness name and built up a few televised wins against the likes of Alex Wright and Scotty Riggs before tasting a quick defeat to the Giant (now Big Show) at the Uncensored PPV.

Haystacks then returned to the UK for a short break and conventional wisdom has it that he was scheduled to return to WCW to feud with Hogan. It's not clear if this was a firm plan, or simply an assumption given that Hogan had been in a "monster of the month" booking style for the past year or so. In fact, Hogan didn't wrestle on pay-per-view again after this point until the infamous Bash at the Beach show in which he turned heel and formed the nWo.

Whatever future booking plans were for Haystacks, they proved sadly irrelevant. Whilst back in the UK he suffered serious stomach pains and, when he sought medical help, was diagnosed with lymphoma, a cancer that affects the immune system. He was quoted by one journalist as saying " I don't want to thrash the world anymore or beat the living daylights out of my ring rivals. My greatest joy these days is just waking up, seeing the blue sky and hearing the birds sing." After battling the condition for two years, he died on November 29, 1998 aged just 52.

"When I think back to his life, the one thing that doesn't get enough credit is his sheer brute strength," Noel Ruane says. "He never did any training like bench pressing or anything, but he had such raw power." That strength and size is certainly genetic, though it appears it may have skipped a generation. "My brothers and I are all a little over six foot and about 17 to 20 stone, so we're big but not unusually so. But some of our kids are already very large: one of my nieces is 13 and she's already six foot -- though I should mention she's absolutely stunning with catwalk looks!

"I'm 42 now and still miss dad telling me all his stories. I truly think there's an epic film to be made about his life."

# JACKIE PALLO

By all rights Jackie Pallo should have been a boxer rather than a wrestler, which makes it all the more ironic that so many fans wanted nothing more than to see him punched in the face.

Pallo was born Jack Gutteridge in 1926 above an Islington boxing gym owned by his father and uncle. His grandfather is believed to have been in the first professional bout at the National Sporting Club, which was the original home of the Lonsdale belts awarded to British champions and the birthplace of the British Boxing Board of Control. Cousin Reg went on to be the voice of ITV boxing for more than 35 years.

Although Jack had a brief amateur boxing career as a teenager and coached for many years at a local school, he also learned amateur wrestling and carried out odd jobs for pro grapplers who used the gym. After working as a cornerman and referee for professional bouts, he was attracted by the money on offer for wrestlers and stepped into the ring under the Pallo name, taken from a brother-in-law.

After several years of paying his dues at the bottom of the cards (later claiming he won just one fall in his first four years), Pallo began making his name through a series of outlandish gimmicks -- or at least outlandish by the standards of 1950s Britain. He bleached his hair and grew it long enough to add a single pigtail, tied with a velvet ribbon that he would throw to female audience members, a set-up somewhat reminiscent of the American Gorgeous George and his "Georgie pin" hairpins.

And hard as it might be to believe today, Pallo was able to stand out further simply by wearing striped trunks rather than a solid colour. Years later this led to a memorable incident when notorious in-ring joker Les Kellett took off his robe at the start of a match with Pallo to reveal an identical pair of trunks.

It was television that helped Pallo really make his name, however. He worked briefly with Kent Walton when ITV began televising bouts in 1955, filling what would now be known as the colour commentator position. Inside the ring, he made sure viewers remembered him when he brought one match to an eye-watering end by missing a dropkick and appearing to catch his groin on a ring rope.

Jackie Pallo

Pallo's personality was simply made for television: in the first half of the 1960s his number of appearances in TV matches was second only to his most famous rival Mick McManus, but Pallo was better able to translate his wrestling fame into other appearances on screen and stage.

An early appearance on the hugely popular Sunday Night At The London Palladium show led him to adopt the nickname "Mr TV", an initial boastfulness that became justified with later spots on Emergency Ward 10 and The Avengers. The latter show memorably saw Pallo as a gravedigger wrestling Honor Blackman's character for control of a spade. Unfortunately Blackman let go of the spade without warning and Pallo took an unplanned tumble into an open grave, knocking himself out for several minutes.

In the early 70s, Pallo even released a couple of songs ("Everyone Should Get What I Got" and "One Little Packet of Cigarettes") before teaming up with wife Trixie and son Jackie Jr) to release a covers album, "Ring-A-Long With The Pallos".

As a top star, Pallo was no longer confined to making regular appearances on a local circuit and regularly criss-crossed the country to headline. He and fellow grapplers had a major advantage in that they could draw fans in smaller towns who would rarely have the opportunity see a television star in person, let alone appearing in their "TV character" rather than simply playing a pantomime role or switching on Christmas lights.

Although a genuine celebrity, Pallo was still able to enrage audiences, with his matches as much about flamboyance and verbal interaction as legitimate grappling. He would regularly exchange insults with the crowd, for example answering one woman's cry of "If I was your wife, I'd poison you" with "If I was your husband, I'd drink it." Ironically that response was lifted from a near-identical exchange between Winston Churchill and fellow politician Bessie Braddock, who later appeared at ringside for a famous 1963 Royal Albert Hall show also attended by Prince Phillip. Pallo decided to give press photographers something to enjoy by throwing opponent Johnny Kwango out of the ring at the Prince's feet.

While Pallo's exchanges with the crowd were often good-natured, other audiences -- most notably in the North and Scotland -- were openly hostile. One heated moment came as Pallo was wrestling Peter Maivia, grandfather of The Rock. The story goes that as Pallo took an "unfair advantage" in the ring, it became clear that Maivia's wife Lia was not entirely aware of how the business worked as she jumped into the ring to give Pallo a beating.

Life has a funny way of balancing out however. Melvyn Eyres, who later wrestled Steve Serene and the masked Solitaire, recalls that as Pallo made a trip to a show, Peter Maiva's presence proved a definite advantage. "A large lorry cut them up and nearly drove them off the road. Sometime later when stopping in a transport cafe for a cup of tea Jack spotted the offending lorry with the driver sitting in his cab. Jack drove over and got out of his car to give the lorry driver some polite pointers on his driving skills.

"The lorry driver, a rather large gentleman, got out of his cab and walked menacingly towards Jack shouting 'You're not big enough to take me Pallo'... at which time 20 stone of Tattooed Maori warrior alighted from Jack's car and shouted back 'He may not be big enough but I am!' The lorry driver then decided to get back in his cab and disappeared at great speed."

Pallo's ability to anger the public was well documented in newspapers of the time. In September 1963 fan Eva Mile, who had been a ringside regular in Carlisle every week for five years, received a lifetime ban from the venue after attacking him with her shoe.

But even supporters got heated by his bouts. The following year Corby resident Raymond Gribble made the headlines when he was watching a TV match and, according to a news story syndicated worldwide "picked up a table knife when one his favourite wrestlers, Jackie Pallo, got into difficulties. Then Pallo gained the upper hand and Gribble stabbed himself [in the side] with excitement."

While Pallo's gimmick seemed custom-made for battling local heroes and television fan favourites, he will forever be associated with a fellow villain. As The Wrestler magazine said in its end of decade review, "For many wrestling enthusiasts, the sixties will stick in their minds as the age of Mick McManus and Jackie 'Mr TV' Pallo... both have become top sports personalities in their own right... both have become household names throughout the country." Indeed, there's little serious debate that the pair were the most famous British wrestlers ever until the Big Daddy era.

Though the pair had wrestled on occasion in the 1950s, including one TV match (won by McManus), the feud proper started on 21 April 1962 at a televised show at Wembley Town Hall where McManus was wrestling Bob Anthony. At some stage in the show (accounts vary on whether it took place before or after the bout) Pallo came to ringside and challenged McManus to a match with both men putting up a £100 stake: equivalent to six weeks' wages for the average working man.

Pallo later claimed the move was spontaneous and initially angered promoters, though this hasn't been verified. Either way, the pair were booked to wrestle at the same venue on 5 May as part of the FA Cup Final special, the biggest TV wrestling show of the year. Both men kept their cash with the match ending in a one fall apiece draw.

According to Pallo, such heel vs heel affairs caught the crowd's imagination because they meant "the punters could have a good time trying to decide which they hated the most." While recollections vary, it appears crowds may have wavered towards McManus with fans respecting his perceived in-ring toughness more than Pallo's naturally irritating flamboyance.

After another draw at the Royal Albert Hall the next month, this time without the cameras, the pair met in a televised rematch on 25 May 1963, again on the Cup Final day special. This time McManus took a 2-1 win, though it was Pallo's celebration of his own pinfall that became widely remembered. Photos of the match clearly show Pallo kissing his own wife Trixie who sat at ringside, but the move was considered so shocking at the time that in later recollections it evolved to Pallo kissing McManus' wife or vice versa.

Save for one non-televised match, the pair didn't meet again for another four years. In part this was careful booking designed to avoid overexposing the feud or being forced to have one man lose, but it was also down to the pair's schedule. Both were usually the biggest name on the bill, so in many cases it would be redundant to have both men appear on the same show, let alone against one another.

The feud reignited on 20 January 1967 when the pair appeared on the Eamonn Andrews show on ITV, one of the first successful chat shows on British screens. Alongside fellow guests including singer Petula Clark and former Conservative leadership candidate Quintin Hogg, the pair discussed their rivalry before staging a raging row with (in Pallo's account at least) McManus walking off stage.

This time round the pair did capitalise on the exposure with a series of matches around the country over the next couple of years, though these were mainly away from their "base" in Southern England and they never again met on TV. The Wrestling Heritage site notes that generally Pallo would only ever win to set a rematch where McManus would prevail

The real showcase bout came at the Royal Albert Hall, where monthly shows were the closest British wrestling in this era had to a "big event" rather than the usual weekly appearances in every major town. (Indeed, in 1966 a show at the venue featuring both men in action against other opponents had been shown live in cinemas nationwide via closed circuit.)

On 24 June 1967, in what was billed by Joint Promotions as "Wrestling's Night of The Year", Pallo took the first fall only to forfeit the contest when he was cut open by a series of headbutts by McManus. So out of the ordinary was this brutality at the venue, the that artist Peter Blake, creator of the Sergeant Pepper album cover, later expressed his belief that unlike most wrestling bouts this was "a genuine fight to the finish."

The final round of the rivalry began five years later with a series of matches at the Royal Albert Hall. The pair first met on 31 May with Pallo teaming up with his son JJ against McManus and his new regular partner Steve Logan. On 13 December 1972 Pallo finally won a high-profile victory; though McManus now held the

European middleweight title, this was a non-title affair. On 7 February 1973 the pair had a title match without a clear outcome, while McManus ended the controversy on 16 May, successfully defending the title with a knockout.

Despite coming out on the short end of the feud, Pallo's celebrity status certainly wasn't affected. On 18 April 1973 he had again appeared on television with Eamonn Andrews, this time as the subject of This Is Your Life, making him the first grappler to star on the show. (A decade later, Shirley "Big Daddy" Crabtree became the only other man to receive that honour.)

The following year, Pallo fell out with Joint Promotions, which had been taken over by boxing promoter Jarvis Astaire. After a spell working mainly in Scotland, Pallo began promoting independently where his fame proved both an advantage and a disadvantage.

The advantage was that he was a recognisable figure to managers of prestigious venues across the country and was thus able to book dates even in towns on the regular Joint Promotions schedule. The disadvantage was that this put him in direct competition with Joint: indeed, some grapplers later theorised he became obsessed with beating his former employers rather than making cash in smaller markets.

Dating back to its cartel heyday, Joint had always had a curious relationship with independent promoters. Those who stuck to smaller towns or areas such as Wales and parts of Scotland, and didn't try to book the wrestlers with TV stardom, were generally left to their own devices. Those who were seen as encroaching on Joint's territory (both figurative and literal) were in for a fight that could be described as "by fair means or foul" -- a fight Pallo certainly faced now.

Neil Evans, a diminutive grappler who was given the Tom Thumb character when wrestling for Pallo, recalls that the new promoter didn't let geography stand in the way of ambition. On one occasion Pallo and JJ wrestled the Borg Twins "in Redruth, Cornwall on a Thursday, Kelvin Hall, Glasgow on the Friday and finally at Kings Lynn Corn Exchange on the Saturday." Despite having driven nearly 1,200 miles in a two-day period, "their tag match on the Saturday was just as electric and at full pace as any other time I had seen them."

Under the banner "The Show You Can't See On TV", Pallo promoted some top-line talent including Adrian Street, Johnny Kincaid and a young Dave Finlay, as well as following fellow independents All Star in featuring women, a 'gimmick' shunned by Joint Promotions. Pallo and JJ generally headlined, creating something of a dilemma. As Eyres recalls, "If Jack wrestled on one of his own shows and won the crowd would shout fix he's the promoter he's bound to win," but Pallo himself noted that if he did lose the crowd often turned out to be secretly disappointed.

It was Pallo's attempts to treat both fans and wrestlers fairly that may have been part of his undoing. As Eyres explains "He treated the wrestlers far better than a lot of the more unscrupulous promoters of the time and paid wages above the going rate. Even when the shows were poorly attended and Jack was facing big financial losses he would insist the boys were paid. This was one of the things that led to his eventual downfall: other promoters after a bad house would just say 'Sorry boys, there's not enough in the pot to pay wages tonight.'"

This generosity became a particular problem when, as appears to have happened on several occasions, Pallo and JJ weren't quite on the same page about who was responsible for booking performers for a show. This could either mean being short-staffed, or having an excess of grapplers arriving and expecting payment. Unfortunately, word of this pattern spread among less scrupulous grapplers and, as Eddie "Kung Fu" Hamill puts it, Pallo "was probably 'done' a few times when it was known that he would pay the wrestlers he had overbooked and too many turned up", including those who'd not been booked by either man.

By 1985, Pallo had largely abandoned his promotional efforts and, dejected with the transition of Joint to the Big Daddy era, released a tell-all book titled "You Grunt, I'll Groan" that explained how wrestling worked. Looked at through modern eyes, it's almost comical the extent to which Pallo has to insist that bout outcomes really are predetermined and that wrestlers are working together in the ring. For fans at the time it was hardly shocking, largely confirming suspicions rather than shattering illusions, though the precise details of how moves worked or how wrestlers used a blade will have been revelations for some.

In 1989 Pallo had one last roll of the promotional dice, running a mammoth one-night taping under the Wrestling Around The World banner. Though he was able to sell the resulting tapes to Central TV, the event proved a major money loser. Like other British promotions, it simply wasn't possible to compete with the likes of the WWF who could supply European stations with well-produced programming without incurring any extra expenses other than the cost of posting a tape.

Pallo's battles with Joint Promotions and his breaching of kayfabe with his book had left him on bad terms with some industry veterans, but he remained highly regarded among most of his colleagues right up until his death from cancer in 2006. Even those who'd had personal disagreements with him had few bad words to say about his work in front of the crowd, and his attitude to the business was summed up best by Eddie Hamill:

"Pallo was one of the top wrestlers around and a great showman: all he ever wanted was a good show as a wrestler or promoter."

# JACKIE TURPIN

Second generation performers are hardly a rarity in the British wrestling business. But Jackie Turpin is perhaps the only British wrestler to follow in his family's footsteps in two separate sports.

Turpin's father, also named Jack, was one of three brothers from Leamington Spa to box professionally. While all three tasted success, with a combined total of more than 200 wins, it was youngest brother Randy who reached the greatest heights. After capturing British, Commonwealth and European titles, he beat the legendary Sugar Ray Robinson at Earls Court to win the World middleweight crown in 1951.

Although Randy lost the title in a rematch in New York just two months later, he continued fighting throughout the 1950s. Upon his retirement from the boxing business, he was struggling for money, having sadly fit the age-old cliché of a pugilist who hadn't kept an eye on his finances.

Randy turned to professional wrestling, first competing in "boxer vs wrestler" bouts (including knocking out Brian 'Leon Arras' Glover) and then turning to traditional grappling. He began working a reasonably regular schedule, with a highlight being a match at the Bradford football ground where he took on the supposed aristocrat Lord Bertie Topsham. Tragically Turpin's financial situation didn't improve, and he was later declared bankrupt before, in May 1966, taking his own life.

Born in 1949, Jackie Turpin followed in the footsteps of both his father and uncles, turning professional in 1967. After an initial string of wins followed by a more difficult period, Turpin really hit his stride with a stunning 1971. Throughout the year he won all 11 of his contests, 10 via knockout, with only opponents surviving past the third round.

The record was enough to earn Turpin a young fighter of the year award from the Boxing Writers Club and he still questions whether his management did enough to lobby for any form of championship match, which he never received: "To be honest, by today's standards that sort of record would get you a world title match," he told FSM.

Jackie Turpin

That debate became redundant in December 1972 when the British Boxing Board of Control withdrew Turpin's licence on medical grounds. He embarked on a lengthy court process, arguing that the licensing system was unlawful because it did not allow fighters the right of appeal.

Nearly three years later Turpin prevailed, but after just two more fights (a win and a loss) he decided to call it a day. It was initially a disappointment to his family, most notably his mother who had spearheaded the legal battle, offering both much-needed energy and practical measures such as organising a petition. However, Turpin was clear in his decision: "I couldn't fight if my heart wasn't in it. I wasn't going to carry on and get hurt just for the sake of the money."

Still in his late 20s, Turpin turned to the wrestling business. It was not an intentional plan to follow Randy's career path, but rather was sparked by a close friendship with grappler Tony Walsh that went back to childhood. As with Randy, Turpin began by doing the circuit with boxer vs wrestler contests. These peculiar contests initially saw an unaware Turpin legitimately trying to win, while in most cases his wrestler opponent tried to make it an entertaining show without getting knocked out too quickly.

Eventually Turpin was let in on the secrets of the business and schooled in the basics of showmanship. Still, he concedes that "I found it very difficult at first to learn how to pull a punch, so even though I was wearing gloves there was still a good chance of me hurting them by mistake." Promoters ran out of opponents willing to take the risk and so, with fresh match-ups hard to find, it was time for Turpin to learn the grappling game.

Here he was "surprised just how much hard graft it was." In a television interview with Gary Newbon he explained that he still got injured in wrestling, but it was to the body rather than -- as in both boxing bouts and more significantly in sparring -- blows to the head, which were more of a long-term worry. Turpin tells FSM that it wasn't just serious injuries that wrestlers had to watch out for: "There were lots of silly things that could go wrong, like when you did the finger interlock at the start of the match, if one of these big guys turned his hand too quickly, you could break a finger."

Much of Turpin's early education came not in working matches against other grapplers, but rather taking on members of the public on the fairground circuit. Working alongside Tony Walsh on Ron Taylor's booth, Turpin competed in both boxing and wrestling matches. Amazingly, although the crowd was always told of his professional experience and family heritage, he was never short of contenders.

"I think a lot of them simply didn't believe the MC was telling the truth and assumed it was all hype. In other cases, it was because I was a middleweight and 15 stone guys thought they could take me. And of course, a lot of them were just drunk!"

Jackie Turpin

On the booths Turpin learned a lot of showmanship, often livening up a bout by allowing an opponent to survive until the third and final round before putting him away, "though I had to keep my wits about me and watch out for ringers like local amateur boxers." He recalls that one particular skill he learned here and transferred to more traditional pro wrestling was the ability to fight a much larger opponent (both for real and as a show.)

Back in the halls, Turpin's existing stardom meant he quickly found favour with promoters, making his television debut in March 1976, a mere five months after his last pro boxing match. Walsh, although not holding it against his friend personally, admitted in his autobiography that "I was more than a little pissed off when the Joint Promotions boys snapped him up without a second thought."

The pair were regular opponents, particularly in their mutual hometown where they built up a fierce storyline rivalry. "Even to this day, people in Leamington Spa think we're enemies," Turpin notes. "It was a 'well known fact' that Tony and I didn't like each other in Leamington."

Their feud involved several stipulation matches including a ladder match for a supposed £500 prize and an infamous hair vs hair contest. With Turpin the logical (and indeed planned) winner, a local well-known businessman offered Walsh £100 if he could win the bout. The pair didn't question why such a bounty was on offer: the most likely explanation is that the businessman found a sucker willing to offer a bet with favourable odds on the upset. Instead they took and split the money -- a welcome bonus given they were being paid only £25 by promoters. The resulting crowd outrage when Turpin had his head shaved was enough to earn Walsh a suspension from the venue for several months.

Such extra paydays aside, Turpin recalls being "disillusioned with the payoffs", which were far below his boxing prize money, albeit with more opportunities to earn. "I worked about four shows a week unless there was something local, but if you wanted to you could work seven nights a week." Being both a husband and a father, Turpin didn't enjoy being away from home, particularly when working the holiday camp circuit where the venues were so far apart that he could go a week without seeing his family.

That said, some of his most treasured memories involve the humour of travelling with Walsh. "This one time a bloke cut us up in a lorry, so we chased after this chap and made him pull over. And the guy got out with a crowbar in his hand. Tony got out and picked him up and then threw him on the ground."

In the heat of the situation, Walsh reacted instinctively -- well, instinctively for a pro wrestler: "He went to stomp but he never actually [connected]. The bloke must have thought 'What happened there?' He pretended Tony had hurt him and crawled under the lorry. Tony shouted at him and threw his keys into the hedge and then got back in our car and we drove off."

Jackie Turpin

"I told him 'Do you know what you did? You picked that guy up and did a working move on him?" Tony said 'Did I?' I said 'Yeah, you pretended to stomp on him and the bloke didn't even realise!"

By around a year into his professional career, Turpin felt he'd not only earned the acceptance of his fellow wrestlers, but his family had come to terms with his new profession, particularly the fact that despite his legitimate combat skills he was allowing himself "to be thrown about the place. But when they saw I was doing OK and was on TV they were happy for me."

As well as the physical toll wrestling took, Turpin had been surprised at "how people in the audience got so excited, so involved, and how they sometimes turned nasty. The villains took a lot of stick after the bout. I wouldn't want to be a villain!"

This wasn't a problem given Turpin's clean-cut look, sporting legacy and developing technical skills. This and his specific experience working against Walsh made him an ideal tag partner for Big Daddy, a role he wound up playing on more than 400 occasions. It's likely this may have made him Daddy's second most frequent opponent behind only Greg Valentine (not the US grappler but rather Daddy's nephew Steve Crabtree who had adopted the moniker.)

With Walsh usually partnered by a giant, Turpin recalls that he and Walsh "did the selling of it, we did the work, we were the workhorses. The matches were OK, they were just... fun matches if you know what I mean. I much preferred singles matches. I got more enjoyment out of good wrestling matches where you had to work, and you had to think about the moves.

"The Daddy matches were just the same old stuff: repetition, repetition. After a while you got fed up of it.... well I did anyway. OK, you made your money, but I enjoyed going in and having a good workout and that's what you get when you worked with people like Jimmy Breaks. There was a lot of skill involved."

Turpin recalls enjoying wrestling the likes of Steve Grey, Pat Patton and Johnny England for their technical skills, with a particular fondness for wrestling Jim Breaks where he was able to display his ability while still having a heated crowd. On occasions when Turpin worked the undercard, he'd often have to work longer bouts to make up for the Daddy tag match being relatively short. "I'd do eight rounds and even ten rounds a couple of time. I even once wrestled Steve Grey in a match without rounds and we just did 25 minutes straight."

Aside from his technical contests, Turpin's most memorable match came at a Leamington show taped for television where he inflicted a rare defeat on Mick McManus: "Admittedly it was by disqualification, but I still beat him!"

Looking back, Turpin is proud of his time in the ring and his ring style. "Today's American stuff has a lot of very athletic moves, but they aren't really believable. We had to do more wrestling type moves rather than hitting each other with chairs and belts -- though of course, we weren't allowed to do that on TV anyway. But I wish we'd been able to get some of the big money like in America."

One man who did make his fortune across the Atlantic was Chris Adams who, coming from a judo background, was introduced to the wrestling business by Turpin, who shared his own experience at switching from pure combat to something with more showmanship. "He was a truly lovely guy. I couldn't believe it when I heard he'd passed away." (Adams died in Texas in 2001 from a gunshot wound suffered during a fight with a friend.)

By the late 1980s, after ten years in the business, Turpin concluded it was time to leave the ring. "The travelling just got to me, and I was starting to feel unwell all the time from taking all the bumps. It comes to a time when you think 'I've had enough of this.' I just thought 'I'm going to get a proper job.' That [may sound] a terrible thing to say, but as much as I loved it, I had to get a proper job."

Like many former wrestlers, Turpin misses the "buzz of the dressing room and being around the lads. I enjoy the reunions, but there are less and less people there every year because somebody has always passed away, so it reminds you you're getting older. I also really miss the punters -- I used to love being in front of the fans and then chatting to them afterwards."

With his in-ring career over, Turpin applied for roles in the police and ambulance services, taking up an offer from the latter where he worked until a back injury forced him into retirement. Ambulance work may have been an ironic career move for a former pugilist and grappler, but it was an earlier side-job that Turpin often likes to recall when recounting his life story. "I've been a boxer, a wrestler, and a gravedigger. So I can honestly say I've knocked people out, I've thrown them around, and I've buried them!"

■ ■ ■ ■ ■ ■ ■ ■ ■ ■ ■ ■ ■ ■ ■ ■ ■ ■ ■ ■ ■ ■ ■ ■ ■ ■ ■ ■ ■ ■ ■ ■ ■ ■ ■ ■ ■ ■ ■ ■ ■ ■ ■ ■ ■ ■ ■ ■ ■ ■ ■ ■ ■ ■

## *Lacing Up The Gloves*

Jackie and Randy Turpin are not alone as boxers who made the switch to British wrestling rings. An early example was Irishman Jack Doyle, known as the "Gorgeous Gael." A talented fighter who received title matches before large crowds, he was at one time the biggest draw in the British fight game, as well as becoming a celebrity who released several records and married a film actress. However, he enjoyed alcohol and cigarettes too much for his own good, with several key defeats blamed on him entering the ring drunk.

Jackie Turpin

After his boxing career ended, he turned to wrestling and became one of the bigger draws in the brief period between the end of the war and the start of televised coverage. He became a regular top attraction at the 10,000 seater Harringay Arena in London where he wrestled a series of challengers billed as from Eastern Europe, most notably a high-profile bout against the alleged Estonian champion Bucth. The bout failed to impress sportswriters and the resulting coverage led to the decline of the venue, though not before Doyle had suffered cracked ribs at the hands of Tony "Two Ton" Galento, an American boxer who struggled to grasp the degree of cooperation preferred in the wrestling game.

Another Harringay star was Primo Carnera, a former boxer who racked up more than 50 wins in five years en route to the world heavyweight title. It was later widely reported that Carnera's career had been controlled by the Mafia, with opponents either pressured into losing or hand-picked for their lack of talent. Despite his success, he ended his boxing career virtually penniless, a situation blamed on corrupt management and loosely portrayed in the film Requiem For A Heavyweight. With little money and finding boxing much harder without the Mafia influence, Carnera had a 16 year wrestling career in Britain and the US. He also appeared as a wrestler in the British film A Kid For Two Farthings.

Stockport's George Nuttall, who racked up a 23-18-2 record as a pro boxer, found a creative way of avoiding any embarrassment in switching to the wrestling business: he became the Black Mask, the first hooded wrestler to appear on television.

Leading star Jackie Pallo came from a boxing family and was the cousin of ITV commentator Reg Gutteridge. Pallo boxed as an amateur and trained local schoolboys, admitting that from a legitimate combat perspective "I was a much better boxer than I was a wrestler."

In 2004, British boxer Danny Williams -- fresh off knocking out Mike Tyson -- took part in a physical angle with Alex Shane at an FWA show. On this occasion the idea wasn't to set up Williams wrestling a match, but rather refereeing the main event of the promotion's Uprising show at the Coventry Skydome. Although the incident attracted national media attention, the refereeing appearance was cancelled when Williams received a world title shot against Vitali Klitschko.

Jackie Turpin

# JIM BREAKS

"The secret of life is that something is only hard work when it's something you don't like," explains Jim Breaks. "For me, sitting down and writing a letter would be hard work, and it would be different for every person. But every job I ever had I've loved, and I always loved wrestling."

It's fortunate that Breaks had that attitude to the grapple game, because his was a lengthy career. Of his 33 years in the business, 28 were spent as a regular on ITV wrestling, a longevity unmatched on the small screen. In fact, aside from the ever-present Mick McManus, no man had more televised bouts than Breaks.

Having taken up amateur wrestling with some success in his early teens and continued the activity during a three-year stint in the army where he served as a physical fitness instructor, Bradford-based Breaks was invited by local promoter and Joint Promotions mastermind Norman Morrell to try out as a professional, an audition he passed.

Noted shooter Bernard Murray trained Breaks for the professional business but, while the amateur sport is usually described as the best grounding for professional wrestling, Breaks isn't so certain, noting that many of the instincts such as avoiding being on your back for even an instant didn't translate well.

"To be honest, I would have been better off not being an amateur. Bernard showed me how to fall and things like that, but in the ring, I was very stiff. I'd wrestle guys and nearly screw their heads off, and they'd tell me: 'Jim, take it easy... we're entertaining.'"

Breaks debuted against Murray in February 1959, a few weeks short of his 19th birthday. Although he didn't have much to worry about from a technical standpoint, he admits that "I was frightened to death before my first match. Not of my opponent, but of the crowd and doing the right thing."

Eventually he made the breakthrough however. "After matches wrestlers would always tell me 'You did this wrong' or 'You did that wrong', but one day they just said, 'Well done'. I knew then that I could do it and after a while I could do it with my eyes shut."

With the wrestling itself under control, Breaks could begin working on his character. "Starting off, being very small and quite good looking, I was naturally a blueeye (babyface.) But I looked at the likes of Mick McManus and Jackie Pallo and realised the baddies get on better, especially when they have a bit of a gimmick, so I tried different things.

"That's how I came up with the 'cry baby' stuff. One day I just jumped up and down in the ring and the crowd went 'Whoa, whoa!' They got so excited, so I started doing it every night and always had a good time!" The routine got over so well that some fans even began bringing dummies to throw into the ring during the tantrums.

According to Breaks, the onus is on wrestlers to develop their personas in this way. "I don't think anyone is underrated. It's up to yourself [to get over] and if you're not getting to the top of the bill, it's your own fault."

Breaks' character was that of a man who could turn vicious in the ring, but would make a major song and dance the moment the tables turned: as he explains it, the crowd hated the hypocrisy that "I could dish it out, but I couldn't take it." That was often the case with his signature submission, the Breaks special, in which he lifted an opponent by one arm and then bent back the wrist, a move that was often reversed to the crowd's delight.

Speaking to the F4WOnline website, William Regal recalled the influence Breaks' antics had on his own career. "I loved Jim Breaks – I talk a lot about wrestling, but I don't think Jim Breaks gets enough credit. I obviously do when I watch him, and I realise how good he was. He might have been the best heat getting wrestler out of all of them. He used to be able to get English people to hate him by doing very, very little. The heat that he had was incredible."

Breaks recalls that at times the crowd anger got out of hand. "The heavyweights didn't have to worry so much about the crowd, but when there'd be trouble, people would be more likely to have a go at me because I was small. I remember one time at Cleethorpes on the pier my son was in the crowd and we wound up having to get escorted off the pier and then have a bunch of police cars make sure nobody went after my car. I knew I'd done a right good job!"

And while wrestlers are often able to read a crowd and ease back if the heat looks like turning dangerous, Breaks admits that he didn't always manage this. "Sometimes my adrenaline would really get up when I got into it with the crowd, so I didn't pull back."

At times though, the heat faded away for other reasons. "At one match an old woman and I got into it: we were giving them a right good show and the crowd was laughing. She tried to hit me with her handbag, so I kicked it away, but I kicked it so hard that it flew open and the stuff inside went flying everywhere. The problem was that for the rest of the match, the crowd wasn't watching me, they were watching this woman walking round ringside going 'Have you seen my lipstick?' and 'Have you seen my cigarettes?'!"

Breaks' rulebending had now moved from the halls to the small screen, with his debut on television coming in May 1960 against Alan Dennison. Viewers soon had even more to get wound up about, with Breaks capturing the British lightweight title in 1963. His longevity, combined with being active in the lighter weight divisions where European and World titles were billed as the almost-exclusive preserve of the technically skilled Brits, meant he was likely the most decorated wrestler of the TV era.

By the time wrestling departed ITV screens in 1988, Breaks had held the British lightweight title 11 times, the European lightweight title 14 times, the World lightweight title twice, and the British welterweight title seven times, an amazing haul of 34 championships. (Perhaps less prestigiously, he also won a TV tournament for a giant chocolate egg in Easter 1981.)

While most of his title reigns involved the pendulum of audience joy as he was unseated, shortly followed by frustration when he regained his crown, two of his title losses in particular wound up spectators. In 1977 he dropped the British welterweight title to Vic Faulkner, only for the title to immediately be held up thanks to interference by Faulkner's brother Bert Royal; Breaks won a televised rematch for the belt. A few years later, Young David (the future Davey Boy Smith) captured the same title, only for the decision to be overturned because Dennison had distracted Breaks.

He didn't always get away with it though. In one memorable televised match, Breaks won the deciding fall against Jim Cortez by holding the trunks, only for ringside commentator Kent Walton to break his usual neutrality by alerting referee Max Ward, who reversed the decision into a disqualification loss. Thankfully for Breaks, he didn't have a championship on the line on this occasion.

Perhaps the ultimate example of Breaks' "poor sportsmanship" came against Kamikazi at a TV match from the Preston Guildhall. With the scores level, the masked man suffered an accidental injury. Breaks was offered the opportunity to accept a no contest verdict -- an offer any decent-minded grappler would be expected to take up -- and instead gleefully rejected the idea and announced himself the winner.

By this stage, Breaks had earned a reputation as a professional. "[Booker] Mick McManus didn't have to tell me much about my match: he trusted me to organize it." It helped that Breaks didn't have any problems with finishes. "Whether I won or lost didn't matter to me because I could always keep myself strong."

He had also become particularly popular with other wrestlers from the Yorkshire area for reasons other than in-ring action. "Though I liked a drink, I wasn't a big drinker, so I'd often drive people to and from shows with me. They could have a few beers and a bit of a sleep and I'd wake them up when I was by their home. It worked for me as they'd give me some money for the driving and if I had a full car, it was a good bit of cash."

Ironically one of Breaks' regular passengers was among the very few wrestlers he didn't get on with. "People [watching on TV] didn't know Les Kellett: he was nasty. He couldn't help himself and it wasn't a case of 'why doesn't he stop being like that?' -- he couldn't change." Although the two never wrestled, Breaks noted that Kellett had a bad reputation: "He took liberties in the ring. He'd give you a right good thump on the nose [without warning] to get some blood and liven up the match. Of course, it was your blood, not his!"

Ironically, it was just such an incident that made for a memorable televised moment in Breaks' 1973 Cup Final day match with long-time rival Johnny Saint that left Breaks with a bloodied nose, footage that even today stands out as looking more vicious than many more elaborate blows and throws. Breaks explains that this was a rare case of things getting out of hand.

"Saint and I always had good matches because we felt the same way about wrestling, and there'd be no nasty stuff. But sometimes you'd lose your temper if you missed a move, or something happened like you [accidentally] put your fingers in the eyes." Breaks notes that if this happened once in a match, it was OK, "but if it happened twice, you were getting a receipt!

"I always put it that wrestling wasn't all straight, but it wasn't all bent either. If something happened the night before, or somebody had done something wrong, you might have some trouble in the match the next night." And while wrestlers were working together, sometimes emotions got heated "and before you know it you're in a struggle.

"We tried to make it look like a genuine fight, although it was show business. For instance, if you did have a nose busted by accident, the other guy would always work on it. If you've got something, you might as well use it, and often the audience would see that and think "well, this [match] must be straight."

Ironically, while the audience may have been uncertain about the competitiveness of pro wrestling (as Breaks puts it, "when people watch cowboy films, they know the people aren't really being killed"), the real con job was the idea of Breaks being a nasty piece of work. Those who met him outside of a wrestling setting recall his friendly, engaging attitude, something FSM can certainly attest to.

This lent itself to a lot of extracurricular activity. "I did a lot of charity football matches. I used to play in a game, jump straight in the car and drive to somewhere like Newcastle and then have to shower all the muck off before I got in the ring."

Breaks also took on many sideline jobs both before turning pro and while wrestling, to top up his income. "I worked as a window cleaner, which I loved. I had a market stall and a pub. I owned a hotel -- it wasn't anything grand, but we took in a lot of homeless people which was guaranteed money [from the local authority]."

And most amazingly of all: "I even worked as a kissogram!"

As well as taking on a few background extra roles in small productions, Breaks had a minor part -- in which he arguably stole the show -- in the show Send in the Girls. As detailed in our previous profiles of Tony Walsh and Kendo Nagasaki, the drama about a group of promotions girls had an episode set at Belle Vue. Breaks' appeared as a particularly cheeky wrestler who took the opportunity to spy on the women as they got changed in an adjoining room, an experience he remembers was not quite so glamorous or alluring as it appeared.

"I was supposed to climb up on a table and look through a hole in the wall and say something like 'Wow, there's some real beauties in here!' I got up and spent ages looking for the hole until the director asked what the problem was. I said I couldn't find the hole and he replied, "there is no bloody hole, just imagine it!"

That's not to say the day wasn't without real drama. "I had to do a bit where Giant Haystacks was rushing to the ring and I'd duck out of his way. He was going so fast I only just managed to do it in time. The speed he was going at, if I hadn't ducked, he probably would have killed me!"

In his final years in the business, Breaks began working for All Star Promotions, an appropriate move given that promoter Brian Dixon's first entry into the business had been as a youngster who started up a fan club for Breaks. Breaks made his final TV appearance in July 1988, defeating the 16-year-old Peter Bainbridge. The story of the veteran Breaks taking on a teenage star was a popular one as he had done a similar routine with Davey Boy Smith, Dynamite Kid and Danny Collins.

After a few years off television, Breaks decided it was time to call it a day. Although he was only 51, younger than many British wrestlers at the end of their career, Breaks' business sidelines had allowed him to put enough by to ease into retirement. "I started to get the odd shout from the crowd about me being past it. There was something in that, and I didn't want to get to the point when they'd start shouting "retire, you old bastard."

Dixon allowed Breaks to pick the venue and opponent, and he opted for Bristol's Colston Hall and, almost inevitably, Johnny Saint. Although it was well publicised that it was Breaks' last bout, he tasted defeat -- at his own request. "We were talking about what we'd do in the match and I just said, 'You're still going to be wrestling, so you should win.'" Following the bout, and despite three decades of antagonising the audience, Breaks received a standing ovation.

He eventually retired to Gran Canaria where he spent his remaining working years selling timeshares. Despite his in-ring image, it was a natural role. "I like to be the life and soul of the party. I did it for 11 years and absolutely loved it. I could do it straight away without practicing and I didn't have to be pushy."

Breaks also took on several gigs as an after dinner speaker for tourists ("it made a change to them listening to yet another person talking about golf"), taking on the role when fellow Canary Islands ex-pat Mark Rocco was unable to make a requested date.

Today Breaks is enjoying his retirement, noting that despite his in-ring image, "I've always been happy doing anything where I can mix with people." Looking back on his career, he recalls that "I always wanted to give 100 percent on every show, and when you'd come out as a wrestler, as long as they would cheer you or boo you, either was good.

"But I always had them wanting to kill me!"

# JOHN COX

For the most part, ambulance staff don't see people getting injured as a lucky occurrence. For John Cox, however, it was two injuries that began and then revived his wrestling career.

"I joined the St Johns Ambulance and I was doing a duty at the wrestling at York and Gwyn Davies were injured. I and a colleague carried him up the stairs to the dressing room and he looked at me and said 'My god you're strong. Have you thought about wrestling?'"

The answer was no (though Cox had trained in judo), but Davies passed on the details of former British heavyweight champion Ernest Baldwin, who now ran a gym in Tingley, near Wakefield. Cox trained three times a week before what would be a short opening run in the business.

"They put me in three bouts: first at Grantham on October 13th, 1962, then about three weeks later at Newcastle, and two weeks after that at De Montford Hall, Leicester. And then I never heard anything from them for about 10 months. People who knew I'd started it were asking 'How's the wrestling doing' and it were a bit embarrassing to say, 'Well I haven't had any offers [of bouts] recently.'

"And then one day I was on duty at the ambulance station and my father came down and said 'They want you to wrestle at Portsmouth tonight. Someone suffered a fractured arm last night and they want you to go down right away.'" Cox managed to find someone to cover his shift and set off on the 270 mile journey, arriving just in time for what would become the first of regular dates.

As a heavyweight, he was soon wrestling some of the biggest names from home and abroad. Most notably he fought a series of bouts with Kendo Nagasaki and some records even show him winning one match at Halifax by knockout, though Cox notes "I certainly don't remember beating Kendo. I'm sure I would [remember that]!"

He also took on Jean Ferre, who would later be known as Andre the Giant. "He was a huge guy and you couldn't really do much with him. You tried to do something with him, almost like being on with Haystacks, you've got to try and do something, knowing full well that you're not going to succeed."

Outside the ring was a different experience altogether. "He was at Whitby one night and was being driven by the late Brian Glover. Brian said to me 'Are you stopping for a drink on the way back?' and I said 'Yeah' and there was a pub, very isolated, and he said we'd stop there. I followed him, and we stopped and then he said, 'Come on, come on, get in quick' as Jean Ferre was getting out of the car and I said, "What's the matter with you?" and he said, "I like to see people's faces when he comes in!' So we stopped and waited and then this huge giant ducked his head under the door and he was right... people were absolutely shocked then they saw him, such a huge guy."

Cox initially wrestled as a part-timer, recalling an incident when a fellow pro gave advice. "This fellow said to the late, great Ian Campbell 'What qualifications do you need to be a professional wrestler?" and Ian said, 'How long can you go without eating?' meaning that it wasn't going to pay you much. However, after an offer from promoter George De Relwyskow of an extended tour of Greece that would have been too long to take a holiday at work, Cox resigned from the ambulance service in 1965.

It kicked off a five-year run of repeated and memorable trips abroad. Having wrestled Japanese star Shozo Kobayashi at the Royal Albert Hall, Cox was among a crew of Brits sent to wrestle in Japan in 1968. "I was with Colin Joynson, the late Billy Joyce who was a wonderful, wonderful wrestler, and Albert Wall from Doncaster. I remember in the dressing room the Japanese guys were looking at Billy Joyce, who by then was in his fifties and wasn't a big man. He could see them sort of nudging each other and grinning a bit."

The local stars clearly either didn't know who Joyce was or didn't recognise the name as he was not only a former British heavyweight champion as a professional, but a legendary figure at the Snake pit in Wigan where he taught the catch style to the likes of Karl Gotch and Billy Robinson. "Billy went on with the Japanese champion [Thunder] Sugiyama, and Sugiyama couldn't do anything with him. He just dragged him round the ring unmercifully."

As happened for many American wrestlers, the Japan trip also marked an opportunity to visit Hawaii, but in Cox's case the diversion came via a personal relationship. "The reason I got into Hawaii was that some years previously there was a guy on television who was just arriving into the UK, Prince Curtis Iaukea. He started in the ring introduced by Ted Beresford, doing this big spiel which the American wrestlers do and of course wasn't common in the UK. Ted was trying to get the microphone off him but Iaukea was swinging him around and his legs weren't touching the floor. I thought 'I can't wait to meet this guy' because he looked so fantastic.

"We actually met at Queens Hall in Leeds and I said to him 'How do you like England?' and he said, 'Oh John,' because it was winter, 'I am so homesick, I've never been so homesick in my life.' I said, 'Well what are you doing on Saturday?' and he said 'Nothing' so I said 'I'll pick you up and bring you back to York and you can stay. I'll take you round the pubs in York' and of course that became a regular occurrence. Then we used to write to each other and when I said, 'I'm going to Japan', he said to send the details and the work permit, and he'd get me into Hawaii. We became firm lifelong friends: he used to come over here every so often, I'd go over there.

"When I got married in 1972 he flew to London and then up to Leeds and I picked him up from Yeadon Airport and then we had the wedding and then a taxi was waiting to take him back because he was going back to Heathrow and flying back to Honolulu because he was on at the Civic Auditorium the following night. That guy did a 24,000 mile round trip to stay with me about five hours."

Cox also made two tours of Zambia, including working under a hood as Black Mask Bula. That said, his most notable appearance in a mask came in Liverpool, for all the wrong reasons. "I turned up there as a substitute and the name of this masked man was on the bill and rather than announce that there was a substitute on the bill, the promoter gave me this mask and said, 'You've got this.' I thought 'I'm sure everybody will recognise my style'. That proved the case with fans openly calling out to ask, 'How are you doing John?', to which he replied positively. "I remember one guy shouted when I was on the ropes at ringside 'Come on Coxy, sort yourself out.'"

The Zambia trip also led to one of the more memorable moments of Cox's travels. "We were coming back on a night flight and the lightning was flashing and thunder cracking, and I don't like flying, I hate it. My wife never knew me get on a plane without a few drinks. There was a guy next to me on the plane who was a German film director -- he'd been making films out in Zambia -- and could see I was perturbed so he said, 'Do not worry my friend, if the lightning hits the plane, we are carrying so much high octane fuel, you will know nothing' so I said 'Well, it's very kind of you to console me!'

"They made an announcement that we were going to do an unscheduled stop at Luanda. I said to this guy 'Where is this place?' and he said 'It is in Angola. They have a civil war there. They are in with everybody: The Baader-Meinhof gang, the Japanese Red Army faction... if any terrorists are going to get on the plane, that is where they are going to get on.'

"Three guys got on and they made us wrestlers look handsome: they had broken noses and cauliflower ears and I thought 'Hijackers.' I was now hallucinating with the amount of drink I had as well. One of them got up to go to the toilet and I followed him, and I hid behind the door because I thought 'If he comes out of the door with a gun, I'll hit him.' So he went back to his seat and then another one came, and he went, and I did the same thing, and then a third one came and went and I did the same thing.

"We landed in Rome and these guys were standing about and I went up to them and said, 'Excuse me, do you speak English?' and they said yes, and I said, 'What have you been doing in Angola?' and they said, 'We are Greek seamen and we have taken a ship out there and left it.' I said, "Oh my God, I thought you were hijackers!' and this fellow said, 'We thought you were queer!'

Back on the safer shores of Britain, Cox had become a TV regular, making his first appearance in July 1964. While he wrestled many big names on the small screen, from Giant Haystacks to Nagasaki to Mike Marino, it was a bout with the little-known Alex Gaul that proved his finest performance. "When the show was live, there was a standby bout always ready to go on, so we didn't get into the ring until seven minutes till five [when the show went off air.] I did a dive across and we went down, and he banged his head and I suddenly realised he wasn't with it and there was about four minutes to go on live television. So I interlocked my fingers with his and kept lifting his arm up and down until it got near the time and I said to the referee Doug De Relwyskow 'You'd better count him out' and he said 'Why?' and I said, 'Because he's unconscious.' He said, 'Is he?' and I said, 'He has been for about three or four minutes!'

Cox returned to the ambulance service and a part-time wrestling schedule in 1970 as he prepared to get married and he decided to cut down his travel schedule, though he'd continue wrestling for more than 15 years. He'd often help out when wrestlers were injured in a bout, though when his own matches led to medical attention, it made for some unusual moments.

"I remember one night I was wrestling a guy at York called Eric Leiderman – which was his wrestling name -- and he broke his arm. He went to hospital and they asked him his name and occupation and instead of saying 'Eric Leiderman' he gave his proper name and said 'I'm a milkman' which was his day job. The following night in the sports pages in the Yorkshire Evening Press it said, 'Hull milkman injured in fight with York wrestler', so it looked like I'd been a right bully picking on this milkman!"

Aside from Belle Vue in Manchester, Cox considered his home venue of York among his favourites, though certainly not for his win-loss record. "You couldn't win in your home town. Somebody would say 'How did Coxy get on?' -- 'Oh, he lost', and they'd say 'Oh, he's a useless bugger' but if you'd won they'd say 'Oh, they let him win because lives here.'

Indeed, some audience reactions were downright baffling. "There was one night I remember I got my eye cut and went to hospital and got four stitches. I came back and met up with some of the lads and was having a drink in the pub and a guy came up to me and said, 'Excuse me' and I said 'Yeah' and he said 'I've been to the wrestling. Can you answer me a question,' so I said, 'I hope so' and then he said, 'I know it's tomato ketchup, but how do you get it to keep on pouring out like that?' I had to remove my plaster and show him the stitches!"

The ambulance service provided many similarly light-hearted moments, but also some days which were deadly serious, none more so than in 1988 when Cox assisted after a terrorist bomb brought down a large passenger aircraft over the Scottish town of Lockerbie, killing all 259 passengers and crew and another 11 people on the ground.

"In 1988 the Scottish ambulance service hadn't implemented a paramedic scheme. Our service was Humberside ambulance service and we used to train with police and fire service and coastguards and RAF helicopters: we had rehearsals in case something happened like a fire on an oil rig out at sea or something like that, so we'd got a great relationship with them.

"The RAF had been told that they wanted as many medical people as possible to go up there, so they rang and said, 'We want to take some paramedics.' Three of us went and we also picked up an RAF medical team. On the helicopter we were given earphones so we could hear what the captain was saying, and I remember he said, 'five minutes to crash site' and then 'four minutes to crash site', then 'three minutes' and as we came over the town of Lockerbie and came down, all you could see was blue lights and sporadic fires. I just thought 'Oh my God.'

"I was put with six ambulance technicians and we went into the Sherwood Crescent area where a huge crater was in the ground. I remember saying to some firemen what a good job it was that they landed on the allotments, and they looked at me and said, 'There were houses here.' I said 'Well, where's the debris?' because you would expect a bath, or a sink or bricks, but there was nothing there, it was just a big hole. And the firemen said, 'It's all gone up into the atmosphere.'

"We spent several hours that night looking everywhere we could in damaged houses and garages and things, but we didn't find anybody. I found an aeroplane window and if we found anything we had to attach a label to it with your name, where you were from and the time you located it and leave it there. Later the Humberside police interviewed us and took us out and that was to find out if anything had been looted, someone coming along and thinking 'I'll have that for a souvenir', because to the police it was a crime scene and it was all evidence.'

As he wound down his in-ring career, Cox found an alternative source of income as an after-dinner speaker, sharing his stories first with local branches of the Round Table and then on the sportsman's dinner circuit sharing the bill with the likes of Jackie Charlton and David Bairstow. He also worked as a councillor and even became mayor of Pocklington, the small town where he now lived.

"I've often thought that I'm so fortunate that the whole of my life, I've never done anything that I didn't like. I loved the wrestling; I loved the ambulance service, both teaching because I was a training manager, and operational; and I enjoyed the council, so those things... when you think about people putting wheelnuts on at a conveyer belt at a car factory, zip zip zip and then the other wheel comes along, I think how fortunate am I that I've had a wonderful career in wrestling that's taken me all over the world and I've thoroughly enjoyed myself."

Today Cox keeps in contact with many of his former colleagues and is a regular at the reunions. "I made a lot of friends in the wrestling. I still get letters from friends abroad. There's nobody you can talk to and have more fun with than the wrestlers. It's just wonderful, it really is, the funny things that you remember.

"I can honestly say I'd have trouble counting on one hand the people in all the years I was in wrestling that I didn't actually like."

# JOHN FREEMANTLE

"I'm not saying that what I do is right and what everybody else does is wrong. What I am saying is that what I do is right for me. I wouldn't want to do it any other way."

So says John Freemantle, Britain's second-longest running wrestling promoter behind only All Star's Brian Dixon, and the last man regularly running shows in the traditional best-of-three-falls, rounds-based format. Both the structure and content of his Premier Promotion shows are a deliberate homage to the wrestling scene that attracted his attention as a youth.

"I first saw it on television on a Saturday afternoon. I remember my dad was in the garden and I saw this on the television and thought 'Good grief.' I called him, and he said he used to watch it in the all-in days after the second world war. Because I showed an interest he took me to my first show in 1960.

"In those days in Brighton the venue was the old Ice Rink, alternatively called the Sports Stadium. Top of the bill was Primo Carnera and Jackie Pallo was on as well. I could tell you what the whole bill was whereas I probably couldn't tell you who was on my show last week!"

Freemantle left school the following year and began a lifetime career in newspaper journalism. He kept his interest in wrestling and turned his writing skills to a freelance position for The Wrestler, a magazine sold both at live events and in newsagents. "It was only done on a contributory basis. Largely speaking I just used to go and talk to a particular wrestler at a show, knock it into shape and send it off to them and they'd probably use it a month or two later. Nobody ordered anything, and you didn't get paid much for it, so it was a hobby."

Among the stories he covered was the charity show at the Royal Albert Hall in 1963 that made headlines with the attendance of Prince Phillip and where both Mick McManus and Jackie Pallo appeared days before their second Cup Final Day bout. Freemantle co-authored a report on the show with another grapple fan and local newspaper journalist, Russell Plummer.

"I often used to go to the Albert Hall, as indeed Russell did. It was a fantastic venue and the atmosphere was electric with the seating all the way round. The sound was amazing. Even with a good wrestling contest [without the crowd heat], at the end of the round when the bell rang, and people applauded, the sound just went round and round and round."

Once that writing came to an end, it would be another two decades before Freemantle returned to being involved in the business beyond being a fan. Now the sports editor of the Brighton Evening Argus, he promoted a show in 1987. "They used to run, every Christmas, a charity appeal for underprivileged children and the elderly that needed a little bit of help. I just happened to say to them one year 'Have you ever thought of doing a wrestling show as part of the charity appeal?' and they said 'Oh, that's a good idea, you can organise it.'"

He brought in something of a package show headlined by Big Daddy and the event proved a great success, due in part to the newspaper's estimated readership of 250,000. "In those days, not like now, everybody read the local newspaper. With all the publicity, the show was extremely popular. For that first show at Hove Town Hall, the attendance was in four figures.

"I ran two or three more for shows the Argus into 1988 and all the money went to the fund. After that we continued to run the Xmas ones for quite a number of years, but they didn't want to run shows in between. I enjoyed that side of it, the organization and running shows. Because I'd got quite involved in it and interested, I decided I'd run shows without them. I didn't set out initially to be a wrestling promoter, it just sort of snowballed and it's carried on ever since."

Freemantle says that two men in particular were key to his early success: semi-independent promoter and former wrestler Ken Joyce, and Max Crabtree, who was by now the main man at Joint Promotions. "Ken was a huge help and mentored me for the first two or three years. He was instrumental in establishing me as a promoter and how to deal with situations that arose. I worked a lot with Max in terms of most of the shows involving Big Daddy. After Big Daddy, Max did a couple of tours with Davey Boy Smith and I was involved with him in those as well and my first show at Worthing in 1994 was a British Bulldog show."

While Freemantle's preference for traditional technical wrestling wouldn't seem an obvious fit for Big Daddy, he has only positive things to say about the times he used him as an attraction. "Whether you liked his style or not, you just had to put your hand up and say people wanted to come and see him, especially youngsters.

"They never ever let me down. If you booked him, he was always there, and Max was always there with him. I enjoyed working with him: he was good to work with. Seriously good to work with. It's not the classical, technical kind of wrestling which I'm known for and which I actually like, but the guy got people into arenas and what you did the audience after that was up to you."

What Freemantle did – and continues to do – with that audience is present a style of show unlike that offered by most promoters today. Usually involving four or five matches, it strictly follows the rules and format most commonly associated with the 1960s boom of TV wrestling. That doesn't just mean matches contested over five-minute rounds with two out of three falls deciding the winner, but also a 10 count whenever a wrestler is knocked down and a ban on wrestlers attacking a grounded opponent unless it is part of a continuous sequences of holds.

"The overriding factor is that my shows are completely different to any other shows that [people] do. I am the only promoter that has stuck religiously to the style that I have. I've always said that if I couldn't survive or draw an audience without doing what I want to do, I'd stop. I don't want to do bizarre stuff, I don't want to do cage matches, I don't want people hitting each other over the head with dustbin lids. If that was the only way I could get people to come to wrestling, I'd pack up."

As well as the unique format, Freemantle prefers using wrestlers willing to practice a more technical style, whether that be World of Sport veterans or up-and-comers. "I like to think that all the wrestlers that appear on my shows are professional and can wrestle, they can actually wrestle in the ring. They can properly wrestle rather than just jump off the corner post or swing off the chandeliers. There's a lot of guys these days that copy the Americans, but the type of action that they do is not sustainable over 6 or 8 five minute rounds. You have to have the basics. I like to think that all the wrestlers that I use can wrestle first and foremost. Then if they can do the spectacular stuff, that's brilliant, but the spectacular stuff is no good without a basic ability to wrestle."

That said, he believes the style is not the barrier to performers that it might appear. "If you use good professional wrestlers, they can adapt their styles. There isn't any problem. Nobody comes on to my shows and says afterwards 'Oh, I couldn't do that.' Good wrestlers can adapt to any style. Over the years I've probably had over a thousand different wrestlers wrestle for me, some of them many times, others perhaps once, but I'm sure that they enjoy wrestling my type of show. It doesn't mean they don't enjoy other types of shows. It's totally different."

That roster has included several US visitors including Colt Cabana, who tells FSM that "I really loved wrestling for Premier Promotions. I think I liked it so much because I got to work for John and Premier just as I was starting to really understand and appreciate the World of Sport wrestling. Here I am, right from watching hours and hours of 70s and 80s British wrestling, going directly into this time warp in 2004 where I'm on shows with Mal Sanders, Steve Grey, Brian Maxine, Dave Taylor and even wrestling Johnny Kidd. I loved doing the rounds for that reason. The reason I came to the UK that time from America wasn't to wrestle the American style. It was to learn about a different wrestling culture.

John Freemantle

"John was running the promotion that he wanted to see. As the wrestling tides were changing to a more American style of show, you could see in his determination that he liked the ways of old, it was his show, and that's the way he was going to do it. I always admired him for that."

Working the rounds format would often mean wrestling 25 to 30 minute matches, something that's proven a valuable experience for many younger British wrestlers. One notable example is Paul Birchall who made his name on the British scene working for the FWA where he was mainly used for storyline reasons in short squashes, but was able to gain experience of longer matches in the lower-profile Premier setting.

Danny Garnell, a British wrestler who has worked regularly for Premier, says the experience stands out. "It's such a step back into the past that you can actually tell a story with the wrestling match instead of being a spotfest. You can literally tell a story around a hold or a lock or a submission. It's refreshing, especially when you are working at other places where you can't always do that. It's a nice contrast."

He also explains that the rounds format has some benefits as a performer. "If you were working five or six rounds you could tell five or six miniature stories that culminate in a whole match. From a worker's point of view, it's a nice way to be able to structure a match. Some of the old school guys that John would use wouldn't want to plan to the finest detail, so you could literally have "Round one, we'll work an arm; round two, we'll work a leg" and then work on the fly.

"You definitely needed the break at times to be able to tell a convincing story. The older guys know so many finishes and false finishes and their timing is just to perfection -- they could plan it so well that if they wanted the round to end while you were just about to tap out or something, it would always happen that way. It's such a refreshing way to be able to work with people.

However, it wasn't without its hiccups. "At Worthing, there was a huge clock in the hall and if we were doing a five minute round, sometimes you'd look at the clock and it was more like a seven or eight minute round. You'd have to say to John 'the bell, the bell!' because he was so caught up in it. Sometimes you'd be drifting into stuff for the next round. He'd definitely give you a bit of leeway on time, but I don't know if it was always intentional. Sometimes I got the impression that he was watching as a fan again!"

While throwing a "British style" rounds match on a US show has often caused confusion, Garnell believes Premier Promotions audiences were able to grasp the concept. "You would get some confusion with younger fans: normally after the first fall you'd get the pop as if it was the finish and then you'd see the mums or dads tell them 'No, no, it's going to carry on.' Because every match was a rounds match, by the second match they were well with it and knew what to expect."

John Freemantle

Dean Ayass, who appeared as Garnell's manager, echoes his enjoyment of the rounds. "In between rounds, I'll be playing the part of giving advice, but quite often we'll be talking about what to do in the next round. The benefit of the rounds system is that you can divide up the match in neat compartments in your mind. Or loosen the corner pad ready to pull it down when the next round starts..."

Indeed, while technical wrestling is very much the centrepiece of a John Freemantle show, there's still a strong hero vs villain element in many bouts, particularly in Worthing where the promotion appeared most regularly and where the local population is heavily skewed to an older demographic. Ayass recalls that "When I worked with Martin Stone, we got tons of heat, especially in Worthing. I'd frequently get people trying to stop me from interfering, and one time we needed four members of staff from the hall to form a human barrier to get us back to the dressing room while the fans threw rubbish at us.

"John also once had to wait about five minutes before he could do the introductions because the crowd were just shouting abuse at us and he couldn't get a word in above all the noise! But the worst one was during a match between Martin and Ricky Knight, which was heatsville as you can imagine. I was choking Ricky on the ropes and I saw someone approaching out of the corner of my eye. I held my arm out to fend him off but the next thing I knew, he'd punched me in the face!"

Garnell has similar memories of an audience that at the very least was accomplished in suspending its disbelief. "I was run over by a fellow in a mobility scooter once! Another time a guy who must have been well into his 70s took his jacket off and wanted to fight me after the show. It's still real in Worthing! It's nice to be able to work in front of a crowd that still looked at it that way.

"When Dean was managing me, a guy was really furious after the show once and he was saying to me 'What percentage of your wage are you giving him because he's not a good man!' I just carried it on and said 'Oh, forty percent' and he said "Forty percent! You're being robbed. You're good enough to not need a manager!" It's nice to maintain your character so that people still believe it and they will come back hopefully. You knew that if you looked out from the ring that the same faces would be sitting there every single time because they never missed the show if they could help it."

Sadly a 23-year run in Worthing came to an end earlier this year with a change in the venue's management. "[The new owners] have a complete different view of events like wrestling," Freemantle explains. "It appears to be financial. I've had an agreement for 23 years with Worthing Theatres, which has worked perfectly well for me and has worked well for Worthing Theatres under previous

John Freemantle

management. They've now changed all the rules and the financial deal which, in my view, makes it uneconomic to run wrestling.

"I'm not packing up. I've not agreed anything at the moment but I'm looking at other possibilities. I did seriously consider whether it was a good time to retire but I've decided after quite a lot of thought that I do want to carry on doing some shows. That's the plan at the moment.

"I just think what I do, which is as near as I can get to the old style of British wrestling, it gives a different perspective to what wrestling is in general nowadays. That's one of the reasons I want to carry on doing what I'm doing. If I don't do what I'm doing, I don't think anybody else will because everybody wants to copy the American style.

"What I try and do, once you've got the audience there, is 'educate' them to my sort of wrestling. They might come to see a bloodthirsty hell of a bash type of match, and that might be top of the bill and draw them in in the first place. But once you've got them there, I like to put on a pure wrestling match, which always goes down very well and always gets applause. It's my way of saying to people 'This is what wrestling is all about, it's what I was brought up to watch, and I hope you like it.'"

John Freemantle

# JOHN KENNY

"I was always in the gym, always working out. I did all the sports at school. I didn't really want to do anything else other than sport." That was the childhood mentality of John Kenny and, thanks to pro wrestling, he would achieve his goal. Like many of his era, though, it wasn't an easy path.

"I used to go to a gym in Widnes and the lad ran the gym was a part-time wrestler called Harry Palin. I got friendly with him and was working out with him and he was telling me things. He took me in the back room one day and showed me a few things. He beat me up actually! He showed me how hard the job was and give me a good hiding.

"I went back, and he gave me another good hiding, and I went back and gave me another good hiding just to see if I was interested. He just kept beating me up until one day I managed to do something to him that he was surprised about and then he sort of showed me a few things in the wrestling business and explained to me a few other things."

At this stage, Kenny still wasn't thinking of a wrestling career, but a chance meeting changed that. "Me and Harry Palin helped put up the ring for the show at the Queen's Hall [in Widnes] and while we were in the ring putting it up, Harry was doing some throws on me and I was cartwheeling. I was a good gymnast in my day, rolling and doing backflips and stuff. [Promoter] Brian Dixon had seen this from the back of the hall unbeknownst to me."

Dixon approached Kenny after spotting him in the venue's toilets later that night and – after a momentary misunderstanding as to the nature of the approach – suggested the youngster might have a future in the business. "I worked hard then in the gym and at a little wrestling place in Widnes and worked my socks off until I became average at the job, just a young lad who could do a little bit and it went from there. Within six months I was a full-time pro because I worked every day I wanted to."

It wasn't the easiest of starts however, with his debut against Buddy Ward at the Queen's Hall being memorable for the wrong reason. "I was something like eleven and a half stone wet through: I worked hard, but never seemed to put enough bulk on. He was this seventeen and a half stone villain with a bald head, cauliflower ear, and a busted nose. My parents and family came to the show because it was my first one and my mum fainted when she saw Buddy Ward: she actually lost it and slid down the seat and was really, really frightened."

While Kenny progressed, he says it took time to gain his confidence. "It's always nerve-racking before you walk into the ring where the public are: no matter how old you are or how long you've been in the job, people will tell you, if you've not got nerves when you do something like that, there's something wrong with you. It took four or five years before I really felt I was as good as a lot of the other people around and I was comfortable with myself."

Even when that day came, it was still a surprise. "You'd go somewhere and be top of the bill with big names, big stars from television. That's where the nerves really started kicking in: you'd think 'Blinking heck, I'm in with somebody here who's a star.' You didn't realise that you were a star also and that's why they put you in with this people. You'd made a name for yourself to warrant being able to wrestle against bigger people in the job."

Just such a match came in 1973 when Kenny made his TV debut against Rollerball Rocco who he describes as "a man who was miles ahead of his time in the wrestling business. I've got to say that was the most butterflies I've ever had in my life. Even though I'd been in the job quite some time, to go in to the arena where you knew it was going to be on television in a couple of weeks and everyone in the [country] that liked wrestling was going to see you [was intimidating.] But it was fantastic, a great feeling to know that you're good enough to be asked to go on TV with a man of that stature."

What may well have been Kenny's most memorable match came a couple of years later and was, to say the least, much lower profile. "Me and Monty Swann, my old tag partner, were in London doing a show. A guy approached us and said would we come to a hotel in London he worked in and do a show, just one match. He said, 'I'm a wrestler from Greece, I'm a waiter there and I'd like to show everybody how good I am.'"

With a fee agreed, the pair went to the hotel for the unorthodox show. "I was going to referee, and Monty was going to wrestle the lad. We came out and they just had a load of judo mats they'd put on the floor in this hall. All his mates and the staff were round the mats. We went in and had a makeshift bell, just a tray and a spoon, and one of them banged it. I said 'Wrestle on' to start the match.

"Monty stepped out and this lad ran and hid behind me. He didn't want to wrestle; he just wanted to show off. Monty was trying to get to him and about five times I tried to get away from him and he kept hold of me. I think he'd seen wrestling and maybe been involved in one thing in his life and thought he could do this, but his bottle went. In the end, I had to throw Monty onto the floor and throw this lad on top to pin him just so we could get out of the place, otherwise we'd still be there wrestling now!"

Like many wrestlers on Brian Dixon's books, Kenny also took dates in Wales and Ireland for Orig Williams, who repackaged him around a decade into his career. "I was driving to Rhyl to do a show and saw a poster on a board. I took a second glance and then backed up in my car to look at it and it said had Dave 'Fit' Finlay vs 'Gypsy' John Kenny top of the bill. So, when I walked into Orig's office I asked, 'Who's this Gypsy John Kenny?' and he said, 'You are son, from now on.'

"I don't know why the hell he picked it! I had long hair and tassels and he just said he wanted a gypsy on the bill, I fitted the image he had in his mind, and get on with it! That name stuck from that day to this. In fact, in my hall I have the poster from that show in a frame. That's just a treasured memory."

Rhyl was not only a regular stop on the circuit, but home to some passionate fans. "I was wrestling Kung Fu and I had a habit of putting a headlock on the floor and [illegally] leaning up on the ropes. A lady this day took umbrage as usual: they'd hit you over the head and things. I just felt a sharp pain and I got up quick and said to the referee 'What's happened?'' and they said, 'You're bleeding.'

"She'd just stuck an umbrella, the point of an umbrella in my back, just getting excited. We got through the match and I went in and the worst thing for me was I had a lovely pair of white trunks on and they were covered in blood and ruined. That was more worrying to me than the pain!

"I was married in them days and I was walking down the beachfront at Rhyl the next week with my wife when the lady that stabbed me in the back came running up, threw her arms around me, told me how much she loved me and that I shouldn't get her so excited at the shows!"

Another memorable moment came when Kenny was working shows at US army bases in Northern Ireland alongside Giant Haystacks. Normally Haystacks would sit in the front of a car where there might be a little more room for his mammoth frame, but on this occasion the delicate security situation meant the vehicle was being driven by an army officer and Haystacks was in the back with Kenny.

"We were trying to find the way with this army officer who was driving us: the roads were blocked off and there were army men following the car and all this. I just leaned up against Haystacks, snuggled up in his arms and he said, 'What are you doing?' I said, 'Can you imagine if a bullet comes up against this car, who it will hit?' He just tapped me on the side of my head and I flew across the car and banged my head against the window on the other side!"

Kenny also wrestled in Europe where he completed something of a clean sweep of TV appearances. As well as making a return to ITV in 1987 after Dixon gained a share of the TV contract, he worked on early cable and satellite channel

Screensport and was a regular on S4C, the Welsh station for which Orig Williams provided the 'Reslo' show. In the early 90s he appeared on shows run by French wrestler Flesh Gordon that aired on the continent-wide Eurosport network. "It was through Orig Williams and me and Scrubber Daly drove over to France, I was on with Flesh Gordon one night and the following night we were on in a different part of France and I was on with a Belgian. They were great memories, fabulous memories. The crowds were fantastic because they were televised. I don't know what it was like for just a normal show there, but the two shows we were there the houses were massive, they were packed."

Among Kenny's opponents on Screensport was Rob Brookside, who viewed Kenny as a mentor and today warmly refers to as his "wrestling dad." Kenny says he clearly had a bright future. "Young Brookside, he had everything, he had the determination, the passion, he just wanted it so much and he was given the opportunity. When he worked with different people, the lad shone. He was always going to be a star in the business. I hope somehow in his mind that I was a big help to him: he does actually call me Dad sometimes and it's a lovely thing."

That's not to say Brookside escaped Kenny's sense of humour. "I used to pull a lot of pranks on him when he was very young, things that probably you can't print a lot of them! He was sat in the car one day and when Rob sat in the car he always had his trainers off: he didn't like travelling in them. I was sat next to him and he fell asleep. We had a rule that we didn't allow people to fall asleep in the car.

"So, I picked his trainer up and tied it to my finger and held my hand out the window with the trainer tied to it. I woke him up as I had it dangled out and he realised the shoe was missing and went 'Jesus, they were my good trainers you daft so-and-so.' And the he went 'Don't suppose this is any good' and threw the other one out the other window! At that point, I just casually pulled my finger up and his trainer appeared!"

With a new generation taking over, Kenny turned to thoughts of retirement, but it proved easier said than done. "When I got to the age of 50, I thought it was getting a bit harder, I thought that the body was taking an extra day to heal after a bad bump. Then I was 52 when I saw a lot of fit young lads coming into the business: they were harder to wrestle, a bit faster and I'd slowed down a bit. I got it in my head that it was my time and I went to Brian Dixon and said 'Look, I think it's time to call it a day, I'm struggling with this.' I'd hurt my shoulder and it was taking a little bit too long to heal and I was having a rough time. I said, 'I'll finish this week off.'

"But believe me, it was so bad not wrestling. After six weeks, I phoned Brian Dixon and asked if I could have some work! He gave me some more and I went back and did another stint. A year later I thought I'd had enough and packed in again. I gave up, and after three weeks I phoned again! He gave me some of the nicest jobs in the world: Plymouth, Croydon, six of the top venues he had. I did three of them and on the third one I went in the room he was in and said 'Brian, I'm not doing any more.' It was just one of them nights and I decided that was it for me. I never went back."

Kenny kept his hand in the business as a referee, but admits it doesn't give quite the same buzz. "I did some in the early days and I learned to be a referee quite easily because you knew the job. A couple of years ago I spoke to Brian and said I'd love to do a bit of refereeing. I did a couple of seasons at Butlins and I'm always available if anyone wants a referee!

"But no matter what people tell you, it's not half as good as being a wrestler. When you're a wrestler you're all hyped up for going out and doing your thing and showing how good you are, and you come out and feel a million dollars and got loads of applause or boos. Once you're a wrestler, you feel like a star and when you're a referee, you're just a third man in the ring in a striped shirt."

Instead Kenny now gets his wrestling kicks as a trainer at the Infinite Promotions school in St Helens run by Ciarán McConnell. "I get in the ring twice a week every week and help teach and I'm loving teaching, loving giving something back. I teach the old-fashioned wrestling, the World of Sport type wrestling. I give them the idea of when you start this is how you stand, this is where you won't make a fool of yourself, knowing about wrestling, putting on holds and moves and submissions and counters to get out of holds We also have two trainers that work with us who are still wrestling on the circuit today and they bring the up to date type of wrestling.

While first appearances matter, Kenny says it's not always obvious which trainees will make it. "There's some that come along and catch your eye right away and you think 'Ooh there's a bit of potential in this kid.' Others come along, and they can come for the next 10 years and you think they won't ever make wrestlers, but you never know. In wrestling, sometimes you'll find lads are hopeless -- no matter what you tell them to do, no matter what you give them, no matter what you show them -- and all of a sudden one night they'll do it right. And they say to you then "Well that was bloody easy, why couldn't I do it before?!" And they are the lads that seem to get the idea and maybe will go forward to be the wrestlers we see in the future. And girls: we have a young lady that's absolutely marvellous in the ring, absolutely fantastic, Lizzy Styles, who's making a real good name for herself."

While it's no substitute for past glories, Kenny says training at least gives him some of the thrills he had as a wrestler. "You get in that ring and it's a different world. You're a star for the half an hour that you're in the ring. That adulation and the adrenaline you get is incredible. When you're walking out the ring and you've done things right and you're getting a load of applause, there's no better feeling. I miss it every single day of my life and I'm really grateful to young Ciarán that he's opened this school. It's gave me another lease of life to get back in the wrestling business.

"It's so deep to have in your heart when you've been a wrestler."

# JOHN NAYLOR

"If you're a shooter, you can get on, can't you? They treat you right if you're a shoot wrestler."

So found John Naylor, a grappler who bridged the great divide of British wrestling, displaying a fast-paced acrobatic style while earning respect for his legitimate background. It would earn him dozens of bouts on ITV, but it was an appearance on another channel that proved his most infamous bout.

Living in Wigan, Naylor embarked on one of the tougher routes into the business via a local gym. Though formally known as Riley's Gym and under the management of shoot wrestling legend Billy Riley, it didn't take long for Naylor to discover its nickname as he quite literally got to grips with the combination of legitimately battling for both pinfalls and submissions.

"It was catch-as-catch-can wrestling there. You used to get ripped and things like that. They'd get hold of your hands and put them up your back or wrap your own legs around you. That was why it was called the Snake Pit." In the early years, it was more a case of surviving than competing. "It took a while [to hold my own]. Billy Riley wouldn't tell you anything until he thought you was ready."

Despite the pain, Naylor considered it a worthwhile experience. "It was hard going there and wrestling, but once you knew it, you could go in the professional job and everybody treated you right."

The entry into the pro game came via Riley, who had a working relationship with independent promoter Jack Atherton. That in turn led to Naylor getting on the books with Joint Promotions, which meant a full date sheet. "You could be working seven days a week all over the country. You could be anywhere and see anything. Come back the day after and go somewhere else. You'd come from working for Max Crabtree in Scotland for three or four days, then be down in London maybe a couple of weeks. It was a good job at that time."

The switch to the pro style and working before the crowd didn't prove too much of a challenge. "It weren't hard really: you just, like, wrestled! There's showmanship in it, you had to be a bit of a showman, but it didn't worry me."

Naylor acquired a nickname, the Golden Ace, selected by Max Crabtree. It's unclear if it was coincidence or plagiarism on Crabtree's part, but the name had been used by wrestler Laurie Chapelle in the 1940s, leading to an unlikely confrontation. "This old fellow came in to the dressing room at Harrogate and said he was the Golden Ace so don't use the name like. He was an old man then, but Max just [verbally] lacerated him. [Chapelle] even sent me a letter through the post telling me not to use his name, but Max wasn't bothered though."

As part of his pro work, Naylor soon became known for some speciality moves that most certainly were not on the Riley's Gym curriculum, most notably a finisher that involved escaping a hold by climbing the ropes and flipping backwards to put the opponent down and in a pinning position. It was similar to what modern fans would recognise as the Bret Hart-Roddy Piper finish from WrestleMania 8, but with some added athleticism as the climb was up the middle of the ropes rather than up the turnbuckles.

"That move came from Ted Betley in Warrington," Naylor recalls. "He trained Steve Wright and I used to go to his gym on Sunday mornings and wrestle Steve. I could keep up with him, like." Betley also trained Tom 'Dynamite Kid' Billington, who became friends with Naylor and, in his autobiography Pure Dynamite, recalled an amusing incident the pair shared.

Naylor ran a smallholding farm including several goats, which attracted the attention of wrestler Honey Boy Zimba, who originated in Sierra Leone and for whom a freshly-slaughtered goat was the ideal centrepiece for Christmas dinner. Naylor agreed to sell him a goat but, shortly before Zimba's arrival for the scheduled collection, he and Billington discovered the animal had not only died but was in the rigor mortis stage. Thinking quickly as Zimba came into view, Naylor began hammering the corpse in the head before Billington surreptitiously kicked it over to give the appearance of its demise.

As well as working the halls, Naylor became a TV regular after debuting as a teenager in 1972 with a drawn bout against Marty Jones. Among his early high-profile appearances was a match with France's Jacky 'Frank' Rickard on a special show pitting British grapplers against continental counterparts. Billed as 'Fanfare for Europe', the show commemorated the UK's entry earlier that week into the European Economic Community, the forerunner to the European Union.

He also appeared on the 1975 FA Cup Final broadcast in which he followed up earlier victories against Colin Bennett and Steve Grey to beat Leon Fortuna and win the "World of Sport trophy" tournament. Indeed, while Naylor never held a British title (coming after the era where the championship picture was dominated by Riley's students), he was always good value in tournaments, reaching the semi-finals of eliminator events to fill vacancies for the lightweight and welterweight crowns.

For all the World of Sport exposure, Naylor's most memorable appearance was a Royal Albert Hall bout broadcast on BBC 1. It was against a man named Keith

Rawlinson who was making his professional debut. Rawlinson was no grappler, but rather a teacher and church organist.

His unusual debut in such a high profile slot, alongside the likes of Big Daddy, Johnny Saint and Mark Rocco came because he was the participant in an episode of 'The Big Time', a documentary series produced by Esther Rantzen. Each week a member of the public would attempt to work at professional level in a job after a brief training period. Other episodes included a then unknown Sheena Easton trying her hand as a professional singer and a would-be professional chef who failed to impress celebrity cook Fanny Craddock, whose criticism was so excessive it harmed her own public image.

While he'd never competed, Rawlinson did teach his schoolchildren amateur wrestling, something that proved of little help when Max Crabtree took him to a gym for an initial try-out. As with the majority of the show, it appeared very much as if Rawlinson was given little to no inside information about the workings of the wrestling business. Invited to attempt to take down Sid Cooper, who did not cooperate with the moves, Rawlinson blew up in a matter of moments. He was then asked to attempt a series of dropkicks that had a similar lack of effect, other than to cause an exhausted Rawlinson to vomit outside the ring.

Rawlinson was then shown meeting reigning world champion Johnny Saint who made a dire, though accurate, prediction of what his training period would entail. "They'll break his heart. They'll plow him in the deck... they'll scurf him. He'll be underneath and die a thousand deaths in a couple of minutes."

The amateur was then sent for training with Peter 'Tally Ho' Kaye and, judging by what was shown on screen at least, was taught some of the basics of surviving in a pro ring but under the guise that he was learning to compete. For example, Rawlinson learned that when thrown into the corner he should run towards it, turn and hit the padding with his back. The explanation he was given – and happily accepted – was that to do anything else would risk sliding either side of the cornerpost and injuring himself on the outside.

Similarly, he was shown learning that when slammed he should take a flat back bump to spread the impact. Judging from his hand placement, he was neither shown any way to resist the move, nor to make the slam easier for his opponent, leading to slams that were lacking in visual smoothness.

In what was billed as his first competitive gym contest with Kaye, Rawlinson refused to submit to a single leg Boston Crab (which Crabtree noted would be unusual for a pro) but was forced into a hammerlock that finished him off.

The cameras showed Crabtree selecting Rawlinson's opponent for his Royal Albert Hall match, supposedly rejecting Alan Dennison and Sid Cooper as too powerful, instead selecting Naylor as that might be a fair match in which Rawlinson "won't feel over-awed." Crabtree later claimed that the scene was constructed and in reality Rantzen had been fooled into selecting Naylor herself after looking at photographs of him along with wrestlers who looked more imposing but lacked his shooter pedigree.

Crabtree was also seen creating a ring name for Rawlinson, reasoning that "Keith" wasn't an imposing moniker for a wrestler. In something of an inside joke referring to jargon for a wrestler with the ability and desire to legitimately hurt an opponent, he noted "We can't call him Ripper Rawlinson, because he certainly isn't a ripper." Instead he settled on Rip Rawlinson, noting ominously it was spelt "R, I, P."

Come the big night, Crabtree had an off-camera request of Naylor that went unheeded. "They wanted me to make him look good, but I didn't want to. It's wrong isn't it?" Instead it was a completely one-sided affair. "That was catch as catch can. It was straightforward, that. There was no conning people there."

Whatever Rawlinson's beliefs about pro wrestling were after his training, Naylor took complete control of the bout. He may not have aimed to finish it as quickly as possible, but he most certainly was not giving Rawlinson any opportunity to shine. In the first of a scheduled six 3-minute rounds, he put on a leglock similar to a single leg Boston crab. With Rawlinson hanging on, Naylor kept applying pressure for a good thirty seconds till the end of the round.

The second round began with the crowd booing, presumably disappointed by the lack of theatrics, and Rawlinson was already limping. In training he had been shown how to apply a full nelson but struggled to get in position to put it on while grappling, something he assumed was simply his lack of experience in timing. Here he went for the hold against Naylor and was simply brushed aside before being put back in the leg hold for an instant submission.

Despite cornerman Kaye's somewhat obvious advice of "Don't let him get hold of your leg!", the limb came under further attack in the third round, with Naylor cranking hard on a stepover toehold facelock (STF): while it later became known as a working hold for Masa Chono, it had been a favourite of Lou Thesz in legitimate gym contests. Rawlinson was saved only by referee Joe D'Orazio pulling his hand to the ropes and calling for a break. Naylor continued to go after the leg for the rest of the round, with Rawlinson's attempts to kick him away being more spirited than effective. The prospect of returning for round four was too much and Rawlinson quit on his stool.

With the image of wrestling very much protected, Naylor got a mixed response backstage. "The wrestlers were fine, it was just the promoter. If you fell out the promoter, you don't get no work, do you. I probably got less work [from Max] but I thought I were doing right.

Nevertheless, Naylor continued wrestling for several years, making his final TV appearance against Peter 'Tally Ho' Kaye in 1985. He hung up his boots reasoning that "Well, you know, you get sick of it. You get older.

"I got out at the right time. Les Kellett, McManus and all that lot carried on for longer... Jackie Pallo, they went on too long. But to their credit, they still got houses full."

Some years after leaving the business, Naylor had an unexpected reunion with a former colleague, Tommy Billington. The pair had not seen one another for around 20 years and Billington had left the public eye following his globetrotting ended with physical decline.

"I found out where he was living. I didn't know he'd come back here. He come from Golborne near Wigan, which was where when we were kids we'd be playing football. I found out he was in Wigan, so I went and saw his mother, she told me where he lived, and I went to see him."

Today Naylor continues to enjoy life outside the limelight and still looks after the animals on his farm. He looks back with pride on his days as a Wigan shooter and believes that his colleagues from Riley's gym would have thrived in today's mixed martial arts. "If you understand catch-as-catch-can, it's a better wrestling. I don't think anybody could beat somebody if they knew catch-as-catch-can."

John Naylor

# JOHNNY KIDD

"Never forget that you were in [wrestling] when it was good," were the words of advice from wrestler Mel Stuart for Johnny Kidd whenever there was any danger about him feeling down about the state of the business. But while today's crowds may be smaller, Kidd's career is hardly in decline: despite recently turning 58, he becomes the first still active performer to appear in FSM's Greetings, Grapple Fans series.

Ironically for a man portrayed as one of the cleanest technicians in the business, John Lowing spend his childhood watching World of Sport and admiring an unlikely figure: "Mick McManus was my idol. To me, he was wrestling."

It inspired him to start exploring his own career path into the grapple game in 1974. "I kept wondering just where the hell you go to get into the business. It was very much a closed shop then and you couldn't just walk in: it was very much not what you knew but who you knew."

Lowing tried visiting shows in the venues near his Luton home and was advised by MC Freddie Downs to send promo photos to Dale Martin, the promotional company that controlled the area, something he did but received no reply. Instead he tried turning to a different style of grappling and wrote to the British Amateur Wrestling Association, which informed him of a local amateur club in Ampthill. Here Kidd learned the amateur style, training regularly for around four years. As well as learning the type of grappling seen in the Olympics, he also got an unusual introduction into working before a crowd.

"We built our own ring and even ran our own shows in places like hospitals and working men's clubs and at fetes. It was amateur wrestling, not so much the style but in that we didn't get paid!"

That changed in the unlikely location of supermarket Sainsbury's, where Lowing was now working. "There was a phone directory at work and one day I saw it and decided to see if I could find any wrestlers who might help [me turn pro]: this was at a time when most people weren't ex-directory."

Among those listed was Ken Joyce, the wrestler behind Deveraux Promotions. While Joyce was not a formal Joint Promotions member, he was on good terms with the group as Lowing explains. "Once Joint had sorted out all the shows for the month, they'd send Ken a copy of the booking sheets and say, 'These guys are booked on these dates, but you can pick up the rest."

After an introductory chat with Joyce, Lowing heard nothing back for around six months before getting a call in October 1978 to say that if he could make it to South Wimbledon tube station the next day, he would be booked on a show. Lowing made the trip and found himself sharing a car with Joyce, Pete Roberts and Lee Bronson to Salisbury where he wrestled Tony Scarlo.

Although it was only a one-fall affair, lasting just three rounds, Lowing was grateful for the support. "Tony was a very good wrestler and helped me tremendously in the match." It proved a successful audition as Joyce informed Lowing that he could take on dates on the weekly circuits run by Max Crabtree, now the boss of Joint Promotions. He was soon working with the likes of Sid Cooper and the intimidatingly-named 'Ripper' Derek Collins. It was at one early bout, at Hanley's Victoria Hall, that Lowing discovered his own new moniker.

"I was looking at all the big names on the poster and wondered where I was. Then I saw 'Blackjack Mulligan vs promising newcomer Johnny Kidd' and wondered if that was me!"

That was indeed his new ring name, as laid down by Crabtree. Kidd says he remains unclear whether Crabtree simply picked it for its neat ring, was inspired by the frontman of the 1950s and 60s band The Pirates, or was trying to hint at a link to lightweight legend George Kidd.

As his career developed, Kidd recalls that "I never felt uncomfortable in the ring, but it was a case of gradual progress. There weren't any formal training schools, so I picked up things as we progressed through matches. But I loved the technical side and most of that came from Ken Joyce: he taught me so many tricks."

Kidd's rookie years came at a time when catchweight contests -- those featuring opponents from two different weight divisions -- were becoming more popular. He notes that this proved a great benefit to his development as it allowed him to experience working with a wide range of opponents with differing styles.

That was certainly the case once he started appearing on television, debuting in 1981 against Jim Breaks, then facing Johnny Saint and Mick McManus, the latter a bout Kidd describes as "the highlight of my career." The following year brought appearances against Jackie Turpin and Ken Joyce, in what proved to be the final TV outing for Kidd's mentor.

A pattern was starting to develop, however, with Kidd having a 0-5 record on the small screen at this point. Dedicated followers at the time noted he appeared particularly unfortunate as TV match number six saw him finally get a win, against Blondie Barratt, only for the bout to not make the air.

"It wasn't unusual in those days that the last match at a taped show wouldn't actually be recorded. It actually happened to me three or four times and you always knew about it: you'd walk out to the ring and as soon as the opening bell went, you'd see the cameraman turn off the camera, swing it round so it pointed the other way, and walk off!"

Over the course of his seven-year TV run, Kidd would wrestle around two dozen times and only avoided defeat three times: a draw against Jim Fitzmaurice, a victory over Eddie Riley, and a win in a six-man tag match (albeit one where Kidd dropped a fall.) But today he shows no disappointment in that record, instead focusing on his good fortune in making so many appearances and taking a note from a good friend who knew the importance of a good performance. "Sid Cooper always used to tell me the matches that felt like his biggest victories were ones that he lost. We knew that as long as the crowd went home happy, we'd done our jobs."

Kidd's own win-loss record certainly picked up when he began working regularly at live events as Big Daddy's tag partner, something he did more than 100 times over a 12-year period. And while some wrestlers might have felt frustrated that such a gig meant doing most of the work and getting little of the glory, Kidd was more than happy in the role. "I wouldn't change a thing about it. We tagged all over the UK and it was always fun times and you knew you'd great reactions. It also meant you'd work with a real variety of opponents from Sid Cooper to Giant Haystacks to [Dave] Finlay."

Indeed, Kidd maintained a good relationship with Daddy and was among just a handful of wrestlers to attend his funeral in 1997. He remained loyal to the Crabtrees as promoters during their run and, although he worked a few independent dates and did a title match with Jim Breaks on an All-Star show in Croydon, he never entertained any thought of jumping ship completely.

Given how often and in how many places Kidd wrestled, it may be surprising to discover that he has never been a full-time wrestler. Since the same year he turned pro, he has worked continuously at Vauxhall Motors, first spending several years as a paintsprayer and now working in the after sales department that takes care of supplying spare parts.

Kidd notes this was a deliberate decision. "Ken Joyce told me 'Never give up your job for wrestling' and I've never needed to, and never thought of going full-time. Being based in Luton was very handy given where Dale Martin used to promote, so I could usually get to shows after work without any problems. Back then the roads were much less congested, so I could be finishing work at 4.30, drive down to Portsmouth and get on the ferry, and wrestle that night on the Isle of Wight -- as long as I was on in the second half!"

That isn't to say foreign travel was never on the cards. Kidd recalls working in Germany, the Netherlands and Malta over the years before, in 2011, making his US debut against Johnny Saint for the Chikara promotion, the teaming with Colt Cabana and Mike Quackenbush the next evening.

Cabana, who had previously wrestled Kidd on British shows, tells FSM that Kidd is deserving of high praise. "While studying hundreds of hours of World Of Sport, I personally came to learn of only a couple of other guys who had a similar style [to Saint.] Johnny Kidd was a stand out in his smoothness and delivery. This style takes hundreds, if not thousands of hours to perfect and craft.

"I loved the fact that I could wrestle another wrestler in this day and age and almost get to go in that time warp and wrestle in a style that the country loved for decades. Even though it's basically a dead style, Johnny Kidd still being in the ring and wrestling these style of matches, he's helping keep a tradition alive."

That has certainly been a challenge since 1988 when wrestling was removed from ITV screens. It proved a particular bittersweet farewell for Kidd, who picked up his first win in a televised singles match at Rickmansworth at the last event ever taped for television. "We'd guessed the end was coming for a couple of years, ever since World of Sport stopped and wrestling was moved to a different timeslot, but we still didn't know what to expect. We were losing our shop window."

Although it wouldn't be long before crowds were indeed dropping off, it wasn't an immediate death as the Daddy roadshow rolled on for a few more years. In 1990, Kidd teamed with Daddy on two straight nights in Aberdeen in an event taped for broadcast on regional ITV stations. "It was a Friday and a Saturday night. On the Friday we had 1,100 and the Saturday had 1,200, which were the biggest crowds I ever appeared before."

Working on those shows, Kidd recalls wearing a kilt in a somewhat unsubtle attempt to win the crowd's affections. That's in contrast to one show where a fan recalls Kidd was billed from Scotland as a way to capitalize on passions fuelled by an England-Scotland football match taking place on the same day.

"I don't remember that particular match, but I did work as a villain now and then, maybe 10 percent of the time at most. I never wanted to work as an outright villain all the time because it didn't fit my style: most shows had at least one completely clean match, which was my speciality.

"Rather than wrestle in a full-on villain style, I could make things a bit more aggressive, crowd my man in the corner rather than let him out, that sort of thing. A few times [in recent years] promoters have asked me to be a bit more aggressive when I'm in with the local hero."

And it wasn't unknown for Kidd to adopt two different styles on the same show, as once happened when he worked a show with perennial rival Blondie Barratt. Both men had masked outfits, allowing them to put on three 'different' matches on the same show: Barratt vs Spiderman, Kidd vs Grim Reaper and Barratt vs Kidd. "I remember that show, but it must have been on a holiday camp because you couldn't get away with that at a regular venue. We'd have been stuck if they asked us all to come out at the same time!

That wasn't Kidd's strangest match however. That came on a show at a pub owned by grappler Ringo Rigby. Although the venue hosted wrestling once a month, on this occasion the ring failed to arrive, and the wrestlers were forced to perform on some makeshift mats. Once again Kidd was on with Barratt and recalls "There wasn't much we could do, but we managed to do a lot of stuff on the ground and put on a show."

Ironically ring positioning and making use of the ropes for something other than backflips is something Kidd now emphasises when invited to run training seminars. In an experience that will be familiar to many veteran wrestlers, he finds that when it comes to the complexity of moves, "many young guys can run but they can't walk, so I concentrate on basics like locking up, wristlocks and headlocks. Sometimes I show them simple moves and they say, 'I've never seen that before." But you never stop learning -- sometimes they'll show me a move, or a way into a move that I've not seen."

According to Kidd, it's certainly not the case that there's a lack of talent today. He cites Zack Sabre Jr and Doug Williams for their technical skills, while describing James Mason as "the best in the UK today, and has been for some time. He's totally competent and never in a bad match, and completely at home with my style. I'd go on with him seven nights a week if I had to."

But Kidd notes a telling change in his experiences working with Mason. "Guys like me, Steve Grey and Mal Sanders wrestled him back when he was starting out at just fourteen and he still always says thanks now and 'I never forget you always looked after me in the ring.' Now, [at my age] I always have to say, 'Just look after me in there!'"

Although benefiting from a clean lifestyle, Kidd is convinced it's his style that has allowed him to continue wrestling for so long. "If I did the modern style, I couldn't have lasted so long. We didn't do as many big bumps and throws, but the crowd still reacted. Now they are more impatient. Back then Steve Grey could be in a wristlock the whole round and then when he escaped, that's where you got your reaction. Sid Cooper had the right idea, though: he'd just pull a face and bring the house down!"

Kidd's career has had something of a boost from the revival of interest in the traditional style and he now considers himself something of a special attraction who will be brought in by a host of promotions to give a show an added dimension with a World of Sport-style match. In particular, Kidd still prefers the rounds-based format: "It gives a bit of an edge to the match and allows you to tell a story.

As well as giving you a breather, the breaks between rounds gives the audience a chance to take it all in."

According to Kidd, there's another big difference behind the scenes. "The fun and enjoyment backstage doesn't seem to be there as much today. That's probably because you don't have everyone working for the same promoter all the time and wrestlers seeing each other every night. If you told normal people about the way we'd talk and play jokes, they'd look at us as if we were daft."

More than thirty years in, Kidd continues to combine wrestling with his work at Vauxhall, where he notes workmates are aware of his sideline and the only real misconception is "when they used to say 'Wow, you must be getting paid a fortune to drive to all these places and wrestle!'"

One long-time (and current) Vauxhall colleague can empathise with the wrestler's lot however: Mohammed Butt, who Kidd introduced to the wrestling business in the early 1980s, and who specialised in one-arm powerlifting, setting what was billed a world record before one televised bout.

Kidd has been gradually reducing his wrestling schedule over the past five years or so, but concedes its far from certain he'll make a formal farewell: "In wrestling, you don't really retire, you just drop out the scene, and you always might do one more match."

Whenever it ends, it will be a career with few regrets, his biggest being that he never wrestled against the late Mike Marino, but numerous happy memories, the proudest being when he received an award at the British Wrestler's Reunion presented by childhood hero Mick McManus. But within the business itself, it's another man Kidd credits for his 33 years (and counting) as a professional:

"Ken Joyce was the man to me. It's all down to him. Without Ken, my career would have been nothing."

Johnny Kidd

# JOHNNY KINCAID

When Johnny Kincaid first asked how to break into the wrestling business, he got a simple answer from grappler Seamus Dunleavy: "Take it from me lad, you never want to get in."

At the time, that was enough to deter a curious youngster who had only come to be in a position to ask the question thanks to a quirk of fate. Kincaid, the eldest of seven children, had a troubled upbringing in Battersea, spending time in care homes and a young offender's institute.

Once his sentence ended, Kincaid returned to lodgings in Brixton with a landlady who also occasionally put up Northern-based wrestlers who had come down to the capital to do a stint with the locally-based Dale Martin promotions. Grapplers Eric Sands and Jim Moser both took him to live shows, which led to the Dunleavy question.

"I'd watched wrestling on TV -- everyone had -- but never really thought about whether you could get into the business," Kincaid told FSM. "I remember how you'd meet these stars off TV and realise they were just normal guys who didn't have ideas above their station, though they were very different in the ring. Eric left me a pair of his trunks when he left the digs: I always wondered if that was an omen!"

Having been discouraged, Kincaid had no serious interest in becoming a wrestler but wound up in the business through another of life's chance encounters. After attending a local fair with friends looking for labouring work, he began travelling around the country working on putting together and repairing equipment on rides.

On a trip to the Nottingham Goose Fair he came across the boxing booth and won five pounds (almost a week's wages) when he became one of the few challengers from the audience to beat the resident pugilist by knockout. The fair crew were unaware he had been boxing as an amateur at his various schools since the age of 11.

Word quickly spread among the fairground community and the following year Kincaid finally gave in to requests to join another travelling boxing booth run by

Harry Wood. The booth also featured wrestling challenges with future TV stars Tony Scarlo and Abe Ginsberg among those facing the audience.

On one occasion John Hurley, who performed as John Monk, asked Kincaid to act as a training dummy so that he could more easily show some moves to a trainee grappler. "Being in there at such close proximity, I was absolutely fascinated. There were so many moves and so much variety compared with boxing, so I wanted to learn it. You never stop learning new things in wrestling, particularly when you go overseas."

After a series of sessions with Hurley, Kincaid tried his luck at a local amateur gym where his first try-out bout didn't quite prove as successful as it first seemed. Kincaid thought he had triumphed by using a figure-four armlock to force his opponent to give up. An angry trainer asked just what exactly he thought he was doing before informing Kincaid that, unlike the violent world of the fairground booths, Olympic-style grappling did not feature submissions.

Hurley also wrestled on professional shows at more traditional venues and, as so often happened with stars of the era, Kincaid was roped in at late notice as a substitute. He was hooked by the experience and began picking up regular dates for independent promoters such as Wales' Orig Williams as well as working on a tour of Greece.

Eventually his persistent enquiries paid off and he was brought in by Joint Promotions for a bout, again as a late replacement. To his surprise, Kincaid found he was facing Jackie Pallo, one of the biggest names in the business. Fortunately, the match went well (albeit with Pallo advising Kincaid afterwards that he needed to slow down his moves so the audience could see what he was doing) and Pallo personally recommended him to management.

Around a month later Kincaid was offered a place on the Dale Martin books, with promoter Jack Dale deciding to bill him from Barbados rather than Battersea, a decision that somewhat contradicted a claim made by partner Les Martin who told the BBC Grandstand annual that "I challenge anyone to prove that a man in one of my promotions is falsely billed."

It only took six months before promoters decided Kincaid was ready for his television debut which came with a bout taped on 15 January 1969 and aired a week later. "I was absolutely petrified: not just because I was on TV, but because I was on with Mick McManus. He wasn't just the top guy, but also worked as a matchmaker. I knew that if I screwed up here, I'd probably never be booked again.

"Fortunately, the match just flowed. Some wrestlers didn't want you to shine and blocked everything you did, so you'd have to keep learning until you could block them back. McManus wasn't like that: he made you look a million dollars because he knew it made him look even better when he beat you."

As Kincaid continued making his name, he started looking for ways to become more memorable. "Even being a black wrestler didn't stand out because there were quite a few of us. Then I decided to bleach my hair and I stood out all right. Stood out like a Belisha beacon!"

The dye job also created an embarrassing moment when Kincaid made a trip to Israel. Having been warned that immigration officials there would likely challenge the fact he no longer resembled his passport photo, Kincaid added a new snapshot which, for legal reasons, had to appear beside the original in the document. Upon arriving in Israel, Kincaid realised that fellow wrestlers' jibes that his blond do aged him had some substance: a straight-faced official noted "It's very unusual to have father and son on the same passport."

Overseas trips quickly became a big part of Kincaid's schedule as he capitalised on his TV exposure as tapes of ITV wrestling were sold around the world. He worked across Europe, Africa and Asia in at least two-dozen countries, leading to some memorable experiences both in and out of the ring: "I never took any notice of politics in Britain, but I became an expert in places in India just from talking to people and meeting dignitaries.

At one show in India, Kincaid teamed with John "Killer" Kowalski (no relation to the US grappler of the same name) to take on Dara and Randhawa Singh. Dara wasn't just a wrestler, he was a movie star and genuine cultural icon. "We're in the ring and conferring in the corner. Bear in mind Kowalski was a huge guy and we're fighting the local heroes. One of us happened to wonder out loud what would happen if John or I just walked over and kissed them on the lips. Of course, we didn't do it, but just the thought of it made us crack up laughing. There's nothing like seeing somebody who's meant to be fighting in a match but is doubled up on the floor in giggles!"

Kincaid soon found that wherever he went, wrestlers were largely the same. "Once you're a wrestler, you can spot a wrestler anywhere in the world just by looking at them. They don't have to have cauliflower ears, it's just their presence and the way they carry themselves and walk with a bit of a swagger. One time I was flying to Nigeria with (MC) John Harris and when we changed in Paris I spotted these two guys and knew instantly they were wrestlers. We wound up on the same plane and I went up and asked if they wrestled. This one blonde guy said 'Yes, how did you know... hey, you're wrestlers too, aren't you?' It turned out I was talking to Dusty Rhodes: I knew his name but had never seen what he looked like."

His international demand meant Kincaid was less vulnerable to the 'office hold' enforced by Joint Promotions and he was even able to work better-paid dates for rival promoter Brian Dixon without them following through on the standard threat that this would mean an end to his Joint career. "I didn't really fear that because I'd already had the benefit of establishing myself on TV. I found the way they ran their business a bit funny at times. Once I was at Croydon to wrestler Jimmy 'Tiger' Ryan and Jack Dale came over to me and said '2-1, you over in four', [meaning Kincaid would win by two falls to one, the winner coming in the fourth round.]

"A couple of minutes later, he rushed back in and said 'I've just heard you're going off to Germany. 2-1, Jimmy over in four.' I said, 'I am coming back you know!'"

By the late 1970s, Kincaid decided it was time for a change and actively set out to make himself a villain. It was partly through curiosity, but mainly "because there weren't any other black villains at the time, let alone a tag team, so I saw an opening." He recruited relative newcomer Dave Bond, offering to help make him a star but warning him the experience might not always be pleasant.

"I knew we'd get abuse just like other villains, and that where Mick McManus and Steve Logan got 'You dirty bastards!' we were going to get 'You dirty black bastards!' I figured if we knew it was coming we could let it go in one ear and out the other and concentrate on making money."

At first it seemed crowds didn't want to believe the popular Kincaid had turned to the dark side and the pairing -- dubbed the Caribbean Sunshine Boys -- struggled to earn boos. Amazingly things changed at the Royal Albert Hall, a venue traditionally filled with well-to-do fans from a professional background who might have been expected to be more gentile.

"I used to write a lot of short stories and poems, particularly when I was in Germany and we were in the same venue for weeks on end, so we had time to kill during the day. Before the Albert Hall show I wrote a poem about me and Dave and how we didn't care about the rules. Doing poetry helped develop the image I wanted in the ring where Dave was the brute and I was more of a suave guy who wound people up.

"I didn't know that the promoters had decided to print the poem in the Royal Albert Hall program, but I think that's what pushed the crowd over the edge. We came out and there were people shouting abuse and making gestures and even throwing fruit at us. Instead of getting upset, I caught a banana, peeled it, bit off a chunk and said 'thanks' to the crowd, which got them even angrier!"

Now firmly established, the team began experiencing heated receptions at other venues, many of which spilled over into physical violence. "We had cigarettes stubbed out on us and somebody even sliced my arm with a knife in Liverpool -- I went looking for them afterwards and, perhaps luckily, didn't find them." Kincaid faced three court appearances during the Caribbean Sunshine Boys run, including one for an incident at the Catford Hall in Lewisham.

"This guy kept pulling our legs away when we were stood on the ring apron waiting for a tag, which was incredibly dangerous because we could have smashed

Johnny Kincaid

our heads on the ring. Eventually I wound up hitting the guy with an uppercut. A couple of days later I saw the paper and it had a picture of Dave captioned 'A hell of a kick to the groin', one of me captioned 'A hell of a punch' and one of the guy, stood posing with his wife, captioned 'Ex-policeman attacked by tag team.' I thought 'Uh oh, this is trouble."

The case led to a £75 fine for Kincaid and a six-month ban from the venue. However, it was an incident that didn't lead to a court case that proved the final straw. "We were on with Mike Marino and Lee Bronson and the crowd got so out of hand that a guy was in the ring about to hit me on the head with a chair. It was almost funny because a lightweight wrestler ran out and grabbed the chair, but the guy was so determined to crack me that he was trying to lift both the chair and the wrestler. I can still picture his face straining as he tried. He'd left himself wide open, so I was able to punch him in the sternum.

"Back in the dressing room the steward said he'd known there was going to be trouble that night. I asked why, and he pointed out that the guys who came after us were wearing National Front badges. When I left the venue, I found a National Front sticker on my car: they obviously didn't know it was my car, thank goodness!"

Two days later promoter Max Crabtree, who now headed Joint Promotions, phoned Kincaid and said he and Bond would never team again. Despite Kincaid's insistence that they had done nothing the likes of McManus and Logan hadn't used to do and that their antics "put bums on seat", Crabtree was insistent that they attracted the wrong type of fans and, more importantly, risked venues dropping wrestling altogether.

The team with Bond wasn't the only time race played a role in Kincaid's career: he cut short a trip to South Africa without wrestling after discovering that not only was apartheid rife within the country, but that it extended to promoters to and that he would only be booked to wrestle black grapplers. That said, sometimes skin colour led to moments memorable for lighter reasons such as the time Kincaid wrestled Alan Turner.

Thanks to his extensive spider-based tattoos, Turner normally worked as Tarantula but on this occasion, he was trying a different gimmick. With a need to cover up his entire body to avoid recognition, he opted to be a wrestling mummy complete with bandages, talcum powder and chalk. "The dust nearly choked me," Kincaid recalls, "and by the end of the match so much of it had stuck to me that I looked like a tabby cat!"

In the early 1980s Kincaid had suffered a serious hip fracture that required a total replacement, surgery he knew would likely end his career. In 1986 he finally made the call to hang up the boots, bowing out on television with a match against world mid-heavyweight champion Marty Jones: "I always thought that having my first TV match against the big star of McManus and my last TV match be for a world title was pretty good going!"

As he prepared for the surgery, Kincaid was alerted to the fact that TV documentary series Jimmy's, which covered the St James University Hospital in Leeds, was featuring footage of a hip replacement. "When I watched them dislocate the leg, I was OK. When I watched them pull the bones out, I was OK. When I watched them cut through the bones, I was OK. When I watched them drill through the bone, I was OK.

"When I watched them put the new hip in and started whacking it into place with a mallet, I have to say my backside started twitching and I made it very clear that anyone who thought I was going through that was very much mistaken!

"I put it off for another three years, but by then I was living on painkillers morning, noon and night and eventually it became too much. I called the doctor and he said he could do the surgery on June the 4th. I turned that down because it was my birthday and I wanted to dance the Twist one more time. Instead I rescheduled for June the 6th: I remember that date because it was my very own D-Day."

Thankfully the operation proved a success, though it would be followed by a knee replacement, a shoulder scraping and treatment to his elbows among other medical procedures. This wasn't enough to stop Kincaid making a brief comeback in 2008 including an appearance at the LDN Legends Showdown event against Jon Ritchie. "I should never have done it. I quickly found that my mind is young, but my body isn't and I wasn't as good as I thought I would be. That said, it was great to be able to stand in the corner of the ring and look out at the crowd, and I think I still looked good on the outside, even if everything inside my body wasn't so great."

Still, Kincaid's career is one with no regrets, as illustrated by an incident a few years ago at a wrestler reunion. "It was held in a Birmingham pub that was owned by Seamus Dunleavy. I went up to him and said, 'You don't remember me, do you?' He said no, so I told him 'When I was young I asked you how to become a wrestler and you told me 'Take it from me lad, you never want to get in.'

"He replied 'Yes, but I said that to everyone! But you got in and did OK for yourself, didn't you?' And I thought about it and replied, 'You know what, I did bloody well!'"

# JOHNNY SAINT

While some professional wrestlers get into the business to fulfil a childhood dream, others find their way into the squared circle through quirks of fate. Johnny Saint, though, is surely one of the few wrestlers whose career stemmed from a woman's haircut.

John Miller grew up in Failsworth, Manchester as a keen athlete with a particular interest in amateur boxing, winning the Lancashire championship in his age and weight division. Despite his athletic abilities, he left school at 15 and, as was expected of most boys in that time and place, followed his father into factory work. Ironically, given his flexibility and resilience in the ring, the job was in a rubber factory.

Miller continued boxing training at a local gym until he received a tip-off from his mother. She'd just returned from what had previously been an empty corner shop across the street from the family home, but had just been opened up as a hairdresser's. The new owner had a husband who owned another gym, along with a son who regularly trained there, and she suggested Miller might give it a try.

When Miller arrived, he did indeed receive boxing training from the owner, but found few sparring partners, with most of the regulars in the facility preferring to learn grappling. He decided to give the mat game a go and began learning from the son -- none other than future amateur and professional champion Billy Robinson.

After two years learning both grappling and submission skills from Robinson, Miller was one day told to report for training in a different gym, at which he wrestled competitive sparring sessions with several different men. It wasn't until the workout concluded that he discovered that the onlookers included several pro wrestling promoters and that he had just had -- and passed -- an audition.

His first pro match followed quickly, taking him across the country to Tynemouth where he lost to a grappler called McDonald. As well as providing an in-ring education and a lengthy ride to the venue, McDonald also suggested Miller adopt the name Johnny Saint -- an appropriate choice given his career long babyface run.

Saint went on to wrestle on the independent circuit for around a decade. He soon found that with payoffs ranging from £3 and 10 shillings to £5 depending on the size of the venue, it only took a few bookings each week to earn more than the basic wage of £8 to £9 plus overtime at the factory. Within three years he took the decision to make a full time career of wrestling.

Although Saint was able to pick up more lucrative work further afield, including for the leading independent promoter Paul Lincoln, he tells FSM the independent circuit had its drawbacks. "You'd often get different promoters trying to book you for the same night and then you'd have to figure out which ones to take and who you couldn't afford to upset in the long run. It was a very cut throat business and whenever there was a clash it was always the wrestlers that came off worse."

Such problems would ease when Saint eventually got the call to work for Joint Promotions, but he recalls his hiring came as a surprise. "I'd written to promoters like Dale Martin and Best/Wryton challenging them to take me on, but never got any reply. Then one night I was wrestling in a working man's club and it turned out [wrestler] Abe Ginsberg happened to be in the audience for a night out. He was working in the Best/Wryton office at the time and remembered my letter so after my match he suggested I come along to the Wryton Stadium in Bolton where they had a training gym. I turned up and had to wrestle about half a dozen fellows in a row and obviously made the right impression because they took me on."

Not only did this mean more opportunity for work, with 25 dates a month not an exceptional schedule, but it made life a lot simpler. "You didn't have to arrange your bookings any more or worry about clashes. You just got a booking sheet once a month telling you where to go. It was exciting as until then I'd mainly stuck to the Manchester area but now I'd be doing one week a month for Dale Martin [in London and the South], one week for Morrell & Beresford [Yorkshire], one week for Best and Wryton [Lancashire] and one week for George de Relywyskow [Scotland]."

Joint Promotions also meant television, with Saint making his first appearance in June 1969 against Vic Faulkner. He quickly made a name for himself, holding his own against the top stars in the lightweight (10 stone limit) division and facing heavier superstars Jackie Pallo and Mick McManus. "I was quite tall for a lightweight, so it looked fine when I wrestled in catchweight matches" says Saint, referring to bouts between two wrestlers of different weight divisions, a common set-up often portrayed as meaning there was no shame in the lighter wrestler losing.

In May 1971, Saint took his first championship, beating perennial rival Jim Breaks in Sheffield for the British lightweight crown before losing a rematch in Manchester three months later. Although the two would clash numerous times on television and at halls around the country, it would be another five years before Saint wore a title belt again.

That came after the retirement in 1976 of George Kidd, the long-time world lightweight champion and the innovator of a style Saint called "escapology": using speedy reversals and tricks to surprise and counter an opponent, rather than relying solely on offensive moves.

"I only wrestled him a couple of times, and it's one of my big career regrets that I didn't wrestle him for the world title on TV," Saint recalls. While Saint had done some training with Kidd, the extent of his direct influence was somewhat overstated by announcer Kent Walton, who made no secret that Kidd was his favourite wrestler and thus was paying a huge compliment in portraying Saint as a protégé.

According to Saint, there's nothing to a theory discussed among some long-term fans that he deliberately held back on adopting some of Kidd's moves until after his retirement. "Anything like that was purely coincidence. I evolved my style over a few years, but I wasn't intentionally waiting to claim some of his moves. My style was my style."

Among those trademark moves was one in which Saint would roll himself up into a ball with his head and limbs all out of reach. It's a routine that baffles some modern or overseas fans, but made sense under the British rules which banned a wrestler from attacking a downed opponent, instead limiting them to carrying out a continuous series of holds (hence the foreign description of the British style as chain wrestling.) A perplexed opponent would have no option of attack other than to bite on the bait of Saint sticking out an arm: going for a wristlock would inevitably see the opponent flipped on to his back.

Many of Saint's more elaborate routines were not only recognisable to fans, but became well known backstage. "I came back to the dressing room after doing one of my tricks and a wrestler said 'That was a real "now you see me, now you don't" trick wasn't it. Later on, wrestlers started giving my sequences nicknames and it almost became a cliché. One of them came about because somebody commented 'that looked like something Russ Abbot would do.'"

The name of the television comedian, known at the time for elaborate physical comedy, did indeed become a backstage shorthand for the routine. It was part of a curious backstage custom by which Saint would not need to explain a particular sequence of moves to an opponent: instead a simple mention of "the Lady of the Lake" or "Roll over Beethoven" sufficed.

With Kidd retired, Saint ascended to world champion status by beating Breaks for the vacant title in Bolton in November 1976. It kicked off two decades dominating the championship, during which -- in the same way as Ric Flair during his NWA glory years -- Saint was involved in every title change, losing the belt and then regaining it from his conqueror. He Saint exchanged the title with Steve Grey (twice), Jackie Robinson, Breaks (twice), Jon Cortez (three times) and Mike Jordan, claiming the crown until 1996.

Saint notes that although he's best associated with Grey and Breaks, he's faced a wide variety of particularly skilled opponents, citing Alan Sergeant, Bob Anthony, John Naylor, Alan Woods and Zoltan Boscik as his most notable underrated foes.

Despite his numerous lightweight rivalries, it was a December 1976 clash with middleweight wrestler Mick McManus that's best remembered by many fans of 1970s TV grappling. The bout concluded with the referee turning his back on the action to inform the ring announcer that McManus had received his second ("and final") public warning for throwing a punch, only to turn back and discover Saint suddenly prone on the mat.

Saint appeared to have intentionally exaggerated the damage caused by a punch, lying down in the style of Eddie Guerrero, with the referee instantly disqualifying McManus to his surprise and fury. Saint then said that if he couldn't beat McManus "fair and square" in a rematch, he would never wrestle again on English television -- a stipulation that never came to pass.

Sadly, Saint has no explanation for the finish, which stands out given his lifetime portrayal as an honest and sporting competitor. "I honestly can't remember that match at all. I can only assume the idea was that McManus was getting a taste of his own medicine!"

In 1982 Saint followed in the path of several of his colleagues by switching to All Star Promotions, meaning he was off terrestrial television for more than four years, though did make appearances on Screensport's "Satellite Wrestling" show. "By this point the people behind Joint Promotions had sold out and the business was in the hands of one person [Max Crabtree], so I could see it was losing a lot of its former power. Others read the writing on the wall, but I was a bit slower before it dawned on me. I became aware I could get much better money by leaving, and by now I wasn't giving up as much security with Joint."

Saint had also come to feel that in the era of Big Daddy and company having necessarily short main events, he was being taken somewhat for granted by promoters who needed to fill out a card. "I termed myself a time machine: it seemed the promoters always said to themselves 'John's fit, he can put some time in with his bout' and they just expected it of me every night."

The move also allowed Saint more flexibility to take lucrative overseas bookings across Europe, the Middle East and Africa. However, it wasn't until 1996 that he made his first trip to Japan, something of a surprise given his technical skills. Saint had wrestled on the undercard of a show at Croydon headlined by six wrestlers from the Michinoku promotion and impressed the tourists so much that he was invited to appear at the group's third anniversary show in Tokyo's Sumo Hall, a card that also featured the final match of the Dynamite Kid.

The warmly-received win over Naohiro Hoshikawa wasn't -- as sometimes claimed -- Saint's final match. He actually wrestled several dates until 1999, but now in his late 50s decided it was time to hang up the boot. He was firmly retired until 2007 when the LDN promotion held a "Legends Showdown" event and invited Saint to wrestle Steve Grey in the main event.

A late injury meant Johnny Kidd replaced Grey, but the bout was still a confirmed hit. Saint wrestled as if he'd never missed a day and the action received a legitimate standing ovation. It's since been uploaded in full to YouTube and has been viewed more than 60,000 times, thanks partially to appreciative tweets from William Regal. The bout led to Saint wrestling several matches around the UK over the next few years, taking on both World of Sport veterans and younger grapplers such as Andy Simmonz and Robbie Dynamite.

However, Saint says he was a little disappointed in changes in the wrestling business by this time. "There was so much razzmatazz and I felt that if I wanted to see that sort of stuff, I'd just watch the soaps on TV. It seemed like some guys spent more time with a microphone to their mouth or hanging over the ropes shouting and jeering at the audience than they did actually wrestling."

Ironically, while Saint was detecting the American influence in British rings, it was this final run that led to his US debut. He had sent promotional packages to US promoters in the 1970s in the hope of broadening his travels but never heard back, something he assumed was down to his size. What he didn't know was that he had become something of a cult favourite on the US tape trading scene, which only increased when the expansion of Internet video made it easier for overseas fans to see vintage bouts.

Some of those tape trading fans had become wrestlers themselves, most notably Chris Hero (now WWE's Kassius Ohno) who not only studied Saint tapes to learn new moves, but made a concerted effort to hunt down the retired Saint during a British tour and persuade him to come out for a pint and a chat.

Saint went on to work two matches against Chikara promoter Mike Quackenbush in Germany before being invited to the US in 2009 where the pair teamed with Jorge Rivera in a six-man tag tournament as "The Masters Of A Thousand Holds" taken from one of Saint's promotional nicknames. The team won their first match but lost a quarter final to "Team Uppercut", comprising fellow Brit Dave Taylor, Bryan Danielson (Daniel Bryan) and Claudio Castagnoli (Antonio Cesaro).

Two years later Saint returned to Chikara for a two night run, beating old rival Johnny Kidd in a truly amazing singles match performance for a man who had just turned 70, before teaming to Quackenbush to beat Kidd and Quackenbush. As pleasurable as the experience of performing before a US crowd was, it proved the beginning of the end for Saint's wrestling career.

"I got back from the US and almost straight away I was out to France again for another match [against Tony Trivaldo]. When I got back from that I felt quite weary and washed out and realised how much I hated traveling. I decided it was time to call it a day.

"I can honestly say I don't really miss anything about wrestling itself, but I do go to the reunions to catch up with people and I miss the camaraderie. As a full-time pro you don't really have a normal social life and it's very difficult to make and keep friends where you live, so in a way you have a social life in the business itself.

"It meant when I retired that I had to work to create a new band of friends. Fortunately, I'm a total motorcyclist enthusiast and I've enjoyed being part of biker clubs for about 15 years now." Saint now lives in Rhyl, North Wales, which is also home to Eddie 'Kung Fu' Hamill: "I moved there to be closer to my family, and it's also near to some brilliant biker roads."

Looking back at his own beginnings, Saint has some clear advice for pro wrestlers starting out today. "I know this won't go down well with everyone, but I really think people should do a few years of amateur wrestling before turning pro. It's the best grounding and I really wish I'd been able to stay training longer myself. I'm still amazed how many pros there are today who've never spent a moment on a catch wrestling mat."

# KENDO NAGASAKI

It's sometimes argued that to be a successful professional wrestler, you need to believe in your character. Bret Hart's insistence on following this philosophy helped him achieve greatness despite a comparative lack of size. Mark Callaway has achieved a staggering 23 year run in WWE by ensuring fans only ever see the Undertaker in public settings and know little of the man behind the persona.

But no wrestler protects his character to the extent of Peter Thornley, who to this day maintains that he does not portray the wrestling character of Kendo Nagasaki, but that he literally embodies him. Of course, to be precise, this claim comes through associates as Thornley does not give direct interviews or indeed speak in public.

Thornley's background before entering the professional ring remains a closely guarded secret. It's claimed he held national titles in weightlifting and was highly successful in judo, though no records appear to confirm these claims. It does appear he met and was heavily influenced by Kenshiro Abbe, a Japanese martial artist who introduced the UK to aikido, a particularly spiritually influenced form of combat which aims to deflect an opponent's momentum and thus act as a form of defence that minimises injury to the attacker.

Other claims include that Thornley worked as an apprentice for a firm making horseboxes, where he lost part of his index finger, an incident later used to build his character with allusions to the punishment dealt out for transgressions by members of the Yakuza, Japan's answer to the Mafia. Fans have also speculated for years that Thornley worked at a Crewe garage owned by local man Geoff Condliffe.

What is known is that Thornley first appeared in the ring as the masked and bodysuit-clad Kendo Nagasaki on 13 November 1964, knocking out Jim Hussey (the father of Mark Rocco.) He then went on a string of victories over several big name heavyweights, often winning by knockout. It's a pattern that stands out as unusual in three ways: a debuting wrestler decisively winning the majority of his bouts, a new wrestler appearing under a mask as anything other than a makeshift gimmick, and a new wrestler going straight into major matches with wrestlers allied to Joint Promotions. Despite this, there's yet to be any credible evidence of Thornley wrestling before adopting the Nagasaki character.

Despite his early successes, Nagasaki's real breakthrough match came in 1966 when he had an in-ring falling out with his tag partner Count Bartelli. The two were signed for a match where both men would put up £500 (the equivalent of nearly £8,000 today) along with their masks. Among those in attendance was future wrestler Keith Myatt:

"Although I was only seven years old, I remember like it was yesterday. My parents had queued for two hours on the Saturday morning to get tickets to what was going to be one of the most famous matches in Hanley for many a year. The Victoria Hall is a majestic hall and this night it was full to the rafters with over eighteen hundred people in attendance. The match itself was a titanic battle with both men fighting hard for the victory.

"One of my memories was the hall smelling of smoke and the crowd roaring as Bartellis nose was split open and blood was seeping through his mask. The roar of the crowd was deafening, shouting for their favourite, Bartelli. The end came when Nagasaki threw Bartelli over the top rope and amongst the chairs. We all thought he would make the count of ten, but he couldn't, and it was the end of an era as he had to unmask after over twenty years as a masked wrestler I remember the referee Stan Rylands untying the laces at the back of Bartelli's mask to reveal Geoff Condliffe from Crewe, his face a mask of red from the bloody nose."

It's generally accepted that Condliffe had been a mentor to Thornley and that the match was designed to help make him a superstar. It didn't seem to do Bartelli much harm as he began appearing unmasked on television and stretching his career out for another 20 years.

It wasn't until 1971 that Nagasaki made it to the TV screen himself. In the meantime, he made a trip to Japan for the IWE promotion. It's the only known time in which he appeared under a different name, "Mr Guillotine", promoted with the outlandish claim that he had killed an opponent in Saudi Arabia with a chop to the head. Back in the UK he continued to build his name, with magazine adverts offering £100 in gold sovereigns to any wrestler who could defeat him. Perhaps wisely the ad made clear that only pinfalls would count, with submissions exempt from the deal, something that may have deterred any troublemakers considering a double-cross.

Although Nagasaki's TV debut actually came in the high-profile FA Cup Final day slot against Wayne Bridges, his best remembered early match came against Billy Howes, who spent much of the match attempting to unmask him. In the end, with his nose bleeding heavily, it appears Nagasaki was forced to briefly unmask himself before attending to his injuries and covering up with a towel. Viewers thus got their first glimpse of an unusual tattoo of an eye inside two interlocking triangles.

Kendo Nagasaki

In 1972 Nagasaki toured the Stampede territory accompanied by manager George Gillette (billed in Canada as Lord Sloane) where he followed the usual pattern of a star tourist working his way up the card before taking the title, in this case the North American championship from Geoff Portz, and then dropping it back a couple of months later.

Nagasaki continued a string of TV victories in the UK, accompanied by George, winning every match by knockout. That led to an inevitable clash with Shirley Crabtree, a fellow heavyweight who was also chalking up the KOs. Nagasaki's standing was shown by the fact that he took the win, putting Crabtree down for the count with a knee to the head.

After a brief spell on the independent circuit (where he wrestled Johnny Kincaid for what was curiously billed as the WWF world championship) Nagasaki returned to television and beat Crabtree -- now Big Daddy -- in a tournament semi-final, again by knockout. In a rematch, Daddy managed to remove the mask but still fell to a pinfall defeat.

Not only did Nagasaki remain undefeated on television (with the possible exception of the disputed Howes bout), but he followed up his win over Daddy with a tag match in which he and George -- very much a non-wrestler -- overcame fellow villains Mick McManus and Steve Logan at the Royal Albert Hall. As testament to his ambiguous character, fans at Belle Vue (Manchester's leading wrestling venue) voted Nagasaki as both their most popular and most hated grappler.

Arguably the most famed moment in Nagasaki's career came at the end of 1977 when he announced he would voluntarily unmask. The real reason he chose to do this is unclear, though part of the storyline was that it would allow him to challenge British heavyweight champion Tony St Clair. With no world title recognised in the heavyweight division in the UK at the time, the story had it that Nagasaki could not wrestle for either the British or European crowns because he refused to unmask and thus confirm his geographic eligibility. So momentous was the unmasking, the ceremony received top billing on local posters for the television taping in Wolverhampton, with the show airing on New Year's Eve.

Nagasaki went on to make several appearances without the mask in 1978, changing to a cleaner in-ring style. On the Cup Final day show he ran to the ring to save Eddie "Kung Fu" Hamill from an attack by Mick McManus. (Ironically both Nagasaki and McManus had taken Hamill's mask, depending on which venue you attended.)

Hamill tells FSM the incident was indeed meant to cement a Nagasaki turn. "He wanted to be a babyface and thought that teaming with me would make it work. At this time, I was coming to the ring wearing the mask and then took it off before I wrestled. The idea was that we'd team up and both do that together as the unmasked masked tag team!"

The team never came about as Hamill became one of the first wrestlers to jump ship to All Star Promotions. Later in the year Nagasaki stopped taking bookings, citing medical issues, and save for a short run with All Star himself, did not appear again until the end of 1986.

With Brian Dixon's All Star having secured a share of the ITV slot for the first time (the show airing the first week of 1987), Nagasaki's return was a key selling point at the taping at the London Hippodrome nightclub. In one of the strangest matches in ITV history, he defeated Clive Myers in a disco ladder match. This was hardly Nagasaki's first ladder bout (he'd actually had a series against Big Daddy at non-televised events) but was surely the first to be played underneath disco lights while classical music played over the building's sound system.

That wasn't the only outlandish Nagasaki moment on ITV. In the final All Star broadcast he teamed with Blondie Barratt to defeat the "Golden Boys" of Rob Brookside and Steve (now William) Regal after supposedly hypnotising Brookside into turning against his partner.

Fortunately, Nagasaki did have some more conventional action, defeating Wayne Bridges for what was billed as the world heavyweight title and teaming with Rocco only for the pair to split up and engage in a violent rivalry that continued around the country after ITV dropped the wrestling slot. Those in attendance at live bouts remember the matches becoming so heated that supporters of both men wound up in physical confrontations with one another!

Around the turn of the decade, George Gillette died. Nagasaki decided to replace him as manager with Lloyd Ryan, a session drummer and instructor who numbered Phil Collins among his pupils. Ryan was a long-time Nagasaki fan and had even composed a song called "Kendo's Theme" that received airplay and was adopted as entrance music by Nagasaki. Ryan was one of several Nagasaki fans who eventually worked for him in a professional capacity.

Following Rocco's retirement through ill-health, Nagasaki's main rivalry was with fellow villain Giant Haystacks, as documented in the BBC 2 Arena documentary "Masters of the Canvas". The show was built around the fact that artist Peter Blake, the man who produced the cover of the Beatle's Sgt Pepper album, had spoken of his desire to be Kendo Nagasaki himself.

It was one of many mainstream media appearances by Nagasaki over the years. Most involved the novelty of him appearing on a chat show but refusing to speak (Danny Baker being among those baffled by the experience), though he did have a brief speaking role in the drama Send In The Girls. He played the Death Angel, a masked grappler who followed the night's action by successfully picking up a character played by Floella Benjamin. His brief few lines was enough to inspire debate that rages today about exactly where his accent placed him.

In 1993, shortly after the start of a feud with Ryan, Nagasaki again withdrew from the ring, returning for a short run with All Star in 2000, kicked off by him having been voted Wrestler of the Millennium by callers to a premium rate wrestling news phone service. He made a final return in 2008 for the LDN promotion where he put up a "sword of excellence" (which he'd previously said would be awarded to a wrestling apprentice) for the winner of a tournament, only to refuse to present it to said winner, his old rival Brookside. It led to several in-ring appearances, with his final bout coming on October 29 teaming with Barratt against Travis and Hakan. The run ended prematurely over what both sides portrayed as artistic differences about Nagasaki's in-ring style.

Though retired from the ring, Thornley continues to use the Nagasaki character as a faith healer, an interest profiled by the TV Times as far back as 1976. His insistence on maintaining the character continues, with the explanation that Thornley is merely a physical conduit, referred to publicly as Yoshenga, for the spirit of Nagasaki, who is said to have inhabited several forms with his last physical appearance being in 16th century Japan.

Real life events have brought about a more mundane portrayal. In the 1970s a plumber discovered Nagasaki's true identity when working at Thornley's home and noticing George Gillette was visiting. The plumber reportedly went on to harass Nagasaki by handing out leaflets and even placing newspaper advertisements revealing his identity. In 2002, Thornley made headlines after falling out with a neighbour in a dispute about ivy plants on a land border, a rivalry newspapers were quick to contrast with his ring battles.

Still, while it's certainly unusual for a wrestler to be so committed to his character after almost 50 years, it can't be denied that in Kendo Nagasaki, Peter Thornley created genuine legend in the British wrestling business and sparked mysteries that continue to intrigue fans today. While he was a skilled grappler who clearly held great sway with promoters, losing just a handful of televised matches (all with controversial outcomes), his appeal was perhaps best explained by documentary director Paul Yates in an interview with The Sun's website:

"People put their own projection on the Nagasaki persona and I'm afraid I can't add to that: it is very much in the eye of the beholder."

■ ■ ■ ■ ■ ■ ■ ■ ■ ■ ■ ■ ■ ■ ■ ■ ■ ■ ■ ■ ■ ■ ■ ■ ■ ■ ■ ■ ■ ■ ■ ■ ■ ■ ■ ■ ■ ■ ■ ■ ■ ■ ■ ■ ■ ■ ■ ■ ■ ■ ■ ■ ■ ■ ■ ■ ■ ■

## *The Imposters*

As Eddie Hamill has previously detailed to FSM, one of the major drawbacks of being a masked grappler is that it becomes much easier for other performers to ride your coattails by imitating you once you become a star. That's certainly the case with Nagasaki, who has "inspired" numerous imitators.

During Nagasaki's peak television run in the 1970s, independent promoter Terry Goodrum (also known as Sandor Kovacs) put wrestler Bill Clark under the hood and billed him as Nagasaki to fool unsuspecting fans. While a brief irritation to the real performer, the move backfired as Thornley had registered "Kendo Nagasaki" as a business name in 1972. He obtained a High Court writ to stop the practice and eventually tracked the pair down and served it in person. Goodrum failed to appear for a court case to answer the claim and spent a brief spell in prison for contempt of court.

When Thornley retired from Joint Promotions, promoter Max Crabtree briefly tried billing an inexperienced grappler named Nick Heywood as Kendo Nagasaki II. He had a noticeably slimmer build and lacked the in-ring abilities of Thornley, and the gimmick quickly died off with Heywood failing to show up at several billed dates.

Bill Clarke had by now rebranded himself as King Kendo, though maintained the same costume complete with ceremonial sword and helmet. Their legal differences settled, Thornley and Clarke agreed to work together for All Star Promotions with George Gillette doing the rounds of the group's regular venues and coming to ringside after King Kendo matches to issue a challenge. Nagasaki would then return at the following show in each hall, soundly defeating King Kendo and removing his mask.

Although Clarke dropped the gimmick at this point, he was persuaded to revive it by Joint Promotions once Nagasaki was appearing on television with All Star. Although still billed as King Kendo, it certainly appeared Crabtree was attempting to cause confusion, with Big Daddy getting a symbolic TV win over the masked man.

Following the axing of the TV slot, All Star decided to revive the King Kendo character. This time the story was that Nagasaki and Lloyd Ryan had split, with Ryan bringing King Kendo in to get revenge. By this time Clarke had passed on both the gimmick and the costume to another wrestler, Dale Preston. In the event Nagasaki quit before the rivalry could really get going, though Preston carried on as King Kendo for several years, notably feuding with Giant Haystacks who was working in a rare babyface role.

Kendo Nagasaki

As well as British performers copying the Nagasaki character, Thornley's creation sparked one of the few occasions where a US-based grappler "borrowed" the name of a British performer (something that happened the other way round on numerous occasions." Kazuo Sakurada had worked for Stampede (helping train Bret Hart) and most likely picked up the name there. He went on to work for several promotions across the US as Kendo Nagasaki, though had a different character and wore face paint rather than a mask. Later in his career he worked for the NWA as the Dragon Master, part of a stable managed by Gary Hart. He also wrestled as Nagasaki against Jim Duggan in a Tokyo bout released on the WWF World Tour 1991 videotape, much to the confusion of many British buyers.

# KID CHOCOLATE

Originally from the West Indies, Alan Bardouille came to England as a teenager in the mid-1950s, following his father who had come to the country a few years earlier. He was part of a wave of immigrants from the Caribbean who filled a vital role, not only dealing with a shortfall in working age men after the losses of the second world war, but filling roles in a rapidly expanding public sector.

The younger Bardouille was a fan of wrestling and took up the amateur sport at a club in his hometown of Bradford. It was one man in particular who inspired him to make the switch to the pro business. "I saw Earl Maynard, the West Indian Mr Universe, at St George's Hall in Bradford. When I saw him, I decided 'I want to be the one who's wrestling.'"

Maynard, who originally hailed from Barbados, was a true two-sports superstar. As well as wrestling in the UK (and later the Pacific Northwest and Stampede territories), he was legitimately world class in bodybuilding. In 1964 he won the professional division of the Mr Universe championships, the same title which Arnold Schwarzenegger would win just four years later.

Bardouille's initial attempts to follow him into the ring would come to nothing, but the impression Maynard left would prove valuable in getting his break. "After seeing Earl Maynard, I went to see Norman Morrell, the promoter, but I only weighed nine stone. He said, 'Look lad, go put some weight on and come back in 12 months' time.' So I started bodybuilding."

After bulking up, he then approached another Joint Promotions bigwig, George De Relwyskow, who arranged for him to begin weekly training with former grappler Ernest Baldwin. There were few trainers at the time with a better resume than Baldwin, who had been the first British heavyweight champion of the Mountevans rules era and would claim the title on four occasions as well as challenging Lou Thesz for his (somewhat unofficial) world title in 1957. Based in Tingley, Yorkshire, Baldwin numbered John Cox and Peter Preston among his other trainees.

As with many other grapplers, it wasn't as easy a transition for Bardouille as might be expected. "Pro and amateur was like chalk and cheese: totally, totally different." In particular the use of submission holds and striking stood out in training, which was very much about the sport rather than the showmanship. "Amateur was one thing, but professional was anything goes."

That was at the forefront in Bardouille's first match. "My debut is something I will never ever forget. It was in Newcastle at St James's Hall against Alan Colbeck, ad ex-champion and a fantastic wrestler. I went into the ring with him and for three rounds he used me as a mop and bucket to wipe the ring with. After three rounds I said 'Look, you will never, ever, ever do that again.' From that I [was ready to go] to the big, big time."

Bardouille's willingness to stand up for himself – which may have felt like a risky move for a newcomer dealing with a veteran in aggressive mood – proved the correct response. "When you were a young wrestler in those days, the first opponent was a tester to find out if you have or haven't got the guts to do it. It didn't take me long to (be comfortable). After that first bout with Alan Colbeck, I really, really went into it and got to know all the tricks of the -- well not all -- most of the tricks of what to do. And after that I was alright at going with the crowd."

He soon found that the Joint Promotions set-up, with the dangers of falling out of favour across the board if you upset one promoter, could also bring positive momentum with word of mouth securing bookings. "All the promoters were very good to me: De Relwyskow and Morell and Ted Beresford was very good."

As well as working across the northern-based promotions, Bardouille got experience in other settings. Like many he worked on the holiday camp circuit and sharpened his interactions with the public – "it was more intimate with the crowd on the camps" – and would even return a couple of decades later in a different context. "I was part of a group of sportspeople who'd go round the camps together for appearances with people like Sharron Davies, Tessa Sanderson and Duncan Goodhew. It was an opportunity for holidaymakers to say 'Well, I've seen these people.'"

He also worked at the infamous Eldorado Stadium in Edinburgh, but didn't face the hostility that many non-Scots would get from the passionate crowd. "I was the only Afro-Caribbean in the All Stars team that would fight twice a month on a Tuesday Night." A unique set-up for wrestling – though not dissimilar to the way 'sports entertainment' event Roller Derby worked in some US cities – the All Stars were marketed as the venue's home team and would face a different set of challenging villains on each show.

While his career spanned several peaks and valleys for the business, Bardouille deliberately chose to maintain a day job and the novelty of his second life meant he was able to get time off to travel to shows as needed. "I was trained as a skilled engineer and worked for Rolls Royce as a chief inspector. They had a worldwide newsletter and they featured my wrestling in one of their issues. I'll always remember the heading: 'The people you find working for Rolls Royce!'"

After many years working under his real name, Bardouille opted for a change of identity, taking on the ring name 'Kid Chocolate'. Uncomfortable as that moniker may be in these more culturally enlightened times, it was a homage of his own making rather than the work of a politically incorrect promoter. Having debuted on television in 1971 against Steve Best, he'd begun making more regular appearances in the middle of the decade when he decided on the change of image.

"While I was wrestling as Alan Bardouille, my children were just starting at school. I didn't want my wresting to interfere with their schooling and [my name be recognised] and used in a bad way at school. Kid Chocolate was an old boxer in Bradford and I knew his family, so I asked them for his permission and they gave it."

It was effectively a second-generation tribute as the boxer in question was a Yorkshireman whose real name was Walter Melgram. In turn he had taken the ring name from Elgio Montalvo, a black Cuban boxer who is recorded as racking up 136 professional wins and held the world junior-lightweight title. He had his own wrestling connection, having been promoted in New York by Jess McMahon, grandfather of the current WWE chief, who had a reputation for ignoring the racial divide when matchmaking.

The Chocolate name would prove popular for Afro-Caribbean combat stars. As well as Melgram, current American middleweight boxer Peter Quillin has used the name. Meanwhile in wrestling the British grappler best known as Jamaica George (among at least half a dozen monikers) briefly worked as Kid Chocolate, as did an American midget wrestler of the 1970s and 1980s.

As the 70s rolled into the 80s, Bardouille wrestled a veritable Who's Who of stars on the small screen. His most prestigious bout came partnering Big Daddy against the masked Marauders on the 1983 FA Cup Final broadcast, where he clearly made the right impression. "It was a big, big match because I started being Big Daddy's regular partner after that." Bardouille laughs as he remembers the division of labour in the pairing: "I did the work... and he'd get the glory!"

Other high-profile clashes included a match with Wigan's John Naylor, which was a culture clash for the audience, but not on racial lines. "It was not just John Naylor and I: it was Yorkshire vs Lancashire!" He also wrestled Mick McManus and found a similar experience to others in that the superstar was very willing to make his opponent look good, safe in the knowledge he'd be getting his hand raised: "He knew I used to put on a good show with my wrestling."

At one point he even wrestled Jackie Pallo in a non-televised match and recalls a surprising outcome. "Pallo had a special move where he used to leapfrog over people, but he didn't realise how tall I was. When he tried to leapfrog me, he hit his privates right on my forehead!" While Pallo had famously intentionally crotched himself on the ring ropes to gain attention on his first television appearance, one thing made it clear this was an unplanned incident: "I won via technical knockout!"

As well as heavyweight brutes and ring veterans, Bardouille also wrestled on television against some future superstars in Mark Rocco and the Dynamite Kid, but singles out the technical abilities of the less-celebrated Zoltan Boscik for particular praise. "We used to have a fantastic, fantastic match. It wasn't a grudge, it was a matter of who could get the better of each other."

Bardouille was among a generation of grapplers who hung up their boots at the end of the 1980s. "I retired once they took it off TV. I had a full time job and I thought: right, it's off television, I've had 20 years of glory: it's time to retire." He believes his part-time status made the transition to life outside of the spotlight easier to handle. "A lot of the wrestlers who wrestled full-time [didn't know anything else]. Because I always kept a job, I'd already met a lot of people in the outside world."

Leaving wrestling didn't mean the end of his physical activities. Bardouille moved on from engineering and finished his career in a very different field. "My last job was anger and aggression training. I was teaching doctors and nurses, anyone working in mental health, how to look after themselves when they are working and dealing with mental health patients. When the patient loses it, they only have 10 seconds to take control. I used to be one of chief instructors and even did six weeks training at Broadmoor."

After officially retiring from work, Bardouille actually expanded his athletic endeavours at a local fitness centre even well into his sixties. "I did personal training and took a lot of fitness classes: bums and tums, pilates, body pump and things like that. I was doing six or seven fitness classes a week." He also completed the 13-mile Great North Run three years in a row, raising nearly £50,000 for Macmillan Support. In 2009, he was even honoured by Bradford council for his work for charity and the community.

Still fit today, he attends wrestler reunions and meets up with former colleagues, at least one of whom has privately joked to FSM of his frustration that Bardouille doesn't share the visible signs of ageing of his peers. But while such gatherings may include the inevitable banter, Bardouille has only happy memories of the time he spent with them in the ring.

"I enjoyed working with all the wrestlers. There was no wrestle I could say I didn't like working with."

## The Black Knights

As well as teaming with Big Daddy, Kid Chocolate often worked as part of the Black Knights tag team. A generous reading was that this was an ever-evolving partnership, though at times it certainly appeared as if the name would be applied to any two Afro-Caribbean grapplers booked on the same bill.

The original line-up, formed during a period of tag team mania in the UK, featured Barbadian Ezzard Hart, a regular in the sixties known for his dyed blonde hair before passing away unexpectedly early in 1971. He was joined by Honey Boy Zimba of Sierra Leone: while the name might not have been politically correct, it certainly beat his original ring moniker of Nigel The Warrior.

Zimba was joined in the most common later incarnation of the Black Knights by Masambula, who was billed as hailing from the Gambia. He had off-screen victories over Mick McManus and renowned shooter Gordon Nelson, aka the Outlaw. Masambula suffered a career-ending injury in a 1975 bout leading to a controversial court case against Joint Promotions over the condition of the ring.

Other occasional members of the Black Knights included Linde Caulder, a bodybuilder from Antigua; Jim Moser of Trinidad; Lenny Hurst of Jamaica; and Bobo Matu, who was billed from the Friendly Isles (now Tonga), though this has been questioned.

# KLONDYKE KATE

When an older wrestler complains about today's trainees having it easy, there's sometimes a touch of the Monty Python "four Yorkshiremen" sketch about it. But it's safe to say that youngsters taking their first steps in today's wrestling training schools do so in more welcoming surroundings than the location of Klondyke Kate's grappling education.

"I trained in a garage and the 'ring' was literally a piece of canvas on a concrete floor with no padding: the ring posts were built straight into the concrete!"

Still in her mid-teens, it was an unlikely event that led to the girl then known as Jayne Porter making a life in wrestling. She sat ringside at a show in Blackpool and, because it was a special occasion, wore her best white dress. That proved an unfortunate choice of clothing as wrestler Crusher Mason (also known as the Mighty Chang) bled profusely in his bout and splattered her dress with crimson.

However, in the long run the dress proved a life-changing piece of luck. She complained to the promoter, Bobby Barron, about her ruined clothing after the show, only for the conversation to turn to her interest in becoming a wrestler. That led to an invite to the training 'facility'.

"On my first day there, I got a broken ankle. It didn't put me off, and when I walked back in six weeks later, they could tell I was serious about it."

Porter debuted in a tag match in 1977 and from a technical perspective was still lacking. "I was diabolical: really, really bad! Then again, I've never professed to be an amazing wrestler. But I interacted with the crowd and showed some idea about the psychology side of wrestling." Of all people, it was Crusher Mason who spoke up for her. "He told Bobby that I had something about me. He could tell I really, really wanted to do this."

Although initially billed as Big Bertha because of her comparatively bulky physique, Porter soon received a new moniker from Barron, one that would stick for the rest of her career: Klondyke Kate. Although there had already been two British grapplers named Klondike Jake and Klondike Bill, "Klondyke Kate" was more famous as the nickname of Kathleen Rockwell, a famed vaudeville dancer who performed for miners in the early 1900s gold rush in the Yukon and had been the subject of a song released by Suzi Quatro in 1974.

As well as wrestling her fellow pros in the halls, Kate joined a lengthy tradition of competing for real against members of the Blackpool public, something she didn't particularly enjoy. "It certainly helped make you tough, but not necessarily in a way that's good for being a pro wrestler. I really didn't like hurting people, but sometimes you had to: once I took on a woman with a real bodybuilder physique who was totally full of herself and I wound up having to break her leg. I didn't want to do the booths any more after that and luckily I had the choice about whether or not to do them, so I stopped."

That wasn't the last time Kate would scuffle with a member of the public however: later in her career one outraged fan stabbed her in the hand during a match. Although he later received a jail sentence, the man also got some instant justice at the hands of Dave Finlay.

Kate had fought men on the booths and continued that approach on traditional pro shows. "I always wrestled men right from the start and it was perfectly normal for me to do mixed tag matches. As a woman I knew I had to be really good to earn respect from the men, but then that's true of everyone. I was always accepted as one of the chaps, probably because I had the same mentality and sense of humour."

As her career took her further afield, Kate began working shows for independent promoters such as Orig Williams and Brian Dixon, who used a lot of women wrestlers, something that Joint Promotions avoided. This led to a particularly memorable bout on a Williams show in an Irish parish hall. There'd been some miscommunication and upon arrival the crew discovered venue management would not allow women to wrestle on the show. This proved a major issue as Williams had already planned on putting together a show with just six grapplers, most likely using additional tag bouts to stretch the evening out. This meant doing the show without the women wasn't an option, leaving only one solution.

"Crusher Mason took some bandages and rolled them round me tightly to strap down my bits and pieces and then I put on a mask. He managed to change my shape, so it wasn't obvious I was a woman, though you couldn't really change the fact that I didn't look like the other wrestlers because I'm only 5'3" and had stubby little fingers. I suspect it was half a way for the show to go on and half a joke on me by Orig.

"I think the priest sussed what was going on, but somehow the crowd didn't seem to notice I was a woman. Well, that was until about round four when the bandages had worked their way loose and I realised it was time to say goodbye!"

Klondyke Kate

The foreign trips with Williams helped Kate get bookings even further afield. "Instead of listing which countries I've been to, it's quicker to say that the only continent I never visited was Australia. There are so many memories, like the time we wrestled in Beirut and then had to rushed to catch the last plane out before the latest war started up again and the airport closed."

Although the huge success of the full-time All Japan Women's promotion in the early 80s might seemingly have made it a dream destination for female grapplers, Kate has a very different recollection of her initial experience there. "I loved seeing all the beautiful cities -- I think we went to 36 in forty days -- but the first week of the tour was absolutely horrid, really vile in every way. It was the first time I'd had to wrestle in such humid conditions, and only [fellow Brit] Sue Keegan and a wrestler called Mimi Hagiwara spoke any English.

"I was still in my late teens and every night I was working in six-girl or eight-girl matches. In every match I was getting an absolute pasting, and not just from my own partners. I was always teaming with Devil Masami, who'd whack her opponents with a big stick, but every time she lifted it up behind her, she made sure to whack me as well.

"Eventually one night I was in the ring with Jumbo Hori who was about six foot and she had me in a figure-four leglock. She was really cranking down and with my legs being so short it was so much more painful: I was wondering if I'd even be able to walk properly afterwards. I completely lost my rag and just punched her as hard as I could. I had no more problems after that! If I'd gone back to Japan when I was older I'd probably have stood my ground from the start, but it was all good experience."

Closer to home, Kate came as close as any woman to wrestling on ITV in the 20th century. She was part of two special tapings in Aberdeen in 1990, two years after the national slot ended. The bouts were originally shown on Scottish ITV stations and later aired in a late-night midweek slot in the Granada and Tyne Tees regions of England. Kate was a ringside manager for the teams of Anaconda & Kamikazi and Count Von Zuppi & John Wilkie as they unsuccessfully challenged Big Daddy and Johnny Kidd on consecutive nights. She even stepped into the ring after the former bout and attacked Daddy with scratches, only to find herself at the wrong end of a belly butt and an Irish whip.

As well as a series of wrestling appearances on Reslo, which aired on S4C (the Welsh Channel 4), Kate distinctive presence brought her numerous media appearances over the years. This included a guest role in the Margi Clark boxing film Blonde Fist and a cameo in the concept musical movie It Couldn't Happen Here, starring the Pet Shop Boys. A newspaper report on one of her matches formed the centrepiece of Klondyke Kate And Other Non-fiction Texts, a 1995 anthology designed to promote literacy. In 2007, she was portrayed in the short comedy World Of Wrestling by a pre-fame Miranda Hart.

Kate's biggest mainstream media appearance came in 1989 when she was the subject of Raging Belles, a documentary in the BBC series 40 Minutes. The show featured both her personal life and her participation in a tournament for the British women's title that had been vacated when Mitzi Mueller retired.

Kate believes the documentary proved a major positive for female grapplers. "Reality TV hadn't taken off then, so it was quite rare that you'd get a show like this that was so genuinely true to life. It had about three million viewers, which might not sound much but was great for BBC 2. I'm still very proud of that documentary because it showed people women's wrestling wasn't just for dirty old men in macs, it was suitable for families. I definitely noticed more women coming to shows after it aired."

"I still get lots of requests to do TV and media appearances, but I'll only do it if I think it's good for wrestling. I'd never go on daytime TV like Jeremy Kyle and have a go at wrestling just to get on screen."

Had the timing of the Raging Belles recording been a couple of years different, the documentary might have had a spectacular surprise ending. After a match Kate felt ill and still had pins and needles the next morning. On visiting the doctor, she was shocked to discover she was eight and a half months pregnant. Amazingly, despite having wrestled a regular schedule throughout the pregnancy, there was no damage and two weeks later she gave birth to a healthy son. Two weeks after that, Kate was back in the ring.

Wrestling has become something of a family affair for Kate over the years. Her partner Justin Hansford wrestles under names including Justin Starr while her daughter has wrestled as Connie Steele since 2007, though is currently considering her long-term career plans.

Kate and Justin even ran a training school for several years in the mid-2000s, only closing the High Impact Wrestling Academy when they moved from its Stoke base to the south coast. Although there were no concrete floors this time round, it was a business she took deadly seriously. "I hate hearing about uninsured schools, or places where you just turn up and pay a fiver and then call yourself a wrestler even though you look like a bag of shit, or people who set themselves up as a trainer and claim years of experience when they've only done thirty or forty matches themselves. There's far more to experience than just time.

"I'm not saying there's a right way or a wrong way to train people, but I do believe there's a safe way and an unsafe way. If people who don't know what they are doing start training people themselves, you get a vicious circle and end up with substandard wrestlers."

"I also never bought the idea that if you train with someone, they can decide who you work for. My philosophy is that I trained people to work in a professional job and when they are ready they can work for anyone. I treat wrestling as a business and that's why I'm totally against people wrestling for free."

Despite her concerns about some training set-ups, Kate has changed her outlook on the state of female wrestling in Britain today. "Back when I started, Brian Dixon was doing a lot of all-women shows [because they couldn't work for Joint Promotions] and I remember I used to stand out, particularly once Hellcat Haggerty retired, because I was the only really big girl there. But it died away over the years so that you only usually had one women's match on a show.

"I must admit that a few years ago I'd have hated the thought of an all-woman show. At that point it seemed like anyone and their sister could get in their business and it absolutely sickened me. I didn't really enjoy watching shows because it felt too much like a busman's holiday.

"Now though, I'm very proud of the women coming in now in places like [all female promotion] Bellatrix. They don't just rely on gimmicks, but they can entertain and are real allrounders. Girls like Skarlett and Destiny are both coming on really well. Watching shows from the viewpoint of an insider means nothing really thrills me, but some of the matches today make me feel that tingle as a fan and get me going.

"All the credit goes to Julia [Hamer, aka Saraya Knight] for training the girls right. Her and [daughter] Paige are the best women wrestlers this country's ever had. It really sticks in my craw to say so, but it's true. I certainly brought something to wrestling -- psychology, you'd call it -- but they really are all-rounders.

While Saraya may one day face a challenge for the title of queen of the ring among active British grapplers, it won't come from Kate. After several false finishes, she finally retired on 12 December 2010 when she teamed with Faith Lehaine to defeat daughter Connie Steele and Erin Angel. "I retired a few times, but that really was the end because the injuries caught up with me. [That match] meant I wrestled in five different decades, which always sounds odd to me being that I'm only 50!"

Although leaving school in her mid-teens, against regulations, Kate returned to education at various points in her career and took several courses that have qualified her as a youth coordinator. Hard as it might be for people who've only seen her vicious character in the ring to imagine, she began fostering children in her late 20s. She's also working on an autobiography. "I want to make it a book that isn't just for wrestling fans, but something that will appeal to the rest of the public, so it'll be more about my life rather than just concentrating on the business."

Klondyke Kate

Like many retired wrestlers, she misses the buzz of being in the ring. "I miss the thrill of winding people up and picking on fans!" But more than that, she misses the way wrestling brought about a transformation beyond literally switching from Jayne to Kate. "When I was working a show or backstage, I had so much more confidence. In wrestling you're surrounded by people who are like you, with the same sense of humour and the same way of thinking. It really was like having a bubble around me.

"In real life I'll speak up for myself, but I'm more quiet and I'll get upset if somebody says something about my size. In the ring I wasn't bothered at all by people staring at me and I didn't care what they thought or shouted. There's nothing -- not drugs, not sex -- that compares to the high of getting in the ring.

"I felt invincible."

# KUNG FU

"I'd tell any young wrestler starting out today not to wear a mask." Eddie Hamill made his name as the masked Kung Fu but now tells FSM that working under a hood isn't viable in the long run.

Born Edwin Hamill in 1943, he grew up in Northern Ireland, the son of a blacksmith in Belfast's Harland and Wolff's shipyard, birthplace of the Titanic among other less ill-fated ships. His father secured him an interview for a similar position but looking back over his career Hamill notes "I failed the interview -- thank god!"

It was sport rather than work that attracted Hamill's attention, initially through a keen interest in judo. After buying a "Teach Yourself Judo" book and practicing by throwing his brother on a makeshift mat made of coal in his back garden, he began training at a local YMCA. He later saw an advertisement in the Belfast Telegraph inviting would-be professional wrestlers to join a local gym. "I'd watched the likes of Mick McManus and Jackie Pallo on TV, but not really been a massive fan. However, when I saw the word 'professional', I thought 'there might be some money in this.'"

When Hamill arrived at the accurately named "The Pit" in the Sandy Row area of the city, he discovered the facilities were not quite what he associated with the word professional: "It was a right bloody hovel, a dingy old place." The training itself was no more glamorous, but Hamill's judo background proved invaluable. "They screwed us over on the mat because they wanted people who could take punishment. I'd been injured and hurt before, so that wasn't a problem. I'd never have even tried wrestling without knowing judo: it meant I already knew timing and how to fall when I was thrown so I was put in a more advanced class. In the end they could see I could take the pain and said 'right, you're in.'"

Hamill wasn't the only graduate of The Pit to turn pro. Eric 'Tug' Wilson was a contemporary, as was Dave Finlay Sr (father of the WWE wrestler and agent) who became one of Hamill's closest friends. By coincidence Finlay's own father had also worked at Harland and Wolff's where he is reputed to have wrestled for beer bets during his lunch breaks. Finlay told FSM that Hamill was "the most naturally gifted guys I know. Promoters didn't know how talented he was."

Finlay also believes Hamill could have been successful in mixed martial arts if he had come along a generation later. Having learned legitimate grappling moves in his training, Hamill says he would indeed have tried that form of combat if it existed at the time. "I'd have loved to have done UFC: it's a marvellous sport. While we did shooting in the gym, I only ever really used it in pubs when I'd take on guys who claimed what we did was all showmanship. I only ever had to go after another wrestler in the ring for real once. The promoter didn't know we had such a dislike for each other when he booked the match!"

Turning instead to the pro wrestling game, Hamill began working around Ireland, though shows in the Republic were largely confined to the border region where viewers could pick up ITV broadcasts and were familiar with the stars, and more importantly the concept of pro wrestling. During this time Hamill's pay was usually withheld by promoters to cover the cost of his training as students paid no money up front. "I'd only have been on about three quid a match anyway, so I didn't really mind!"

Despite a knockback when Joint Promotions' Arthur Green attended his third pro bout and declared he would never make it in the business, Hamill quickly improved. His most frequent opponent was Finlay, who was able to contrast the judo influence with his own combination of natural gymnastic ability and a newly found interest in amateur wrestling; after retirement Finlay became a keen advocate of coaching youngsters in the sport.

While Finlay opted to stay local rather than relocate his family, Hamill eventually decided to travel to the mainland where he settled in Rhyl, working as a lifeguard while building his pro career, starting with local promoter Orig Williams. The pair toured Turkey where Hamill recalls being introduced to a more outlandish side of the wrestling business.

Always on the lookout for some extra cash, Williams allegedly looked at the huge crowd on hand one night and decided it would be a smart idea to quietly book a second night in the venue and have it announced just before his scheduled main event against local hero Ordulu Mustafa that he was injured and the match had been postponed until the following evening. Told they would have to buy new tickets, the crowd opted not to call Trading Standards or write to Watchdog, but instead began smashing up wooden seating and starting a series of fires. (For his part, Williams claimed the Mustafa match did take place as scheduled and the trouble started with the cancellation of an advertised women's' bout.)

Hamill did get something from the trip beyond an education in the limits of crowd manipulation. "I met an army fellow who showed me a new martial art called Kung Fu. I thought to myself 'that's a bloody good gimmick." Having previously wrestled as "Judo" Mike Hamill and then under his own name, he eventually made the switch to the Kung Fu character, adding Chinese characters and designs to his judo-style ring jacket.

"A while later I saw a newspaper advert for a kung fu class where the guy in the photo was wearing a mask, the idea being the techniques were so secret he couldn't reveal his identity. I thought "that's another good gimmick: I'll nick that one too!"

The mask proved a success, despite initially causing confusion as previously hooded grapplers had nearly always been ring villains. Eleven years after Arthur Green's poor review, Hamill began working regularly for Joint Promotions and debuted on television against future tag partner Clive Myers. He protected his masked identity, leaving the venue unmasked and with his hair slicked back, a tactic that sometimes left him feeling guilty when he had to tell autograph-seeking children that Kung Fu had already gone home.

This did lead to an unfortunate incident when police officers knocked on his door and explained they were investigating an armed robbery at a post office and that he not only matched the description of the robber's stature, but that they were looking for a man with an Irish accent and a mask. Fortunately, Hamill's particular collection of hoods were distinctive enough that an identity parade was not required.

The success of the Kung Fu gimmick led to developments that explain Hamill's advice to young grapplers not to bother with a mask. "Eventually, if you're good enough, people will start to copy you. At one stage there were at least four imposters. Some of them were good wrestlers like Alan Miquet who was better than I was and I couldn't understand why he felt he had to do it. But other guys weren't so good and it really hurt me when people would go to see 'Kung Fu' and leave thinking 'That fellow's fucking rubbish!'"

At one show at Hanley's Victoria Hall, an impersonator had the misfortune to appear on the same bill as Hamill. Although he was working under his own name that night, he was carrying the knock-off ring gear in his bag. "It's a nasty thing to admit now and I do regret it," Hamill says "but I took out a knife I was carrying and slashed the mask and outfit to pieces. I remember Mick McMichael was in the dressing room at the time and when the other wrestlers heard what I'd done they asked him why he didn't stop me. He quite reasonably replied: 'Would you try to stop an angry Eddie Hamill who was carrying a knife?!'"

The imitation eventually came to a head when Hamill was wrestling at one of his favourite venues, the Liverpool Stadium. "I heard people in the crowd shouting 'That's not the real Kung Fu.' I thought 'It bloody well is!' and decided it was time to give it up."

On 24 March 1976, Hamill lost a match to Kendo Nagasaki at the Royal Albert Hall. An unspoken rule of British wrestling was that a masked man must unmask if he lost cleanly. This was sometimes given the condition that it only applied to TV matches, but not in this case: Hamill removed the mask.

While this was the most high-profile bout, according to Hamill, he actually lost the mask on several different occasions around the live event circuit over the next few weeks, with either Nagasaki or Mick McManus taking the prize. The change of appearance then went nationwide with a loss to McManus in Woking taped on 21 April and aired on ITV three days later, the bout ending in the memorable scene of McManus wearing the mask himself and looking a right plonker. (In an unusual twist, McManus was beating down Hamill after the final bell in a rematch two years later. Nagasaki, now unmasked himself but wearing sunglasses, made the memorable save.)

For the first few weeks after losing the mask, Hamill would wear it to the ring but take it off before the match: "It was meant to show I was indeed the real Kung Fu, but it seemed to confuse people, so I dropped the idea." Hamill did retain his martial arts ring gear and continued to work barefoot, something he was very comfortable with thanks to the judo background.

The barefoot style allowed him some creative moves such as gripping an opponent's fingers or even his ears between his toes. He also used his feet in a creative twist on Johnny Saint's routines, feeding his foot to a gullible opponent who, once grabbing the foot, would be caught up in a fast-paced series of rotations that saw them end up on the floor in a headlock.

Ironically Saint himself had fallen victim to an unfortunate incident wrestling Hamill back when he did wear boots. Hamill tried to jazz up the look by spraying them with silver paint, but the paint didn't dry as anticipated and Saint returned from the ring after their match resembling a very low budget version of a living statue street performer.

Hamill went on to increase his popularity on TV in the tag team scene, first partnering Pete Roberts as the Kung Fu Fighters, then pairing with Clive Myers as the Martial Artists. This led to the strangest booking of his career when music group Manhattan Transfer contacted promoters and asked for two grapplers to appear in a promotional video. "Me and Clive turned up and wrestled on a bare mat for three minutes while the band played live behind us. There was also some weird storyline with a coffin that I didn't understand. I've never seen the video, but as we did the whole thing in two takes, it was a damn good payoff for six minutes' work!"

He later followed a raft of grapplers in leaving Joint Promotions to work for Brian Dixon's All-Star Wrestling and is straightforward about his motivations. "It was for the money, plain and simple. We were in wrestling for the money, not the glory." Although it meant giving up the biggest paydays, £60 for a televised match and £100 for headlining the Royal Albert Hall, All Star was paying double his basic match fee. "Between TV and the Albert Hall, you're only getting the 'big' money once or twice a month; the nightly jobs were your bread and butter."

The move didn't mean an end to TV exposure as Hamill appeared on cable channel Screensport along with other All-Star talent, and made several appearances for Orig Williams' Reslo show on S4C, the Welsh version of Channel 4. His international journeys continued, taking him to Africa, the Middle East and most memorably to Sicily. "We wrestled in Palermo where there was always a mysterious man on hand at every show. It turned out he was from the Mafia and collected a cut of the takings. So indirectly we were working for the Mafia, though as their cut didn't come out of our payoffs, we were happy!"

Hamill had previously toured Stampede twice, teaming with Bret Hart and Davey Boy Smith. He was asked to revive the mask for these tours, eventually dropping it to the Dynamite Kid. Hamill didn't particularly enjoy these tours, struggling to adjust to both the altitude and the fact that the absence of the rounds system meant he didn't have breaks every few minutes to catch his breath.

While work in the US wasn't on the cards ("I didn't have a work permit, and I was only about 12 and a half stone, so I wasn't big enough for the promoters to want to get me one), it's perhaps more surprising that Hamill was never offered any tours to Japan where his ring style might have been a good fit. Then again, "I'd have been a white fellow doing a martial arts gimmick in Japan, so I don't think it would really have worked!"

Hamill finally hung up his boots in 1990 as injuries took their toll and he began to fear being put out of action and left unable to earn. He returned to his full-time lifeguard role at Rhyl where he made national news with an impassioned plea for holidaymakers to avoid using inflatable dinghies at sea. Although he would have liked to open his own wrestling training school, knee problems prevented him from doing so.

While Hamill doesn't miss the injuries, he does miss the backstage atmosphere. "I went to a show in Rhyl recently and couldn't believe it when I went in the dressing room: all the wrestlers were sat there staring at the floor and there was no personality. When we were wrestling we were like a bunch of kids and there was always somebody up to something, whether it be playing pranks or telling jokes.

"Steve Logan [partner of Mick McManus] always used to crack me up with his droll comments. On the coach to one show Mark Rocco of all people was pointing out the window to a field and saying how beautiful the lambs were. Logan waited long enough to drawn on his pipe, then just drily uttered 'Yeah... with mint sauce.' Another time a wrestler was going on and on about how his backside was in a horrendous state because he'd had a particularly hot curry. Logan paused for effect and then said, 'You fool, you're meant to eat it, not stick it up your arse.'"

Kung Fu

Dave Finlay Sr remembers that Hamill himself was happy to take part in pranks, particularly where the victim was deserving. "This one guy was living proof that the easiest part of your body to grow is your head: he was so big-headed it barely fit through the door. We hid a sanitary towel in his trunks and kept quiet as he walked about with the strings hanging out the back.

"Another time a guy was making a song and dance demanding to be allowed to wrestle earlier on the show than scheduled so he could make a sharp exit. While he was in the ring we switched all the clothes in his bag and managed to find stuff that looked the same but was much smaller. He was far too confused to get off home early!"

Today Hamill relives those days as a regular at the various annual British wrestler reunions. As he told FSM Editor Brian Elliott in 2008, "We talk about those good times, and all those things we did... I guess I miss the in-ring stuff a little, but I miss the dressing-room camaraderie and fun with the other wrestlers even more so than that."

And while Hamill is more than satisfied with the way his career went, Finlay Senior maintains he could have been even bigger on the international stage: "Without doubt, he could have been a star anywhere he went, including WWE, but I respect that he chose to stay at home with his family and be happy. He was a pioneer of moves seen today and talent-wise, nobody could touch him."

# LEN IRONSIDE

From an early age, the writing was on the wall for Len Ironside's lifetime fascination with the wrestling business. Literally so as his uncle was a signwriter whose weekly tasks included updating the display board at the Aberdeen Music Hall each week with details of the main event contest at the next wrestling show.

The perks of the job included free entry to the shows, with the pre-teen Ironside allowed in without charge as long as he sat on his uncle's shoulders. The only downside to this deal was that said uncle would usually enjoy a few interval drinks and be unable to continue the arrangement for the second half of the show.

Having decided he wanted to be a pro but with no obvious road in to business, Ironside later began hitchhiking from Aberdeen to Perth each weekend for amateur training. He competed in a series of amateur bouts as well as taking part in various Highland Games open competitions.

The amateur training led to a meeting with Scottish lightweight legend and perennial world champion George Kidd who, along with Joe D'Orazio, showed him the professional ropes. When Kidd deemed Ironside experienced enough to earn his recommendation, he helped set up a debut bout in 1973 at the Eldorado Stadium in Edinburgh under promoter Max Crabtree.

Ironside recalls being "thrilled to bits" to debut at arguably the most prestigious venue in Scotland, though in his bout with Dave Ramsden he struggled to win the crowd's approval. That was partly because he adopted an aggressive style but largely because, despite being from Yorkshire, Ramsden was part of the Eldorado All-Stars. A Crabtree creation, this was the wrestling equivalent of a 'home team' that would take on outsiders in a series of matches across an evening, creating a partisan and often overheated atmosphere.

While the crowd reaction wasn't initially warm, Ironside impressed his peers enough to be invited back and start a series of regular appearances on the Scottish circuit, this time in a more heroic role. As one of the shorter wrestlers on the scene, he found that catchweight bouts against heavier villain opponents worked better for crowd appeal.

"Speed was the thing I used, and I loved to run rings round them and it was easier if they were bigger and heavier when I'm nipping through their legs, jumping over their backs, tripping them up." Indeed, even with an unfamiliar crowd, having a size difference meant "they would look and say right away 'We know who we support there.'"

Although he wrestled regularly, Ironside maintained a day job working on benefits management for what was then the Department of Health and Social Security. It was a deliberate decision based on the experience of others. "I had known about Clayton Thompson who when he first wrestled broke his leg in his first match and he couldn't wrestle for months. Nobody paid him, he'd no income, and nobody insured wrestlers in those days. So I thought 'Right, I'll keep on a job so if anything does happen, I've got a fall-back position.'"

With the long distances on the Scottish circuit, it meant some short nights. "I used to travel in the car with an alarm clock so if I ever felt tired I could sleep in the car for a bit and have the alarm wake me and then I'd get shooting up the road again. It was just something I got used to. In fact, even today I find it difficult to sleep early in the evening; it has to be early morning before I go to bed because you just get used to that travelling around."

In 1976 Ironside made his TV debut in a 2-1 loss to Jim Breaks. It was the deciding bout in a Scotland vs England series put on to coincide with the two nations clashing in an annual football match that was in those days a major rivalry. (The following year's game infamously ended with triumphant Scottish fans invading the Wembley pitch and destroying the goalposts.) Despite the wrestling show coming from Sheffield, it was the Scots who had the support of the crowd, which Ironside recalls was an unusual occurrence: "People like Andy Robin, they were really just Scottish wrestlers because in England they were looked on as villains, they weren't really looked on as heroes."

The small-screen exposure helped Ironside's recognition when he wrestled occasional dates in Northern England, but it would be his only TV appearance. During the ITV years wrestling was rarely if ever televised from Scotland, partly because of promotional politics, but also largely because venues needed to be conveniently located for ITV film crews who would be coming from or going to other sports events.

While Scotland's biggest star George Kidd made a conscious decision not to wrestle much on television (believing the fixed payoffs did not reflect the value star wrestlers brought to the show), Scottish wrestlers were underrepresented on TV thanks to the logistics of them travelling to venues where shows were recorded.

"A number of guys that we wrestled didn't really make it big. One of the guys that I think was grossly underrated was Jimmy McKenzie, who when I started wrestling was the lightweight champion of Scotland. Jimmy was a fantastic character and had an unusual style. He didn't get the recognition for what he did.

Maybe Bill Ross should have got more recognition for what he did because he was a fantastic wrestler."

In the following years, Ironside had a change of employer with Max Crabtree leaving Scotland to take over Joint Promotions nationally and Brian Dixon taking the opportunity to begin running some of the abandoned venues. According to Ironside, it was a different experience.

"Brian was much better at it: his shows were good, good top of the bills, good exciting shows. He was a joy to work for and he never stung me of any money or anything like that: he was straightforward. I found him good to work with.

"Max was slightly different. Max was a ruthless businessman, you had to admire his business skills because he made money for himself but for nobody else unfortunately! He put on good bills as well, but it seemed he did better before he took over Joint Promotions because he was a struggling promoter then and he was fighting for everything. When he took over Joint and had a wealth of people to deal with, it didn't seem to work the same for him."

Ironside also worked for independent promoters such as Orig Williams and Jackie Pallo, who he recalls favourably. "One of the bouts we had to go to was cancelled but he paid for our flights and paid us the money as if we'd been there and I thought that was a decent thing to do, a really decent thing to do. I suppose not everybody had the same experience with Jackie Pallo, but he was fair and straight with me and that's the only way I can judge him."

While Scottish wrestlers in the late 70s and early 80s in particular would jump back and forth between promoters, officially anyone working dates for Joint Promotions was strictly barred from working for the opposition. "If you worked for anyone else they would sack you and I worked for a group of [independent] guys from Dundee. They were struggling guys, they would never be stars but they were good in their own way and they liked having me on the shows and I had a good friendship with them." Wanting to work with the likes of an up-and-coming Chic Cullen, Ironside got round his employment difficulties by donning a mask as The Avenger. "I really didn't like wearing it and I had to change my style to not be recognised, but I think I got away with it: nobody said anything."

Another potential gimmick change was not to be, despite fellow grappler Alan Dennison arguing that Ironside's distinctive eyes presented an opportunity. "He was full of ideas was Alan, quite a character and a lovely man. He thought 'If you could put this yellow dye on yourself and crop your hair really short, you could pass for a Chinaman and we could call you the Chinese champion.' I rejected that! You can just imagine [the dye running off] when you're sweating in the ring!"

Outside of the ring, Ironside began a lengthy run as a councillor in Aberdeen. "I've always been interested in politics, particularly in the politics of working people, and if anything goes wrong it's always working people who suffer. I had

Len Ironside

that attitude from an early age and I joined the Labour party. I was invited to stand as a candidate, I accepted, and it was 35 years before I decided to pack it in."

During that time Ironside found his wrestling background did offer some help. "You do get the confidence, it does build that confidence in you. It gives you a feeling of what's going on because you do hear from a different group in society of things they come across, things they hear. It does give you a wider view of life having travelled and so on."

There was one occasion where the two parts of his life did directly cross over. "At the Aberdeen Music Hall the ring was placed on the stage so one side of the ring had a seven foot drop beneath the ring. One opponent threw me over the top rope, so I landed just completely falling down about 12 feet, landed on my back winded. When somebody fell out of the ring, the crowd used to rush and pick them up and throw them back in.

"As I'm being picked up to be thrown back in, this woman said to me 'Is there any word on that house you were getting me yet?' I just thought that's incredible, how could anyone think that [was a good time]: that's so Aberdonian!"

As well as winning nine consecutive elections, Ironside spent a decade leading the Labour group on the council and four years leading the council itself. He notes the nature of the work changed dramatically during his time. "There's much more politics in local government now. I think there's much more interference from national government in local councils. At one time it really was just about local issues but now there's a political line to it that takes you into having to put in the politics of the government of the day. That's not helpful because you can't have a one-size-fits-all with local government."

The 1980s brought several in-ring highlights. In 1980 he beat Tony Borg for the vacant British Commonwealth middleweight title. He went on to exchange the championship with arguably his greatest in-ring rival Mike Bennett. "I think Mike Bennett was so underrated. Any of those matches with him would have been great because we did everything: we did last man standing, [we had bloodbaths], we did a straight match with no villainy at all. He was a guy I respect."

He also had a world lightweight title match against Johnny Saint in Aberdeen which was an exception to his preferred 'David vs Goliath' format. "It was just holds and counters and the people loved that because they were clued up on wrestling. They'd come to shout and bawl at the bad guys, but they enjoyed some clever stuff too."

Ironside originally retired in 1992 but made an unlikely comeback in 2014 at the age of 58 for the WrestleZone promotion. "I wrestled a young guy in his mid-20s, Aspen Faith, who was quite a clever wrestler actually. It was a challenge [to me] to see if I could keep up with this young guy. I thought if I could do maybe 10 minutes it would be fine, but I managed at least 20 minutes, so it was a great night and I enjoyed it.

"I lost two stone in weight in preparation. I was doing a lot of running to lose weight for that match; and I did train hard for it and I really enjoyed that. I was quite surprised how well I did in that ring, the amount of time we did.

"I think people generally underestimate that wrestlers are very skilful people, very fit people - they have to be fit. They're quite clever and athletic in their own way and they never get the credit for that. If you run out of steam in the middle of a bout, that's the loneliest place in the world."

Ironside then had his final match the following year teaming with Bob Holly against Faith and Johnny Lions. Today he keeps a keen interest in the Scottish wrestling scene and is hoping to open an amateur club in Aberdeen, noting that "It's just in your blood: you can't leave it."

Len Ironside

# LES KELLETT

"If he liked you, you got a good match. If he didn't, by god you got a bad match." That's how Les Kellett is remembered by frequent opponent Mel Stuart and it's indicative of a man whose reputation as one of the hardest in the wrestling industry oversimplifies a far more complex individual.

Although at least a couple of people in the industry believe he shaved a few years off his age, Kellett's obituaries record him as having been born in 1915. He was born and bred in Laisterdike, a suburb of Bradford close to the "border" with Leeds. After training in engineering, he went into the merchant navy, which was a commercial rather than military occupation.

Writing in his autobiography Sadist In Sequins, Adrian Street recalled Kellett telling him of an experience during this period that would shape his character and approach to life. Confronted by a would-be attacker late at night in a dockyard, Kellett used his experience from a brief spell at an amateur wrestling club to pin the man down. Kellett then told the thug that if he promised to behave in future, he would let him go without further incident. The thug made such a promise, only to wait until Kellett released his grip, kick him in the groin and unleash a violent assault that knocked Kellett out.

According to Street, Kellett explained the lesson he learned was that "You've got to hurt them for them to know they've been beaten." It was a philosophy he would later unleash on would-be grapplers unlucky enough to meet Kellett at a professional try out.

His own professional career was rudely interrupted: after learning the basics from a friend who was already in the business, Kellett debuted in 1938 and quickly had to put wrestling on hold when the second world war broke out. Eddie 'Kung Fu' Hamill explains that this too shaped his attitude to life.

"When we were wrestling together, there was a referee who Les absolutely hated and I could never understand why. It turned out the referee used to be a military policeman. Les had spent some time in a military prison for refusing to fight and was given a particularly hard time." (In other tellings of the story, Kellett reportedly said he was happy to fight but refused to wear a uniform.)

Following the war, Kellett returned to the wrestling business, this time trying to get regular bookings from local promoter Norman Morrell, who'd go on to spearhead Joint Promotions. Accounts of Kellett's try-out vary, but the most common version is that he had to legitimately wrestle Arthur Belshaw and wound up with his finger bent backwards. Told that he would have to submit to avoid having the finger broken, Kellett simply said to go on and break it.

In some accounts Morrell himself had the hold on and it was an arm rather than a finger, though it's certainly possible this may have been a separate incident. In any case, it appears Kellett was let go with his bones intact and his reputation cemented.

Morell certainly appeared to take to Kellett, not only giving him work in the ring, but also making him a popular referee in one of his key venues, St James' Hall in Newcastle, where Kellett also took on local organizational duties.

Kellett debuted on television in September 1957, though only made occasional appearances over the next few years. He was a skilled technical performer: Tony Walsh says, "I would put him right up there with the likes of Eric Taylor," referring to the first British heavy-middleweight champion, a hugely respected grappler with submission expertise.

But Kellet's reputation went beyond the ring, and as an interview segment in the "Best of ITV Wrestling" DVD showed, it had a consistent theme. "He was probably the hardest man ever in the wrestling business," said Jackie Pallo. "A hard nut. A very hard nut," was Mick McManus's take. And Max Crabtree believed that "He was a hard man, hard in every way."

Speaking in the same segment, Kellett himself said that "I was hard in this respect: I wouldn't stand any nonsense from them. That wasn't just in the ring, that was in the dressing room."

Indeed, there are numerous tales of Kellett's toughness, among the most gruesome being when he suffered a hand infection and, after the hand swelled with a build-up of pus, demanded another wrestler stamp upon it to burst the foul pocket.

Street wrote that he believed Kellett, although undoubtedly tough, went out of his way to do things the hard way to boost his reputation as somebody to be feared. He noted it was so effective that at one stage wrestlers had a genuine debate about who would win a fight between Kellett and Georges Gordienko, who no less than Lou Thesz ranked as a contender for the world's greatest legitimate grappler.

Johnny Kincaid tells FSM that he believes Kellett had a genuine physical condition that meant he didn't feel pain in the same way as others. "We were staying overnight in Plymouth and a guy was causing a nuisance of himself in the bar. He started talking to us and then said to Les that 'Now I know it's all fixed:

how can an old fucker like you wrestle?' Les grabbed him and held his face to a radiator. I went to break it up but Les just looked at me with [an expression] of evilness, so I went back to the bar.

"The next morning, he came down to breakfast and I noticed a huge burn running down his arm. I pointed it out and he hadn't even noticed it. I don't think he really felt pain. That's partly why he was such a good wrestler!"

Kellett's reputation built in the dressing room, partly as a result of his eccentric behaviour. "He was an odd fellow," Hamill recalls. "He'd sit there in his pants reading the paper. I think half the time he did it just to get a reaction." Stuart has a slightly different take however: "He was very quiet and liked to sit there and read books. He'd really only have a problem if you invaded his privacy."

Kincaid noted that although Kellett could be stand-offish in a crowd, that tension quickly disappeared when he was in a one-to-one situation with somebody he trusted. Several wrestlers recall Kellett having some unlikely interests including collecting tarot cards and touring car boot fairs looking for toy steam engines and fire engines. He also ran a transport cafe near Bradford named The Terminus, along with a smallholding farm.

A common theme among wrestlers who worked with Kellett is that he quickly made up his mind whether or not he liked somebody and then stuck to that belief. That wasn't always the case, however, as Hamill explains.

"Another wrestler had been winding me up about Les's attitude towards me and eventually I decided to stand up to Les and offered him out to fight. The next day he came down to breakfast and I was convinced we were going to go at it. Instead he put his arms around me and said, 'I can tell you and I are going to be friends.' I think he respected me for being willing to stand up against him.

"Some time later we were sat in a restaurant and I saw a wrestler who'd done the dirty on me once and we'd fallen out. I mentioned this to Les and he simply got up, walked past the guy and pulled his chair right out from under him. That's how strong he was."

Kincaid notes that earlier in his career Kellett had a reputation for taking his curmudgeonly attitude into the ring. "He almost rode himself out of the business because people didn't want to work with him and sometimes wouldn't even turn up if they were booked against him. [The story was] if you accidentally poked him in a match, it was time to get out of the ring because he was going to hurt you. He had these big calloused hands and fingers like bananas and even broke [referee] Max Ward's jaw just by slapping him."

Despite his reputation, there's only one account of Kellett actually fighting a wrestler in the locker room, with Jackie Pallo describing his futile attempts to break up a brawl between Kellett and Clayton Thomson. Perhaps not so coincidentally, a TV match Kellett and Thomson is recalled by long-time fans as particular violent, as was another with Peter Rann.

Those matches stand out even more considering that when Kellett really made his name, it was as a comedy performer: indeed, the contrast between Kellett's persona in and out of the ring is a key part of the enduring interest in his career.

The comedy wrestling appears to have developed after a bout in the late 1950s against heavyweight Sheamus Dunleavy in which Kellett felt he was taking too much legitimate punishment. Eventually Kellett began ducking out of the way of the mighty Irishman's blows, only to discover the crowd found his evasion hilarious. He made it a key part of his routine, taking advantage of his truly impeccable timing that allowed him to continue as a star performer into his 50s and beyond.

Stuart notes this part of the routine was no act. "The way he could do it was completely genuine. You'd go in to link up for the referee's hold and at the last moment he'd suddenly be out of the way."

Kellett expanded the comedy routine by developing bouts of selective deafness when the bell ran for the end of the round and he had the advantage. He also came up with an eye-catching move in which he would appear to fall backwards between the ropes and be headed for a dangerous tumble to the floor, only to rebound into a surprise headbutt.

It's a move British-born grappler Nigel McGuiness borrowed decades later, modifying it to end with a running clothesline. He tells FSM it led to a more unintentional comedy experience. "I always called it the 'Les Kellet lariat' and no one [in Ring of Honor] could understand what I was saying so they called it the 'let's kill it lariat'."

Kellett was also a huge influence on Colt Cabana, who has often noted Kellett stood out on tapes he viewed during his early British tours and led to his own adoption of a comedic in-ring style. In an interview with the Huffington Post, Cabana noted of Kellett that "the way he manipulated a crowd with comedy is one of the most beautiful things I've seen in my life." So enamoured was Cabana that he even commissioned US artist Rob Schamberger to produce a painting of Kellett.

So popular was the act that Kellett became a regular on the small screen from 1964 onwards including a run from 1969 to 1974 when he averaged more than one appearance a month (making him the most featured performer) and appeared on three FA Cup Final day spectaculars in the space of four years.

Arguably his biggest individual bout came in May 1969 when he wrestled Mick McManus as half of a double-header with Jackie Pallo vs George Kidd at the end-of-season show at the Royal Albert Hall. That said, Kellett was more of a special attraction than a wrestler engaged in more traditional feuds or title chases. Perhaps his best remembered match was in fact a 1974 TV clash with Leon Arras (better known as actor Brian Glover) that is certainly a contender for the greatest ever comedy-based wrestling match.

That's not to say crowds saw Kellett as a novelty however. Mel Stuart notes he was "always top of the bill" and an attraction on the level of Big Daddy. Tony Walsh goes as far as to call him "the biggest draw in the country. A phenomenal crowd puller. Unbelievable."

With that ability to sell tickets, Kellett was free from the usual stranglehold that promoters had over their talent, giving him a power he happily exploited when he felt it appropriate. Stuart recalls an incident when, upset by something a promoter had said, Kellett ordered the bus carrying the Dale Martin crew to a show to stop and simply walked out and made his own way home without explanation.

Eddie Hamill notes Kellett could be particularly obstinate with promoters he disliked, giving the example of a promoter who asked, "Could you go on last tonight?" and got the dry reply, "Yes, I could. But I'm not going to." He also recalls that Kellett could be particularly smart when getting his revenge.

"Les was wrestling at Bradford Town Hall. The promoters there had treated him like shit during the many years before he became a star and he decided tonight he was going to get his own back. The hall was packed and before the show started he walked out to the ring and began pulling the ropes and banging on the canvas as if he was checking the ring.

"He then came back to the dressing room, said 'I don't think I'm going to work tonight', and walked out. Of course, all the fans had seen him, so the promoters were stuffed: they couldn't just pretend he was injured or stuck in traffic."

Kellett didn't just use his status for his own benefit, however. Hearing that Stuart had received no extra pay for not only refereeing a Kellett-Marino bout, but carrying out a gee (a British term for what American wrestlers call an angle) to build up a future show, Kellett took it upon himself to persuade Dale Martin's office figure Mike Judd to make sure a bonus was in Stuart's next pay packet.

Eventually it seems Kellett tired of battling Joint Promotions and decided to move over to the independent circuit where it was certainly possible to make a decent living if you had already established yourself as a TV star. That was the case for Kellett, despite the fact that his last Joint Promotions match came at the end of 1975 when he was now 60 years old. He had made at least one appearance for an "opposition" show before formally leaving Joint and there's some dispute about the exact circumstances of his departure.

Kellett continued wrestling until 1983, working shows for promoters including Jackie Pallo, Brian Dixon, Orig Williams and the Klondyke brothers. Although his physical condition and timing both had an inevitable decline, it seems his comedy-based ring style certainly helped him carry on much longer than if he'd stuck to more traditional grappling.

He maintained his power over promoters, in particular insisting on choosing which wrestlers he worked with rather than take the risk of getting in the ring with an unknown grappler who, particularly on the independent circuit, might lack experience. This wasn't necessarily bad news for the promoters however: not only did it ensure Kellett was comfortable in his performance, but in any case, his ring style meant he was best suited to working with particular types of grappler, specifically those who could afford to look foolish in the ring and still maintain their heat.

At least one independent promoter has noted Kellett wasn't always a headache and in fact once insisted on taking a lower payoff than originally agreed when the crowd proved disappointingly small.

On several shows, mainly in the north of England, Kellett was accompanied by a young grappler Dave Barrie who was in fact his son. That Barrie wrestled under a false name was far from unusual: on the British circuit it was usually considered that whatever benefit would come to the son from the family name would be outweighed by the risk that the audience would come to view the father as much older than they realised.

Barrie died unexpectedly young in 2000. In the same year Kellett moved into a nursing home in Ilkley, around 12 miles from Bradford, where he died in 2002 aged 86.

Les Kellett's reputation as a hard man to be feared has lived on, aided in part by his portrayal in Simon Garfield's 1995 book The Wrestling which included numerous stories from his peers, many of them negative, along with a linking device throughout the book of Garfield's failed attempts to persuade Kellett to be interviewed.

Many have commented on the disparity between the clown prince of the canvas and the hard man of the dressing room, but it appears Kellett was a more nuanced, if no less memorable, character. As Johnny Kincaid puts it, "He was a cantankerous old soul, but there was a nice part about him."

# MAL KIRK

It's a well-worn cliché that wrestling villains are often the most pleasant people in real life, but by every account this was most certainly the case with ring ruffian Mal Kirk.

Manager and commentator Dean Ayass recalls an experience from his youth that illustrates Kirk's ability to distort reality. "When I was about seven my dad took me to the wrestling at the Brighton Dome. The Dome complex is situated right next to the Royal Pavilion and we were walking through the Pavilion Gardens when I spotted big Mal Kirk sitting on his own on a bench. I was too scared to approach him, but my dad assured me it'd be OK, and he started to talk to Mal, who smiled and was really nice to me. I remember that he was facing Big Daddy on TV in the coming weeks and he asked me how I thought he'd get on. I replied, 'Big Daddy will put you in hospital!' and he roared with laughter, smiled again and ruffled my hair. He was just a lovely man and obviously great with kids.

"Yet when he came out for his singles match on the show, he was such an amazing villain that I just got caught up in the atmosphere of the crowd and booed him relentlessly. King Kong Kirk was a million miles away from the pleasant gentleman Mal Kirk that I'd met just a couple of hours beforehand. It's a memory that has stuck in my head over 30 years later."

Indeed, Kirk's daughter Natasha later recalled hearing stories of his frustration at going out for a quiet pint only to have a "good guy" wrestler enter the pub: on orders of promoters, he would be required to start a slanging match and even throw his drink at any future opponent.

Kirk began his sporting career in rugby league, one of the few professions other than wrestling where a cauliflower ear is an occupational hazard. He played for several Yorkshire-based teams between 1955 and the early 60s, most frequently for his home side of Featherstone Rovers. However, he is perhaps best remembered in the rugby community for a spell at Doncaster where he formed what must be the only front row made up entirely of future wrestlers.

The prop on one side was George Goodyear, a man who at that time was bulkier than the future behemoth Kirk. Indeed, club folklore has it that he wore the number 8 shirt (rather than the other prop option of 10) as this made it easier to sew together two jerseys to produce something that could fit his frame.

The central position was taken by Ted Heath, who was no relation to the future Prime Minister, but instead was said to be the son-in-law of another grappler named John Foley, with whom he teamed in the United States as the original 'British Bulldogs' team. Heath's position on the field was hooker, which ironically described his wrestling skills after a spell at the notorious Snake Pit gym.

Kirk completed the trio, though it was his mother who was at the centre of two much-discussed incidents. She was known for bringing an umbrella to the games to stand by the entrance tunnel and point to players that she believed Kirk should target with game-ending tackles. Doncaster fanatic Geoff Roebuck recalls one occasion when, at the end of the game, the umbrella was redeployed to chastise Kirk, the mother being upset that the opposing team had emerged unscathed.

Meanwhile wrestler John Cox retells the story of the time it was Kirk who left the field early. "He'd been sent off and had just got to the touchline when his mother told him to get back on. He turned round and walked back at which point the referee asked him what he was doing. Mal said his mum had told him to stay on and the referee took a look at her and said, 'OK then, you'd best stay!'"

When he moved into the grappling game, Kirk initially wrestled as 'Mucky' Mal Kirk, carrying a lamp to the ring and presenting himself as a coal miner from Pontefract. The name stuck behind the scenes, but in time he refined the in-ring image, being known at various stages as Killer Kirk, King Kong Kirk and even Kojak Kirk during the height of popularity of the TV show with a similarly shaven-headed detective.

After a spell on the independent circuit (including working on shows produced by future opponent Shirley 'Big Daddy' Crabtree), Kirk joined the books of Joint Promotions in 1967, making his TV debut against Albert 'Rocky' Wall two years later. He soon became a TV regular, earning a strong reputation behind the scenes for his agility and stamina, while fans of the era remember him standing out by not selling a whip to the cornerpost that would normally result in wrestlers clutching their back and feign fighting for wind. As evidence of his standing among promoters, he even earned a win over headliner Mike Marino en route to losing the final of the 1971 Royal Albert Hall tournament."

Mac 'Scrubber Daly' Hardiman, at one time a regular partner when Kirk had bulked up, recalls that "He did his share in the ring. Somebody like Giant Haystacks was so big that he couldn't do a lot and you'd have to work most of the match as his partner, but Mal could even roll up like lightweights and end up on his feet."

Meanwhile Dave Taylor notes coming off worse in a cardio battle. "He was a giant of a man, about 28 stone to me at 17 stone, but I couldn't keep up with him.

Mal Kirk

He used to challenge you to see how many times he could take an armdrag. The problem was that he could do it 10 or 15 times in a row and by then you'd be blown up!"

Kirk was also known for his ability to deliver a seemingly devastating 'guillotine' elbow-drop to the floor without any serious impact. Indeed, noted fan of snug-but-safe performances Bret Hart wrote in his autobiography about the experience of taking on Kirk in his first ever match in the UK. "Kirk turned out to be a great worker and bump-taker, and when he collapsed on top of me, he was as light as if he'd covered me with a blanket."

A skilled British heavyweight in Kirk's era was always in international demand and he made several trips abroad. In the early 70s he wrestled for Stampede Wrestling as well as the All Star Wrestling group that promoted in Western Canada and Washington state, and made several appearances in California. Notable opponents included Greg Valentine, the Wild Samoans and the future Sgt Slaughter, Bob Remus. (There's also an unconfirmed report of a run as 'The Mummy' in the Southwest territory around San Antonio in 1984.)

He was also a regular on the European tournament circuit and toured India and Africa, sparking off a series of memories from his fellow travellers. Dave Taylor recalls sharing a room with Kirk in India. "In the middle of the night his bed broke: the headboard stayed in place, but the bed was sloping down to the floor. I asked if he wanted to move the mattress flat on the floor, but he said 'Nah, I'll be right lad, I'll stay as I am.' When he woke up in the morning, his head had turned blue from sleeping on a slope!"

Meanwhile John Cox remembers an unwieldy incident in Dortmund. "We had to walk back from the hotel for some reason and Mal was complaining because he was so big, his thighs were chafing. We came to a big road where you had to come off and go a bit out of your way to an underpass, but he was so fed up he said there wasn't much traffic and he'd rather run across. The problem was it was so dark than we didn't know there was a big fence in between the two carriageways. So we end up sat there in the middle of the night in the dark and I'm having to lift him right up, so he can get over the fence!"

Cox also noted a memorable, if not entirely politically correct image in Zambia. "He'd disappeared, and we wondered where he was. It turned out he'd gone off with Crusher Mason and they both came back on a jeep. It was an old German army model from World War II and had a raised platform at the back, so they were stood higher up than the driver." Suffice to say, when the former army jeep came round a corner into view, the pair were both giving an appropriate – or rather inappropriate – salute.

Another African adventure came in Egypt where Kirk and Taylor were among a crew who were looking for a traditional tourist experience – albeit one not usually suited to the bulkiest holidaymakers. "We all wanted a camel ride, but there were only so many and there were none left for Mal. Instead he went off on another trip on one of these horses they call dancing horses. When we came back later Mal was stood there and said 'The bloody thing was supposed to dance but I got on and it just went... uuuuuuuuurgh.'"

Kirk didn't just wrestle in Africa but also had a role in the Italian comedy film "Io sto con gli ippopotami" (I'm for the Hippopotomus) that was set in the continent. After appearing alongside boxer Joe Bugner and stars Terence Hill and Bud Spencer, he took a liking to safari suits and picked one up in South Africa, as Taylor explains.

"I picked him up in Featherstone for a drive to Nuremberg, about a thousand miles, and he decided to wear the suit the whole way there. It was white when we left... when we got there he'd spilled so much food and dirt on it, it looked like he had a row of medals!"

Kirk was also known for his post-show entertainment. As Tony St Clair put it, "He was very boisterous: it was always party time after a show." Others recalled that he would get up to sing anytime the crew were in a venue with a stage and he would even play drums if a kit was available.

Even on quieter nights in the UK, Kirk liked a post-match pint according to Hardiman. "He was always happy if he could get back after the show in time for a pint of Tetley's. Back then you could only get it up north, so for him it was a good night if he made it back to a pub or club for the last pint."

Travelling around the UK also presented opportunities for amusement according to Marty Jones. "There was a time when we were all into CB radio to keep ourselves occupied while driving. Mal's handle was 'Chicken Legs' and he'd get into it with all the truckers until they started getting riled up and threatening to sort it out at the next services. They'd pull up and come out ready for a fight with the image of this 'Chicken Legs' character in mind only to back away when Mal stepped out of the car!"

Taylor notes that Kirk was a particularly trusty travelling partner. "If I had no vehicle, he'd come 30 or 40 miles out of his way just to pick me up. One time I was going to Austria and taking a caravan with me because I was staying for the season. Even though I was going from Rotterdam to Vienna stuck at 50 miles an hour, about 20 hours altogether, he followed me the whole way."

Inside the ring, Kirk developed into a true monster heel, growing a small patch of hair on the side of his head to add to his unusual appearance. Hardiman explains that "He should have been world champion: he had it all, looked the part and could do the job. Just the look he'd give would make people shudder. You know people would like to have said 'What the hell has he grown that odd bit of hair for?' but he just had one of those looks that could make people think 'Oh shit.'"

Kirk put on a substantial amount of weight in his later years and became known as one of a line of monster heels who were built up to – unsuccessfully – challenge Big Daddy. Appropriately he was a successor of sorts to Hardiman in this lineage: the unmasking of Scrubber Daly was immediately followed by an unusual 'run-in' with manager Charlie McGee introducing Kirk and Tiny Gallaghan as his next contenders.

Daly and Kirk also teamed on the live event circuit, with Hardiman recalling "he really did help me. He was one of the most underrated in the world." On one occasion Kirk kept some of his experience to himself however.

"We were teaming at Hanley where you come out on the stage to climb into the ring. It was my first time there and Mal said 'I'll come out on the right and you come out on the left.' I asked why, and he insisted 'Just walk out on the left.'

"I did so and suddenly felt a bang on the back of my head. It turned out this old woman had a jar of Vaseline in her handbag and she'd always sit in the same place and lean over the balcony to crack a wrestler on the head. I looked over at Mal and he was nearly wetting himself."

Unfortunately, it would be Kirk's final match with Big Daddy that would be his most memorable, for all the wrong reasons. Teaming with King Kendo against Daddy and Greg Valentine (Daddy's nephew) in Great Yarmouth on 24 August 1987, Kirk fell unconscious at the end of the match and died at the venue. Though media coverage at the time questioned whether Daddy's finishing splash was somehow responsible for the death, a pathologist concluded he had an existing heart condition. Many wrestlers who spoke to FSM recalled their shock and genuine feelings of devastation upon hearing of the loss of a man who had only just turned 50.

The combination of the press interest, awkwardness in the industry about how to address the question of whether Kirk and Daddy were legitimately competing to win, and complaints by Kirk's widow about his low payoffs left an unpleasant tone in the subsequent coverage and somewhat overshadowed his career in the public's eye.

Kirk's daughter Natasha was just three years old at the time of his death and thus has only a few memories of his life. However, she has since begun trying to find out more about his times both in and out of the ring, attending wrestling reunions. Earlier this year she visited the Leeds reunion (organised by FSM historian Darren Ward) and accepted an honour on Kirk's behalf from his colleagues and friends.

Their appreciation for him can be summed up by the words of Dave Taylor – who is certainly not one to give unwarranted pleasantries. "He was a great, great fellow. Truly one of the nicest guys in the business."

Mal Kirk

# MAL SANDERS

"I'm still hanging on. But I'm hanging on to the edge of my windowsill by my fingertips," is how Mal Sanders describes his continuing involvement in the wrestling business. It's an acknowledgement that his career has seen him go from pupil to teacher and beyond.

A keen Crystal Palace supporter, Sanders admits that "I always thought my destiny was to be a footballer," and at 13 he spent a year on the club's books. Sanders was told he needed to build up his body to stand up to the pressures of playing at a time when dropping to the floor at the slightest hint of contact was not an option.

"From being around the bodybuilders, it was a natural progression to the boxers and then the wrestlers," Sanders recalls. He wound up at the United Club in Stockwell, an amateur gym that produced numerous grapplers who later turned pro. "The Borg Twins, Lee Bronson, Bully Boy Muir, John Hall, Clive Myers: they were all there."

Sanders quickly became entranced by the "glamourous, glitzy" offerings of pro wrestling and football took a back seat. He turned pro after many months of training in the pro style under the teaching of Mike Marino at the Brixton Road gymnasium run by promoters Dale Martin.

As he explained to FSM in issue 94, Sanders considered Marino as something of a father figure, something he credits to Marino recognising his combination of amateur skills, charisma and a willingness to "get stuck in." It proved fortunate timing as Marino took over matchmaking roles previously held by McManus and engaged in an intentional program of pushing young talent in the hope of creating new stars.

The necessity for such action was explained by a TV Times article reporting on a small but noticeable drop in ratings in the mid-1970s as the leading names of the peak era remained in the ring into their late 40s: "The trouble is, they've all grown old together, and, unless some star names begin to emerge shortly, wrestling is going to be desperately short of the very commodity which keeps the sport alive - the men in the ring who deliver the goods, combining their fighting skills with colour and character."

Mal Sanders

Adjusting to what he calls "showbiz with an athletic twist," Sanders recalls being particularly nervous before his pro debut at the Catford Halls in Lewisham, worried both about the crowd and the prospect of making a mistake in the ring. However, "I soon got over that and after five or six matches it felt as easy as shelling peas."

That quick-found confidence was aided by working with men such as Steve Grey, against whom Sanders made his TV debut in November 1977 aged just 19. "I was lucky to be working with guys like Grey and Zoltan Boscik who were so talented at making people look good. I could wrestle Zolly [Boscik] and come out of the ring hardly knowing I'd been in there."

Sanders's development benefited from his coming along in a period where a traditional insistence on wrestlers sticking to a pre-determined weight class (regardless of how their body had changed over the years) was phased out by the booking of first Marino and then Max Crabtree.

"Anyone could fight anyone: you'd almost expect to see Tom Thumb against Giant Haystacks. With Mike, whatever he wanted, you took as gospel. And with Max when the Big Daddy era started, it could be you versus anyone: you'd either do that or get out."

Sanders recalls enjoying the experience of working with heavyweights such as John Elijah and Pete Roberts. "Pete was one of the greatest workers in the country, a fantastic worker and I had the deepest respect for him." Although Roberts was well regarded in Japan, Sanders believed Roberts was hugely underrated in the UK. "He should have been the world champion."

Wrestling the heavyweights wasn't always fun though. "I worked with Ray Steele and came out feeling like I'd been in a real fight. Let's just say he was... solid. The Northern wrestlers used to joke that we were all soft Southerners because we worked lighter!"

It was against a fellow Londoner that Sanders achieved true fame and the tag of "Superstar." At this stage Mick McManus had only lost two matches on television in a small-screen career that dated back to a pre-war appearance on BBC. In what was only Sanders' fifth televised bout, he defeated European Middleweight champion McManus by two falls to one in a non-title bout.

The conclusion was certainly controversial: Sanders, held in a submission hold, tapped McManus on the back. McManus released the hold, wrongly believing the referee had made the tap, which was the traditional signal from a referee that a grappler's opponent had given up. Sanders then capitalised on the confusion with a quick pin.

Three weeks later TV viewers saw Sanders capture the title by disqualification: the UK did not have the "pinfalls and submissions only" rule for championship changes. With the victory, Sanders ended a seven-year title reign and became the first and only man to ever beat McManus on TV twice

Sanders wasn't portrayed as dominant over McManus -- only the following month, McManus won a non-title TV rematch by knockout -- but merely being portrayed as in his class was a major boost to his standing. Speaking to FSM for our bio of McManus in issue 97, Sanders stated that " It was an absolute privilege to be able to work with him for so long. Wrestling Mick was every wrestler's dream and I'll never forget people like him who looked after me when I started."

The pair worked around the circuit for much of the next year, including headlining at the Royal Albert Hall in a bloody affair, and exchanging the title a further four times. In total Sanders would claim the middleweight crown nine times, later beating the likes of Keith Haward and Clive Myers in the 1980s and Steve Grey and Danny Collins in the 1990s.

Being based in the capital and working for the Dale Martin group worked out well for Sanders. "You could wrestle every night of the week if you wanted, without even leaving London." In fact, he usually wrestled further afield, noting the schedule became particularly diverse in the summer season. "You might be wrestling at Great Yarmouth on Mondays and then go back there on Wednesdays. The problem was that on Tuesday you'd be in Weymouth!"

Unconventional as the schedule may have been, it still allowed Sanders to hold down a full-time job for much of his career, starting out in the architect's office of the Greater London Council. This somewhat curtailed his ability to take advantage of his TV fame with overseas tours, though he still managed to fit in trips by carefully booking his holiday allocation. "I wasn't as prolific, but I visited Africa, Iceland, Dubai and Germany. I did one six-week run in Hamburg where you wrestled in the same place every night, which certainly sorted out the good wrestlers from the bad -- though if you were bad, you wouldn't usually be invited!

"The craziest was when I was flown into Nigeria for one day. I was wrestling a local guy and there were 10,000 people there, so that was pretty scary!"

Back in the UK, unlike in many areas where wrestlers searched for colleagues to share cars, at the start of Sanders's career Dale Martin still took its main crew to shows in a large group in a minibus from Brixton. It made for some particularly happy memories.

"You'd spend more time with the boys than your own family. I couldn't wait to get in the bus: it was like a school outing or a party. Even though there were plenty of big name TV stars, there were no egos on the bus and we were all mates. Mark Rocco and Max Crabtree were great storytellers and we always had fun. Every day there'd be something different happening."

Despite his newcomer status, Sanders recalls he was among the practical jokers of the group. "I'd always have my ant buzzer out, giving Daddy an electric shock and stuff like that. I've been told about some shows today where the wrestlers spend two hours working out their match, go in the ring and wrestle, then go straight to watch the match back on tape. We'd have been far too busy mucking about for anything like that!"

It was another example of Sanders learning from his mentor. "Mike [Marino] was a great prankster himself. I'd physically have an aching stomach from his antics. I truly felt like I was in Disneyland every day just being around Mike."

That warmth made it all the more tragic when, in 1981, Marino died while being driven home from hospital by Sanders, having been admitted earlier in the evening feeling weak, but discharging himself. Marino suffered a seizure in the car and, despite Sanders's best efforts, he died on the side of the M20 late at night. Although the cause of his death was unconfirmed, Marino had recently had medical tests; he'd yet to get back results that diagnosed him with leukaemia.

Appropriately Sanders was given the honour of defeating John Naylor, Pat Patton and Syd Cooper in a one-night tournament in Croydon to win the Mike Marino Memorial Shield the following month.

By this stage, Sanders was working with one wrestler more than any other. "Steve Grey and I were almost married at one point! I always knew if I listened to him, I couldn't go wrong: he had such great timing. Eventually we'd be able to have a match without even saying a word: we didn't need to.

"Our styles just went together, a bit like how Mark Rocco and Marty Jones always had great matches. I was told Big Daddy even said that if me and Steve were wrestling each other on one of his shows, he wanted his match to go on first so that he didn't have to follow us!"

One bout with Grey in Salisbury proved to be particularly influential. "I'd done something a bit aggressive and against the rules and the crowd reacted to it. Afterwards Steve told me to carry on doing that at the venue, so for a while I'd be more of a villain just in Salisbury. I liked it and found it a lot easier."

Eventually Sanders adopted the bad attitude across the country, a marked change for the previous golden boy. It allowed him to add a verbal edge to his feud with Grey, earning the nickname 'Mouth of the South'. "Steve, bless him, will admit he's no good on the mike. But I have the type of personality that can rub people up the wrong way, so it added to the bouts. It's a lot like being a live comedian: you learn to know what gets a reaction and you can try stuff out each night and keep the parts that work and drop the parts that don't."

"Just a couple of weeks ago I was wrestling on Ricky Knight's retirement show and came out and said how great it was to be in Norwich and how much I always enjoyed coming there. The crowd started cheering and I knew I had them. Then I hit them with 'I enjoy coming here because it reminds me how lucky I am to live in London.'"

Mal Sanders

Sanders gradually developed his heel act, at one stage coming to the ring in an American football shirt and helmet, something referees seemed to object to for some reason. He also added a manager/valet at the suggestion of the Crabtrees, who had seen Lois Hyett -- mother of teenage grappler Stevie Hawk -- at ringside and persuaded her to become a performer, explaining that "You're just the sort."

Hyett, billed as Loretta, tells FSM she was happy to follow the more experienced Sanders's lead. "I did exactly what he told me to! We'd speak in cockney rhyming slang so the crowd couldn't understand and he'd tell me to distract the ref, grab the opponent or whatever.

"My favourite routine was when Mal suggested I use my stiletto heel on the opponent. I didn't want to try hitting them myself in case I missed, which I probably would have a lot of the time! Instead we came up with the idea that I'd stay in the ring in the break between rounds and be protesting to the referee about the opponent, but be edging my shoe off with my other foot and slide it across the canvas to Mal. He'd use it and slide it back and then by the time the referee had seen the opponent down and asked what happened, the shoe was back on my foot and I was denying all knowledge!"

Having a manager certainly proved an advantage when Sanders and Grey engaged in a series of blindfold matches. Sanders recalls that unlike in some US bouts, the pair's vision was genuinely limited because members of the audience were invited to tie the blindfolds tight for the sake of credibility. Loretta therefore proved useful in storyline and reality: she gave Sanders an "unfair advantage" by letting him know Grey's positioning, and, as Sanders explains, "there wasn't much we could do for real in the bouts, so it helped having her to play stooge outside and liven things up."

Much as she enjoyed her time in the business, making an entertaining change from her day job as an accountant, Hyett does recall one night when she felt conflicted about the role. "Mal was having a match with [my son] Stevie and I did my usual trick of loosening the corner pad so that Mal could whip him into it without protection. On the way home Stevie was having trouble breathing and I eventually persuaded him to go to hospital where he turned out to have broken several ribs. I felt like such a horrendous mother!"

Fully established as a heel in the mid-90s, Sanders began wrestling the post-television generation of new grapplers, including numerous bouts with the teenage James Mason. The parallels with the McManus feud were not lost on Sanders and he was aware of his career turning full circle.

"Me and the other [veterans] took James under our wing because we could see he had potential. He turned into a fantastic wrestler. He always took notice of what you said and wanted to learn more, like ways he could play to the crowd."

Wrestling for two decades after British wrestling came off television, Sanders officially retired in March 2008 on his 50th birthday. Among the crowd were dozens of senior citizens from a local Age Concern centre where, contrary to his in-ring image, Sanders was now working to help people suffering conditions such as dementia.

Quitting the business gave Sanders a chance to take stock of his career. "I had no time to really think about it while I was wrestling. I'd been so busy having a great time, training and working. When I retired I realised I didn't even have any posters or programs from my career. Fortunately, one of the guys who used to be a second was kind enough to give me some mementos at a reunion."

Like many veterans of his era, Sanders has made some guest appearances at training seminars and shares a common complaint among those teaching today's students. "Too many guys want to do somersaults before they've even learned the basics like linking up or doing headlocks. They can't do the technical stuff that was on World of Sport with guys like Alan Serjeant, Johnny Saint, Alan Colbeck, George Kidd and Jon Cortez, who was absolutely fantastic and a big hero of mine.

"There's also too many cases where there's no psychology like working an arm. Guys just want to go bang, bang, bang."

And it seems even those wrestlers who do go to the right place to learn the basics sometimes experience problems. "I still spend some time at amateur clubs and they do get people walking in who think it's going to be American [pro] style wrestling. They get a shock, especially when they find out amateur wrestling can actually hurt a bit!"

Although he stayed out of the ring for a year, the lure was too much for Sanders to resist and he has returned for several bouts, largely against fellow veterans. "When you know you can still do it, it's tough to stop. It's difficult to be sat at home watching TV rather than walking out in front of three or four hundred people. You lose the buzz: nothing turns you on and you're not being stimulated.

But asked if the day will come when he really does hang up his boots, Sanders's adamant response is reminiscent of a Daniel Bryan promo. "Yes... yes, yes, yes. Yes!

"It does ache when I come out of the ring and I'm no longer as supple. I've had a very privileged life and although it's nice to be involved in wrestling, [retiring] won't be too long off.

"I saw James Mason wrestle recently and he's now in his mid-thirties and [a veteran] himself. So it may be time!"

Mal Sanders

# MARK ROCCO

When Mark Hussey went into the wrestling business against his father's initial wishes, he set out to prove he was willing to put 100% into being the best performer he could. That drive led him to become Rollerball Rocco, Britain's most intense, and arguably best ever, in-ring performer.

Wrestling has a strong background in the Hussey family: Rocco recalls that his great grandfather worked in fairground booths facing challenges from the public, while his grandfather was a skilled amateur competitor. His father, "Jumping" Jim Hussey, had achieved success as a professional performer, known to fans as a hard-hitting and ultra-athletic grappler and to fellow wrestlers as a notorious prankster. Upon Hussey's death, Tony St Clair noted his versatility, allowing him to work credible matches against opponents as diverse as Andre the Giant and the lightweight George Kidd.

Mark's first professional training came in a particularly informal manner: aged around five or six, he accompanied his father to the German tournaments and worked out in the ring with a group of visiting midget grapplers who matched him in height and lent him some suitable footwear.

For the most part, though, Hussey was not keen on having his son follow him into the business, instead encouraging him to pursue an interest in equestrianism. Hussey owned a wrestling gym and was unaware that whenever he was away working shows, Mark was receiving training on the quiet from local professionals, most notably Colin Joynson.

The first Hussey knew of the training was when he worked on a show where heavy fog led to a severe shortage of performers. An 18-year-old Mark had come along for the trip and chose this moment to reveal his ring education, volunteering to fill the bill. Entering the ring "in a pair of borrowed trunks that were almost falling down" Rocco put on a decent enough performance for an inexperienced grappler that he was able to pursue a professional career. He began working regularly early in 1970 under the Rocco name and made his TV debut that November, losing to Brian Maxine.

Rocco would only return to the small screen a couple of times over the next two years as much of his early wrestling career took place overseas. Speaking to

FSM's John Lister, Rocco explained that it was Hussey's influence that led him to make full use of his passport:

"My father said it's a hard game and you can't be in the business unless you learn the job properly. I tried to impress him by doing as much as I possibly could [to gain diverse experience.] I went to the Snake Pit in Wigan and learned submission wrestling. I went to the Canary Islands and did the local Canary wrestling [a similar sport to Sumo]. I wrestled in India, Turkey, France: everywhere I could think of to give me credibility."

"I learned my trade and anyone who told me I didn't know my job was incorrect. I learned it the hard way, from the ground up." To become a success, Rocco reasoned, a wrestler has to "keep fresh. You have to be totally dedicated with a one track mind. I wanted to learn my job and be better at it. I wanted to please the crowd and make them go home thinking they had a good night."

Back on British shores, that drive eventually paid off with championship success in 1977 when Rocco defeated veteran Bert Royal for the British Heavy-Middleweight title. He would go on to dominate the division for the rest of the TV era. His first reign ended in a champion vs champion clash against perennial rival Marty Jones in 1978. Jones immediately vacated the title, choosing to concentrate on defending his light-heavyweight championship. Rocco then regained the belt in the resulting tournament, defeating Chris Adams in the final.

He went on to hold this title for another three years, at which point promoters considered him worthy of an even bigger championship boost. Until this date heavy-middleweight had been one of the divisions where no world champion wasn't billed in the UK, the logic being that it would be implausible for Brits to hold every world title. The original plan was that Rocco would defeat Sammy Lee (Japan's Satoru Sayama) for the "vacant" title on the undercard of the Giant Haystacks-Big Daddy clash at Wembley Arena, but the match was cancelled when Sayama was forced to return to Japan for personal reasons. Instead French grappler Joel De Fremery was brought over to wrestle Rocco in Southport in a match confirming the Brit as the world titleholder.

Rocco and Sayama were by no means done however. Back in Japan, Sayama had been repackaged as Tiger Mask, a real life recreation of a long-running Manga comic book character. In a series of bouts with the likes of Dynamite Kid, Tiger Mask helped change the concept of junior-heavyweight wrestling: where once it had simply featured smaller performers working a traditional wrestling style, it now became a showcase of fast-paced, high-flying athletic action.

New Japan's Hiroshi Shinma then began looking for another rival for Tiger Mask, creating the character of an alter-ego dark side version known as Black Tiger, who had not featured in the comic books. According to Dynamite Kid, the character was created with Bad News Allen (later Bad News Brown) in mind, though this story seems hard to believe. Instead the role went to Rocco.

Having previously toured the Orient with some success for the smaller IWE group, Rocco now became a semi-regular for New Japan across the rest of his career, calculating that he made 38 tours in total. The gig proved such a cash cow that Rocco opted not to pursue other opportunities that might have appealed from a purely artistic perspective, such as the "shoot-style" promotions that sprang up in the era: "I was very interested in the UWF style, but I was on such a good deal with New Japan that there was no point leaving." Similarly, the seemingly natural fit of Stampede wasn't a financially viable destination given Rocco's Japanese schedule and regular headline slots back home.

That's not to say working for New Japan didn't bring new international opportunities. In December 1984 Rocco wrestled fellow NJPW regular The Cobra (George Takano) at Madison Square Garden for the Japanese-controlled WWF Junior-Heavyweight title. Five years later he wrestled Jushin Liger on New Japan's first and only show at Moscow's Lenin Stadium, just months after the Soviet Union began allowing professional sports events.

According to Rocco, he intentionally set out to further develop and change junior-heavyweight wrestling with Sayama, following on from the Dynamite Kid matches. "I'm certain the Tiger Mask matches helped change wrestling. Just look at Eddy Guerrero [who took over the Black Tiger character in the 1990s]: he ended up as world champion and he was only my size."

On World of Sport screens however, Rocco's ring style was making an impact in both a good and a bad way. Good in that he was winning acclaim for his combination of speed and aggression, but bad in that sometimes his matches stood out for the wrong reasons:

"I had the same idea for wrestling whether it was on TV or in the halls. I gave my best every night, gave my all. I had these ideas for how wrestling should be, and I put it into plan. Not everyone was happy with my style. The TV people thought I was too strong for the wrestling audience, but it did work.

"They didn't want the blood, sweat and tears, the intense wrestling. They wanted something more suitable for the mums and dads and grandmas. I never listened to that: I carried on and did my own thing. Not every match I did for tv got shown; a lot of them were cancelled because of the blood and violence."

That caused problems for promoter Max Crabtree who had become the main man in Joint Promotions. Speaking to Simon Garfield, author of "The Wrestling", Crabtree recalled that "Mark was crazy. He couldn't help it Mark believed that to be a good wrestler you had to dismantle the ring, hit the referee with the bell, throw your opponent into the audience. Nobody slept when he was on, but he was dangerous because he could kill someone. So I kept having to pacify the television people who said they didn't want him on no more, and I had to go back to Mark and say, 'Silly fella, you're off for three months."

ITV bosses would soon be free from the headache of a rowdy Rocco match however. In 1982 he decided to leave Joint Promotions, taking bookings with independent promoters Orig Williams and Brian Dixon. Like Tony St Clair before him, Rocco took his world title with him, taking full advantage of the fact that the championship was billed as being outside of the control of individual promoters.

While most wrestlers who made the switch to All-Star tell FSM it was purely a financial decision, Rocco was influenced by artistic issues as well. "At Joint I was getting a lecture every day about not to do this, not to do that. I was already friendly with Dixon and Williams. In fact, I was very friendly with all the promoters: I was very friendly with them because I was putting arses on seats! I was putting a lot of people in a lot of seats in a lot of venues on a lot of nights.

"All Star treated me a lot better, paid me a lot more and gave me a lot more freedom on what I could do. They didn't try to restrict my continental exploits or my Japanese tours."

Rocco also noted that leaving Joint meant his status wasn't overshadowed by Big Daddy. "When I went with All Star, I was the big star with them, so I had more freedom. Joint had pressure not to be too violent, which I couldn't help. My aggressive style was what it was: I couldn't tone it down, it was all or nothing. Dixon's opportunity was a light at the end of the tunnel because I knew the enthusiasm of the public was going in the direction of the American style rather than the English soft style.

"The Americans were throwing chairs, jumping up and down doing somersaults, and dressing up like Red Indians. The English guys were coming out in a black pair of trunks and sitting in a hold for 20 minutes. That wasn't what the English public wanted to see: the wanted to see the more dramatic stuff, which was what I was doing."

Leaving Joint certainly didn't end Rocco's television experiences. He appeared on broadcasts on French television and on Williams' Reslo show on S4C (the Welsh version of Channel 4). He also memorably appeared on "Satellite Wrestling" on the satellite and cable channel Screensport where broadcasting regulations were much looser, something Rocco took full advantage of. The prime example of this was a clash with Eddie "Kung Fu" Hamill which might as well have been a public information film showing everything you couldn't do on ITV: the pair used the foulest of language, fought outside the ring, used chairs and electrical cables as weapons and engaged in a full-blown post-match pull-apart.

Rocco then returned to ITV in 1987 when All Star was given a contract to fill several of the Saturday afternoon wrestling slot. Back under the control of the broadcasting authorities, Rocco was again upset with ITV when they aired WWF programming kicked off by a Hulk Hogan-Randy Savage clash. "It was a big contention for me: you're telling us to tone it down, but you're showing the American stuff which was full throttle such as this lumberjack match."

Still, he played by the broadcaster rulebook (if not the wrestling one) and took on the likes of Chic Cullen (with whom he had previously exchanged the world mid-heavyweight title) Danny Collins and Johnny Saint. Having had a series of matches on the arena circuit with Fuji Yamada (later known as Jushin Liger) where the title switched back and forth, Rocco finally regained the title in a televised show in Catford.

The best-remembered part of Rocco's final TV run came in 1988 when he teamed with fellow arch-villain Kendo Nagasaki only for the two to fall out and feud. They clashed in a heated tag match on television (Rocco partnering former rival Wayne Bridges against Nagasaki and future "WWF tribute show" promoter Shane Stevens), though their encounters at All Star's regular venues were even more violent and rowdy.

This was one of the very few occasions where Rocco heard the cheers of the crowd after establishing himself as a top star, and he admits he was sceptical such a role would work: "When promoters first put me and Kendo together, I thought 'This will never happen.' I thought that even if I went in the ring and chopped his head off with an axe, they would not be interested in watching two bad guys fight each other. But the crowd went along with me and supported me for about a year. I had no problems hurting him and he had no problems hurting me."

As the ITV era came to a close, there was just one last chance for Rocco and long-time rival Marty Jones to clash on television again, the match ending in a double disqualification. Rocco continued headlining for All-Star as the 80s turned into the 90s and business held up surprisingly well for a couple of years, perhaps because dedicated television viewers were now forced to leave their homes to get their grappling fix.

In 1991, Rocco's career came to a sudden end when -- working his second bout of the day -- he wrestled Fit Finlay in Worthing, a match that arguably paired up the two most aggressive, hardworking grapplers in the British business. Collapsing in the dressing room after the match, Rocco was taken to hospital with pain in his neck, back and kidneys that he assumed stemmed from the combination of a mishap the previous night and a stiff piledriver outside the ring from Finlay.

In fact, his problems were far more serious. Medical examination showed Rocco's heart was severely damaged, most likely as a simple result of the strain he had placed on it through his wrestling career.

Rocco had no choice but retire, eventually moving to the Canary Islands where he has been involved in a series of successful businesses including restaurants and car hire services. His family remains part of the ring business with his son Jonny racking up a 15-2 record as a light-welterweight boxer.

While his business skills have helped make retirement comfortable, Rocco notes that he was fortunate in being able to make a good living while in the wrestling industry. "The English promoters were the foremost in the world at making money. They were running six or seven shows a night and making thousands of pounds every night in the 70s and 80s and didn't put one penny back in the business. There's a lot of money in the wrestling business, always has been, but unfortunately the wrestlers don't get it.

"I've been lucky enough to get some of it. For a period of time when I was in the business, if I ever saw anything less than a full house I was devastated. We used to turn people away and there was real money on the table."

That's not to say Rocco's approach to wrestling is purely mercenary. "I remember one time at Belle Vue with me and Marty Jones we turned away 1,400 people on a Saturday night. The following Tuesday I went back there to see the amateur wrestling world championships and there were about 100 people in the audience. I was so sad because I looked up to these guys as icons of wrestling."

It's the combination of legitimate skills and showmanship that Rocco believes is the key to up and coming wrestlers making a success, such as the crew of TNA's British Bootcamp series who underwent his scrutiny before moving on to the US. "You need to learn the basics, know the job inside out and keep a balance. You have to learn all the wrestling techniques and styles to get a broad base, then you can work anywhere in the world. If you're in with a southpaw or somebody working a different style, you aren't left with your finger in your mouth wondering what's going to happen next.

"But you have to be different. There's no point being just another guy who's like everyone else. Those people don't make money."

Fittingly, Rocco's number one piece of advice for new wrestlers mirrors the approach he took in those early years trying to live up to the high standards set by his father:

"Learn your business and make your money."

# MARTY JONES

When you hear tales of a TV star who was bullied at school, the story usually involves them fighting back with quick wittedness and growing up to be a comedian at school. Marty Jones fought back with his fists and it led to a very different career path.

The bullying in question came because Jones had suffered a serious eye injury in an accident at the age of three and grew up wearing "Milky Bar kid glasses." The constant teasing led to him frequently losing his temper and getting into fights, to the point that Jones's father decided a local amateur wrestling and boxing gym would be the best place to channel his aggression.

This was no ordinary gym: the facility in Failsworth, Manchester was the home of Billy Robinson, one of the legends of Britain's "catch" style of submission grappling. Robinson, who'd previously taught Johnny Saint at the same venue, trained Jones in amateur wrestling and helped him achieve success at several tournaments around the country.

Eventually Jones began looking at getting into the pro game, but admits "at first I thought it was a bit of a joke. Then I got in the ring with Tony Charles and quickly found myself with my own head shoved up my ass!"

Jones stuck it out and learned the ropes at several north-west gyms including one based at the Wryton Stadium in Bolton, the permanent home of the town's weekly professional shows. "I was introduced to the crowd at one show as a former amateur champion just to get me known, but I wasn't scheduled to debut yet. Later on the show Abe Ginsberg (of the Black Knights) had beaten the local heroes Bert Royal and Vic Faulkner and the crowd got incredibly heated and went after him. I ran out and helped fight them off. That impressed the guys and I turned pro the next week!"

Debuting in his late teens, Jones says it took three years before he really felt comfortable in the ring. By this time, he'd made his first overseas trip where a three-week booking in Mexico turned into a three month stint. "It was very eye-opening. One day you'd be enjoying sitting on a beach in Acapulco and then the next you'd be looking at the extreme poverty in Mexico City."

Marty Jones

During the trip, Jones made it to main event status against local top star Perro Aguayo. Although Jones pulled off a win, the feud ended in inevitable fashion: on his last night before returning to England, Jones lost a "hair vs hair" bout. "The trip was a great experience, but my family and girlfriend weren't too impressed when I came back home with that haircut!"

The trip kicked off a domino effect of international travel: "Everywhere you went, there were wrestlers from all over the world. If you showed you could do the job, they'd put in a good word for you in their country and you'd end up moving on from place to place."

This included regular trips to Germany and a tour of the Stampede promotion in Canada where Jones teamed with the Dynamite Kid as part of English manager JR Foley's stable in a feud against Bret and Bruce Hart. Jones and Bret worked particularly well together, and the pairing was revived back in the UK where Jones was victorious in a match on the historic final show at the King's Hall in Manchester's Belle Vue facility.

Jones also picked up bookings for New Japan thanks to the legendary Karl Gotch, with his first tour bringing a memorable moment. "We were there right around the time they first started bringing the American guys over, so I was there to help fill up the undercard and make sure there were some decent matches. Chief Jay Strongbow was on the tour and everyone thought the crowd would love him because gimmicks like his often go down well with the Japanese audience.

"He got in the ring and did his usual routine: run the ropes, stop, stare out his opponent, run the ropes again, stop, do a war dance, then hit him with a 'Tomahawk' chop. The problem was that this made his Japanese opponent look foolish by just standing there, so the guy waited till Strongbow threw the chop, ducked, and then hit him with a real chop of his own that actually left a crease! Strongbow fell out of the ring, slid under the ring for a minute, then ran back to the dressing room and flew home the next day."

Jones himself didn't have any problem with the stiff style: quite the opposite. "I absolutely loved working in Japan. You didn't know who you'd wrestle until five minutes before the match, then you shook hands, went in and beat the crap out of each other, then came back and shook hands again!" His liking for hard-hittin action was particularly beneficial when he later switched to the UWF promotions, one of several "shoot-style" groups that deliberately employed a more believable ring style.

During his time in New Japan Jones teamed with a diverse group of American stars including Pat Patterson and Nikolai Volkoff, but the most memorable both in and out of the ring was Andre the Giant. Jones recalls that Andre's size meant even a trip to the cinema became a logistical issue. "First we'd get a taxi there, but he had to lie down on the floor because he was too big for the seats. Then we'd have to pick up a bench from the street and carry it in to the cinema, so he could sit down to watch the film. When we did get inside, he'd go up to the women carrying trays of ice cream, throw a couple of hundred dollars at them and just take the entire tray and sit there eating the whole lot during the film."

Andre always attracted attention thanks to his size, but he made a particular impact among the generally smaller Japanese people. "One time we were standing on a railway platform and I swear there were five thousand people on the other side of the track just staring at him. Andre bowed to them and there was a pause and then they all bowed back in unison. Andre turned to me and said, 'Well I've never seen that before... five thousand backdrops at once!"

The Japanese trips also led to an invitation to wrestle in Korea, but it's the trip he turned down that remains strongest in Jones's memory. "Vince McMahon Senior asked me to come to his promotion (the future WWE) but I decided against it because I didn't think it was really my style. Of course, this was just a few years before his son took it worldwide."

Still, America's loss was Britain's gain and the now seasoned traveller began establishing himself on television. His most celebrated rivalry was with Mark Rocco: the pair had 11 singles bouts on television, which may well make it the most repeated TV match-up. Arguably biggest bout came in 1978 when Jones, then the reigning British light-heavyweight champion, dropped down a weight division to capture Rocco's heavy-middleweight championship.

It was only the second time (the first being Brian Maxine) that a man had held two British Mountevans titles simultaneously, though Jones immediately vacated the heavy-middleweight title. By the time ITV dropped British wrestling in 1988, Jones's championship haul consisted of seven world mid-heavyweight titles, three British light-heavyweight titles and the British heavy-middleweight crown.

Writing in his autobiography, the man now known as William Regal noted "I recently watched a video of Marty Jones wrestling Rocco in 1977 and it still stands up today. You wouldn't know it wasn't a modern match -- in fact, it was better than a lot of what you see today. Incredible wrestling."

It was appropriate that such bouts inspired Regal as, although he learned the basics of the business on the Blackpool fairground circuit, he went to Jones to develop a style more suited to regular arenas. Jones's family owned an equestrian centre and he used a spare barn to set up a ring where he trained would-be and current wrestlers alike. "I treated people the same whether they were in the business or not. Max Crabtree used to send a lot of seemingly useless big lumps over to me so I could test them and see if they were good enough to work with Big Daddy. Regal was a scrawny kid, but he wanted to get bigger and better and said his ambition was to make it in America. I said at the time there was no way he was good enough then, but he stuck with it and the rest is history."

The same uncompromising welcome went to any member of the audience who fancied their chances. At a show in Stockport one spectator made personal comments to Jones, who replied that he was welcome to get in the ring and have a go if he thought he could do any better. Other fans on hand remember the subsequent clash lasted for approximately 10 seconds. "I waited until the exact moment he put his hands on the ropes," Jones recalls, "and then I cracked him. I really liked defending the game when I could, even to this day when people don't respect it. I've got arthritis from it now, so it upsets me when people attack wrestling. It's one of the hardest jobs going and frankly you've got to be mental just to do the miles of traveling."

In taking on more conventional opponents, Jones arguably had quality bouts against the widest range of performers on World of Sport. He names Rocco, Dave Finlay, Skull Murphy, Pete Roberts and Danny Collins as some of his favourite foes, but says "It really didn't matter who I wrestled because the international experience with the different styles meant I was comfortable working with people of any style or size. I could wrestle heavier men like Pat Roach or smaller guys like Collins."

The wide range of TV match-ups also helped Jones secure a full calendar when cameras weren't present. "TV was your shop window as a wrestler so whenever you had a good match, all the local halls promoters wanted to book it."

Sometimes that wasn't possible, most notably on the occasion Owen Hart made a flying visit to the UK, wrestling Jones for the vacant world mid-heavyweight title in Bradford. It was arguably the greatest match ever shown on ITV, combining mat-based grappling, power moves and high-flying. When The Wrestling Channel began showing old World of Sport tapes in 2004, it was included in the very first edition, a deliberate (and successful) attempt to attract younger viewers with Hart's name value and then hook them with the quality of the action.

Shortly after this, Jones began working for All-Star Promotions who would eventually be his major employer for the rest of his career. While previous stars such as Mark Rocco had jumped ship completely, giving up TV exposure, Jones was able to continue wrestling for Joint Promotions. "By this time the business at the halls was dropping off, rents were going up, and fans were tight for money. It meant management couldn't argue with us taking bookings from different promoters because they knew we had to, so we could keep our calendar full." The All-Star connection allowed for one final Rocco-Jones TV bout, meaning the pair had clashed on-screen over an amazing 15 year period.

Jones had previously had the occasional bout where he dropped his sportsmanlike style, for example against Pete Roberts on the undercard of the Big Daddy-John Quinn Wembley Arena show, with Jones's aggression portrayed as "needle" rather than outright villainy. It wasn't until he was with All-Star about a year after the end of TV wrestling that Jones began wrestling as a full-blown heel though, and he notes that the beginnings of his turn to the dark side were very much unplanned.

"We were at Norwich where you had a lot of gypsies in the crowd who liked it violent and always booed clean wrestling. Ricky Knight and Jimmy Ocean were really getting into it with the crowd, so I had to run out there and help save them, then start laying into Jimmy myself to try to calm things down. Then some guy in the crowd starting shouting abuse at me about my eye [Jones has a squint from his childhood injury] and it wound me up so much that I poked him in the eye and told him we were now even!"

Once it was decided Jones should officially turn to villain status, he was billed in a tag match against Danny Collins that appeared on paper to be a clean and sporting contest. However, on the night Jones's advertised partner was "revealed" as unable to appear so long-time rival -- and firm heel -- Dave Finlay took his place despite Jones's protests. The pair remained at odds until Collins threw a punch at Finlay but hit Jones by mistake. Jones responded by throwing Collins into the crowd and joining Finlay in a violent beatdown before unleashing the first of what proved to be hundreds if not thousands of verbal attacks on audiences.

The Collins rivalry led to an incident that is among the most memorable of Jones's career, albeit for all the wrong reasons. "The Americans were doing a lot of steel cage matches, so the British promoters copied them, only we used the type of metal fences you see when they are doing repair work on the motorway. We had a match at Bristol and it all went OK: not a great match, but the cage got plenty of heat."

The set-up was similar to WWE's Hell in Cell (without the roof), with the cage several feet from the ring, leaving space to brawl on the floor. That worked fine in Bristol but not in Croydon. "The ring there was bigger, so there wasn't as much room between the ring and the cage. As I got on to the apron at the start of the match, Danny hit me with a dropkick and I flew back and hit the cage. Unfortunately, the top of the cage was covered in spikes and I caught one of them right under my arm in the armpit. I was hanging there, and my feet were just above the ground, so I was literally impaled.

"I managed to get myself free, and stupidly I didn't go back to the dressing room because I thought I had to be professional and do the match. The moment I got in and the referee rang the bell, Danny put on an arm submission, so I could give up right away, but it meant we'd actually done the match. I looked at my arm and it was like a pound of mince -- they took me straight to hospital and I had 96 stitches."

Fortunately, it wasn't a career-ending injury and Jones was able to carry on wrestling for another decade, with his last recorded bouts coming in 2003. In his retirement he followed in the footsteps of many wrestlers by taking over a pub. Jones believes there are two reasons why grapplers are attracted to the licensed trade: "It's partly because we love being in the public eye and it's partly because we can use having been on TV so much as a way to draw people in." Jones's establishment, the Angel in Royton near Oldham, had a brief moment of television fame itself: the exterior was used for filming scenes in the BBC's Life On Mars where the detectives in the show went to their station's local.

Looking back, Jones says that he now appreciates just how much the wrestling career sparked by a schoolyard bully truly changed his life. "In some ways the life of a wrestler is shit. You don't get any social life with your family because you are always working in the evening, you don't get paid enough, and even if you make enough to take them away for a nice holiday they have to put up with you always being recognised and people wanting to talk about wrestling.

"But I've also been very fortunate, and I've been able to use wrestling to improve my life. I wasn't the brightest kid at school -- I was more sport mad -- but wrestling has meant I've learned several foreign languages and been able to tour the world, which I'd probably never have been able to do otherwise.

"When my wife died of cancer when she was 42, I was left to look after my two kids who were 12 and 9. It was a tough thing to do, but one of the reasons I was able to manage it was because I didn't have a normal, easy job: wrestling had taught me how to struggle and work hard.

"My ambition was to be top of the bill in every place I wrestled, and I managed it. Even though I'm in pain every day with the arthritis, in a weird way it's a reminder of my life in the business. I don't have any regrets about wrestling -- except regret that I can't still do it."

Marty Jones

# MEL STUART

"I could do villain matches, I could do happy [comedy] matches and I could do wrestling matches," recalls Mel Stuart, "but I was a wrestler first and foremost." Such versatility is the hallmark of a man who really has done it all in the British wrestling profession.

While many of his peers struggled to find a way into the closed shop of wrestling, Stuart answered a call. "I started going to shows at the Co-op Hall in Gravesend in around 1959 and would go whenever it was on. A couple of years later I saw an advert in the local paper, the Gravesend and Dartford Reporter asking, 'Are you athletic?' Well, I was -- in them days! It said if so you could learn to become a wrestler, so I replied and went along to a gym in Northfleet."

While Joint Promotions had a tough entry policy for its shows in major venues, work was a little easier to come by on the "opposition" circuit. "There were always plenty of shows at working men's clubs," Stuart recalls, referring to social clubs aimed at manual workers where affordable entertainment was a key part of the attraction."

While Stuart worked around the circuits, he really began to make a name for himself when he picked up a spot with Len Britton, a leading independent promoter in South London. "I'd met Steve Grey by then and we did a try-out at a gym for Len. We must have done something right because he turned to two other wrestlers there and said 'You know that job I gave you at Dulwich Baths? Cancel it: these two are on.' We did a tag match with me and someone against Steve and someone, and that was my first really big opposition match."

Originally Stuart wrestled under his real name of Malcolm Clifton but "it didn't really gel. I decided to take my middle name to make Mal Stuart, which eventually ended up as Mel Stuart for some reason." The change led to some confusing situations. "I got so used to signing autographs that I'd often catch myself signing legal documents as Mel Stuart, handing them over, and the other person looking confused.

"Eventually I started doing everything as Mel Stuart, even my bank account. I didn't really think anything of it until my daughter asked why she had a different name to me!"

Mel Stuart

When local promoters stopped running the Co-op Hall where Stuart had first become a fan, he began promoting the venue himself. While the independent scene lacked the formal structure of Joint Promotions, there was still a territory system of sorts. "I promoted Dartford, Gravesend and Swanscombe, but didn't go into the [neighbouring] Medway towns because someone else was there. It wouldn't even dawn on you to promote elsewhere."

His attempts to fill the bill led Stuart into a new venture. "I used guys like Steve Grey, Johnny Kincaid, Peter Kelly and Tony Scarlo. I also started my own gym to train guys and would send them to other promoters, like Bruno Elrington in Portsmouth, and they'd trust my recommendations. While drawing depended on who was on the show, using guys from my gym meant you'd get their friends and family coming along: even my mum came to every show! I guess you could call them 'internal punters.'"

However, Stuart's successful model came to an abrupt end in 1968 when Gravesend got a new civic centre complex, complete with a theatre that attracted the attention of a Joint Promotions member. "Dale Martin started running the new Woodville Halls and that killed me stone dead. I'd been running monthly, often selling out, but nobody wanted to see the small cheeses when they could see the likes of Mick McManus and Jackie Pallo. I'm kind of half-joking in saying I found out punters are turncoats!"

As one door closed, however, another opened in the form of the fairground circuit where fellow pro John Hurley introduced him to the world of wrestling challengers from the public. "I spent many years on the booths with guys like Johnny Kincaid and the boxers. To be honest, the money was not that clever, but you made up for it by bulk: sometimes I'd wrestle up to 10 times a day."

Whether it was his growing name on the opposition circuit or the evidence that he could handle himself in a genuine grappling contest, Stuart finally got his biggest career break in 1972. "I'd been writing to Dale Martin for years and finally got a letter from Joe D'Orazio who was in the office at the time. I didn't have to do a gym try-out, but instead they told me to come for a try-out match at a show in Weston-Super-Mare. When I got there, I couldn't believe it: I was in the main event with Mike Marino. He told me afterwards that he'd put in a good report and tell them I was a good wrestler and a hard wrestler, and he liked my style."

Marino was as good as his word and Stuart earned a spot on the regular roster where he no longer had to worry about piecing together a monthly schedule across promoters: instead Joint sent a monthly date sheet with everything planned out in advance. "In the 70s and 80s there was so much work, you were glad to get a day off. Even if you had been allowed to work for the opposition on your day off, you wouldn't want to."

Mel Stuart

"The rings back then were very hard and were a design we called gate rings because the main parts looked like metal gates. The way they were designed meant every single part of the ring [below the canvas] was touching the floor, so there was no give, no spring.

"I don't mean to use the word in a bad way, but I think the promoters were ignorant of the fact that caused problems. They just thought rings had to be done the boxing way. I remember the first time I saw a new ring put up in Margate and each corner was a big plank of wood on top of four lorry tyres: it doesn't sound much, but it made such a difference to have a bit of suspension."

By 1973, Stuart was deemed ready for television. His first TV recording bout was a victory against Johnny Czeslaw at Wembley, though it's unclear if it aired in all regions. That was unfortunate as his next TV appearance, a knockout loss to Les Kellett, was the start of a 20-match run of consecutive small-screen defeats the spanned the rest of the TV era. That's not to say Stuart had any complaints or felt it harmed his appeal

"I knew I was very, very popular with promoters or I wouldn't have got the amount of work I did. Yes, the TV wrestling punters only knew the big stars, but the ones who went to the live shows knew you and respected you, and to them you were almost as big a star as 'the stars.'"

Indeed, regardless of his domestic exposure, Joint respected Stuart's abilities enough to have him act as a representative on numerous foreign trips. "Whenever people knock the job, I ask them where their work has taken them. Wrestling took me to Zimbabwe, Kenya, Spain, Germany, Greece, India and Bangladesh."

Stuart would also become a talent scout of sorts. "I wasn't organising foreign tours as such, but the local promoters would ask me to find them wrestlers to come on a trip and fill a role." On one such trip to Greece, Stuart picked Johnny Kincaid as a late replacement, and it was this experience that Kincaid credits with earning him a much-anticipated try-out for Joint Promotions.

During this trip, Stuart suffered an injury at the hands of an over-aggressive opponent, something he recalls as an occupational hazard overseas. "I didn't really get into any hairy situations outside the ring, but you'd sometimes come up against a few big, hairy, hard ugly guys in India or Pakistan. The trick was to show no fear and make a good accounting of yourself."

On another occasion, Belgian wrestler Bert Mychel paid the price for taking advantage of Stuart. "He suplexed me over the top rope to the outside without warning. He thought he was being clever. I was hurt, but I just smiled and didn't let him know.

"In the dressing room afterwards, Tibor Szakacs asked me if I was OK, and I told him I'd been hurt by it. He asked Bert why he'd done it, but Bert just laughed. Tibor said 'Well, you're on with me tomorrow at the Royal Albert Hall.' Bear in mind Tibor was the number one shooter at the time. Suddenly Bert's going 'Please, please, we don't need to fall out!'

"There was a dressing room code: you only do to another wrestler what you'd be prepared to have done to yourself."

That code would come into play much later in Stuart's career when, in 2000, he was booked to wrestle a tag match for Premier Promotions teaming with Dick The Bruiser against Pat Roach and the Red Shadow. Roach's partner was not a masked grappler, but rather sportswriter Ian Stafford, who was working on a book in which he competed as a novice in a variety of sports.

Writing about the experience for Esquire, Stafford noted that however pro wrestling worked, it certainly wasn't easy "as my bruised back, abdomen and jaw, scratched neck and shoulders, cut nose, ripped-out hair and nasty whiplash injury can testify. It's a rough old game, all right, played primarily by some rough old people, but they're much fitter than you could possibly imagine, and far more professional, too."

Stuart explains that Stafford didn't receive any special treatment either way in the match. "Pat had taught him the basics, but told us to do what we normally do, just be careful not to injure him. The guy said afterwards that it was one of the hardest things in which he'd ever participated.

"I remember Pat's specific words were 'don't take liberties.' You have to remember we could have done anything with that lad. We could have broken his nose or bloodied him up, but we didn't."

Stuart had experienced extreme physicality as a regular opponent of Les Kellett, particularly in the 1980s when an ageing Kellett became very choosy about who he would work with. "Les was a funny old bugger, very reserved in the dressing room. A lot of the boys didn't like doing his matches because they didn't like the comedy, but I just looked at it as me going on to do a job."

But while he was equally at home in a comedy role or a more traditional villain performance, Stuart explains that he'd evolve his approach during the match. "I'd always do some straight wrestling at the start of a match, throw in some fancy counter moves. The psychology was much easier that way.

"Five rounds is a long time to hold the crowd's attention doing the same thing. By wrestling at the start, when I started the villain stuff after a couple of rounds, they crowd would be asking 'Why would he do that?' and be seeing another side of me.

"Later on in my career, a lot of the new guys couldn't out-wrestle a peanut: all they did was punch. I'd always come across as arrogant, but show I could wrestle. After all, the name of the game is wrestling."

Stuart's versatility made him a valuable utility player for promoters. "Dale Martin had a simple four-match format for shows, but it worked. You'd do a clever [technical] match first, then the next one would have a bit more villain stuff, then you'd have the top of the bill match, and finish off with a 'send them home happy' match with somebody like Catweazle, Billy Torontos or Johnny Czeslaw. That way the show would cater for every person in the hall. Now you'll often see every match on a show doing the same thing."

While Stuart could fill multiple roles, he was aware of his place in the presentation. "I did one match with Spencer Churchill where we were on right before Mick McManus. We were getting loads of reaction and Spencer said 'Mel, take it down a step.' I was being too much of a villain and getting too much reaction. I understood because I'm not top of the bill: they came to see Mick. So we simmered it down because you don't want to scream the people out."

One particular setting where villainy and comedy were both useful skills was the holiday camp circuit where Stuart regularly worked by promoter Jimmy Hagen. While he always played the heel role, it didn't work all the time. "For some reason, disabled kids like ones with Down's Syndrome seemed to love me. I think it was because I always played up so much in matches. I used to frighten them during the match, but would always go up to them afterwards and show I wasn't all that bad."

Sometimes this support presented its own problems. "I used to do a bit where I'd get hit on the head with a tea tray at the camp shows. After one show, there was a lad banging himself on the head over and over. Somebody asked him what he was doing, and he said, 'I'm being like my friend Mel Stuart.'"

Hagen's son Robbie was also a pro and he would wrestle Stuart in what would become a historically notable bout, the last of the night at an October 1988 taping in Rickmansworth. Although the broadcast running order varied so that Pat Roach vs Caswell Martin was the last match aired during the 33-year ITV run, Hagen and Stuart was actually the final bout recorded for television.

Stuart recalls the atmosphere in the venue that night: "We all put our heart and soul into it. We wanted to show that we loved it and make sure we stayed in people's minds. But it was within a few years of going off TV that crowds started to dwindle. TV was like an advert and when fans start not seeing your faces, they lose enthusiasm: TV acted like a reminder for the live shows in your town."

That's not to say Stuart disappeared from the small screen. His distinctive appearance and physical performing abilities earned him a range of TV roles and an Equity membership, both as a background extra and in wrestling-related skits. "I did EastEnders, The Bill, Casualty, Lenny Henry, The Vicar of Dibley, and even did a Gotcha Oscar with Bob Holness on the Noel Edmonds show.

And while the visit of the Duke of Edinburgh to a Royal Albert Hall wrestling event has been much discussed, Stuart is among the very few wrestlers to perform for the Queen, albeit in an unconventional manner. "My biggest accolade was the

1991 Royal Variety Performance where I was dressed as a sumo wrestler in the background when Eric Idle did Always Look on the Bright Side of Life. I still have the letter from the organizers saying the Duke of Edinburgh had called it the most enjoyable show in over 20 years."

Stuart wrestled for more than 15 years in the post-TV era, becoming a regular on Premier Promotions' shows which used the traditional style and format. He decided to call it a day in April 2005, retiring with a match against old friend Steve Grey. "I was 65, which was at retirement age, and it felt like the right time to go. Nobody was shouting 'come on Granddad', and I always felt I should get out of the business while I could still do the business. It didn't get to the point where people were saying 'Don't put me on with him.' When you get too old, your body breaks down and you start blocking people and the match doesn't flow."

While Stuart doesn't attend many live events today ("It's a different ball game now, and I catch myself starting to pick fault, which I don't like doing"), he remains in touch with his former colleagues and is a regular at the wrestling reunions. It was at one such event that he got confirmation that despite rarely receiving top billing, he was appreciated by his peers.

"I got an award presented by Pat Roach, who everyone respected. I said to him that I felt odd being given the award because I wasn't one of the stars. I'll always remember Pat told me: 'You are as good as any of us stars. You are worthy.'"

Mel Stuart

# MICK MCMANUS

"He was portrayed as a villain, but outside the ring he was an absolutely lovely fellow," is how Eddie 'Kung Fu' Hamill remembers Mick McManus, the man who took his mask and dominated TV wrestling for three decades.

Long after the way wrestling matches worked had become public knowledge, some wrestling secrets remained: McManus's real name and date of birth were hotly disputed until his funeral when son Tony confirmed he was born William George Matthews in January 1921. He is believed to have adopted his ring name into reality by deed poll after becoming a star.

McManus began his working life as a printer, something he later used when running a side-line business producing posters (or "bills") for upcoming wrestling shows. He took part in several sports in his youth, including learning amateur grappling at the John Ruskin Amateur Wrestling Club.

Hamill recalls that, contrary to his public perception, McManus was actually a skilled grappler: "He could really do the business, but that didn't appeal to fans. He just didn't show his skills because of his villain image."

Debuting as a pro in 1944 against Al Fuller at Belle Vue, McManus's lengthy TV career actually began before ITV even launched: he was featured against Al Lipman on 26 May 1947 as part of an occasional series of bouts shown on BBC. Once ITV got in on the grappling game, McManus appeared on the fourth ever show, against Chic Purvey, starting a 26-year run on the channel during which he was the most featured wrestler with more than 200 bouts, more than 50 ahead of anyone else.

Perhaps the ultimate example of McManus's standing and longevity was his record on the FA Cup Final day broadcasts when wrestling aired before the football in what was the most prestigious slot of the year. Between 1963 and 1978, McManus appeared on every broadcast except for one, a record no other wrestler even began to approach.

With his pre-ITV career receiving little publicity, and with up to seven years shaved off his billed age at times, it's easy to forget just how old McManus was during his fame: when he began his famed feud with Jackie Pallo in 1962, he was already safely into his 40s. The fact that he never seemed to age was in part due to what was an open secret in the business: his trademark dyed jet-black hair.

Mick McManus

Hamill recalls that the hair wasn't just an ego boost, but part of an overall image: "Mick always looked absolutely immaculate, from his appearance, to his ring gear, to the clothes he wore outside the ring. He always looked completely professional."

FSM detailed the Pallo feud in our profile of "Mr TV" in issue 84, but it bears repeating that, although the pair clashed less often than you might think (with both men major stars, it usually made more sense for them to headline separate shows), it remains arguably the best-remembered rivalry in British wrestling.

The pair clashed on the FA Cup Final day specials in 1962 and 1963, followed by a 1967 nationwide run sparked by a slanging match on the Eamonn Andrews TV chat show and finally a series at the Royal Albert Hall in 1972-3 where one match attracted a capacity crowd despite ticket prices being raised to three times their normal level. Such hikes weren't that unusual for McManus: in some venues prices would go up by a third when he appeared, something that was normally reserved only for championship matches.

The 1963 Cup Final day bout marked the conclusion of what must surely be the most historic week in the ITV wrestling era. It came just three days after a Royal Albert Hall show attended by Prince Phillip as part of a charity fundraiser, with McManus defeating Linde Caulder. (Prince Phillip returned to the venue for a televised bout pitting McManus against Mick McMichael in 1968: the fact that the Queen noted watching that show on TV to cabinet minister Richard Crossman, who mentioned the discussion in his published diaries, is the source of the likely over-hyped claim that Her Majesty was a dedicated fan.)

Exactly how many people watched McManus and Pallo on the Cup Final Days is the stuff of legend. Any figures and comparisons to the football audience must be taken with a pinch of salt as a newspaper clipping from 1963 shows a famous story has its origins in careful hype. Despite being published several days before the bout, the article notes as a matter of fact that "Eight million viewers will be tuned in for this Cup Final speciality -- in fact, more ITV viewers than for the Cup Final."

Questionable timelines aside, the article does show the way in which the pair's clashing personalities made the feud so effective. McManus is reported as saying of Pallo that "He's a well-known big-head with a matching big mouth. What's more, he's flash. Never liked him. Can't stand him. Delusions of grandeur. Wants cutting down to size and I'm going to do it."

In return, Pallo is said to have described McManus thusly: "He's a horrible piece of work. Rotten fighter. Bad tempered. Jealous of my fame. I've hated him for years and my life's ambition is to beat him and forget him."

Despite the perception of a vicious feud between the two, there wasn't any real personal grudge, and claims by celebrity fan Peter Blake that one of their Royal

Albert Hall bouts was a genuine fight are merely a sign of a job well done by both men. Writing in his autobiography "You Grunt, I'll Groan", Pallo explained the relationship was more complex: "Although there was never any wrestling needle between Mick and me (the whole thing was an act), we were not mates outside the ring. Neither were we enemies. But there was a little 'feeling'."

Pallo followed up those comments by complaining that although the pair worked well together, McManus would often overly-dominate other opponents. That's an experience that isn't shared by Eddie Hamill: "Kendo Nagasaki once told me 'I'm a taker, not a giver', but that wasn't the case with McManus. I like working with him because he'd let you do what you wanted and then you let him do what he wanted, which is the way it should be."

That mirrors comments made by Johnny Kincaid to FSM last year. "Some wrestlers didn't want you to shine and blocked everything you did, so you'd have to keep learning until you could block them back. McManus wasn't like that: he made you look a million dollars because he knew it made him look even better when he beat you."

While the majority of McManus's bouts were examples of two professionals working together to please the crowd, the same can't be said of one his most infamous bouts, his first televised defeat. It was to Peter Preston, a Bradford based wrestler who worked mainly for Norman Morell. Although Morell was the Joint Promotions representative in Yorkshire, he operated one venue in London, the Lime Grove Baths, at which Preston was booked as a late replacement in a televised bout with McManus.

It's never become public knowledge whether Morrell was intentionally trying to harm his colleagues at Dale Martin (which ran the rest of the capital and was McManus' main employer) or simply trying to build up Preston, but either way the promoter was behind the incident. According to Preston, speaking to the Wrestling Heritage site in his first public discussion of the issue, Morrell did not explicitly tell him to take an unplanned victory, rather that he should "go in there and make yourself known", the only limit being that he should not hurt McManus enough that the star wound up missing future bookings.

Preston won the first fall (which may have been the booked outcome) but it soon became clear he was not co-operating with McManus, leading the latter to eventually conclude that despite his own amateur background, he couldn't contend with Preston's legitimate skills. Instead he simply struck Preston in the groin, concluding that the controversy of a disqualification loss was the best available outcome.

It appears that although the bout aired in full later that day for Northern viewers, the bout was cut off before the conclusion in the Southern ITV region. Such an event wasn't unheard of on ITV in this era, but it does at least raise the possibility that Dale Martin was able to persuade broadcasters to make the face-saving move.

It wasn't just a case of his ability to draw fans making McManus a favourite at Dale Martin however. For a lengthy period, including much of the 1970s, he was the booker for the promotion. Hamill notes that this meant "a lot of people were frightened of him, because he had the pen." As a result, wrestlers were careful not to take the risk of involving McManus in the practical jokes that were commonplace in the business.

Pallo claimed that "All the lads used to call him Paramount because they reckoned all his bills were like a mountain with a star on top, just like the film company's trademark. Our Mick, of course, was the star, and the mountain was the supporting cast."

But while there may have been resentment among those passed over for top spots (Mal Sanders recalls that "some wrestlers found him hard work"), the consensus appears to be that although McManus used his power to protect his own position, his ability to attract crowds justified such behaviour.

Hamill notes that as a booker, McManus' manoeuvring was less about holding down other talent and more about carefully promoting himself. "He usually made sure to have other big stars on the show as well, like a Mark Rocco or a Tony St Clair, who helped draw the fans. But Mick always made sure he was billed as the main event, so he could make out the fans had all come to see him, even though there were lots of attractions on the show. He was pretty clever like that and he got away with it, so fair play to him!"

Although billed as the headliner on posters, McManus was also noted for using his power to make sure he got his favoured positioning in the second bout on the show. This meant that, having allowed the opening bout to warm up the crowd, he could have his match and then get home at a reasonable hour, something that was particularly attractive as he wrestled into his 50s. Hamill noted another benefit to the positioning: "Because he left while the show was still going on, he didn't have to worry about being hassled by fans or held up by being asked for autographs."

Despite his age, McManus remained a regular headliner throughout the 1970s, with notable moments including teaming with regular partner Steve Logan against fellow villains Kendo Nagasaki and Gorgeous George at the Royal Albert Hall, and taking the mask (on television at least) of Kung Fu.

As the decade went on, however, it became accepted that it was time for McManus to begin winding down and do his bit to promote some younger talent: with viewing figures on the slide, Joint Promoters made a specific effort at this time to push some new faces. While this may have been overdone at times, with a lack of star power on some shows, McManus was careful to make his losses meaningful rather than dilute the effect by losing to all and sundry.

Mick McManus

In April 1977, Tony St Clair handed McManus his second televised defeat, and the first to conclude with a pinfall. The following year McManus began a lengthy program to put Mal Sanders over, first losing a non-title match on television by 2 falls to one, then dropping his European Middleweight championship in a TV rematch, albeit by disqualification.

What made this so impactful was that not only had Sanders become the first (and as it turned out, only) man to twice beat McManus on the small screen, but at the time he was just 20 and had been on television for less than a year.

"We were on together almost every night for a couple of years," Sanders recalls. "Mick was a fantastic professional and when it was time for him to lose the belt, they saw a little bit of promise in me and it was definitely a case of right place, right time."

It proved a great learning experience for the rookie. "Mick just had to walk to the ring and people would react. He knew when to bring the crowd up, when to bring them down and when it was time for me to make a comeback. He was just a fantastic tradesman. He got so much heat just waving a fist or throwing an elbow that a lot of the time the promoter would have to arrange the card with a clean wrestling match on afterwards just to let the crowd calm down."

McManus would also wind up audiences by dishing out all manner of dirty moves, only to complain bitterly when he got a taste of his own medicine. One of his trademark spots was to plead with opponents not to go after his ears, which led to an inevitable outcome.

Sanders believes that McManus's ability to manipulate the crowd helped extend his career to an age long past his natural athletic prime. "He never got out of first gear because he never needed to. I remember one time at the Cambridge Corn Exchange when he suddenly shot up into the air. It turned out a woman had come up to the ring and stuck a lit cigarette into him. It was a horrible thing to happen of course, but I do remember it being so obvious something had happened because I'd never seen him move so fast!"

McManus finally called it a day in 1982 with his last television match being against ring comedian Catweazle, a frequent opponent in his final years. His final arena match, the following day, came against Steve Logan -- though it was a younger grappler of that name, rather than his famed tag partner.

In the two decades after retirement, McManus kept his name in the public eye, something that he had managed to do throughout his career thanks to all manner of public appearances and celebrity photo-ops. As well as pursuing an interest in antiques, running a pub and working in public relations, he made several guest appearances at new wrestling promotions and events. Following on from lending his name to a column in The Sun, a book and even vitamin pills during his active career, he hosted a video tape release in the late 80s and was featured in the

British edition of the Legends of Wrestling videogame. Unlike many of his counterparts, McManus never openly spoke about the way wrestling matches were put together.

Although appearing in relative good health as he appeared at wrestling reunions into his 90s, McManus was devastated by the death of his wife Barbara earlier this year. Living in a nursing home popular with retired actors, he sunk into a depression and eventually refused food and drink. He passed away on May 22nd, making headlines worldwide and attracting a flood of reminiscences and tributes. Ironically this final moment in the spotlight came exactly 50 years to the day after the Royal Albert Hall show with Prince Phillip.

While there's an argument that Big Daddy was a bigger star at his peak, Sanders sums up the respect and standing McManus had within the industry. "It was an absolute privilege to be able to work with him for so long. Wrestling Mick was every wrestler's dream and I'll never forget people like him who looked after me when I started.

"He was the best villain British wrestling ever saw, bar none."

# MIKE MARINO

"That man was 120% professional wrestling," is how Marty Jones remembers Mike Marino, who was one of the most consistent and reliable performers of the golden years of ITV wrestling.

Indeed, Marino's TV stardom went right back to the beginning: he faced Francis St Clair Gregory (father of Roy and Tony St Clair) on the first ever ITV wrestling show on 9 November 1955 at West Ham Baths. His TV involvement actually started a week earlier as he spent several sessions demonstrating holds on Kent Walton so that the commentator could more accurately describe.

In total Marino would become one of the few grapplers to appear in more than a hundred televised bouts, a figure that might have been higher had he not been off-screen for several years during his prime.

Although born Michael Harrison and a London resident, Marino liked to play up his Italian heritage, something that often left other grapplers unsure exactly what to believe. Johnny Kincaid recalls visiting Marino's house for dinner one night and finding "he was sitting there in front of me talking Italian to his dog! Well, until his wife walked in and said, 'Speak English, you silly sod.'"

Marino is reported to have had a spell boxing in Europe in his younger years, though records don't exist to confirm this. What is known is that his first recorded pro wrestling bout came on 22 April 1948 against Sonny Wallis. In his early years he wrestled in Spain and he also had at least one tour for the Japanese IWE promotion in 1969.

On the British circuit he quickly made his name as a highly-skilled technical grappler, working out in gyms with the likes of Bert Assirati and Billy Robinson. Kincaid recalls that Marino preferred a more credible, wrestling-base style: "He was a wrestler's wrestler. He liked to wrestle straight, and his moves were very feasible."

Marty Jones recalls that Marino didn't use his legitimate skills to take advantage of younger grapplers. "He was what I think of as a great [technical] worker, along the lines of a Pete Roberts or Terry Rudge. He could make anyone look good and he wanted you to look good. He gave me a lot of respect, partly because I had the Wigan training background, and I wish I'd spent more time with him."

Tony Walsh recalls getting a first-hand experience of Marino's abilities. "I was on with him on one of those nights where a lot of wrestlers hadn't shown up at the hall for various reasons. To try to fill the show until they arrived we had to wrestle on and on. I think we wound up doing five 10-minute rounds in the end. I learned a lot but that was a hard night!"

Writing in his autobiography "Thumbs Up", Joe Cornelius recalled an incident showing Marino's ability to maintain credibility. After Cornelius hit Marino with a particularly stiff knee to the head, Marino offered to show him how to hit a realistic but safe knee, despite the fact that the venue layout meant fans were right up against the ring. "The crowd hadn't got a clue what was going on: they didn't know he was teaching me in their time."

In another memorable bout with Cornelius, the crowd began booing the straight-laced action, prompting Marino to take extreme measures. "I took him into a headlock and he just lay there... We had raspberries and booing for five rounds and Mike just wouldn't do a thing." Johnny Kincaid notes this showed Marino's approach to the business: "Some wrestlers panic if the crowd doesn't respond right and start throwing themselves about. Marino made sure the crowd had what he wanted to give them."

With credibility still a major part in earning champion status, it was appropriate that Marino took the world mid-heavyweight title in 1960, beating Norman Walsh to kick off two decades of championship glory. Marino was also among the few grapplers deemed worthy as an opponent during Lou Thesz's tour of the UK in 1957.

In the early 1960s, Marino left Joint Promotions to become one of the leading stars for the recently-formed independent group Paul Lincoln Promotions, cutting short his television exposure. Between 1961 and 1966 he only had one TV bout, appearing as a special attraction on the 1963 Cup Final Day broadcast underneath the famed Pallo-McManus rematch. During his time with Paul Lincoln, Marino exchanged the world title with Al Hayes as well as having a high-profile match with Dr Death (Lincoln himself under a mask) at one of group's main venues, the 3,000-seat Granada Cinema in Tooting.

By the end of 1965 the promotional war came to an end, with Paul Lincoln joining forces with Joint Promotions. Just two days after the legal paperwork was complete, the New Year's Day 1966 ITV broadcast returned from an ad break with Marino, Al Hayes and several other wrestlers from the independent circuit invading the ring despite the protests of the MC.

Exactly which wrestler or wrestlers spoke is a subject of diverging memories, but one of the key points made was that Marino had not received any television exposure despite being world champion. Although the angle wasn't explicitly followed up on television (it took a couple of months before Marino returned to the small screen), it did lead to a series of "inter-promotional" bouts at some of the leading Joint venues.

With promotional wrangling out of the way, Marino was able to establish his utter dominance of the mid-heavyweight scene. Already a world titleholder he succeeded Bill Howes as holder of the European crown in the late 1960s after a brief spell of confusion where both men laid claim to the title. In 1966 he became British champion after previous titleholder Geoff Portz vacated the title through injury.

Marino would famously go on to hold all three titles throughout the 1970s. In a lesser-known honour, he also captured the Commonwealth title from Andy Robin in 1976, meaning he spent the rest of his career as a quadruple-champion.

Although a star around the country, the Royal Albert Hall was undoubtedly Marino's wrestling home where, as covered in last month's FSM he appears to have been the most frequent performer. Marino had a particularly strong record of being featured in main event matches that led to a profitable return bout at a later show. One example came in 1960 against Ian Campbell where historian and former Dale Martin publicist Russell Plummer recalls ticket touts asking for £40, equivalent to £780 at today's prices. From a storyline perspective at least, his most celebrated night came on 26 January 1976 when he beat Shirley Crabtree (Big Daddy) and Mick McManus in consecutive bouts.

During the 1970s Marino had a spell in the Dale Martin office working alongside Mick McManus and then taking over booking duties. Wrestler and fan attitudes to his performance are certainly mixed, with Tony St Clair posting on a discussion forum in 2005 that "as a matchmaker he was living in the past. People wanted to see good wrestling as always, but they also wanted excitement, not three matches of good guy versus good guy every show."

Other critics pointed to a lack of follow-up for hot matches and putting too much emphasis on filling cards with young inexperienced talent, though some have questioned how much of this was down to financial constraints.

That said, the criticism certainly isn't universal. Tony Walsh tells FSM that "Mike's booking really gave me the chance to show what I could do, unlike during the Daddy years. Sometimes it's nice when you are a professional wrestler to show you can wrestle!"

Meanwhile Johnny Kincaid points to Marino breaking tradition as a matchmaker. "He came up with the Caribbean Sunshine Boys name, which certainly helped my career. But one thing I really remember is that before then if you started out at a particular weight, you often stayed billed at that weight for the rest of your career, even if it looked silly when you piled on a few pounds and clearly weren't a welterweight any more. When Mike was matchmaking he gave me the chance to move up divisions and wrestle some of the bigger guys."

Whatever the view of his office work, wrestlers appear unanimous in recalling Marino's personality. "He was a hell of a guy," says Johnny Kincaid. "When he was serious he was really serious, but when he joked, he really joked.

"I remember one time Mike, Wayne Bridges and I were in a pub in Guildford and we were stood behind a bunch of proper old school Irish navvies with sideburns and donkey jackets. Mike took one sip of his beer, grimaced, said 'Ugh, that's vile' and calmly poured it into the pocket of one of the navvies. I was stood next to the guy, so I quickly took a few steps away and made sure Mike was in the way!

"Eventually the beer started leaking through the pocket and the guy could feel it dripping down him, so he turns round all angry. Well, you have to picture that Mike was a big guy who looked tough with those cauliflower ears, and he always had his head tilted to one side because of an old neck injury. As you can imagine, the guy turned round ready to kick off, looked up at Mike, then just walked away without saying another word!"

Marty Jones has his own memories of Marino's pranks. "About 40 years ago KFC was just starting to come out in Britain, so fried chicken was a new thing. We got back to Brixton (the Dale Martin base) on the bus after a show and all went along to KFC. Mike walks in alongside John Elijah and asks for 'two front legs, two back legs and a bit of breast.' John looks confused and starts arguing with him that there's no such thing as front legs on chicken.

The guy running the place steps in and says 'No, it's true. How do you think they pick up their food to eat?' John listens to him and then says "Oh right. I'll have a couple of front legs then", which cracks us up and we were teasing him for weeks after that. What he didn't know was that Mike had been into the shop a few days earlier and set the whole thing up!"

Although in no way questioning his honesty, wrestlers also recall that Marino certainly had a gift for tall tales. "He'd tell you the same story 10 times and every time it had a different ending," says Johnny Kincaid. "We used to call him Mick the Fib."

Tony Walsh recalls another nickname that shows the high esteem with which Marino was held. "He was sometimes billed as the Golden Boy, but in the dressing room we just called him Golden. Everyone loved him, and he was a real comic, even when he didn't know it. He was a legend in the business and one of life's characters. That's one of the things I miss most about that era -- all the different characters you used to get."

Mal Sanders remembers a trip to Kings Lynn for one of his first matches, with Marino driving the Dale Martin bus. "It was about five hours there and five hours back. I remember that by the end my stomach was actually aching with laughter at some of his antics. They don't make them like him anymore."

Sanders is the man best placed to describe yet another aspect of Marino's career: as a trainer of several stars including future world heavyweight champion Wayne Bridges and Sanders himself. "I used to train at the United Amateur wrestling club in Stockwell alongside the likes of Lee Bronson, Clive Muir and Ian [Big Bully] Muir. Mike Marino was in charge of recruiting and training new talent for Dale Martin at the time and he picked me out as a good prospect. He gave me a solid grounding and I was at the gym with him three or four times a week for a full year before my first pro match."

As well as showing him the holds, Marino took Sanders under his wing and acted as a mentor in the business. "You spend more time with wrestlers than your own family in this job, and Mike really was like a father to me. I think that as well as my amateur background he saw I had a bit of flamboyance and charisma about me. He could also see I wasn't frightened to get stuck in against some of the big names in the business. I'd never say I was as good a wrestler as him, but I like to think I followed his legacy and I certainly took over from him as a joker!"

By now in his late 50s, Marino for the most part remained active despite a spell away from the ring at the turn of the decade. The most high-profile bout of his final years came, appropriately enough, at the Royal Albert Hall in May 1980 when he lost to John Quinn who was being given a renewed push to set up a second Wembley Arena clash against Big Daddy (this time in a tag bout.) The match ended with a decisive Quinn victory as the referee stopped the match after Marino bled from the forehead, an appropriate finish given he had a reputation among ringsiders for having developed scar tissue vulnerable to laceration.

Marino's career would come to a tragic end on 24 August 1981, as Mal Sanders recalls. "He called me and asked me to drive him to the show which was unusual as, other than when we were on the Dale bus, he usually preferred to travel alone. When I picked him up he was very quiet, which wasn't like him. When we got to the building at Folkestone he looked grey and just wasn't Mike at all. We persuaded him to go to hospital to get checked out. It turned out he'd already been in recently for tests but at this point he'd not got the results back -- it wasn't until later we found out he'd got leukaemia.

After working the show, Sanders went to collect Marino from the hospital, where he'd signed himself out against medical advice. "I drove him home and he couldn't speak because he'd had an injection so his tongue had swollen up and he was holding a towel to his mouth. I was driving down the M20 and I remember right after I got to the unlit section Mike started having a fit and banging the roof. His teeth were locked into place and all he could manage to say was "I'm going to die."

Mike Marino

Although Sanders was eventually able to flag down a passing family who called for an ambulance, Marino couldn't be revived. "I went to see him in hospital and I remember thinking just how unfair and wrong it was that somebody who'd spent their life giving so many people so much pleasure should die on the side of the road.

"Many people told me later that if Mike had to pass away he'd have wanted me to be with him, but that didn't make it any easier. I still miss him and every time I get together with the lads for a drink or at a reunion we always talk about him. I was so lucky to have him believe in me."

Amid the tragedy, Sanders does recall a brief moment of levity: "I went to see him in his coffin and they'd embalmed him. He had these huge cauliflowered ears and they'd clearly struggled with them, so they looked like they'd come from a waxwork!"

Dale Martin promotions marked Marino's death a month later with a show at the Fairfield Halls, Croydon which included an eight-man tournament for the Mike Marino Memorial Shield. The tournament's winner was, appropriately enough, Mal Sanders who defeated John Naylor, Pat Patton and Syd Cooper to take the title. Sanders would go on to defend the shield in several subsequent bouts.

Upon his death Marino still held all four of his mid-heavyweight titles. The European and Commonwealth titles effectively disappeared after his passing, while the British title remained inactive until being revived by All Star Promotions in the early 20th century.

The only vacancy filled by promoters at the time was the World championship, with a reported series of elimination matches coming down to a televised title bout between Marty Jones and the Guadeloupe-born and European based Bobby Gaetano. Jones took the title and ensured that Marino's legacy would live on:

"Every time I put that belt around my waist, I thought of Mike and what an honour it was to hold his title. I looked at him as the Joe Louis of wrestling. He would have been a professional wrestler 26 hours a day if he could."

# MITZI MUELLER

"We were walking in Manchester and saw one of these old promoters and then my Dad started talking to him and just jokingly said 'I'm sure my daughter would love to be a wrestler.' And the [promoter] said 'Well, that's no problem' and we just started from there."

Relatives having already been in the business was one of the most common reasons for British wrestlers to get involved, and that's certainly true of Mitzi Mueller, the daughter of Joe Connelly. She would go on to be arguably the biggest female star British wrestling has ever seen.

The chance meeting in Manchester may have been a casual remark, but Mueller decided to follow up on it. "My father knew two old promoters called Johnny Howes and Chunky Hayes. My dad would go down to the gym training and I went down with him one day and they said, "Come on, get in the ring, we'll see what you can do."

Choosing a ring name was no problem as her mother's pre-marriage name of Mitzi Mueller not only rolled off the tongue, but also happened to be reminiscent of American female wrestling supremo the Fabulous Moolah. Debuting in the ring against 'Naughty' Nancy Barton in 1963 was another matter however. Barton, the step-daughter of veteran Roy 'Bull' Davies, was a tough performer, while Mueller was just 14.

"[It brings back] bad memories. I think we went into about the fourth or the fifth round and then she took me on her shoulders in what we used to call an airplane spin. She threw me down and I landed on my face and I got knocked out!"

It didn't take long to get over the rude awakening and become comfortable in the ring. "Only a matter of weeks later to be honest with you. That's life, life goes on -- if you have an injury, you get up and brush yourself down and carry on."

With Joint Promotions having no interest in female grapplers, Mueller was left building her name on the independent or 'opposition' circuit. This regularly involved battles with local authorities and pressure groups who opposed the very idea of women wrestling, as frequent opponent Klondyke Kate recalled.

"The girls had to overcome the preconception that it was all for the dirty mac brigade, rather than something you could bring your family to see. Mitzi was able to do that: she was very ladylike and looked and spoke very feminine: she epitomised what women's wrestling was all about. She always looked like a lady in the ring doing athletic stuff, which is hard to do when you're stomping around!"

For the most part, the novelty of women's wrestling would draw a crowd, leaving it up to Mueller to make sure they returned. "We'd go into towns and you'd see the posters of female wrestlers and in them days it was a new thing, so people would come along and think 'Ooh, this is something different, let's go and watch it.' And we'd give them a good show, so each time we went back to that place we'd get crowds."

On one memorable occasion, the crowds most certainly were not there, as Eddie Hamill explained. "We had a show in Partick in Ireland where the girls were on for the first time and we thought it would be a great draw. When we got there, it was almost empty, and we couldn't understand why. We only found out when a journalist from the local newspaper turned up and told us the paper had simply not printed the advert for the show because it decided it didn't approve of women's wrestling. The amazing thing is that the journalist still turned up and expected to do an interview!"

Even on those shows which didn't run up against opposition, Mueller still faced the occasional hitch. "We were on the way to a show in Ireland and our vehicle broke down, not too far from a farm. Somebody knocked on the farmer's door and he had a tractor and a trailer, and luckily it wasn't too far from the venue, so we all ended up going there in the trailer!"

Further problems came on a tour of Turkey where the prospect of female grapplers was a major draw at what was planned to be a series of consecutive nights of shows at a stadium. Mueller recalls that things didn't go to plan.

"The Turkish promoter got really greedy because he thought 'well, we've filled the stadium. Let's not put the women on tonight and we'll do it tomorrow or the day after' [to draw another crowd.] There were riots and as we all ran on to the bus, most of the people got through the police barrier and they started tipping the bus over."

Mueller was also involved in another memorable incident in Turkey, as Hamill explains. "All the local women wore traditional clothes with only their eyes uncovered, so when Mitzi walked along the road, she brought a lot of attention. With her long blonde hair, t-shirt and shorts, she certainly took the men's' breath away. As we walked through the markets, our gaze followed a man who could not take his eyes off her. We watched him for several seconds until he literally fell from our view. Along the road, we had dodged a very large and deep hole in the ground, and yes, you guessed it, he fell down it."

That tour was promoted by another leading opposition promoter, Brian Dixon, who was now Mueller's husband. The pair had a memorable first meeting when he refereed one of her matches and mistakenly stepped on her hair when she was trying to get up. It prompted an angry first conversation that eventually sparked off a romance. Mueller would go on to be one of the key attractions for Dixon as he turned to promoting himself and needed to offer something that couldn't be seen on ITV's wrestling coverage.

That's not to say Mueller wasn't a recognisable figure. Indeed, she was a regular on television in both acting roles and as a guest in her own right. "The first acting I did was for Muscle Market, a BBC Play for Today. We went to the theatre and the producer, whoever did it then, saw me and said, 'Who's that lady' and then 'I want her in my play."

Over the years Mueller's CV included appearances on everything from Minder and The Bill to BBC health show "Looking Good, Feeling Fit." She was also the first guest when ITV revived the panel show "What's My Line?" and contestants had to guess her profession.

Her most prominent show was not as a performer, but rather as a subject in the play Trafford Tanzi. Still performed to this day, it was loosely based around Mueller's life and was another example of lucky timing. "[Writer] Clare Luckham was on her honeymoon, I think in Paignton near Torquay. At this time of night, it was raining, and they saw a poster, probably with my photograph on it and they came in to watch the wrestling show. She'd never been to a wrestling show before. Sitting down and watching it, she thought to herself 'I can write a play about female wrestlers.'"

That she did, and Mueller not only shared her experiences, but helped train some of the actors who performed wrestling moves in the play, which is staged in a ring and is broken into rounds rather than scenes. "We trained for months and months and months and went up and down the country seeing what these students could do. Then Toyah Wilcox got the part and she was fabulous, she really was. She took to it straight away. There was no stardom whatsoever about her. When she had her break while everyone else was in the ring training, she'd go and make cups of tea and coffee for everybody."

Mueller's comfort with media exposure proved invaluable in what was arguably her biggest battle: to be able to wrestle in London. While reports that London councillors banned 'All-In' wrestling in the 1930s because of its violent content are unconfirmed, wrestling in the capital was certainly hit by a clampdown on entertainment licences during the war years. When hostilities ceased, London City Council expressly omitted women from wrestling and boxing licensing.

That stance was shared by the LCC's successor, the Greater London Council, which took power in 1965. The first real challenge came from Sue Brittain, who wanted to appear on shows run in the capital by wrestler Al Hollamby under the name Verdun Leslie Promotions. She argued that the licensing restriction was a breach of equal opportunities legislation as it meant she was unable to take up an offer of employment that could be taken by a man. The GLC countered with a technicality: London bye-laws were technically Acts of Parliament and thus were exempt from the equal opportunities law.

Brittain's challenge proved successful and she wrestled Jane St John in Wimbledon on 23 August 1979 in what was the first major women's match in the capital for 40 years. However, the GLC appealed the case and eventually won in the House of Lords, reinstating the ban just three months later.

New GLC leader Ken Livingstone, who took power in 1981, continued to support the ban, leading Mueller to launch a campaign to have it overturned permanently. "He didn't want female wrestlers, he said it degraded everybody. My argument to him was that if people don't want to come and see us, then they won't come and buy a ticket. Let us put our show on and we'll see."

As well as debating the issue on television, Mueller released a record to promote her cause. She turned to author songwriter Robert Rigby, who was working as musical director on one of the many stagings of Trafford Tanzi.

"My brief was to write a catchy song that would also get the message over, and from that came 'Let the Girls In To London Town.' It was a big rocky number. I brought in some of my old contacts to play on it, including the drummer from Dr Feelgood and Suzi Quatro's guitarist. We had female backing vocals and I was in the mix too as the ref and MC.

"I wouldn't say that Mitzie was a natural in the studio, but she was a real trouper and worked tirelessly until we were satisfied with the vocals. In those days records had 'B' sides and I'd written a gentle little ballad called Slowly for her - I think she actually preferred singing that one."

While Livingstone wasn't persuaded by the campaign, the decision was taken out of his hands in 1986 with the abolition of the GLC when the relevant powers instead moved to individual borough councils. The following year Westminster City Council agreed to allow women's wrestling, which paved the way for Brian Dixon's to run the Royal Albert Hall.

Mueller made her farewell teaming with Rusty Blair against the 'Bovver Birds' duo of Klondyke Kate and Nicky Monroe. "I remember there were a lot of big stars that turned up. Most of the wrestlers that were on the bill knew a lot of people, so you looked out into the audience and just saw people you recognised."

While it was certainly a fitting finale to headline British wrestling's most prestigious venue, Mueller's departure was somewhat out of her hands. A series of significant injuries had peaked with a back problem in which two of her discs were rubbing against one another and Dixon insisted she call it a day for the sake of her long-term health. That led to a sudden readjustment to 'ordinary' life, particularly given Dixon continued heading out on the road every day.

"It was hard for me because I'd been doing it for so long. When something's in your blood for that many years, it takes a heck of a long time to sit down and think, well, I'm not going to be doing this any longer."

While she devoted much of her time to animal welfare charities, Mueller was able to ease back into the wrestling world without taking physical risks. She began working as an MC for All-Star and appeared on one ITV show in 1988, making her one of just a handful of women, alongside valets Princess Paula and Dr Monica Kaiser, to be featured during the ITV run.

Mueller also became involved in All-Star's training school in Merseyside. As well as making occasional appearances on All Star shows today, she remains firmly rooted to the business thanks to her daughter Letitia, who is All-Star's regular MC, and her son-in-law Dean Allmark, a leading wrestler.

Looking back, she is clear about what she misses most from her time in the ring. "It's the camaraderie and the people. The fans were my number one priority at the time, and when I made my record I used to wrestle and sit by ringside and sell my records and sign autographs. I miss all that -- all the people and how genuine they were."

# ORIG WILLIAMS

"He was billed as El Bandito," says Eddie Hamill of the late Orig Williams, "and he was definitely a bandit. But he was the nice type of bandit!"

Williams was one of the biggest independent or "opposition" promoters of the ITV era, but to describe him solely in terms of his wrestling and promoting career would be a disservice to a man universally recognised by his peers and indeed in Welsh culture as a truly remarkable figure.

He grew up in the tiny Welsh village of Ysbyty Ifan in North Wales which, even today has a registered population of less than 200 people. Evidence of the rural nature of his upbringing comes in his uncle's profession: a collector of urine in order to provide ammonia to professional wool washers. (Redheads have the most productive urine according to Williams' autobiography.)

Leaving school after the second world war, Williams enrolled in the RAF where he regularly fought, both in official boxing and wrestling sessions and in brawls in local towns while on leave. He then moved into professional football, spending time with Oldham Athletic and Shrewsbury before moving into the Welsh leagues where the rules of the game proved no barrier to continuing to fight.

As player-manager of Nantlle Vale he was engaged in numerous physical incidents that would be scarcely believable if the press cutting did not exist. Among the most notable were the time he was sent off just four minutes into a game, and the time his side's aggressive manner caused the opposing goalkeeper to simply walk out mid-match.

Things came to a head when one game was abandoned, and Williams was summoned to a disciplinary hearing at Rhyl Town Hall, which ironically would become his home venue as a promoter. He was given a six-month ban and threatened with permanent exclusion for a future offense. The punishment prompted him to seek an alternative career as a professional wrestler, having noticed that attendance at games was hit hard when wrestling was shown on ITV.

Although Williams turned pro thanks to contacts made via his former Army amateur coach, he struggled initially, and it was only legitimate combat in the boxing booths that helped him make a breakthrough. Although more than happy to take on all comers, he had to be coached in the art of "working for the nubbins"

-- in other words, to deliberately engineer an exciting contest that earned the crowd's approval. With the help of a bogus sob story from the ring announcer about how the fighters were unpaid amateurs and in need of money to support a family orphaned by a mining accident, such contests could encourage the crowd to donate money in appreciation of the "hard-fought" victory.

It proved a valuable lesson in the psychology of the wrestling business, something Williams passed on to Klondyke Kate. "Bobby Barron taught me the moves and gave me my start, but Orig taught me how to be the villain and tell a good story. Cowboys and Indians still enthrals a crowd."

Williams' own education continued when he was invited to wrestle in Pakistan with the Bholus, a family with genuine hero status in the country. He went on to spend several months living with the family. According to Peter Nulty, who went on to wrestle and referee for Williams as Jack 'Flash' Davey as well as being his business partner for many years, "the Bholus taught him everything he knew about promoting. We wouldn't always agree and when I'd suggest something he didn't like, he'd start his reply 'Akram [Bholu] once said...' It didn't matter that it was 40 years ago Akram had said it!"

The friendship continued with Williams bringing the entire family over for a successful UK tour aimed at fans in the Pakistani community, including a memorable show in Bradford where all five brothers were victorious. Williams was also brought in as referee for a memorable show in Pakistan where Akram took on Antonio Inoki. Reportedly disgruntled by an attempted deviation from the booked finish, Inoki wound up breaking Akram's arm, leaving a disappointed Williams to call an end to the bout.

During the initial tour Williams met the behemoth Klondyke Bill who, along with his equally oversized and unkempt brother Klondyke Jake were among the leading figures in his cast of characters, including women wrestlers and midgets, who didn't fit into the more traditional sports-like roster of Joint Promotions. A BBC documentary as part of the Philpott Files series shows how the sheer size of the pair combined with the remote nature of many of the towns Williams ran to allow for some easy promotion: the "brothers" would simply walk around the town in the afternoon before a show, attracting the attention of local residents before explaining the reason for their visit.

Of all British promoters, Williams probably covered the widest territory. While he based himself in Wales (which Joint Promotions largely ignored aside from Cardiff), he also ran dates in parts of England and Scotland, as well as making regular tours of Ireland.

Between 1982 and 1995 he produced regular TV shows for S4C, the Welsh version of Channel 4, under the banner of Reslo (which translated simply as 'Wrestling'), He took advantage of the looser broadcasting standards to present more violent bouts than seen on ITV, often with stipulations. "He was still putting on a family show," Klondyke Kate notes, "but he liked you to show a bit more fighting spirit."

Neither were the British Isles a limit to Williams: he promoted shows around the world, from British army based in Europe to tours of the Middle East and Africa. This led to numerous hair-raising incidents, such as dangerous overcrowding at a Nigerian show run by the infamous "Power Mike" where, having run out of printed tickets to sell, staff simply handed out blank pieces of paper to be accepted as passes, something that perhaps inevitably led to mass "counterfeiting".

Then there was the show in Turkey where fans were enraged, though accounts vary as to exactly what upset them and who was responsible. One version has it that promoters had attracted great interest by billing women and, seeing a sell-out crowd, decided to hold off their appearance until a second show. Another has it that a top star was falsely billed as being injured but ready to fight the following evening, only for the same trick to be attempted the next night. Every version of the tale has the same ending however: Williams and company fleeing for their lives after fans literally set the timber stadium on fire.

Indeed, it seemed that wherever Williams promoted, incident was sure to follow, as Tony St Clair recalls of one trip to Zimbabwe.

"Flying over, I got upgraded to first class, which seemed great until I went to the bathroom and discovered about a square foot of the padding was missing and you could see straight to the outside of the plane. I told Mark Rocco about this and he had a look and then complained to the stewardess saying, 'This is dreadful.' She replied 'Well, what can I do?' Mark then asked what films were playing and she said 'Films? You're lucky we're in the air!'

"We then did the tour and went to a big reception one night. Most of the wrestlers were sat together and then Orig Williams was on the top table with Otto Wanz, [CWA matchmaker] Peter William and then Robert Mugabe and his wife. They were chatting away all night; about what, who knows?

"Then we came to the flight back and directly after take-off the cabin filled with smoke and the warning signs came on. Mark, Danny [Collins] and I downed a bottle of vodka inside five minutes. We had an emergency landing, but it took about 20 minutes because they had to dump fuel to make it safe.

"The airline staff then told us they would put us on their other plane. Not 'another' plane, but 'the' other plane. About three hours later we took off and after five minutes it had problems. There was no smoke this time, but it must have been more serious because we landed straight away. We then had to spend an extra three days in Zimbabwe waiting for them to get a working plane."

Orig Williams

In the early years of his career, Williams certainly was not above pulling a few strokes. "He'd do anything to make money," Hamill recalls. "He'd print up posters with MCMANUS and PALLO in big letters and you had to read very carefully to see the small writing to see it was Mike MCMANUS and Jimmy PALLO.

"Other times he'd list the right name but put 'are invited to appear' -- that was a good one! When the show started he'd announce that they'd been invited but refused to show up. That was pretty embarrassing when you were an unknown youngster and you'd have to go out in the first match and face the crowd after that."

Over the years, Williams mellowed a little in his approach to pulling a crowd, largely because he began running venues regularly and realised you could only fool an audience once before disappointing them. Klondyke Kate says that by the 1980s he was "running a very legitimate, very lucrative business." That said, around the turn of the century he was among those promoters running shows with wrestlers portraying knock-offs of popular WWF performers, justifying the presentation not as an attempt to deceive fans but as a "tribute" show in the same manner as happens in the music world.

To be fair to Williams, he was certainly the victim of some shady practices himself, particularly in Ireland. It became almost a running joke when running small buildings in the Republic that venue owners would demand a last minute price hike knowing that Williams would get the blame from an angry crowd if the show didn't go ahead. Things were even worse further North, as Kate recalls: "We'd have shows where the IRA would turn up, demand the takings and even the raffle money, and then leave us to carry on with the show. It was quite surreal!"

Peter Nulty notes that Williams was also renowned for his aggressive style in the ring. "Deep down he was a drinker and a fighter. He loved to hurt people. He wasn't a bully and expected you to hit him back just as hard, but it was a case of defend yourself at all times. His stomps were like being hit with a concrete block: if he stomped you once, you made sure to grab his foot before he did it a second time."

There was a famous incident in which Williams came off worse, however, involving Tony St Clair who recalls: "I used to throw punches that, shall I say, sometimes connected and sometimes didn't. This time he was getting all excited and leaned in a bit too far, and I threw the punch a little too far -- it was a bit of both -- and I cracked him right on the nose. He slowly toppled over, then looked up at me shocked and said 'You can't do that! I'm the fucking promoter!'"

The old cliché about hard but fair certainly applied to Williams. On one occasion a disgruntled wrestler suckerpunched a rival in a hotel bar after a show. Williams was not upset by the fact that two colleagues had fought in public, but rather that one had taken an unfair advantage. He ordered the pair to meet in his garage the next day to settle their differences in a fair fight.

With fighting out the way, it was time for the drinking. "We always had to make sure the show was finished before last orders," explains Hamill. "Orig couldn't go to bed without a pint. The first thing after the show was the pub, never going back to where you were sleeping. It only took him two pints to get pissed, but he was always a happy pissed fellow." That said, Adrian Street recalls Williams getting into a heated argument with a talking Macaw in a hotel bar. The bird had the temerity not only to ape Williams' solo rendition of 'Danny Boy' but then to repeat back Williams's ensuing curses.

Nulty explains that the pub sessions were a key part of Williams' operation. "He would never shy away from the lads: there was never any 'them and me'. Some of the trips to Ireland were notoriously long, like 32 shows in 28 days, so drinking was part of making us one big happy family to survive the stresses. Sometimes a wrestler would come on tour and not get on with everyone else in the pub and they'd never be invited back again."

Drinking was in turn a gateway for Williams's other big love: talking. "He loved to speak to people," says Nulty." "He was never happier than in a little back street pub where he'd wind up chatting to a couple of random old men about the old times.

"He'd phone me every day, and if I missed a call, he'd leave a message saying, 'I need to speak to you urgently!' When I called back it would turn out he just wanted a chat."

It wasn't just wrestling that Williams could talk about, as St Clair recalls. "The first time I met him in Roy 'Bull' Davies's pub, we didn't speak a single word about wrestling: it was all football, which was a common interest.

According to Kate, "He was very intelligent: he could talk about anything. Unlike some people in wrestling he'd always read and listen to things to keep up with what was happening in the world, right until he died.

"I'd left school at 15 to become a wrestler and after I had my first child I decided to take a break to go back and finish my education with GCSE's, A Levels and even a degree. Even though that meant missing shows, Orig totally supported me because he knew there'd be a time for me after wrestling -- I'm just lucky that time turned out to be way down the line. He taught everyone not to be just a one trick pony with wrestling but to get out and experience life."

Williams certainly did that towards the end of his career and beyond. He took a keen interest in Welsh culture and current affairs and even took up a regular column in the Daily Post titled 'Siarad Plaen' ('Plain Speaking') where he shared his uncompromising views on life and politics. Editor Rob Irvine later noted that "he certainly did speak as he found, even if that left myself and the lawyers twitching a little as the paper went to press."

As his own in-ring career took over, Williams supported the next generation of both family and business. His daughter Tara Bethan became a singer and actress, appearing on the BBC contest 'I'd Do Anything' and taking on a regular role in S4C's flagship soap opera Pobol y Cwm. Meanwhile Williams championed a young recruit in Barri Griffiths who became first Goliath in Gladiators and later Mason Ryan in WWE, signing his developmental deal shortly before Williams' death. Nulty notes that "Orig was so proud of Barri. Finding a Welsh heavyweight with the potential to make it big on the world stage was one of the highlights of his career."

Another of Williams' proudest honours was being named to the Gorsedd y Beirdd (community of the bards), a select group of poets, artists and others who have made a noted contribution to Welsh language and culture. Taking a keen interest in poetry himself, William's final words before dying from a heart condition in 2009 were to recite poetry by the Welsh language writer Cynan.

A reported 500 people attended Williams funeral, an event Kate recalls as "the saddest I've ever been to. As much as it was meant to be a celebration of his life, to see how much people loved him and missed him was devastating."

Eddie Hamill is among those for whom Williams remains sorely missed. "I still go to wrestling at his old base of Rhyl Town Hall and the people there still think of him as being there. He loved wrestling, but I think he could have done anything. He just had that personality and had ideas and was such a big character.

"He'd done things you wouldn't think people could do."

# PAT ROACH

There are few men who have wrestled with Bret Hart, Giant Haystacks and Andre the Giant. But there must surely only be one who has also grappled with James Bond, Indiana Jones and Mr Blobby.

Francis Roach, better known by his middle name Pat, was born in 1937 and grew up in Birmingham. During his younger years he held a series of jobs around the area ranging from delivering coal and working with a "rag and bone" iron dealer, to running a string of cafes and selling one-arm-bandit fruit machines.

It was his sporting ability that was to lead to his first true profession however. As well as competing against the public on a fairground boxing booth, Roach had become a skilled judo practitioner, with several claims that he won one or more national titles. (Suggestions that he made it to the final of the first world championship in Tokyo in 1956, only to lose on a coin-flip, can be confirmed as a typical exaggeration by fellow wrestlers. Ironically the bronze medalist in that event, Anton Geesink, later had a successful career with All Japan Pro Wrestling.)

Roach's athletic abilities weren't limited to combat. In 1979 he was invited to compete in the first televised Britain's Strongest Man, the contest that kicked off shot-putter Geoff Capes' stardom. And in 1986 Roach even played a game for the Birmingham Bulls American football team amid the gridiron mania that swept the country during its initial coverage on Channel 4.

These sporting skills were his entry ticket to the wrestling business, where he was trained by local grappler Alf Kent. His debut on television on 18 June 1966 was no throwaway preliminary bout: he took on Billy Joyce, who would win his sixth British heavyweight title just ten days later. Indeed, historians at the Wrestling Heritage site note that Roach's first three televised opponents -- Joyce, Gwyn Davies and Billy Robinson -- were "probably the top three heavyweights in Britain at the time."

It wasn't just Roach's size and skill that attracted attention. The 1970 "Mick McManus Wrestling Book" revealed Roach's party trick of sticking safety pins into painful parts of his skin including the throat, which he would perform for fans and colleagues alike.

The book also tells of the time Roach was hired to act as a minder for Madeline Hartog Bell of Peru, better known as Miss World 1967, while she visited Birmingham. Unfortunately for Pat he was mistakenly locked outside the building and began frantically knocking on the door, only to hear a voice inside inform him that "Miss World's bodyguard is a big fellow and if you don't push off he'll be called to deal with you."

In all Roach would go on to wrestle on ITV almost 90 times over the next two decades, a figure topped by only 16 other grapplers, and an achievement all the more impressive given how much time Roach spent away from the ring.

Roach also wrestled across the globe, including a 1969 tour of Tokyo with the then dominant IWE promotion (albeit a tour where Roach's hand was rarely if ever raised in victory) and a trip to India where his size and distinctive looks made him an ideal victim for local superstar Dara Singh.

The two men worked together again across Canada in December 1974 before Roach moved down to California where he was dubbed "Lord" Patrick Roach, a gimmick about as far from his Midlands background as it got. After wrestling the likes of Andre the Giant, Dino Bravo and trampolining sensation Dennis Stamp, Roach became one of the "international superstars" making up the numbers in the annual January battle royales in Los Angeles and San Francisco. In the latter bout, Roach's new peerage did him little good as he was the first man eliminated, thrown out by eventual winner Pat Patterson.

Roach also wrestled in several of the lengthy tournaments in Germany, leading to a telling story recalled by fellow tourist Johnny Kincaid in his own autobiography. According to Kincaid, British wrestlers working abroad generally looked out for themselves, but Roach proved a stark exception. After a public dispute with a promoter, Kincaid was told he would no longer be used. Roach immediately threatened to walk out and take the other British performers with him, reasoning "This man is a professional wrestler, he's a star, and you can't have a little fat man pushing him around in front of the public: they would have no respect for him as a wrestler."

He didn't always favour principles over practicalities as Clive Myers, who toured with Pat to Zimbabwe and Dubai, explained to FSM: "I was complaining about the wages we used to get, and I remember Pat persuading me to be satisfied because '10% of something is better than 90% of nothing.' I will always remember him for his cool and compassionate way of dealing with others."

Having been spotted during a match by Stanley Kubrick, Roach was hired to play a bouncer in A Clockwork Orange, kicking off a career as an actor specialising in combat scenes. At a legitimate 6'4" Roach towered over most leading men and his wrestling skills proved a great basis for combat scenes. Roach also had the advantage that although he was physically dominant, his facial features weren't so distinctive that he overshadowed the characters he played: indeed, even regular wrestling viewers didn't always recognise him on screen.

On another early acting job, Roach performed in a TV advert for whiskey aimed at the Japanese market and directed by Ridley Scott, though unlike Bill Murray's character in Lost In Translation, this didn't involve a trip to Tokyo. Instead it was in Arundel, Sussex where Roach met his co-star and future lifetime friend Vic Armstrong, whose voice came alive as he began speaking to FSM about his "fabulous, fabulous" colleague:

"I'm not sure quite what the story of the commercial was meant to be, but it involved Pat dressed up as a Scotsman, picking me up by the feet, swinging me round and throwing me away like I was a log. We ended up doing that move [in other films] for the next forty years!"

On one occasion in a later movie Roach had to toss Armstrong into a narrow mine shaft with little padding or room for error. "I was completely in his hands and it was like asking him to thread a needle with a dart, but he hit it perfectly."

Armstrong is among the world's leading movie fight choreographers and is recognised by the Guinness Book of Records as the most prolific stunt double. He explains that Roach was "very professional and totally legit" when it came to learning film combat and the two quickly built up an understanding of how to best pool their skills.

Armstrong would lay out the precise order and timing of the kicks and punches, making sure every move was in the right position to be caught on camera without exposing that it hadn't connected, while Roach would contribute idea for holds and grappling sequences. "He also taught me the dropkick, which I always remember as being a bit weird: the teacher showing the student how to knock him out!"

Even on sharing a hotel room the first night they worked together, Armstrong was struck by Roach's considered and forceful opinions. "He always had a theory on everything and would tell you all about it, whether it was income tax, how to get a table at a restaurant, or the best way to pull birds."

Armstrong would go on to share many memorable moments with Roach. "The next time I saw him after the job, he arrived in his Rolls Royce, but the back of it was virtually dragging along the ground, as if the car was falling apart. It all made sense when he pulled up, got out, opened the back door and all his training weights rolled out!"

Although the two worked on more high-profile films, it was Red Sonja that provided two of Armstrong's favourite memories of working with Roach. The first came when the pair had been sparring in the gym and Roach mistakenly gave Armstrong a black eye. "The next day the girls were all over me, asking what big brute had done that to me. Next time we went to the gym, Pat stuck his hands behind his back and said, 'Go on, take a shot -- I want some of that loving comfort too.'"

While working on the movie, shot in Mexico City, the pair discovered Andre the Giant was in town to wrestle. Roach, Armstrong and the movie's leading star Arnold Schwarzenegger accepted his invitation to see the show, albeit it with some transportation problems as "Andre took up the entire back seat of a 4x4."

Once at the show, which was first, and only live wrestling event Armstrong ever saw, the trio were introduced to the crowd and received a warm reaction. That soon changed. "Once the match began, we realised Andre was the villain and was destroying all these little guys. First the crowd started booing him, then they realised we were his friends and began screaming and even throwing bottles at us."

The group were escorted by security to the dressing room where Armstrong got a first-hand look at the wacky world of pro wrestling. "The room was full of guys covered in blood. But they were all saying, 'See you next week' to one another and 'Drive home carefully', even though they'd just been out there half-killing each other. I was absolutely mesmerised."

In the foreword of Roach's autobiography If, Schwarzenegger recalls that the trio then accompanied Andre and a group of wrestlers to a restaurant where he, Roach and Andre wound up in a "friendly argument" about who would pay the bill. "The frightened Maitre d' standing between us was thinking to himself: 'I don't care who pays -- as long as I get out of this alive!'"

Roach's best known movie roles are arguably in the Indiana Jones series. He's one of just a couple of dozen crew members to work on all three films in the original trilogy and, like Armstrong, was presented with an exclusive jacket with the dates of the movies and the legend "It's not the years that get you, it's the miles." Other than Harrison Ford, Roach was the only person to appear on screen in all three films, managing to pull off four separate roles.

In Raiders of the Lost Ark, Roach played both a giant Sherpa who wrestles Indian Jones in a bar and, more famously, a bald German who fights Jones (played here by Armstrong as a stunt double) for several minutes on an airfield before being chopped to pieces by a propeller. Though the scene is widely regarded as a screen combat classic, Armstrong considers it his funniest recollection of Roach:

"Because he'd shaved his head, Pat had lost the sensory perception you get from having hair, which you can see in action any time somebody unconsciously ducks while passing through a doorway. All through that scene I kept seeing poor Pat's skin peeling off because he couldn't stop bumping his head on the wing of the plane!"

In Temple of Doom, Roach played a guard who is thrown into a rock crusher, while in Last Crusade he appeared only as a background character who is a

Gestapo member. On this occasion Roach filmed two different death scenes, neither of which were used, both involving the chase of Indiana Jones and his father as they escape a Zeppelin airship by plane. In one version, Roach hitches a ride with a drunken pilot who forgets to switch the plane's engine on before detaching it from the airship. In an alternate take Roach's giant frame means he simply drops through the bottom of the plane.

Roach also appeared in the "unofficial" James Bond movie Never Say Never Again, playing Count Lippe. It took several weeks of rehearsals and filming to put together a six-minute fight scene involving Lippe and a combination of Sean Connery in close-ups and Armstrong as stuntman. Lippe met his doom crashing into a collection of medical syringes, though it was the turning point of the fight that Armstrong remembers most vividly:

"Connery picks up a bottle of urine and then it cuts to me throwing it in Pat's eyes, blinding him and taking control. I'll never forget how bizarre it was to keep seeing that bottle's label: 'Urine sample -- James Bond.'"

Among Roach's other film roles were performances in four separate Robin Hood instalments, playing alongside dwarf actor Warwick Davies as General Kael in Willow, and portraying the evil incarnations of both Clark Kent and Superman in Superman III.

While Roach went on to appear in bit parts in virtually every television show going, from The Bill to Casualty, he truly hit the public eye in 1983 with a leading role in ITV's Auf Wiedersehen Pet where he played Brian 'Bomber' Busbridge. Despite his big-screen career, the lack of outlandish costumes or make-up meant it was the first time Roach had become a truly recognisable celebrity, making him a firm favourite among the wrestling audience after years of suspicious or even hostile reactions.

The fame didn't go to his head, as Keith Myatt explains: "When I first met Pat Roach, I knew of his work in TV and films, and I expected to find a guy with an ego and big head like with so many people that I had met before who were well known through the media. When I first walked through the dressing room door what I saw was a giant of a man a gentle giant with impeccable manners. Pat had learned his trade well and always gave one hundred percent in the ring and was respected by his fellow professionals and he was always there to give you advice after he watched you wrestle. He was a quietly spoken man with a dry sense of humour."

Some wrestlers got a slightly less orthodox introduction to Roach, however. As Sweet Saraya recalls: "He never really spoke much to me and I kept my head down as he was old school hierarchy, just an occasional smile or a nod of the head was about as much as I got out of him. Then this one day I was preparing myself to wrestle and Pat went past my room, stopped, giggled and carried on walking.

"I went out to wrestle and when I got back to the girls changing room (which was a broom cupboard) someone had written on my mirror in my lipstick 'I love you always xx'. It was quite startling, but I thought it was [my husband] Ricky [Knight] and went in to the lads' changing room to find out.

"There sat Pat with a huge grin on his face saying 'I see you got my message then'; he was smiling, and he winked at me. That was Pat's way of welcoming me to the business. Even though by that time I had been in the job around 12 year, he decided that day to accept me. And what an honour that was."

Indeed, Roach was so respected among his peers that he was chosen to be in the final televised match when ITV dropped British wrestling in 1988, beating Caswell Martin by two falls to one. He then delivered a farewell address aired at the end of a highlights programme the following week, telling the viewers on behalf of all wrestlers that "we are very, very, very sad that in the near future we will now no longer be in your front parlour."

Despite his TV success Roach continued wrestling into the early years of the 21st century, as well as becoming heavily involved in the annual wrestler reunions. Among his regular roles on such occasions was to read out the list of wrestlers who had died in the preceding year, making his death in 2004 from throat cancer all the more poignant.

As well as hiding the physical effects of the disease, Roach had kept his lengthy illness a private matter: Vic Armstrong first learned of the cancer when reading his obituary. It wasn't until just six weeks before his death, when he attended a reunion at Ellesmere Port, that the effects of the illness were clearly visible, as Myatt recalls:

"When he entered the room about thirty to forty hardened wrestlers and ex wrestlers rose to their feet to give him a standing ovation, something that I will never forget. A man's man is how I would describe him, and it was an honour to have known him."

# PETE ROBERTS

Each year at the southern wrestling reunion in Kent a string of former British grapplers will accept an honour from their peers. But it's almost a running joke for organisers that Pete Roberts will refuse to take to the stage. As he explains to FSM, it's not meant as a sign of disrespect.

"It's hard to explain really, but I feel awkward about it. It feels like once I finished wrestling, I don't want to carry on performing. The way I look at it, wrestling is a job I did, and I got paid for it. To me it's like if somebody who worked in a factory and retired, they wouldn't expect to get presented with anything.

It's typical of a man whose undoubted successes in the ring were exceeded by the respect he had behind the scenes. As Tony St Clair once wrote, "he was a wrestler's wrestler. Everyone knew how talented he was apart from the promoters, mainly because he understood the business better than they did."

Determined to turn professional, Roberts prepared for a life in wrestling at the end of the 1950s by visiting both amateur wrestling and judo clubs, the latter providing his initial nickname of "Judo" Pete Roberts. "The clubs were packed with people back then because the pro style was so popular on TV -- everyone and their dog wanted to do it. An amateur background was a necessity, while I was very fortunate to have done the judo as I learned things like break falls."

Although hailing from the West Midlands, it was further north where Roberts had his break. "I wrote to the promoters and they invited me up to the gym at Wryton Stadium in Bolton for a try-out with Colin Joynson and Roy St Clair and they decided I'd got what it takes."

The head trainer at the gym was Roy's father Francis St Clair Gregory, an initially intimidating figure for Roberts. "He was one of the top half-dozen wrestlers in the country and the biggest draw for Wryton. I remember he was there the first time I turned up at the gym. I thought 'Oh my god, what have I done? Imagine what he could do to me!'

"But after they put me through the test and I passed, he took to me. He was one of the best and I was very lucky to be trained by him: it really was a case of right place, right time. He also gave me good advice like the importance of getting a trade and finishing your apprenticeship."

Once Roberts had finished said apprenticeship, in carpentry, he continued the slow process of becoming a full-time pro. "It took quite a long time to get comfortable in the ring. With Wryton based in Manchester, you got more work if you were based there. I'd be wrestling four times a month, while somebody like Roy was wrestling four times a week. Like anything, the more you do it, the better you get. It took quite a while to get going and it was ten years before I did it for a living."

At that point things began rolling and Roberts would go on to become a TV regular, making more than 100 appearances over the course of two decades. He recalls Joynson and Ray Steele as being among his favourite opponents, while naming Steve (William) Regal as somebody underrated by promoters: "He was a great talent: I thought he was a lot like me." The feeling is certainly mutual, with Regal telling FSM that "He was the wrestler I aspired to be. Always carried himself with style. My hero."

Writing in his autobiography, Regal elaborated: "Any British wrestler worth his salt would put him in his top three... his stuff was so far above anybody else's... He gave me a piece of advice I've never forgotten. He said: 'Make everything you do in there mean something, otherwise don't bother doing it.'"

Roberts spent time in two regular tag teams based around his judo background: the Judokas with Al Marquette and the Kung Fu Fighters with Eddie Hamill. But arguably his most memorable run came in singles action when he battled world heavyweight champion Wayne Bridges in one of the few long-term storyline rivalries on television.

The series began in late 1981 with Bridges disqualified for repeatedly kneeing a grounded Roberts, an out-of-character move from a man who'd previously been portrayed as a British hero battling the likes of John Quinn. In a non-title rematch, Roberts not only took an unlikely victory against the champ, but did so in two straight falls in the third and fourth rounds, prompting commentator Kent Walton to proclaim the result "unbelievable!"

Just as memorable was a post-match exchange in which Bridges made clear that "two lucky falls doesn't get you a crack at the title," furthering his rubbishing of Roberts' title credentials by asking "Who have you ever beaten?" Roberts gave the obvious answer "I've just beaten you!"

While a simple angle, the upset and the verbal antics proved unusual enough that the subsequent title match headlined at the Royal Albert Hall in February 1982; historian Russell Plummer records that it was the last time a British show sold out the venue. Bridges took the victory by two falls to one, repeating his success in a fourth televised bout in May to settle the issue.

Pete Roberts

It was the closest Roberts ever came to heavyweight title status in the UK, though some records have him making the final of a somewhat mysterious Joint Promotions tournament to fill a vacancy after Tony St Clair jumped to All Star while still holding the title.

Roberts did claim the World mid-heavyweight title, winning the belt from Marty Jones in Croydon, though the win was mired with controversy when some more dedicated followers noted Jones had already lost the title to Dave Finlay on a taped match that had yet to air. At a later Croydon show, fans were informed the Roberts victory had been declared void.

He did at least have one championship win that came without any disputes, defeating Skull Murphy and Tom Tyrone to win the 1987 edition of the "Grand Prix" tournament on television.

Roberts was also involved in a couple of TV bouts that were memorable for all the wrong reasons. The first featured he and Hamill against Dave Bond and Johnny Kincaid in what would become the only televised match for the Caribbean Sunshine Boys. The combination of their villainous antics and a nasty undercurrent of racial tension led to crowd trouble, heightened when Bond was forced to kick away a fan attempting to grab him on the apron.

"I was quite surprised it was shown on television to be honest," Roberts recalled. "Kent Walton had a lot of input to the TV and he didn't like the incident, which is fair enough seeing as the crowd could have been jumping all over him at ringside. It was an uneasy tension and with one more wrong move, there could have been a riot. It was more trouble than the promoters wanted, though funnily enough it's just the reaction some of the wrestlers tried to get in the 1980s!"

Another controversial bout came in Preston against Masambula, who suffered a career-ending injury after hitting the corner; the ring had been set up incorrectly, with the hook between the turnbuckle and post having no "give". Masambula later sued both the promoters and the man who had erected the ring, winning £20,000 in compensation, around £75,000 at today's prices.

Roberts was subpoenaed to give evidence at the trial, which led to unwelcome press coverage that concentrated as much on the booked finish of the match as the unplanned events. "It was very awkward and embarrassing. The footage was shown on the TV news every night, in slow motion and then speeded up. I feel I was dragged into it because of him trying to get money out of promoters. I feel he was not injured as much as he said - he seemed alright in court. Only he knows the truth of that, and I'm not a doctor, but I was very doubtful about his motives."

By this time Roberts had begun wrestling abroad, visiting France, Belgium, South Africa and, in a rare trip even for British globetrotters, Brazil. He'd also become a regular in the German tournaments where, unlike some colleagues, he didn't find wrestling before in the same venue nightly for weeks on end to be a challenge.

"Because it was a round-robin format, the interest built up, and you'd be working with a different person every night. It was really nice to have no travel, the food was good, and there was plenty of time to train. It was one of the best places in the world to work. In fact, some people like Dave Morgan and Tony St Clair even moved there permanently."

He also broke into the Japanese scene thanks to Welsh grappler Tony Charles. "He was a real friend to me and taught me the way to do things, what to do and when to do it. He didn't keep that knowledge to himself and really helped me out. I asked his advice for how to get into New Japan and he told me I had to write to Karl Gotch, who booked the foreigners. I sent off a letter and a picture and he liked what he saw."

Roberts' technical skills and straightforward approach to pro wrestling proved a perfect fit. "It was a very high standard and you had to be in shape. Some guys were just told 'you aren't good enough' and sent home with no more pay, just their flight paid for. You had to be with the program."

One tour began a lifelong friendship with American star Stan Hansen, who wrote in his autobiography that Roberts was "the true brother I never had. His friendship is one of the best things that came out of my years in wrestling." The pair met on Hansen's first trip to Japan, and Roberts recalls fate played its hand.

"Whenever you arrived, you'd have the first day off, so you'd check into the hotel and ask at the front desk who else had arrived among the foreign wrestlers. Stan phoned up to Dave Taylor's room first, but could barely understand a word he said because of his Yorkshire accent!

"He called me instead and because the only other foreigners on the trip were two Canadians who'd paired off, Stan, Dave and I began going round together. However, Dave got peritonitis a week into the tour and was in hospital and then flown back home, so Stan and I paired off.

"We were up in Hokkaido in northern Japan and it was the January tour, so it was very cold. We stayed in traditional Japanese hotels with straw mats instead of beds, and no heating, so we bonded by complaining about it together. I always thank Dave Taylor for getting ill and letting me make such a friendship with Stan!"

That friendship remains in place today with the pair regularly visiting one another's homes, most recently embracing their mutual interest in the Wild West by visiting the site of the battle known as Custer's Last Stand. So close were the pair, Roberts was one of only a handful of people aware that Hansen was secretly negotiating with rival All Japan promoter Shoehei "Giant" Baba.

Pete Roberts

"I was there for the wheeling and dealing; there was quite a bit of intrigue, real MI5 stuff. It was one of the biggest moves in Japanese history. Stan wanted me to come over, but I felt loyal to Karl Gotch. Without him I would never have got started in Japan: I always felt I should go with people who helped me."

For Roberts, working abroad was a business decision. "I had a family to support, so I went where I could get the most money. I'd gone as far as I could go in England. It also made you a bit more interesting to promoters when you came back."

Indeed, it was following one tour that Roberts was rebranded by promoter Max Crabtree. "I teamed with the original Destroyer, Dick Beyers, and mentioned it to Max when I got back. He decided to use the name and started billing me as the Super Destroyer."

The new nickname was accompanied by Roberts beginning to wear elbow and knee pads, a look that was so unusual at that time that Kent Walton remarked upon his "curious elbow protectors" during the second of the Bridges bouts. But Roberts recalls this was a matter of practicalities rather than any attempt to reboot his image.

"I got a bad knee on tour and one of the American guys said 'hey, put on these pads.' Back then British wrestlers normally just wore an elastic bandage. Then I had several chips in my elbows, so I needed to protect them. Still, I consider myself quite lucky: I wrestled 30-odd years without a serious injury."

Roberts would depart New Japan in 1984, but not for All Japan. Instead he followed Gotch to the breakaway Universal Wrestling Federation, which used a more realistic style. "It was called shoot wrestling, with more submissions and the Japanese guys liked the kung fu and kicking stuff. I was up for it: I'd been over to Florida and spent time with Karl getting personal training."

While he made the move out of loyalty, Roberts was aware it was a risk joining a fledgling company. "It didn't last too long: Inoki and Baba squashed them. But again, I was lucky and in the right place and the right time: I just picked the phone up to Stan and got into All Japan."

Here he wrestled for seven more years, teaming with Hansen and Ted DiBiase, which later allowed him to experience a memorable moment with a young fan. "Back in those days we had a milkman and I'd talk to him sometimes. He knew I was a wrestler and he watched the American stuff on Sky with his son and would sometimes tape it for me.

"A few years later when Ted was doing the 'Million Dollar Man' stuff in the WWF he phoned me up and said he was coming to England for a holiday and would like to visit. I remembered the milkman's son loved WWF, so I asked him to bring the son over on some false pretence. He walked into the living room and Ted

Pete Roberts

was sitting on my sofa. I'll never forget the look on the kid's face: it was a picture!"

As fate would have it, Roberts and a returning DiBiase would finish their careers in All Japan within a few weeks of one another in 1993. While DiBiase was forced to quit thanks to a neck injury, Roberts chose to hang up his boots voluntarily in his late 40s.

"My theory, and Stan shared it, was that you did wrestling to a certain standard. When you feel you can no longer reach that standard, you go out rather than hang on too long like some people did - Jackie Pallo comes to mind. People like Les Kellett and even Big Daddy were the same. But it's everyone's choice to make."

Still over a decade away from pensionable age, Roberts fell back on his carpentry training and set up a building business with former grappler Paul "Tom" Tyrone. "I was so pleased I'd listened to Francis St Clair's Gregory's advice. So many wrestlers didn't and were left with nothing after their in-ring careers ended."

It was an easy transition for Roberts who, despite the disparity in public exposure and celebrity status, was able to treat wrestling and carpentry as simply two different jobs to carry out."

"That's just the way I felt about wrestling and everyone's different. I didn't have flashy gowns or dyed blonde hair, I just liked the wrestling side of it. I was an introvert in an extrovert's business."

Pete Roberts

# RAY ROBINSON

British wrestling in the TV era had its fair share of tough guys. Arguably the toughest of all was Ray Robinson, who was honoured in 2011 at the Northern reunion when his colleagues gave him the "Hard As Nails" award. Indeed, he'd later be described by Max Crabtree as "the toughest bit of steel to ever come out of Scunthorpe," a reference to the town's dominant industry.

It didn't start off that way however. While Robinson certainly had a gritty upbringing on a small farm with the arrival of an indoor flushing toilet seen as a luxury, he didn't stand up to bullies for several years. "Up to about 11 years old I was a right wimp and then all of a sudden my dad and granddad said 'You've got to do something about this. You've got to really go for it and start training and make it so that [people] don't want to fight you, they don't want to push you around.' My dad made me some home-made weights taking old bits of iron and sticking them on bits of wood. I knew I was getting really strong. I had three lads that were picking on me in school and I did them all in one day, I just flipped and hurt them."

With his new found love of fighting, Robinson moved on to secondary school where as well as wrestling in the playground ("I'd get submissions with backhammers and things like that,") he thrived in schoolboy boxing. Unfortunately, his potential was cut short after a couple of years when the local authority banned the sport from schools on safety grounds. When he came to leave school, his dreams of a professional boxing career were dashed because the nearest boxing club was more than 20 miles away. "My dad didn't have a car then, so Doncaster might as well have been another country."

Instead Robinson went into the steelworks where he held down a full-time job for most of his working life. While here, he met a couple of local pro wrestlers who would train in a barn and accepted an invitation to come along. "I think they wanted to get rid of me. They knocked the hell out of me. I'm one of those people that don't like to get beat: it's just my nature when it comes to fighting.

"So I kept going back and going back and going back until I started holding my own and they was impressed with me. After a good while of training they took me to various places to pull around with other young wrestlers and eventually they introduced me to [independent promoter] Cyril Knowles."

Robinson made his debut on 12 February 1970 in Goole in a match he remembers as a six round draw with Keith Hadey. He continued working for Knowles, including teaming with him to get more experience. While Robinson normally used his own name -- a gift to promoters given the stardom of the middleweight boxing champion by the same name -- he did occasionally change persona.

"One of the promoters wanted me to wrestle as the Masked Destroyer or something like that. I went in there and the crowd were against me and I had to wrestle a different type of match otherwise people would have recognised who I was because I'd wrestled in that hall as Ray Robinson. My dad had a car and was driving me to shows by now. One time with the mask on, I had trouble with the crowd, I think I hit somebody that was overenthusiastic about it, and we had to get through the back door window to my dad's car. He said, 'If we're going to be messing around like this regular, I'm not taking you because I don't like it.'"

There were some lighter moments working for Knowles however. "He used to always pay you [straight] out of his pocket. He'd have his money ready for you and he'd call you somewhere so nobody could see what you was getting. One time he waved me over and he went in the showers at the dressing room and I thought "What's he waving me there for; the shower's going?" He had cauliflower ears so couldn't really hear properly, and he'd just walked in there. It was hilarious: he came out shouting a moment later, absolutely drenched. All the other lads were trying not to laugh because they knew he hadn't paid them yet and might knock a quid or two off!"

Working the independent circuit also meant meeting some colourful characters. "Cyril said 'Can you go to the railway station and meet Gunga, who wrestles as the Wildman of Borneo. He's a Sikh guy, about 18 stone, he's got a turban, and he has a case with him.'

"I met him and when we got back to the hall he said, 'Is there a back way into this hall?' I always went in the front, but he said, 'I don't want to go through the front dressed like this because I'm supposed to be half man, half animal." He'd not had his hair cut for donkey's years so it would come down to his waist, cover his face and he had a big black beard on. He didn't want people to see him [dressed up smart with his hair up.]

"All of a sudden round the back he sees some market stalls, so he puts his case down and starts taking his turban off and taking pins out of his hair. So I found this door and started turning it, but the caretaker of the place was inside, and he thought it was somebody trying to get in for nothing. He was a right little fellow and runs over and opens the door to stop them and as he opens the door he sees six foot odd, eighteen-stone of Gunga with all hair down to his waist. The fellow just fell over! I ran over, picked him up and said, 'Don't worry, it's just the Wildman of Borneo.'"

After establishing himself on the independent circuit, Robinson began working out at the St Patrick's boxing and wrestling club in Leeds run by Joint Promotions members George De Relwyskow and Arthur Green. After proving himself over a long period, he eventually got a trial match for Joint before making it to the 'big leagues' regularly and impressing Max Crabtree, who was now running wrestling nationwide. "He seemed to take a liking to me and said, 'You always look good, you train very hard.' And I did, I was always training when I came home from the steelworks, I'd be out running or lifting weights or going down to the judo club. Max appreciated that."

While on the Joint circuit, Robinson regularly got talking to Marty Jones and took him up on an offer to cross the country to Lancashire for additional training. "Marty made a big difference, a real big difference. Marty Jones to my mind is one of the best wrestlers I've ever wrestled. I've wrestled some really good ones like Dave Finlay, Alan Kilby, Pat Roach, but Marty Jones was the complete wrestler. He was a great amateur mat wrestler, had balance, everything. I went down to his gym at Shaw and spent a lot of my time mat wrestling Marty there: mat wrestling, pro wrestling, different holds and locks as well as the amateur style. I learned a hell of a lot."

Robinson began gaining national exposure after making his TV debut in March 1982, losing 2-1 to a man would become a perennial rival in Alan Kilby. "I think I've had more 1-1 draws with this fellow than any other, so when I [finally] beat him at a time he wasn't getting beat very much at all, that was a good one!"

He soon became established in the heavyweight ranks, often wrestling straight after the headlining tag match featuring Big Daddy. While this might have seemed a tough position with the potential for a burned out crowd, Robinson recalls he had a specific role to fill.

"Max Crabtree said to me that 'Yours is a different match to our Shirley's. I want you to go on after and I'll put you on with people that really are [wrestlers]. Yours is a completely different match to what they have been watching.' I think the crowd appreciated it because if you are running a wrestling show and you put all the same type of wrestling on, what I call show wrestling, you only got the people in there that was interested in watching show wrestling.

"If you mix the bill up a bit so you get a couple of lads like Dalibar Singh or Ray Steele, me, Alan Kilby, that is real solid hard professional wrestling and there's a certain amount of people that when they see you on the bill, they want to see you, they wasn't bothered about coming to see Big Daddy. There's other people that aren't bothered about seeing you so much, but they want to see the tag. When you put them both together you can fill a hall.

"I found that certain halls I went down very, very well and then the promoters watching you over time they though 'Oh yeah, we'll put him on in a fortnight's time or a month's time, he goes down well here.' Some halls I would be going there regular, time after time, year after year. Other ones you maybe didn't go down so well because they didn't like your type of wrestling so much and the promoters knew that after you'd been there a couple of times, so you didn't get jobs there."

Robinson says that in some ways he'd have preferred to come along in a previous generation when a more credible style was in favour. "That sort of wrestling suited me down to the ground and that's why I maybe I didn't fit in with some people because I didn't do the type of wrestling that some of them was doing. If I put a hold on you, unless you could get out of it, you stayed in that hold until I let you out."

There was one opponent that Robinson refused to wrestle: Giant Haystacks. "I looked at it this way. The sort of wrestling that I did, I used to tear in to people, really have a go at them. If I'd had a go at 'Stacks like that he'd have been too big and he'd have hurt me and maybe put me off wrestling for a week or two, maybe break my ribs or something like that.

"I really was only a light-heavyweight, I wasn't a fully blown heavyweight, but I did wrestle heavyweights because sometimes some of the other lads that was my weight thought I was a bit too much for them, so I was told. So I think Max put me on with people like Ray Steele or Pat Roach because they would [wrestle with] me a lot better than some of the smaller guys."

Robinson was able to give such a refusal largely because he had continued to work full time in the steelworks during his wrestling career. The power that security gave him even extended to his schedule, being exempt from the usual system by which management would send wrestlers a monthly date sheet with the location of their bookings.

"If you was full time you had to go when and where you was told to go. But what I used to do was write a letter to the office at Joint Promotions and put on the days that I was available, ie my days off from the steelworks. If I had two days off a week then the first day I used to put down for a long job: that meant I would travel as far as I was needed, London or anywhere."

The big downside of having a 'real job' was that Robinson had to pass up the globetrotting opportunities available to British grapplers, particularly in the heavier weight divisions. "Gil Singh asked me a time or two to go to India with him. I wasn't keen on that: I'd seen a lot of people do that and come back and they'd lost a couple of stone with the food and the heat.

Ray Robinson

"I'd always had the chance to go to Germany and my sort of wrestling would have gone down really well in Germany. I used to get fan mail from there when I was on World of Sport because they'd sell the tapes there and I had to get an interpreter read what they'd been saying. One guy even said if I went to Germany and was struggling for accommodation, they'd put me up in their house! Barry Douglas used to say to me come over to Germany, them promoters will love you."

But with the German tournament format that could involve being in the same city for six weeks or more, it wasn't to be. "They just said to me at the job we can't let you go for weeks on end, we can only let you take a few holidays." In the long run though, Robinson believes it was the right decision. "I'm pleased I kept that job because it's given me a damn good pension."

Another drawback of Robinson's schedule was that it made it tough to put him in the championship picture. "Max didn't want me to win a belt and then be not travelling around the country. So I promised him that every week if I won the title, I would go twice a week, one long job and one short job, meaning 50, 60 miles. If I hadn't have said that, I wouldn't have got a title shot."

Robinson's championship win eventually came just after the TV era in 1989 when he defeated Ian McGregor in his home town of Scunthorpe for the British cruiserweight title. Not one of the traditional Mountevans championships, it was a division revived by Max Crabtree after the term came back into fashion in the boxing world.

"It was a very good hard match. I always remember the bouncers from the nightclub around 200 yards away from the hall: they said they knew I'd won the match because they were outside and heard the crowd erupt and they said they very rarely heard that!"

By the mid-1990s, Robinson decided it was time to retire thanks to a nagging knee injury. He also moved on from the steelworks and became a guard dog trainer and set up his own security business, working closely with local police. He returned to the ring for several bouts in the mid-2000s.

"I had four or five matches, but I knew that I was on the slide. I really did well, but I could feel in my body that I was getting on a bit in years and it just wasn't working like it used to do. It used to be I could do a match and then wake up with a few bruises and I could do a match again the next day, but now it took about a week to get over it. A lot of people in all sorts of sports find if you're good at it, it's very hard to give it up and you go on as long as you can, and some people go on a bit too long. I think that's what happened with me with my knees!"

He would have one more match in the ring, but not in wrestling. Instead he set up his own gym at home and trained several local boxers, gaining a second's license from the Boxing Board of Control. As well as the regulars, he almost had a visit from a young prospect by the name of Tyson Fury, but the session had to be

Ray Robinson

cancelled when it became clear he would be several inches too tall to stand in Robinson's ring without bumping his head!

While there was no prospect of the then 57-year-old Robinson getting a license to box in a sanctioned public bout, he did finally achieve his dream of a fight against a professional, taking on Davy Jones in a four round affair before a select audience at the gym.

In the months after the fight, Robinson developed serious back pain that was later diagnosed as being the result not only of arthritis from wrestling, but tumours caused by prostate cancer. After a lengthy battle against the disease, he eventually made a recovery. As well as writing an autobiography titled The Sheriff, he continues to work out daily even in his mid-60s.

# RICKY KNIGHT

Patrick Frary was in his early 30s before he became involved in the wrestling business. But since becoming Ricky Knight, that business has been his life -- and that of his entire family.

Frary recalls watching World of Sport wrestling shows as a youngster and going along to live events in Potters Bar, but says he wasn't a particularly dedicated fan. "I preferred football, and watching wrestling was just part of the culture." He spent much of his 20s dividing his time between playing both the British and American forms of football, running a staffing agency for removal firms, and working as a bouncer in nightclubs in East Anglia.

It was in Kings Lynn that he had what would be a life-changing encounter. "I was working at a club which was pretty dodgy and had a lot of aggro. We got a knock on this big metal door and I told the guys it was a private members club and they couldn't come in. They said, 'it's alright, we're wrestlers, we'll be no trouble' and I believed them and let them in."

Whether he thought wrestlers would not be looking for out-of-the-ring violence, or simply assuming nobody would challenge them, it proved an accurate assessment by Frary -- and a fortunate one. "Jimmy Ocean came straight over and got chatting and we clicked straight away. It was like we'd known each other for years. Right then he tried to get me interested in wrestling."

Although Frary didn't follow up on the suggestion, destiny intervened. "A while later I was visiting a friend's house and Jimmy was sitting right there -- it turned out he was my friend's lodger. I guess [me wrestling] was just meant to be!"

Having enjoyed his training with Ocean, Frary debuted against his mentor in Wells, quickly finding that cardio could be more of a problem than pain. "We only went four rounds but I was blowing out of my arris [backside]. I quickly learned there's a difference between gym fit and ring fit."

Although he avoided some of the vicious beatings that newcomers would have faced a couple of decades earlier, it was by no means an easy grounding. "It was a tough business, and believe me I knew tough guys after working all those years on the doors. People [in wrestling then] didn't beat you up, but they really made you work and you had to genuinely fight to get out of holds. You had to earn the right to get out of a headlock or wristlock."

Making friends with Crusher Mason, also known as the Mighty Chang ("the best heavyweight ever to live in my opinion"), he gained another form of combat experience by working on Ron Taylor's boxing and wrestling booth at venues such as the Nottingham Goose Fair. Here he took on members of the public in legitimate combat. "That was a real education and a grounding for the business. Sometimes I did 13 or 14 shows a day. I did both boxing and wrestling, and probably did more boxing. They were always short of boxers because they took such a hiding!"

Now establishing himself on the undercards of wrestling shows as 'Rowdy' Ricky Knight or 'The Superfly', it was another quirk of fate involving Ocean that truly made Frary's career. "I was working for Brian Dixon and turned up to a show one day with a new haircut to make myself stand out. I called it the skunk: blonde in the middle and black on either side. I'd not seen Jimmy for ages because he'd been working up North for the Crabtrees, but he was working on this show and walked in the locker room with exactly the same haircut!"

Promoter Dixon quickly spotted an opportunity and suggested the two form a tag team, adopting Knight's nickname to become the Superflies. With Ocean a fast-paced aerial lightweight and Knight a much bulkier brawler, it made for a perfect contrast, while the pair were both equally skilled at verbally winding up an audience with or without a microphone. "It meant I was main eventing just 18 months after my debut. I wish there was more of Jimmy's stuff on YouTube so people could see how good he was. He was the first lightweight flown into Germany, which shows you how highly they regarded him."

Sadly for Knight, the team came along right as wrestling was coming off ITV and, while Ocean made it onto the final taping, Knight's only small-screen exposure came on the Reslo show on S4C, the Welsh equivalent of Channel 4. "It was a real privilege to be in with top guys so soon, but I do wish we'd been able to hit earlier. We had a good run, but I genuinely believe that we could had been real big [in the TV era.]"

While tag wrestling had been hugely popular in the 1960s, it had fallen from favour somewhat since that time, with fewer regular partnerships. However, the Superflies were an important part of a mini-revival as All Star Promotions adjusted to wrestling in the post-television age, with a multi-way rivalry also including father-and-son team King Benn and Kid McCoy, the Liverpool Lads of Robbie Brookside and Doc Dean, and the Task Force of Steve Prince and Vic Powers.

As the tag scene took off, Dixon created the British Openweight tag titles, with the Superflies wrestling Benn & McCoy to crown the first champions. It proved to be Knight's favourite match of his career. "Driving over to Bristol we never thought we'd win, but results never bothered me and I didn't have any big illusions about winning and losing.

"What stands out is that the match was 44 minutes and we had to wrestle the first half hour or so almost completely straight with no villainy. At that time you weren't allowed to blatantly break the rules in a title match and if you did something that made the ref look a twat, you'd be out [whatever the planned finish.] So after all this straight stuff, I hit McCoy with a knee and he was cut open and then spent the last 10 minutes fighting to get to his dad for the tag while the crowd was going crazy. Eventually [Benn] threw the towel in to save his son, so we won the titles which was a great finish."

Knight considered the win a genuine honour: "There was only one real tag title in the country at the time, not 30 different sets of champions like today, so it meant so much to be trusted by promoters to carry the title." But the win sparked off what would be a major turning point in his career.

"We won the titles, but there weren't any belts. There's nothing worse than winning a title and then going home and your family ask where the belt is! It was just a sign of cheapness by the promoters and we wound up buying belts ourselves. We'd also get pissed off when you'd be on a show and the title match was on first or second." The shortcomings of promoters would be a regular topic of conversation for Knight and Ocean for the next several years.

Later that year, Knight's life changed again when he met an 18 year old waitress while working a wrestling show at the Pontins holiday camp in Hemsby. Not only did Julia Hamer become engaged to Knight within six weeks of their first meeting, but she was soon working as a ringside manager for the Superflies, providing just as skilled as infuriating audiences -- though without the relative protection of being inside the ring.

Given she was inevitably going to be involved in physical confrontations with wrestlers and fans alike, the new couple eventually concluded she may as well train to wrestle. The newly renamed "Sweet Saraya", who took her name from mishearing a rock club DJ introduce a track from Slayer, went on to become the consensus pick for the best British female grappler of the 21st century.

In 1993, still thinking back to the missing belts fiasco, Ocean and the Knights decided to create their own promotion, World Association of Wrestling, based in East Anglia. "We wanted to treat wrestlers right and decided to give it a go or die trying." It was a philosophy based on a common-sense, long-term thinking approach to the business, as noted by promoter Scott Conway who recalled on the WAW forum that Knight was one of the few wrestlers who'd never tried to hit him up with an inflated claim for travel expenses.

Ricky Knight

"Ricky understood that if the promoter made money, he would run more shows, but if the promoter lost money, he would run less shows. He was one of the only wrestlers who, if you ever did badly, would offer to give some of his wages back. Other wrestlers would not care: they thought of today and not tomorrow."

That said, Knight admits he still had some short-term thinking in the early days of WAW, including working several relatively-lucrative dates doing a knock-off Legion of Doom gimmick. "I regret doing the tribute shows and having our events sell lots of US merchandise. I was going for a quick buck and letting myself down. Eventually we decided to sell pictures of our own guys instead. The way I look at it, if you go to see Phantom of the Opera in the West End, they are selling Phantom merchandise, not stuff from Broadway shows."

As well as running their own venues (including once drawing 2,000 people to an event at the Sports Village in Norwich with PN News and Tiger Steele the only US imports), WAW has used other business models. These include offering sold shows, in which a local promoter pays a flat fee for the event to be put on, leaving them only having to worry about promoting the event and selling tickets. WAW also does regular gigs on the holiday camp circuit, one of which led to Knight's most memorable road trip.

"I was going to Camber Sands with Jimmy, Saraya, Ivan Trevors and Morris Atula [an African wrestler who performed as the Golden Warrior.] The van broke down and after arguing about who would walk to a phonebox to get help, we had to wait four hours for the AA to turn up. The guy comes and starts pulling the van up the ramp of the recovery truck and every time we pointed out one of us should be steering the van into place, he just said 'I know what I'm doing.'

"The next thing I hear is a massive 'PING!' and we look round to see the van fifty feet away having gone straight through a hedge into a field. Jimmy and I went into the field to get it. 10 seconds later we're running back in the other direction chased by a big bull!

"It was getting dark and Morris told us that as he was such a dark black guy, he could sneak up on the bull without being seen. He was nearly right, but we could definitely see his wide-open eyes and teeth as he screamed all the way back to us after the bull found him!

"Eventually we found the farmer, who led the bull away, which gave me the chance to have a quick piss round the back of the van. Next thing I see, Morris goes round the back, spots something on the van, touches it, licks his finger and says, 'I think we've got an oil leak.' I said nothing!

"We finally get the van back on the truck and the AA guy drives off, five hours after we broke down. 10 minutes later there's a big bang and it turns out the van's tyre has gone. The driver starts complaining about how this is the worst call-out he's ever done, so Jimmy asks how long he's been doing the job, to which he replies: 'It's my first day!'"

Another memorable camp show came at Hemsby in 2006 when the Knight's returned to the site of their first meeting, this time accompanied by son Zak and daughter Saraya who both wrestled alongside their parents.

Despite their skills, it wasn't possible to run a promotion consisting entirely of Knight's descendants and he decided to launch a full-blown training school, the WAW Academy. As well as training teenagers and adult, Knight adopting the youth policy of professional football teams.

"We realised that teams like Man United and Tottenham get players when they are as young as six, so we run training classes even for the kiddies and let them put on a little show every six weeks. It's an amazing sight when you see an eight-year-old working a match in the traditional British style. I'm proud to say that something like 80 percent of our main show roster now started off in our Academy system."

WAW runs a structured training program, with wrestlers earning martial-arts style grades, with class fees dropping as wrestlers progress further. Those getting grade C can work on Academy shows, grade B qualifies you to work battle royales or tag matches on the main roster shows, an A gets you singles bouts (and is the first point at which an in-ring gimmick is discussed) while those at A+ grade get Knight's recommendation for working for other promotions across Europe. Passing each grade involves a test match before judges such as Ocean or other World of Sport-era stars.

Knight also makes a big point on both his regular training sessions and one-off seminars of stressing wrestling etiquette. "I sent a couple of guys off to do a tag match for Brian Dixon and they walked in with an arrogant attitude. Some things went wrong in the match and afterwards they were in the locker room arguing with Brian's top guys about how it wasn't their fault. That's a lack of respect: it's like reserve players mouthing off to first team players in a football team.

"I'll never forget one young guy who was working with Crusher Mason and just went on and on about all the moves he wanted to do in the match. Eventually Mason just calmly asked 'Is there anything in this match for me, young man?'"

"I don't allow any egos at our Academy. We make sure our champions get to take the belt home and show it off to their family, but they still have to come and train with everyone else and be treated no differently to the newbies. I make sure every trainee knows that wrestling is a hard road, a rough road, a dodgy road and a long road, but it's worth it."

Knight notes that where wrestlers might once have wanted to imitate American idols, he's now got a generation of trainees who want to follow in the footsteps of local performers. "We're getting a lift from kids who see Paige or Nick [Aldis, aka TNA champion Magnus] and realise that you really can make it big."

With the future talent pool well in hand, Knight felt ready to retire last year as he entered his 60s, having the somewhat unusual farewell bout of a three-way TLC cage match against two of his sons. "I was comfortable with getting out of the ring. What helped was that I saw a tape of me and [Zebra Kid] in a match from the FWA about seven years ago and realised that I couldn't physically do now what I did then.

"I do miss being in the ring, but I'm just being selfish. Still, when I go to shows, I can't help looking around and trying to read the audience and work out how I would wind them up!"

## *All In The Family*

After the Harts and the Anoa'is, the Knight family is among the largest wrestling clans with nearly a dozen members involved in the business to some extent. Knight's father Charlie Frary, a former amateur grappler, served as WAW head referee, while brother Julian wrestled at one time as Black Magic. Knight has two children from a previous relationship who've both wrestled: Nikki Best and Roy Bevis, best known as The Zebra Kid.

Ricky and Julia have three children who've wrestled. Their eldest son Zak first appeared on shows aged six when he portrayed the midget Dink alongside "Dunk the Clown", but is now better known as Zak Zodiac. Younger son Asa formerly wrestled as The Mask, while daughter Saraya-Jade wrestled in the UK as Britney Knight and is now a star in WWE's NXT developmental program as Paige. Finally, the couple have two grandsons, Ricky Jr and Patrick Jr, who are both currently in the WAW Academy system.

Ricky Knight

# ROBBIE BROOKSIDE

Speak to virtually any British wrestler of the past couple of decades and they'll tell you they learned as much listening to Robbie Brookside speaking in the dressing room as they did from any training seminar or match. It's the result of a desire to pass on knowledge that stems from Brookside's own experiences breaking into the business.

Brookside's parents were no fans of the business ("Even today my mother asks when I'm going to get a real job, and she's 83!") and he had to rely on snatched moments of watching on television when his father had left the room. That all changed in 1978 when his aunt took him to a show at the Liverpool Stadium, a custom-built 5,000 seat arena, where he saw Jon Cortez win a one-night tournament for the European middleweight title.

"Even now, I look back on it as a life-changing experience. Jackie Pallo was on, there was a fellow named Johnny Palance who was possibly one of the most underrated wrestlers I've ever come across. Tony Borg and Adrian Street were there. Then Cortez came out: I'll never forget the look on his face, the movements, the mannerisms and the reaction of him towards the crowd and the crowd towards him. It was incredible."

Brookside became a regular spectator and took his first steps into the business after a friend told wrestler Carl McGrath that Brookside believed wrestling to be fake. He was invited along to the Liverpool Olympic Wrestling Club to correct his supposed misconception and put through three minutes of utter torture. Despite feeling sheer panic during the experience, Brookside was intrigued enough to return week after week, skipping training sessions as a promising youth footballer to the dismay of his parents.

"I had my first match in Rhyl in 1981 aged 15 and felt like a shark trying to walk along a promenade -- just out of my depth and out of my world. I was on with Joe Critchley: he was an old Wigan wrestler, but he was a very mild guy and kind of looked after me.

"I was quickly on a four-week tour of Spain and really thought I'd made the big time. I was on the same shows as Jon Cortez and Keith Hayward, which was mind-blowing. Then I came back, and the reality of the world really hit me."

Robbie Brookside

With Liverpool Empire promoter Brian Dixon not interested in the inexperienced youngster, Brookside took on work for Bobby Barron in Blackpool. "I didn't feel at all at home, because you're going on with people who don't want you to be in the ring. The more people that step through the ropes, there's one less spot on the card."

The experience still proved a springboard as a holidaying Dixon and partner Mitzi Mueller stopped in at a Barron show, saw Brookside in action and offered him work on the holiday camp circuit before he made his way to the main shows and picked up work with fellow independent promoter Orig Williams.

Brookside's early years in the business were particularly harsh, both in and out of the ring. It's an experience that he finds difficult to sum up in a simplistic fashion, instead simultaneously recognising that it instilled the respect and toughness that made his career, but also significantly affected his confidence and delayed his learning process.

"I was working with guys like Mike Bennett and Terry Jowell, very dour Yorkshiremen who didn't really care too much for youngsters or anyone else for that matter. You had to go five or six rounds and not call anything. Then you come out of the ring and you've taken a bit of a hiding and you're criticised and ridiculed by everyone, then you're travelling four hours home and all the way you're given the height of the abuse.

"You had to get to a certain level and attain that level without any help. If you want to learn something, you've got to be helped and nurtured and shown the way, rather than just being told you're not going to add up to everything and you shouldn't be in the job. One of the common [phrases] was 'you're taking the food off my family's dinner table.'"

The breakthrough came when Brookside began working with a little-heralded wrestler named Mickey Gold. "He was someone I used to watch at the Stadium. He wasn't one of the most charismatic people; he was somebody who used to come on and people would go and get a cup of tea or go outside to the pub. But in the midst of this getting my head ripped off my shoulders on a nightly basis and not getting told the mistakes I was making, Mickey Gold was someone who helped.

"He could be very sarcastic and in-your-face, but he was genuinely a good fellow that helped me on to the next step of the ladder and gave me confidence. He showed me how to reverse things and how to take things, and why I should do particular things. I can never thank him enough. I'd come out of the ring and people would say 'good match'. It was still not enough for me to feel good about myself, but by God that gave me the spark."

Brookside does have one other abiding memory of Gold. "He used to eat these garlic sausage sandwiches and [the stench] would kill me in the back of Brian's car. We'd be driving six hours to Norwich every week and Mickey would get his sandwiches out. I still remember feeling green and queasy, but it was a small price to pay!"

As he continued to establish himself and gain confidence, Brookside would still have tough experiences such as the first time he wrestled Johnny Palance. He just tied me in a knot. It's like when you're used to three foot of water and as soon as you jump in the deep end and it's 12 foot, you sink down the bottom and you're there for 15 seconds bubbling away and you don't know where you are. Well try doing that for six rounds!"

While constructive advice from fellow pros wasn't always easy to come by, Brookside began upping his game when he started appearing on cable channel Screensport and could rewatch his matches. "In the mid-80s, video tapes of your matches were very few and far between. It's not like today when you can record anything on your phone: just to get a big video camera in the building you needed a crane!

"The first time I ever watched myself was a match from Butlins with Sandy Scott and I thought 'Oh God, I've got to improve that... I thought my dropkicks were good, but oh geeze...'"

TV provided another milestone in Brookside's growing confidence when he teamed with Wayne Martin against Bobby Barnes and Blondie Barrett on the first All-Star show recorded for television. "I remember having no sleep for about a week before that. I kept having a nightmare that I was going to come out when they played the music and fall down the stairs or something like that."

Fortunately, it was all right on the night and Brookside went on to have several memorable televised matches. Some were memorable for the wrong reasons, such as the infamous tag match in which Kendo Nagasaki hypnotised Brookside to attack his partner Steve [now William] Regal. Others were memorable for the right reasons, such as a bout with Johnny Saint which wound up as cult classic on the American tape trading circuit and has been cited as inspiration by several big names from the 21st century indy scene.

All-Star's TV run ended after just two years when ITV dropped wrestling, but a combination of a more action-packed, storyline driven product and an audience hungry for a wrestling fix meant the promotion did strong business for a couple of years at the turn of the decade. That was until a night that would change Brookside's career in two very different ways.

He wrestled Mark Rocco, who was scheduled to make two appearances at different venues in the same night. "He slammed me and went up on the top rope. I moved out of the way and as he landed I heard this wincing sound from his lungs that I'd never heard before. The next day Brian called me and said, 'Rollerball's in a bad way.'"

Robbie Brookside

Rocco had dashed off to his second match, against Dave Finlay, only to collapse in the dressing room after the bout. Doctors later diagnosed that severe heart damage had led to a pulmonary embolism, a blood clot blocking the main artery to his lung. It spelled an immediate end to the career of the reigning world heavy-middleweight champion, and opened up a vacancy.

"Brian held a huge tournament over a couple of months. Nobody told me what was happening: you just turned up every night and did our thing. Then we had the semi-finals and finals at Croydon and I beat Danny Collins and got the belt. All of a sudden, that boosted my confidence. When you're repeatedly told you're not good enough, you start to believe that. I'd been wrestling 10 years, getting on for 2,000 matches, but that was the first real time when I thought I knew what I was doing. It was a defining moment, the moment I really realised that people were retiring and now it was down to me to take up some responsibility, take the bull by the horns."

That growing level of comfort with a headline position continued as Brookside began working on the German tournaments, fulfilling a longstanding ambition. "Guys like Mal Kirk and Tony St Clair used to go to Germany and you wouldn't see them for most of the year. They all came back with big cars and stories and always seemed to have money. That was the real Cup Final for me. Once I'd done that, I was boosted in confidence."

Throughout the early 90s, Brookside built his name by teaming with Doc Dean as the Liverpool Lads in a flourishing tag scene against the likes of the Superflies, Task Force One and Double Trouble, but he was growing increasingly frustrated, something he demonstrated in a 1993 edition of BBC 2's Video Diaries, a documentary series where the subjects shot their own footage. Not only was the show's audience hurt by being shown opposite Nigel Benn vs Chris Eubank in one of the last truly major boxing fights on free television, but Brookside felt it failed in its main goal.

"I wanted Video Diaries to be a springboard to knock on a few doors and say, 'we're still here', but to do that you need your promoters to work with you. There were loads of times we'd work a challenge to go back to a place and you'd never go back with the person you'd done the challenge with. There'd be no logical explanation and there's only so many times you can do that. You can't cheat your audience."

This was what Brookside saw as the second consequence of Mark Rocco's departure. "Brian [Dixon] used to have a great appetite for the job: he used to come in and take an interest in the matches. But I truly believe when Rocco retired, a part of Brian retired as well. I'd tell him to believe in us and say, 'If Rollerball's down, we need to think about how to put arses in seats.'

Robbie Brookside

"By the end of the Video Diaries thing, I saw the writing on the wall. By 1995 it was just like when you leave an old door in the back yard and the wind and rain and sun get to it and it corrodes: that's what happened with the job, and then the lookalikes and tributes didn't help. I'd never wanted to leave Europe, but I realised if [promoters] were not going to help us, we had to go further afield when opportunity knocks."

Indeed, Brookside and Dean took on foreign work with an appearance in the 1997 New Japan Best of the Super Juniors tournament where Brookside wrestled the likes of Chris Jericho and Shinjiro Otani. The Liverpool Lads were due to wrestle for AAA in Mexico and, although the tour fell through, the connection with Konnan led to a gig with WCW. What started as a two-week run working TV tapings turned into a three month stint, albeit in an enhancement role for bigger stars. "I wasn't bothered: it doesn't change my wages," Brookside recalls.

While Dean took to the US lifestyle and remained in the country even after retiring from the ring, Brookside returned to the familiar comforts of home, though did make a trip to a WWE developmental territory in Memphis in 2000 where Regal was now a trainer. Here he helped shape the early careers of Daniel Bryan and Brian Kendrick among others.

Brookside remained on WWE's radar and worked on a 2004 Sunday Night Heat taping against Maven in Manchester. "We had a good match and they sat me down and asked if I'd like to come out to the States and give it a go. They had a couple of ideas being bandied around but I decided there were too many things in Europe for me that I didn't want to miss."

He became something of a regular on WWE tapings in the UK and his attitude changed over the subsequent years, with both marriage and a significant knee injury making him rethink his outlook on wrestling. After setting up his own training school in Leicester, Brookside accepted a 2012 invite to help run a try-out at Florida Championship Wrestling and returned in 2013 to take on a full-time training role at the new WWE/NXT Performance Centre. "I can't find the words to describe this place: it's something to be seen."

Teaching wrestlers with widely varying experience, Brookside says he gets something from every student. "There's a lot of job satisfaction when you've got someone coming in that's never been in a ring before and you can mould them and give them a foundation, self-belief and confidence, then hand them on to the next coach: it's a fantastic feeling. But it's also a fantastic feeling when you're working with some of the top liners and you can add your little bit."

Drawing on his own experiences, confidence is the watchword for Brookside's training style. "They need to find self-belief. With the way I came into the job, I can give them that confidence and tell them it's OK to make a mistake. I'm not going to start ranting and bawling at them if they make a mistake.

Robbie Brookside

"I tell them all the time that the hardest door to get in is the door they've got the key for. I got my head ripped off frequently between 1982 and 1984/5 and I don't think any of these guys could handle that, but I seriously don't think if I came back as an 18 or 19 year old I could handle what they do."

In particular Brookside points to the daily physical training sessions that accompany the technical wrestling tuition. "There's a dedicated strength and condition room with the coach, Matt Wichlinski. He's incredible: he's got workouts for everything. He could give you an eyelash workout!"

With his new career a success, Brookside is contemplating the end of his own time as a performer. "I've never been to a wrestlers reunion before because I feel I haven't retired, but I've probably had my last match, I don't think I need to go back in the ring: I've gone beyond anything I needed to do. I don't think I will, but it's foolish to say I never will because you never say never.

"I love this job: you can't come into it and stay in it for 34 years without loving it and being married to it. Now I'm living my life through the people I'm training, but I still live and breathe this job, in fact more so now. It's not a job, it's a lifestyle."

Brookside's life in wrestling has finally come full circle as he looks back to the influence of Mickey Gold. "He helped forge the foundations of what I was, what I became and who I am today.

"I'm really happy to be here for the likes of Mickey, Steve Grey, Mal Sanders -- all the people that helped me along the way. I can now keep their name and their message and style alive and bestow that on to the talent out here. It's an honour passing on the great things that have been passed on to me."

# SCRUBBER DALY

For most of British wrestling' TV era, one could only be trained and enter the business by invitation, with the idea of a paid, open training school not popularised until Hammerlock in the 1990s. However, as Mac Hardiman tells FSM, there was one notable exception.

"I used to go to shows every month at Bedworth Civic Hall and I was really interested. I wrote to Dale Martins with an address I found in one of the programs, to see how I could get into it and they wrote back and said Pat Roach was doing a course. It was eight weekends and it was £150, which back in 1981 was a lot of money. I was out of work at the time, but my friend was a businessman and had a milk round and a window cleaning business. He got some of his friends and they all put some money in and sponsored me."

While entry to the course was open to virtually anyone with the cash, it was far from a sure-fire way to become a pro. "There was about 120 went and only myself and Andy Blair done any good and that carried on into the wrestling. About 60 survived all eight weeks: it was dwindling down because it were hard. Pat came in and even though I was 20-odd stone, he just picked you up and slammed you on the concrete floor. I were black and blue each weekend when I got home but I stuck it out and at the end of it he took us to Digbeth Town Hall and we met Max Crabtree there and I got a date sheet."

The usual approach would be to put a wrestler in with a veteran teacher to carry him through his first bout, but Hardiman – billed as Red Mac because of his hair – instead debuted against fellow survivor Andy Blair. "As far as I know, it had never happened before, two new guys coming in like that that hadn't wrestled properly, only training and they're in, but we had a good match actually. It went down really well."

Hardiman successfully played the villain role in the bout, prompting promoter Max Crabtree to repackage him as Scrubber Daly. "He told me I'd got to grow a beard and let me hair grow longer because I was too good looking to be a villain! Max said there was a rugby league player with long red hair and a beard and he was called Scrubber Daly, so that's where the name came from."

Scrubber Daly

"I started travelling and working quite a bit with Pat Patton and Johnny England, a few of the other Midlands lads. It just took off. Johnny England got the sack from Dale Martin and I ended up with his date sheet which was seven nights a week."

While this was good news for his career, it meant a brutal schedule for Daly, who held down day jobs during his career, working first at a quarry and later as a milkman. While the hours were compatible, it didn't leave much downtime. "Sometimes I used to start at 4am and they'd let me finish when I'd got to go early. Some days I'd gone to work, come home, washed and changed, perhaps gone up to Glasgow, wrestled, come home, changed and gone straight back to work. But I wouldn't change anything."

For a large, unruly looking villainous grappler in the mid-80s, there was one prime slot for Joint Promotions: feuding with Shirley 'Big Daddy' Crabtree. Scrubber Daly not only worked with him regularly in tag bouts, but was in several shows where the pair would face off in singles action before returning at the end of the night on opposing sides of a six-man tag. Daly recalls this could be a creative challenge.

"It was hard because you've got to do different stuff in both matches. When you come into the six man tag, you're working a lot with the smaller guys because you're trying to keep them away from tagging Shirley in and you'd try to work on them. When Shirley got in, you'd have to do different stuff or even just jump out of the ring. That used to wind up the crowd a lot when you wouldn't get in with him."

Not everything went to plan however, with one incident showing just how vital Daddy had become to Joint's promotional strategy. "At Croydon, Pat Patton got in the ring at the start, I think against me and Lucky Gordon. Shirley was still on the outside because the kids used to group round him as he came out. We got hold of Pat and knocked him about a bit and chucked him out the ring. Shirley had got his arm on the side of the ring and Pat landed on his arm and broke it. He still wrestled on that night and the next night Max had got him out and he were wrestling with it in a plaster."

Daly had his own lucky escape in another tag match. "I wrestled all them years and didn't really get any real bad injuries. I was in a Daddy tag at Stockport and Ray Steele pulled me over the top rope. I was so far over I let go of the rope and just landed on the back of my neck. I thought I'd broke my neck, but I'd just ripped all my muscles."

Some mishaps were memorable for more positive reasons however. "We done what they call the double heads. It was Pat Patton and Shirley against me and Lucky Gordon. Shirley got me, Pat got Lucky Gordon, and they ran us together. The thing was we really did clash heads and I got a lump like an egg. But for some reason I just started laughing and thankfully at the time I could pull my hair over my face so nobody could see!"

While Daddy faced a line of foes who often had a short shelf life after audiences had seem them vanquished, Daly and Gordon were able to have a second run as the Masked Marauders with Blackjack Mulligan sometimes filling in for Gordon. Daly took the commitment to the role's mystery seriously. "Nobody knew who it was because I'd get a mile away from the venue and you'd put the mask on just in case there were anybody about. Having to do that was a bit funny. I used to carry a different bag, so nobody knew who it was."

Even in his unmasked guise, Daly stayed in character at venues. "Outside the ring at shows was still the same as in the ring, while when I went out at home, I was just myself. Scrubber Daly was the wrestler and when I went out I was Mac Hardiman. But at the shows, even after or before, I was still the same: I wouldn't sign autographs. There were a lot of women hanging around -- we used to call them ring rats – but I didn't have nothing to do with them and being a villain, you could just tell them to... go away!"

With an unofficial convention that a masked wrestler clearly defeated on television would have to unmask, the Marauder gimmick came to an inevitable end, albeit with an unscheduled encore. Daly originally lost the hood after losing in a lumberjack match to Daddy. "It went well and then when they done the unmasking, when they actually took the mask off, the [heel] wrestlers were all round me and somebody put a towel over me. ITV got loads and loads of mail saying that they didn't know who it was because they couldn't see so we had to do it again."

It took eight full months before he lost the mask for good, losing a tag match with Tony 'Banger' Walsh against Daddy and Patton in what Daly calls his most memorable performance. While Daly stopped wearing the mask (which he still possesses), he and Gordon continued teaming for some time under the banner of the "gruesome twosome" and continued wearing their matching singlets with an Iron Cross logo before Daly reverted to his traditional dungarees garb.

In his various incarnations, Daly made three appearances on the FA Cup Final day broadcasts, which he described as "an honour because there were millions who'd watch the Cup Final and the same watching the wrestling." In 1983, having decisively knocked off Colin Bennett and Eddie Riley a fortnight earlier, the Marauders went down to Daddy and a man whose name would probably not fly today, Kid Chocolate. In both this bout and the one in which Daly unmasked, the conveyor belt booking was in full effect with heel manager Charlie McGhee entering the ring immediately after the finish to bring out a new challenger: Mal Kirk on this occasion and the ironically-named Tiny Callaghan after the unmasking.

Daly was back in the prime slot in 1986 with another losing effort, teaming with Dave Finlay against Daddy and Danny Collins. In 1987 he took part in a battle royale. While not a new gimmick on TV, the match was notable for being an all-heavyweight affair with the likes of Giant Haystacks, Kirk, Roach and Colonel Brody among the field. "It was fun, but you were limited what you could do because there was some weight in that ring when you think about it. It was also good because the villains were working against the babyfaces as usual, but you also had villains against villains because [in storyline] everybody wanted to win and get you over the top rope."

Despite the TV losses, Daly maintained his heat and wore it as a badge of honour. "The worst crowd was in either Maidstone or Norwich, at a cattle market. A lot of gypsies used to go, and they did get quite rough. I did a show there on against Catweazle and had a job to get back to the dressing room: Fit Finlay, Skull Murphy and a couple of others had to help me come back to dressing room."

"Another of the worst I had was in South Africa. I'd been on with the [local] champ, beat him and I had to have a police armed guard on the door because they were trying to get in the dressing room. They smashed all the windows trying to get in and everything, so that was a bit scary. But I still went back, and we did a cage match, I think the first cage match in South Africa. It didn't bother me: I knew I'd done the job right when the crowd were up in the air."

Arguably the most attention Daly every attracted for his underhand tactics was back in the UK, with the unlikely victim being veteran BBC sports reporter Ray Stubbs. "It was a show at Hanley. BBC2 had done a programme on the professional wrestling and the amateur wrestling. After I'd done my match, at the end we were in the ring and he were asking me some questions.

"He said, 'Well the amateur wrestlers think you professional wrestlers are all ballet dancers,' so I just said to him 'Well I'll show you what a ballet dancer can do,' and I put a grovit on him. It's a hold which, if you put on right, it just stops the oxygen to the brain and they automatically pass out.

"I had to loosen it off a bit, so he could finish talking. They'd got the camera underneath looking at him trying to finish talking, then they cut the camera back and the producer gave me the nod to put it on, so I put it on and just dumped him in the corner and he were out cold. Just walked away and left him there. "

The incident became a favourite when repeated on a TV show about mistakes and other outtakes. "I was on 'Aunties Bloomers' so many times that I had to go down to the BBC studios and do a show with Gaby Roslin because it was in their top 10 clips. When they showed the bit where the camera went underneath, she said, 'His lips are going blue' and I said 'Well, that's what happens!'"

Another piece of publicity came when Daly worked with Big Daddy in a TV advert for Daddies Sauce, a very different experience to the one-take world of wrestling. "It took them three days to do a two minute advert. They done the finish before they done the start and somehow they would stop the recording and then they could get you the next day back in exactly the same position you was when they stopped recording."

As the TV era ended and US wrestling became more popular on these shores, Daly began being billed as the UK Earthquake. However, this wasn't an explicit 'tribute' gimmick as posters usually made clear it was Scrubber Daly performing and he continued working in his dungarees. Instead it was more of a nod to the American scene and the fact that Daly also used a vertical splash as a big move.

During this era, Daly had a match that proved surprising even to him. "Brian Dixon rang me up at work and said could I go down to Bristol tonight. So I said 'No, I've been out most nights this week, I'm tired." He says, 'I'll give you double money' and I thought 'There's something funny here.' So I said, 'Who am I on with?' and he says 'I'll tell you when you get down here.'

"So when I got down there he says 'You're on with Giant Haystacks.' I said 'You what? We were here last month tagging with each other.' It turned out he'd brought an American in and he wouldn't go on against Stacks, he said he was too big, so Brian sent him home. I went on against him, I done two rounds and I hit him with my horseshoe on his head and split his head open! Even then, I was still the villain: even thought I was the small guy, people were still cheering Stacks and booing me! It were quite funny actually. It was daunting because at 42 stone, he was a big, big man, but it was an honour to be on against him, work with him and be part of his life."

In 1995, Daly was forced to hang up his boots as a regular. "I changed the job to lorry driving and I weren't getting home till 6pm so it was too late to go anywhere really." In the final years of his career he wrestled only on local shows promoted by Klondyke Jake, occasionally taking a week's holiday when Jake would run a tour of Scotland.

Since then Hardiman has faced and overcome some medical challenges that, combined with no longer needing to maintain the Daly character, means he now has a very different appearance from his wrestling days. "When I finished wrestling, my knees were bad, but I still went to work. They told me when I were 40 that I needed new knees, but they wouldn't do them until you're 60. I was still going to work but my knees were really hurting me, I couldn't go anywhere, I couldn't walk far. Although I was still driving, my knees were really giving me pain, so I had a gastric band fitted and I've lost 17 stone, down from about 36. I've had one knee replaced and I'm on the list to have the other one done.

"Unfortunately just over two and a half years ago I had an accident at work and it crushed my spinal cord. I'm still on crutches and had to have an operation where they shaved the bone away to release the spinal cord but as the surgeon explained, it's like when you squash a pipe: it doesn't spring back. It also crushed my sciatic nerve down my right leg. As I move my foot up I get a burning up my leg and into my back. But I've got full use of it back from working with the physio and I'm going to the gym, so life is looking better."

As well as being a season ticket holder at Leicester Tigers rugby club with fellow former grapplers Pete LaPaque and Ron Marino, Hardiman is a regular at the Northern wrestling reunions. At the most recent such event he received an achievement award from his colleagues, presented by Shirley Crabtree's daughter Jane Wade. "The words she said really touched me. She said 'This is a pleasure to give to one of the men that made my dad look a million dollars."

Scrubber Daly

# SHEAMUS DUNLEAVY

Growing up in the rural Irish town of Charlestown (current population 914), Sheamus Dunleavy followed many of his peers by taking the ferry to Liverpool to find work. He always dreamed of a professional career in the ring, but it was boxing rather than wrestling where he thought his future lay.

Dunleavy began training at the Duffy's Boxing Club, but soon realised that his stocky frame was not ideally suited to boxing: most opponents of a similar weight were taller with a longer reach, putting him at a disadvantage. However, the same building also played host to the Pegasus Wrestling Club three nights a week and he found his raw strength was more suited to amateur grappling.

He eventually progressed to the point of being a runner-up in the Northern Counties championships, qualifying him for the All-England championships at Haringey Arena in London (which happened to have been the capital's major venue for professional shows in the post-war years.) Here he progressed through three preliminary bouts before being defeated by the eventual winner Harry Kendall, a mute grappler who would go on to wrestle Dunleavy in the professional ranks.

The highlight of the event for Dunleavy was the introduction of a special guest. "When I grew up, there was a small little pub in this little country town. At the time I had a set of weights in the back yard which I built myself. This man, a stone mason, used to come in to the pub and knew I was training a bit and said 'When you grow up, you might be a wrestler.' He'd say there was a great wrestler called [George] Hackenschmidt and I often wondered who Hackenschmidt was. I got to read books about him and heard he was a fantastic wrestle who wrestled everyone, all over the world.

"All of a sudden at the British championships, before the matches the lights went up and they said there was a very famous person in the audience who turned out to be Hackenschmidt and I met him and shook hands with him. For me it was absolutely amazing because I grew up hearing the name and didn't know if he was big or small or fat or bald or whatever, and here I am shaking hands with him. It was akin to meeting the Pope!"

Sheamus Dunleavy

After working in a series of construction and factory jobs and moving to Birmingham, Dunleavy decided turning professional would give him a better life. He notes that "I think if the mixed martial arts had been around at the time I would probably have ended up in that street." Instead it was pro wrestling that was his best option.

He had a lucky break when he took on work as a doorman and found that the club's owner was married to the daughter of legendary catch wrestling pioneer Billy Riley. With a good word put in place, Dunleavy began training at the infamous Snake Pit in Wigan where he recalls that the regular crew included four of the eight reigning British champions: heavyweight Billy Joyce, light-heavyweight Ernie Riley, welterweight Jack Dempsey and lightweight Melvin Riss. Perhaps surprisingly he didn't just learn the art of legitimate submissions at Wigan, but – with the aid of a punching bag – worked on some more spectacular moves such as dropkicks.

Once he was deemed ready to work professional shows, Dunleavy was sent to the boxing and wrestling booth circuits. Traditionally this would be where a wrestler would learn the basics of crowd psychology and making an entertaining match, even with an uncooperative opponent. However, Dunleavy was never comfortable with the idea of risking himself for the sake of making his challenger look good. "It was very serious: you had all sorts of idiots and drunks and hardmen and everything. They were egged on by their mates to have a go for five or ten pounds and so you had to be on top of your game to not let them win any money and keep yourself safe."

That's not to say it wasn't a great learning experience and it helped ease him into one particular aspect of turning pro. "[I worked there] for a while to get the feel of the ring: in amateur wrestling [and at the Snake Pit] you only wrestled on the mats and had no ropes or anything"

Dunleavy went on to make his pro debut against Alec Bray in Colne and soon worked his way up to the TV ranks, first facing Bill Howes in 1961. While Sheamus was the bigger star (literally and physically), he was actually beaten to the small screen by a few weeks by younger brother Mick, who had unsuccessfully challenged for Dempsey's welterweight crown.

The brother would eventually tag up with some success, though for large parts of their careers they primarily worked different circuits: Mick in the North and Sheamus for Dale Martin in the Midlands and South. The Birmingham base made him well-placed for venues around the country however, and he particularly enjoyed the travel in the early years.

"I love driving. I used to love driving in the summer. I might be in, say, Doncaster: I'd leave at 12, get there early, find out where the hall was, get my bag in and my gear, then look for a cinema. Growing up at home, the cinema was three doors away from us, so we grew up in the cinema. I had a little Volkswagen car, then when we got married, my wife came with me. That was lovely: we'd always have a Chinese meal on the way back. Nothing beats youth: when you're young, married to a nice girl [and travelling round], that was as good as it got.

Not every trip went quite to plan however. "I went to Bournemouth one night, but it turned out the wrestling was at Weymouth. I had to get across as fast as I could, find the hall, park up and just as I'm walking in down the aisle the MC's saying 'Seamus Dunleavy hasn't appeared, so we have a substitute' so I shouted 'I'm here, I'm here!'"

Another trip that ended with a surprise began when Dunleavy returned from a show on the Isle of Man. "I'd parked my car in Liverpool and when I came back to drive to Birmingham, I met Les Kellett, who said 'I'm on in Birmingham' so I gave him a lift, dropped him off at the hall and went home. When I came back down to the hall I found I was actually wrestling against Kellet. He was a peculiar man and never spoke a word to me on the journey on the way down. We'd travelled down together, you could imagine we were very good friends, but [in the ring] he did his level best to kill me! That was Kellett."

As an ex-pat, Dunleavy would often come across fellow members of the Irish community, some more surprising than others. "You'd wrestle and meet two or three lads from home that you grew up with, particularly in London. I was in Torquay one night and there was the bank manager from my little town. Growing up, we were very, very, very poor and the bank manager wouldn't speak to us much. But here, all of a sudden, I heard someone shout 'Up Charlestown', so I looked through the crowd and there he was! Being recognised gives you a great buzz: it means you've arrived."

Sometimes however it was Dunleavy doing the recognising. "Growing up there was a circus strongman called Young Atlas who came to our town and would lift weights that none of the local boys could manage: they used to check to see if they were real! He also used to demonstrate the sleeperhold and have volunteers and cut the blood off to their head. I don't know why people used to volunteer: I saw him put seven in a row out one night, all lined up.

"He went off to America and I forgot all about him. Then I went to work a show in London and was billed against Timmy Geoghan, who turned out to be Young Atlas. That was amazing, to actually wrestle somebody I'd seen and admired all my life. He wasn't a very good wrestler: he was immensely strong, but his technique wasn't all that good."

Said technique was something Dunleavy would work on when he had a hand in training several wrestlers including Pete Roberts and Pat Roach, "Pete Roberts was an exceptionally good wrestler. Pat was very good, and he was a very good boxer: in fact I don't know why he didn't stick to boxing. There was nothing vicious about him, but he was a hell of a big man. I also helped train another lad, Pete Evans, who I often see today. He's 70-odd now and still trains. I get embarrassed with it, but then I ask myself, how could I train at over 80?!"

While he made his career in the UK, Dunleavy would eventually have a homecoming when he was booked on a show at Tolka Park, the home of several Dublin football teams. It proved a trip of mixed emotions.

"It was peculiar. I was wrestling for the first time in Ireland. When I came to Dublin, my family lived 150 miles away. Nobody had sent me a wire or a telegram and I thought 'That's funny' and nobody had come up to the show: I thought maybe my mum or dad would come up, but nobody appeared at all. Of course there were no mobile phones in those days.

"I wrestled anyway and then got the bus home. When I got to the last town before mine a school teacher got on that lived in my town. He came up to me with commiserations and 'I'm sorry about your mum' and I knew right away and asked 'Is she dead?' I knew she was sick, but it turned out that she died just after I wrestled. It was said she waited until my wrestling match was over. Amazing really, she knew I was there and would be coming home, so that was bittersweet."

As well as wrestling, Dunleavy had begun a side business of buying up properties in Birmingham and renting them to mainly Irish labourers, later moving on to own a series of nightclubs. It was an incident with a troublemaker at one of these clubs that was the most likely cause of one of Dunleavy's most memorable moments, though what really sparked it remains a mystery to this day.

As he was returning home in the early hours and getting out of his car, an unknown assailant fired five shots, hitting the car, the wall of the house and, with one bullet, the top of Dunleavy's head. He escaped without stiches, though that was not so much through a lack of damage, but rather because the bullet had cleanly taken away a chunk of flesh. The incident led to a surprise gift when promoter Jack Atherton approached Dunleavy after a show, mentioned the attack, and gave him what he euphemistically referred to as "material" for protection: two loaded handguns and a machete.

Despite such incidents, the property business flourished, and Dunleavy decided to hang up his boots at the age of 35. "As you get older, your injuries seem to accumulate a lot more and you don't recover from them as quick as you would when you're young and very fit. Plus I wanted to spend more time with my kids and the good lady."

While the businesses proved successful, Dunleavy had heeded the advice of many back home to avoid paying tax in the UK wherever possible. That turned out to be a costly error and at one stage he had to return home for several years to escape the reach of the Inland Revenue. Ironically not only did he return to Birmingham and eventually settle the debt, but the family business expanded into commercial property and he eventually owned the building in King's Lynn from which his annual tax demand was sent.

Dunleavy's son Russell had a successful amateur career, winning several international tournaments, but opted not to go into the pro game. "All he wanted was to emulate me and when he won a title or two, that was enough - plus he had a back injury."

Today Dunleavy looks back on his career with pleasure. "I enjoyed my life: I had both cartilages out through the wrestling but apart from that I didn't end up with any serious back injuries, which is the worst in our game. I'm 83 and still alive and can still throw my missus about, so I'm not too bad!"

Sheamus Dunleavy

# STEVE GREY

Steve Grey's career began with a spell of refereeing and is approaching an end in the same fashion. But between that came four decades as one of the most respected technicians in the British business.

The refereeing stint that began Grey's career was actually carried out by his father, Freddie Green, a merchant seaman who boxed professionally in venues near his postings. Grey himself boxed as a youth and spent several years training in amateur wrestling.

The pair were both fans of professional wrestling and regularly attended shows at Dulwich Baths. With his legitimate combat background, Grey's father often complained that he could do a better job of officiating than the referees at the shows (whose failings were of course often intentional to help the drama.) At one show he decided to take his concerns to promoter Len Britton, who invited him to a local gym for a try-out.

Not only did Grey's father get taken on as a referee (working for independent promoters before eventually joining Joint Promotions), but during the visit Britton invited Grey to get in the ring with some younger regulars. "It was only meant to be a one-off," Grey tells FSM, "but Britton told my dad that I was a natural."

Grey was invited to join the pro ranks and eventually made his debut in a tag match at Dartford in 1970. "I can remember it like it was yesterday. I was incredibly nervous. I had a habit of biting my lip out of nerves, but this time I was biting the inside of my mouth so hard that I was bleeding out of it.

"But the place was heaving, absolutely packed, and like a lot of wrestlers the nerves disappeared the moment I stepped through the ropes. I remember thinking 'I really like this!'"

Unlike some who struggled to make the transition between the amateur and pro styles, Grey recalls being comfortable almost immediately. "I was already good at break falls which helped but, although pro was very different, I grasped it straight away. It was just of learning the rule 'go with it, don't fight against it.'"

Although building up experience on the independent or "opposition" circuit, Grey was determined to get into Joint Promotions, which was a truly gruelling process. Like many hopefuls, he attended a try-out at the Dale Martin gym in Brixton on a Sunday morning.

"There was no pro stuff there. They'd make you take on wrestlers in amateur matches and then shoot wrestling with submissions. They used to call it the sausage machine, the way they'd treat guys who walked in thinking it would be easy.

"I got in with a couple of guys including Lenny Hurst. He tried to turn me over but couldn't because my balance was good from my amateur days, so he wound up sticking his finger up my nose to try to turn me! I always reminded him of that later on when we worked shows together.

"[Promoter] Jack Dale liked what he saw in me, but I had to keep coming back every Sunday for around a year. Things were delayed as Jack had a heart attack, but when he was back in the office he eventually decided I was ready." Grey went on to make his Joint debut at the unusual venue of the Royal Air Force base in Lakenheath, Suffolk.

Joining the Dale Martin roster, and in turn Joint Promotions, not only brought more prestige but improved logistics. "They were incredibly well organised. Every month you'd get a sheet in the post with a list of dates you'd be working. A little after that you'd get a second sheet that told you which venues you'd be at on those dates. In the early years at least, you'd be getting these sheets months in advance of the shows."

It took around four months with Dale Martin before the question of Grey's ring name was settled. His birth name was Steve Green, and he wrestled on the independent circuit under the logical enough variation Steve 'Kid' Green. Upon arriving at Dale Martin, it was decided there was a risk of confusion with the more established star Roger Green, the solution being the minimal tweak to Grey.

That wasn't the end of the problems however. "For whatever reason, the promoters decided there were too many Steves on the books already, so I started out as Stanley Grey. I wasn't too happy being billed as Stanley, though funnily enough some of the guys I was working with back then like Sid Cooper still call me Stanley today."

(As coincidence would have it, the "too many Steves" theory is the reason fellow Brit Darren Matthews changed his name from Steven to William Regal upon joining the WWF in 1998.)

Eventually Grey was established enough that the risk of confusion had subsided, and he had settled on Grey by the time he debuted on television in a losing battle against Cooper in August 1971. In all Grey would appear on the small screen more than a hundred times and was regularly among the ten most-featured performers from the late 1970s onwards.

Steve Grey

It wasn't just inside the ring that Grey was initiated into the Joint roster. "I was on a show in somewhere like Norwich where, even though I was a younger, smaller guy, I was allowed into the heavyweights' dressing room, and this was at a time when they really ruled the roost. There were guys like Mike Marino and Steve Veidor and they decided to wind me up by hiding my boot and replacing it with one of theirs.

"Given I was a size seven and this was something like an 11, it looked absolutely ridiculous. I kept asking for my boot back, but they just kept a straight face. By about five minutes before I was meant to be in the ring I'd given up and had put the large boot on and was panicking about how silly it looked and how I'd work the match. What I didn't know was that the order of the matches had been switched and they hadn't told me, so thankfully I didn't end up having to wear it."

"I was getting very wound up at the time, even though I was trying to keep it all professional. Looking back I can see how funny it was and how they must have struggled to keep it together. Being around the boys and the banter is definitely the one thing I miss the most about wrestling."

Throughout his career, Grey -- like regular opponent Johnny Kidd -- never made the move into being a full-time pro and instead continued working a full-time job. "I'd trained as a carpenter and joiner and done my apprenticeship, so started off with that work. However, in my spare time I volunteered to help elderly people, which I really enjoyed as I love interacting with people. Eventually I started teaching them woodwork skills and went on to make it a job and do the same thing with people with learning disabilities. I still live locally to where I worked, so I often go and see some of the people I used to teach."

One downside of this work-life balance was that Grey's opportunities for foreign booking were limited. "I did Dubai, Spain and France, but a lot of tours I couldn't do because I couldn't fit it around work. I was asked three times to wrestle in Japan, but it was something I could never make happen. That said, I did still manage to wrestle about 20 times a month, which was an awful lot on top of the day job. I do look back and wonder how the hell did I get the energy!"

Despite his "part-time" schedule, Grey still impressed promoters enough to earn championship status, winning a 1978 tournament for the British lightweight title vacated after Dynamite Kid moved up to the welterweight division. In total Grey's title haul during the TV era included five British lightweight titles, one reign apiece with the European and World lightweight crowns, and three reigns as British welterweight champion.

Throughout his career, both on television and on the live event circuit, Grey became known for two distinct types of bout. Against the likes of Johnny Saint and Johnny Kidd, he more than held his own in displays of clean, technical grappling of the type that allowed Kent Walton to reminisce about the days of George Kidd and helped maintain enough sportsmanship to justify wrestling's inclusion in the World of Sport package. At the same time, Grey was also comfortable playing off villains such as Cooper, Jim Breaks and Mal Sanders.

"I didn't really mind which style I worked. I was always happy, no matter who I was wrestling, because I just wanted to perform and have a good match, which I could do either way. Certainly in my early and middle career, I liked to zoom around at 100 miles per hour and I just wanted my match to get a reaction!"

Among Grey's highest-profile matches were appearances on the FA Cup Final day specials, losing to Mick McManus in 1977 and drawing with Breaks in 1978 and 1979. But Grey notes that the stature of such bouts, which at this stage were recorded a couple of weeks before the big day, wasn't always apparent at the venue. "[When we wrestled] it was just another show. It wasn't until you watched the matches on TV that you thought 'Crikey, this is a big slot!'"

One exception to such a rule came in 1979 when Grey wrestled Jim Breaks on the undercard of the Big Daddy-John Quinn spectacular at Wembley Arena. "In the weeks before the show, I saw adverts on the side of the bus which mentioned our match, which felt really big. I guess things would have been very different if we'd had social media and the like back then."

Perhaps the ultimate example of a bout's importance being a matter of perception came with an October 1975 TV match with Clive Myers in Southend. While just another bout for British viewers, it later became something of a cult classic in the US via the tape trading circuit. It acted as almost a gateway for US viewers into the British style and has been cited as an influence by several independent stars.

According to FSM's David Bixenspan, the match had two leases of life among US fans. "The really hardcore, geeky (and I mean that in a good way) fans and indie wrestlers, especially guys like Chris Hero, were already starting to get into whatever World of Sport era British wrestling they could find, sometimes with some Reslo and Otto Wanz's CWA mixed in. One well-known tape trader was best known for specializing in Japanese wrestling, but he also had the best collection of European wrestling tapes in North America. There was a very finite amount though, including Myers-Grey, and it was all stuff that had been converted from PAL to NTSC back in the '80s and dubbed many times.

"Then the 2004 launch of The Wrestling Channel in the UK, with its World of Sport 'classics' show, came along right as a real hunger for British footage had built up among Americans. It was also right as DVD recorders and DVD burners started to become commonplace, so it was suddenly much easier than it had been for decades to circulate this stuff, as you could make a copy in a few minutes without losing any quality. An episode featuring two Grey-Myers matches aired about three months into the run, so a lot of people saw them when the shows were more of a hot commodity."

Grey was unaware of this cult status until informed by FSM, noting "Dear me, that's really quite nice. I do remember that match as we went on last at the TV recording, so we thought it might be very difficult to keep the crowd interested, but we seemed to really wow them. Clive was a real natural at wrestling and really moved around like me, so we'd get so much reaction."

While it was either coincidence or a natural result of working so many bouts, Grey did seem to find himself involved in some unusually memorable matches. One such affair came at the Royal Albert Hall where he teamed with Big Daddy against the Black Baron and Chris "American Dream" Colt. The latter team was accompanied by singer Joe Cocker and Grey recalls a surprising lack of interest in Cocker by wrestling fans. More notably, both Cocker and Colt appeared to be under the influence of some substance or another.

"They were both slumped in the dressing room, which I had a very dim view of. [Promoter] Max Crabtree didn't look pleased, and that's an understatement." While Colt's condition in the ring was noticeable to the audience, Grey recalls he was able to work the match. "There was nothing sensational or grim, and he was fine to work with me, but he definitely didn't want to do anything with Daddy."

Fans recall another Grey match, with Mike Jordan, had another unexpected moment when referee Roger Brown fainted -- albeit with no suspicion of being under Colt-style influences. There was also a tag match with Grey and Daddy against Tony Walsh and The Bulk in which the latter, a behemoth working a similar gimmick to Haystacks Calhoun, somehow managed to fasten up his dungarees with the strap wrapped around the top rope, leading to the inevitable calamity when he tagged in and tried to enter the ring.

While the removal of wrestling from ITV hurt live gates and eventually led to the demise of Joint Promotions, Grey continued to find work from the remaining promoters and, somewhat to his surprise, was still wrestling occasionally two decades later. He is quick to cite James Mason as his most underrated opponent of the post-TV era.

"He is one of the best, a good little grafter who always gives 100%. He lived near where I worked so I often gave him lifts to shows when he was younger, and he really reminded me of myself at his age: it was obvious he'd eat, sleep and dream wrestling."

As he took on more of a veteran status, Grey even tried working a villain role on some shows, with mixed success. "I was quite happy to do it and quite enjoyed it. I remember one show I was on with a teenage lad, so I thought it would be easy to make myself the villain, but the crowd wouldn't have it. In some places it worked, but I'd say I played the villain not very successfully to be fair. Probably the best match I had doing it was where half the crowd was cheering me, and the other half was booing me!"

A niggling neck injury has meant that for the moment Grey has stopped taking bookings to wrestle, but he has made numerous appearance following in his father's footsteps as a referee. "I want to keep in contact in the business and feel I still have something to offer and can contribute with the refereeing. It means I can watch the matches at shows and give advice to the young guys.

"They work incredibly hard, but it's difficult because they can only copy what they see, most of which is the American stuff from TV. I wish it was like the old days for them so that they could work more shows. We'd wrestle five times a week and you'd always be wrestling different people, so you had to learn different styles to adapt and come up with different moves to fit. That schedule was how you built your confidence."

Despite his switch to being the third man in the ring, Grey notes he isn't yet technically retired. "I've not had an official retirement match. Maybe if my neck gets better, I might still have one last match, but it would only be one. It depends on the neck: people tell me I could probably work a match if I just stood around, but I'd only want to do it if I could give it 100%. But either way, wrestling's been good for me, I have had many good times, and I hope I made things entertaining for people."

Steve Grey

# TOM THUMB

Many of the wrestlers featured in Greetings Grapple Fans were fans as a child, but few had the level of devotion of Neil Evans. Part of his early interest was making up for lost time as he didn't actually attend a live show until 1966 when he was around 13.

"Some mates took me to Chelmsford Corn Exchange. I can still remember almost the whole show today: it was Pat Barrett vs Judd Harris, Reg Trood vs Peter Rann, Gordon Quirey vs Clayton Thompson and the Borg Twins against Ray McGuire and somebody else.

"I enjoyed it so much I went to the shows every fortnight until the venue stopped running wrestling. Then I got meeting some of the real superfans of the day like John Curry and Bob Moncrieff who would go to a show every night, which you could do back then. I'd start going to other venues in the area like Colchester and we'd go to some of the TV shows further afield in places like Hertford, Brent and Lewisham, which were easier to do because the shows were on Saturday afternoons.

"I did quite well considering I couldn't drive -- either my dad would give me a lift, or I'd get the train. It wasn't as a big a deal for a kid to be getting a train late at night then as it felt much safer."

Now part of the inner circle of fans, Evans began exchanging results with his fellow supporters through posted letters, building up a picture of who was wrestling where (and sometimes discovering patterns that promoters might have preferred to have remained a mystery.) At one point Evans was also buying a dozen or more programs at each show to exchange with enthusiasts who attended other venues.

In place of WrestleMania or the WWE's UK tours, the biggest event for the dedicated travelling fan was the May or June show at the Royal Albert Hall each year, the "end of season" spectacular before the usual monthly slot was put on hold for the Proms. Among the big bouts during Evans' teens were Mick McManus taking on Ricki Starr and Jackie Pallo.

Just as significantly, the events marked the closest thing to a fan convention, with letter writers meeting up and on one memorable occasion posing for a picture

Tom Thumb

with Adrian Street. It was at one of these meet-ups that Evans' friend Neil Sands revealed he was taking his wrestling obsession a step further.

"He was now calling himself Clive Churchill and part of what they called the Chelmsford Wrestling Club. They were amateur wrestlers, but they used to put on shows working the professional style -- I guess you could call them a semi-pro show. Neil had decided to break away and start his own gym and eventually promote his own shows. I became effectively his right-hand man putting shows together and he even suggested I try training in wrestling myself. I thought that sounded a bit of a crazy idea, but I gave it a go and liked it."

After debuting against Johnny Dennis in Whitton in 1973, Evans spent several years wrestling under his own name for Sands and other independent promoters such as Brian Dixon and Jackie Pallo. "One day I got a call from Jackie and he said Jon Cortez had come up with the idea of calling me Tiny Tom Thumb and what did I think of it? I said it sounded a good idea to me, especially as Jackie said only the name would change and I could just carry on doing what I was doing in the ring."

There are a couple of possible sources of inspiration for Cortez's suggestion. The Tom Thumb name originated in the 17th century in the first printed fairy tale written in English. It was then famously used by showman PT Barnum for a circus performer who reached three feet four inches at his peak. The name had already been used in wrestling by British-born Billy Bowman who emigrated to Canada as a child and wrestled despite standing three feet ten.

Evans, however, was no midget, but stood a hair over five feet tall. Even once clad in a green tunic and hat similar to that worn by the Thumb character in book illustrations, he combined the traditional comedic antics of midget wrestlers with the more technical lightweight style that was popular in British wrestling. "It was a fine balance in the ring. People were there to see wrestling, but my opponent would usually be the type of villain that people would like to see made silly, so it was always popular."

Among his most notable early bookings was one to Nigeria. "The wrestler Bill Clarke used to supply a couple of midgets to promoters, but one of them refused to go to Africa so he asked me to step in. It was quite an experience as we went to places like Benin City where the promotion for the show involved the crew of wrestlers sitting in the back of a pick-up truck that would drive round for two or three hours until people in the street followed us to the stadium! It seemed to work, particularly as we had Rusty Blair, who was the first woman to wrestle in Nigeria, and we had something like 25,000 people one night."

The promoters did also use more conventional publicity, which brought a surprise for Evans. "On the poster me and [opponent] Tiny Brutus were billed as pygmies! It didn't bother me as the money was so exceptionally good: in 10 days I got about as much as an average working man made in three months."

Tom Thumb

It also meant a change in style: "Because I was the bigger guy, we wrestled his match and I was his stooge for the night. I just got on with it and didn't really think about it."

While the British independent circuit wasn't quite such an outlaw scene, there were some shenanigans. "You'd often get called for a sub job [replacing a billed wrestler who had pulled out] on short notice. However, some promoters had a policy that, as far as the crowd was concerned, they never did substitutions, so you'd be billed under the original wrestler's name -- I'd be 'Ian St John' for the night, or whatever. They'd get away with it because if you weren't on TV, most people had no idea what you looked like."

After several years of being rejected by Dale Martin promotions as too short, Evans finally got an opportunity after speaking to promoter Max Crabtree at a local show. Originally scheduled to debut at his home venue of Chelmsford, Evans actually made his first Dale Martin appearance as a substitute -- as Tom Thumb this time -- at Hanley against Ricky Wiseman. It was the start of a run on which he almost always ended the show, though in the British set-up that wasn't the same as main eventing.

"I'd usually be booked in the last match because we'd follow a real blood and guts affair like Dave Finlay and Mark Rocco, so I'd do something a bit more light-hearted to make sure the audience went home happy and calmed down. Although with Dale Martin you had to be there at least 15 minutes before the doors opened, later on with other promoters it meant I could get to the show a bit later. The downside was that you never got home early unless you were on with Daddy [who'd be on before the interval, so he could stick around to sell merchandise] or Jim Breaks, who wanted to get back up to Bradford to his pub."

It was Breaks, whose cry-baby persona was tailor-made to be enraged by Thumb's antics, who was the opponent when Thumb made his TV debut in 1982. "He really set me up. Being on TV cracked it for me. It picked up so much that in July 1983, I worked 31 dates in the month."

That was particularly impressive given that Evans, having been advised to never give up his day job for wrestling, was still working in a full-time office position. "I'd be getting up at 7 to go to work, then going to wrestle and getting home to bed around three. I could only have done the schedule when I was that young and could live on less sleep!"

The busy schedule was relatively short-lived as, with business dropping off in the 1980s, Evans was a victim of Crabtree cutting down the number of shows he ran every night. Still, as perhaps the ultimate in undersized babyfaces, he did have a couple of runs as Big Daddy's tag partner, including two televised matches in 1988.

Tom Thumb

"I'll never forget the crowd at Everton Park Sports Centre for one of the TV matches. There were 2,000 mad scousers in the crowd and they had the feather out of my hat the moment I stepped out of the dressing room. I was lucky to make it to the ring with my hat still on! As for the match... it got a reaction!"

One of the opponents in Liverpool was Drew McDonald, one of many giant wrestlers Evans faced in his career as promoters took the size difference to the extreme. But it was McDonald's much smaller foe that Evans has the highest praise for. "Sid Cooper is an all-time great. He made so many people look like superstars and could have a good match with a broomstick. He had the first match with Sammy Lee [Satoru "Tiger Mask" Sayama] on TV here and absolutely made him in just a few minutes. Sid was a proper craftsman, a star maker."

While the TV exposure was short-lived, Evans kept busy by running his own shows as Four Star Promotions, running holiday camps and summer fetes as well as in town venues. "I learned that the biggest mistake you can make is to go back to a venue or a gimmick too often. We did some of the first rumble matches and they did great business, but sometimes we'd come back with them too quickly and they didn't do as well. Big Daddy was like that -- he'd sell out a venue where you'd normally do 150 fans, but the next show without him would be right back to normal and if you brought him back too soon he didn't do as well."

Some other lessons came behind the scenes. "I realised that wherever possible you shouldn't wrestle on a show you are promoting. It means you can't be concentrating on all the things that make the show run well like getting the music right or making sure nobody gets in without paying. No one knows your own business like you know it.

"Being a wrestler also meant I knew some of the scams to look out for, like when guys would charge you too much for petrol, or you'd send them to a camp show and you found out they'd been selling their own merchandise without permission."

After a few years of easing in and out of retirement and comeback, Evans had what he now expects to be his genuine final match last year against Ricky Knight. While he continues in his office job, Evans has found giving up wrestling to be a surprising experience.

"I appreciate what I had with wrestling, but when you stop you start to appreciate what you didn't have. It's genuinely life changing to be able to do normal things like go out on a Saturday night to the theatre or into London, rather than always be busy travelling to Kings Lynn or wherever.

"But wrestling treated me right and I made a good living. Working two jobs meant my wife could leave her job for five years to bring up our kids, which made their life much more stable than if they'd been in a nursery all day."

Tom Thumb

And although Evans is no longer putting on his tunic, wrestling is never far away. "I still get recognised by fans, though it's a bit off-putting when they ask if I 'used to be' Tom Thumb -- I'm still the same bloke! I also do some training classes for WAW and it's great that their trainees have such respect for the old school style and guys.

"I love still being able to have that involvement. In fact, I'd almost pay them to do it!"

# TONY ST CLAIR

"You had to have luck. It's all about being in the right place at the right time."

That's the modest approach taken to his career by Tony St Clair, a man who certainly caught his share of breaks, but encountered misfortune as well. It's fair to say he made the most of his ups and downs to become one of the more respected heavyweights at home and abroad.

Born Tony Gregory, he certainly had good fortune in the gene pool as the son of Francis Gregory, a seven time champion in the regional competitive sport of Cornish wrestling. It involves wrestlers clad in jackets trying to throw each other so that three out of four points (shoulders and hips) hit the ground simultaneously.

Francis went on to become a highly regarded professional wrestler, writing his place in the history books by opposing Mike Marino on the first ever broadcast of wrestling on ITV. For a touch of added glamour he tweaked his name to 'Francis St Clair Gregory', taking inspiration from his heritage in Cornwall.

"I grew up going to wrestling shows and cheering my dad, even when he was booed," Tony recalls. "He didn't so much have a villainous role in those years as a hard one. The booing hurt me a lot as a youngster: I was always the one that was cheering, even when the people were booing, and my mother said 'Shh, don't let them know who you are.' I was proud of him regardless."

While older brother Roy followed his father by turning pro, Tony instead pursued another sporting interest as a football goalkeeper. This experience was most certainly an example of the importance of luck and timing. "I played for Baguley Lads Club at 15 and their trainer had good connections to Manchester United. One Friday afternoon they rang him and asked if they could borrow a goalkeeper because their fourth team goalkeeper had got injured in training. The coach said 'I've got a goalkeeper that you can have with pleasure, but not for your fourth team, he's too good for that, so it's third team or nothing.' They agreed because they trusted him."

After playing one game for the third or 'A' team, St Clair was invited to train full time as it was the school holidays. On his first day, history repeated itself. "They got a phone call from Old Trafford to say Harry Gregg, the second [reserve] goalkeeper had been injured and they needed somebody for the Lancashire Cup final against Everton at Goodison Park. The other junior goalkeeper was playing a junior cup match, so I was roped in to play for Manchester United reserves when I was just under 16.

"We started the game and after two minutes my right back tried to pass back to me and the ball went straight in for an own goal! We got through the first half at 1-0 and I'll never forget the legendary manager Matt Busby took me to one side and said 'Don't worry son, it happens. Just go out and give your best.' Through a lot of luck we won 2-1, so I got my first trophy after just two games for Manchester United!"

Tony decided to leave school and give full-time football a try, but soon became disillusioned at his lack of progress. After around 18 months he was on the verge of giving up, only for future international star Jimmy Rimmer to get injured, giving him the chance to play in the finals of the European Youth Championships, where he won his second trophy as a late replacement. It was only a brief respite however.

"I decided to stay another season, but halfway through after lots of injuries and disappointment, I moved on to Altrincham and then Nantwich. I had a lot of injuries, especially ankles, and every time you'd get injured you'd have to fight your way back in the team only to get injured again. I just lost heart in the end."

Having left school without qualifications, Tony decided there was only one career path to pursue. "My father had trained me in wrestling since I was around seven or eight, so I dedicated my time purely to training to be a wrestler and had my first professional match when I was just over 18.

"I was very lucky as my father and brother trained me, plus my father was training Pete Roberts and Terry Downes at the same time, so I had the benefit of training with them as well, with my father advising. We had the key to [the gym at] Wryton Stadium and could go whenever we wanted. My father treated me the same as everyone else, but Roy treated me better as he was the older brother. I got away with murder with Roy, but it all worked out in the end!"

Like Roy, Tony decided to simply use the St Clair name when he turned pro, though there was no question of hiding that he was the son of Francis. While many second-generation stars of the era would use a different name or pose as a younger brother to avoid exposing the father's age, that wasn't an issue with Francis already retired.

While St Clair says he felt fully comfortable inside the ring and before the crowd within a week of his debut, he considers this largely a matter of fortune. "I was very lucky that it came like water off a duck's back to me. I just had it. I don't know why but it was directly there. I associated with the crowd. Maybe that was confidence from the football."

He's also quick to point out the assistance of his peers. "When I started I was looked after by numerous old professionals. People like Jeff Kaye or Mick McMichael, who is the best wresting trainer I ever had and helped me a bundle. And I had my first match with Johnny Eagles who was also a great professional and looked after me like a baby.

"I was lucky in a way that my father had so much respect from the other wrestlers that it rubbed off on me and Roy. But on the other side, people expected me to be good from the beginning because Roy was so good and because my father had been so good for 30 or 40 years. As luck had it, I could deliver the goods: purely a fluke."

Whatever the reason for his early promise, St Clair quickly earned the trust of promoters. Not only did he make his television debut a matter of months after his first match, but he did so on the prestigious FA Cup Final day broadcast in 1967, teaming with Roy as The Saints against the Black Diamonds of Abe Ginsberg and Eric Cutler. Tony and Roy returned to the flagship broadcast three years later in an even higher profile bout against Mick McManus and Steve Logan.

As he built a solo career, St Clair began expanding his horizons. He spent several weeks in South Africa, the first of at least 10 African nations that he wrestled in. He also made a visit to Germany that proved a memorable experience for the wrong reasons.

"My son was a couple of years old when I first went, so I wasn't happy to be away that much. On top of that, I wasn't, in my opinion, treated right by the promoters. I only wrestled about twice a week because there were 28 wrestlers and only 12 wrestled each night, plus the promoter had gone back on his word and paid a couple of pounds less a night than he'd offered me. When I said I wanted to go home, he said 'You can go tomorrow then, but you won't get your travel expenses'

"Peter Williams, the booker, told me I should stay and said 'Remember what I say to you now: when the promoter changes I will bring you back and you will be a star for me.' I listened and stayed the month, but I hated every minute of it because I wasn't wrestling: wrestlers want to wrestle."

Instead St Clair's rollercoaster life took him back to South Africa. "My wife at the time was a professional cabaret singer and got an offer to work in South Africa for a longer period of time. We went there with the intention of emigrating. At that time there was no television in South Africa, so all live entertainment was doing great and you couldn't go wrong. You'd wrestle in Johannesburg before 7,000, in Cape Town before 6,000."

Things changed when television was controversially introduced nationwide in January 1976. "Suddenly the crowds were 700 and 600. Everybody bought a TV, and nobody went out any more. The same thing happened to my wife: she toured with Jose Feliciano and Demis Roussos, but the live entertainment in the clubs became very, very hard to get and wages dropped enormously. After 10 months we called it a day and came back to the UK."

During St Clair's absence, Max Crabtree had risen to take full charge of Joint Promotions and St Clair took the opportunity to bolster his career. "I telephoned Max, who I'd always had good contact with, and said I was prepared to wrestle for Joint but not the same as before. I said I didn't want to be in throwaway matches, I wanted top of the bill matches and the possibility of getting a championship belt.

Crabtree invited him to come to a Joint Promotions board meeting and put across his case. "Billy Dale said 'So, Tony, you don't want to be just a fill-the-card man. What can you offer us?' I said 'Well, I can offer you excitement, I can offer you 100% effort...'

"Before I could go any further, Mick McManus said 'Billy, Tony has always, always done well for us at Dale Martin and for Max in Scotland. He works his cobblers off and he's somebody that you can trust, and we should look to giving him a championship match.'

"Max had said nothing up to this point and then out of the blue he said 'The one championship that lacks somebody like Tony has described for us is the heavyweight. We need somebody that touches the people, somebody they can have sympathy for, somebody not too big.' I was totally amazed: heavyweight champion had never entered my head. McManus and Mike Marino both said they agreed 100%."

The decision was made for St Clair to step up to the top weight division, though not before he had a final high profile match against middleweight McManus. "I always worked a lot with him, even though I was nearly a foot taller and a couple of stones heavier." In a match aired in April 1977, St Clair became the first wrestler to cleanly defeat McManus on television, scoring two falls to one.

The following month he took the British heavyweight title from Gwyn Davies at Belle Vue and, save for a four month program with Giant Haystacks, would continue to wear the belt for over a decade.

Meanwhile there had been a change of promoter in Germany. Peter William kept his promise and arranged for new boss Nico Salenkowitsch to watch a St Clair title defence against Pat Roach, which proved enough for him to be added to the Bremen tournament. In turn he caught the eye of Otto Wanz and was invited to Graz.

"That was the beginning of my love for the German and Austrian tournaments and the German way of life. It was relatively easy in your lifestyle. You'd sleep late in the morning, get up, go to the gym, have time to train and eat, go to the tent or hall at 7, and after the show go out and eat. In England you were in the car all the time: you never got home before two in the morning and were always leaving home by 2pm. In between you had to look after your family, train if you could and live your private life as well."

Working in Germany also meant spending more time with Mick McMichael, which always brought humour. "One time we went to a department store and Mick -- who was wearing his kilt as usual -- said 'Come with me, we'll have some fun here.'

"We went to the top floor and he started trying on dressing gowns, so the assistant asked him if he wanted help. 'Yeah, I'm trying this on. Where are the slippers?' 'Oh that's on the second floor; you're on the fifth now.' So Mick started going down the escalator, still in the gown, with the assistant chasing after him.

"We get down there and he tried on the slippers and starts asking 'Where are the pipes?' 'Ground floor, tobacco.' So now we've got two sales people chasing him. He gets there and puts the pipe in his mouth and asks 'Where's the wine?' Oh, it's down in the basement where the groceries are.'

"Down in the basement there's a woman distributing sample of wine, so he asks 'Could I try a glass?' So he's got a pipe, slippers, dressing gown, and a glass of wine, and then says 'Whenever I drink wine, I need a bit of cheese' which ends up with the woman from the cheese counter chasing after him. At the end of all of this, about an hour or an hour and a half, he says 'I'll have to think about it; thank you very much.' He took it all off where he stood, and we walked out of the store!"

St Clair's growing standing and confidence also brought an end to a two year wait to return to New Japan Pro Wrestling after an initial unsuccessful tour. "During that time I improved my physique and improved my attitude. It's not easy to work with the Japanese wrestlers or promoters but I managed to crack it. I also had a bit of luck as I met Andre the Giant again after about 15 years not seeing him. That helped me as well because he was almost in the office as a booker."

Indeed, Andre even recommended St Clair to Vince McMahon Jr, who was visiting Japan. While the introductions were polite, it was clear nothing was coming of the visit when McMahon talked to St Clair after the show about how good Andre's match had been, having apparently not even noticed St Clair had been his tag partner. "His eyes were on different people: he was overawed by big bodies and big men and I wasn't one of them."

Fate struck again on a New Japan trip to the northern island of Sapporo on a flight delayed several hours because of heavy snow. "We took off and levelled off and about 20 minutes in the stewardesses were serving drinks when all of a sudden we went into a dive. The stewardesses ran down the aisle, left the drink wagon where it was, sat down and put their heads between their knees. Nobody told us anything or what to do, not that we could have understood it anyway. Everyone was white, except Masa Chono who was cool as anything.

Tony St Clair

"We then levelled out and you could see the sea and beach, I think no more than 100 feet below us. We were flying at that low level for about 10 minutes before landing. Bull Power [Leon 'Vader' White] pushed his way past all the crew and opened the door to the cockpit. The pilot was sat back in his seat, white as a ghost, closed eyes and sweating like he'd run a marathon."

It's one moment in particular from the experience that still gets recounted at reunions however. "Bob Orton slept through the flight till I woke him up during the nose dive. I woke him up and I couldn't speak, I just pointed. In the end I got out 'We're going down.' Bob looked at me and said 'God, you woke me up just to tell me I'm going to die?!'"

Even without near-death experiences, the travel in Japan was lengthy but St Clair found it a more civilised schedule than in the UK. "You got up at seven in the morning, had breakfast, got on the bus or train, drove or flew to the next town and you were there by midday. You had time to sleep or train, then go to the show. The wrestling started mostly at between six and six-thirty, so by five you were in the arena. After the show you could eat early and go back to the hotel."

St Clair was soon splitting his time internationally. "I was doing seven or eight months in Germany, two tours of Japan and maybe a month or two in England." Those English dates were to be for a different employer as, in 1982, St Clair accepted an offer from Orig Williams to work for he and Brian Dixon for a considerably larger wage than he got at Joint Promotions. While world heavyweight champion John Quinn had already jumped ship, St Clair was the first holder of a Mountevans British championship to depart Joint Promotions. However, the parting had none of the ill-feeling that might have been expected.

"I had to give my notice to Max, at least a month. I went to him and said 'I'm going to Brian Dixon and Orig Williams and there's nothing you can do to change my mind. Do you want to sack me now or do you want me to work my month's notice?' He said 'Work your notice if that's OK, that suits me: that way we can do the matches we've advertised and won't be letting the people down.'

"I said 'OK, but I must tell you that I've told Orig Williams I will be going as the British heavyweight champion, so I'm not prepared to have a championship match on TV before I leave, and I'm taking the belt with me.' He said 'That's great that you've laid the cards on the table, I respect you for that. And when you leave we'll just make another champion and another championship belt!'

"I wrestled the month and left on very good terms with Max. We spoke to each other regularly for the next year at least before it drifted off. I called him up when Fit Finlay was thinking of going back to Ireland and the military because he wasn't getting enough work. I phoned Max and said 'You've got to have a look at this kid, he'll be great for you' and that's how he got [his push]."

Tony St Clair

While Crabtree did indeed crown a new champion in Pat Roach, St Clair continued to claim the British title with All Star and engaged in a lengthy feud with Quinn in which he lifted the world title twice. He continued his worldwide schedule but, as the British and Japanese dates became less frequent, he decided to settle permanently in Germany where he had met a new wife. In 2000 he had his official retirement bout in Hannover, losing to Finlay who, after several moments remaining in character after the match, shook his hand.

In the following years St Clair occasionally wrestled in what were billed as "legends matches" and also turned his hand to refereeing, an experience he didn't find easy. "I kept wanting to clothesline people out of the blue! Refereeing is not an easy job: just because you've been a wrestler doesn't qualify you be a referee."

St Clair's in-ring days came to a conclusive end in 2006 when he suffered a stroke. Although he recovered physically, he was left with an unusual side-effect. "My wife could speak English, but she usually only ever spoke German to me. I didn't realise I was speaking English [in hospital] until the second or third day when she asked why I wasn't speaking German. I realised I'd totally forgot everything and had to learn the language all over again.

"The doctors think it's something to do with me being left-handed. They say normally when a stroke hits, it hits the right hand side of the brain, which is why you get the problems on one side of the body. With left-handed people it can sometimes strike both sides of the brain at once, and the memory loss can come on the left side."

St Clair continues to enjoy his time in and around Germany's wrestling community. He's also had the pleasure of reliving his football days vicariously through his son's stepson Ryan Taylor, a professional who has played in the top flight for Wigan Athletic and Newcastle United, albeit facing similar challenges from repeated injuries.

For all his talk of luck, it's St Clair's choice of the matches he'd most like to relive that highlight that even those with good fortune have to put in the effort to make the most of it. "It's the street fights with Fit Finlay in Germany. By that time I'd matured immensely in my wrestling style. They were hard, really hard matches. Nobody believes it's real any more, which is OK, but we worked hard and without thinking of whether we were hurting each other or now. We were working as hard as we could."

Tony St Clair

# TONY WALSH

"It hurts when people only remember me as Big Daddy's fall guy," says Tony 'Banger' Walsh, who wrestled hundreds of matches against some of Britain's most skilled grapplers. "But at the same time, I was good for Daddy and he made me."

John Sheehan, the man who would eventually become Banger Walsh, was born in 1949 and grew up in Leamington Spa. Though a keen boxer, he had no involvement in the wrestling business until his early 20s when he began working as a doorman for a local hotel under the supervision of Barry Hawkins. The gargantuan Hawkins lived a double life, wrestling and promoting as Klondyke Jake, and one night was short of performers for a local show.

Sheehan volunteered to fill the gap to get a much-needed £5 payoff, taking on "Outlaw" Mike Pritchard. The fact that Sheehan had no wrestling experience, nor an understanding of exactly how the professional business worked, was not an insurmountable problem: Pritchard manhandled him as best as possible before eventually concluding the simplest way to end proceedings was a low blow for a disqualification loss.

Despite the painful experience, Sheehan was hooked by the combination of the athleticism, the crowd recognition and the potential to make money. He set his sights on a career with Joint Promotions and began regular visits to the company's gym in Leeds where, as he wrote in his autobiography Minding My Own Business: "I was less of a student, more of a sparring partner. Less of a sparring partner and more of a punchbag if the truth be known."

Eventually the wrestlers who worked out in the gym concluded he had enough desire and potential to be let into the inner circle and he was taught the counter-intuitive lesson that allowing yourself to be thrown by your opponent was less painful than resisting the move. Sheehan quickly figured out the way matches worked and, while a little disappointed, realised that entertaining a crowd brought a more appealing lifestyle than fighting for real.

With no immediate openings on Joint shows, Sheehan began working regular dates for Klondyke Jake and fellow promoter Barry Potter, known to the public as Duke Badger. Here he was told that the Sheehan name left ring announcers confused about pronunciation and asked to come up with a new moniker. He settled on his middle name of Tony and his mother's maiden name of Walsh. ('Banger' came later after an off-the-cuff remark by Mark Rocco that West Midland grapplers were "a bunch of headbangers.")

Walsh also gathered experience in working a crowd by working at boxing and wrestling fairground booths against legitimate challengers from the audience. He quickly learned that although he needed to win the bout to avoid a costly and embarrassing pay-out, dragging out the contest to make it more exciting would encourage the crowd to throw money into the ring as a measure of appreciation.

Eventually Walsh got his break with Joint Promotions, again filling in at late notice, this time against Steve Haggerty. He tells FSM that "I walked in to the venue and there were TV stars everywhere. I felt like a kid in a chocolate factory. It's still amazing to me that those stars wound up as my contemporaries."

In 1974 Walsh made his televised debut against Bobby Graham. Although initially filling the traditional rule of a youthful hero bravely taking on more experienced foes, Walsh soon became more comfortable in a villain role. This was certainly the case during a hometown feud against fellow Leamington native Jackie Turpin. The older brother of world middleweight boxing champion Randolph, Turpin was himself a boxer until losing his license and turning to the grappling game.

While the boxer vs wrestler feud was billed as a violent grudge, fans weren't told that Walsh and Turpin were in fact childhood friends who had not only trained together and worked at the same fairground booths, but had even been colleagues in the sea cadets. The feud built to a hair vs hair contest where both the audience and the participants expected Walsh to be shaved bald.

However, a local businessman who had found somebody foolish enough to bet on pro wrestling offered Walsh £100 -- four times his payoff for the match -- if he took the upset victory. Walsh agreed but, rather than double-cross his friend, simply agreed the change of result with Turpin and split the cash. The resulting hostile reaction from the audience led to Walsh being barred from future appearances at the venue for some time.

This was by no means the only match in Walsh's career to end in crowd mayhem. Another came with a tag match when he and Haystacks took on two local grapplers who were relatively inexperienced but popular in their hometown. When a promoter asked Walsh to cut open his foes with a razor blade he agreed, assuming they weren't confident about self-mutilation. Unfortunately it turned out the young pair weren't told about their impending blood loss and their response to being cut open was understandably hostile!

Walsh tells FSM that unexpected blood loss was also at the heart of his most memorable bout when it comes to crowd reactions. He took on Wayne Bridges in Southsea and "I was building up nicely to a disqualification finish and went to hit him with the belt. Unfortunately I was so sweaty it slipped out of my hands, hit him full force and cut him open. I think he thought [promoter] Max Crabtree had put me up to it, so the match got very heated, which the crowd loved. We even had a tussle in the dressing room, but at least it worked out well for the match!"

It wasn't just his ability to rile a crowd that earned Walsh his most famous slot: as a regular opponent of Big Daddy. Having wrestled Shirley Crabtree on several occasions before the Daddy gimmick and push hit full steam, he'd impressed Crabtree's brother Max who was now running the show. Walsh had the uncanny ability to wrestle in a style that made Daddy look as good as possible night after night without simply appearing a pushover: "I was a big enough guy at 6 foot and a decent physique that athletically I appeared a credible opponent."

As Daddy aged and he switched to a predominately tag based career, Walsh was cemented into the niche role even further. The common formula was Walsh and a giant villain against Daddy and a young partner, with Davey Boy Smith, Dynamite Kid and Steve Grey among Walsh's favourite opponents. It was here that Walsh's versatility shone: he needed the ability to work the bulk of the match with the youngster, the size to dominate and build up peril, and then the skill to make Daddy's comeback look spectacular without appearing too ridiculous -- the latter being a task many grapplers would later struggle with.

Most notable of all was Walsh's ability to take Big Daddy's double elbows move, which he calls "my favourite finish apart from maybe doing double knockouts from a clash of head with Dynamite Kid." The double elbows resembled what is now known as a back bodydrop, but with Daddy holding on to Walsh's arms and appearing to land with his full bodyweight driving Walsh's head to the mat -- and in this case appearances weren't always deceptive. "It was incredibly dangerous, but I knew exactly how to do it just right. Nobody else could pull it off: poor Bill Bromley, who wrestled as the Emperor, tried it once and broke both of his ankles."

We've previously noted in FSM how Walsh was Daddy's most common opponent, though he points out that our estimate of them having wrestled 637 documented bouts was an understatement as it only counts the number of shows on which the pair worked. "We also worked a lot of shows with a triple tag format: three singles matches and then a six-man tag with the same guys for the main event."

On some variations of this show, which appears to have been a way to save on payroll, Walsh would batter a youngster in the preliminary bout, allowing Daddy to get revenge at the end of the night. Most times, though, Walsh and Daddy would work twice, with the singles bout being a condensed version of their usual tag routine. It presented a challenge to avoid giving the crowd the same thing

Tony Walsh

twice but, Walsh says, "without being big-headed, it was a situation where either you've got the ability to do the job or you haven't, and I had it."

Ironically Walsh's biggest bout against Daddy was as a late substitute for Skull Murphy, teaming with Crusher Brannigan against Daddy and, of all people, Kwik Kick Lee (better known in Japan as Akira Maeda) at Croydon in 1982. Though Walsh wasn't aware of it at the time, the match was being recorded for broadcast 11 days later before the FA Cup final, the biggest TV date of the year. While there are no official figures to verify the claim, Walsh was told the bout attracted around 15 million viewers.

He'd also played a valuable role the previous year when Daddy took on Haystacks at Wembley Arena. Walsh and Anaconda acted as Haystacks' cornerman, but the pair weren't just there for show: "I was effectively on standby to jump in the ring and take some big bumps for Daddy if anything went wrong with the match or they slowed down too much. It was a role I did a few times including, funnily enough, at the end of Anaconda's first TV match."

As the years went on, Walsh's partners became more outlandish. While the likes of Haystacks and Mal 'King Kong' Kirk had the in-ring ability to back-up their size, the same can't be said of the likes of The Bulk. "One moment he was just a punter at Croydon called Terry Thomas," Walsh recalls. "A couple of weeks later he was wrestling on national TV. He never should have been allowed to be a wrestler and really didn't understand the business."

The most embarrassing example of Bulk's lack of natural athletic coordination came in a tag match against Daddy and Steve Grey. Bulk wore dungarees that came undone and somehow while reattaching a strap, it became tied around the ring ropes -- something that nobody noticed until he tried and spectacularly failed to get in the ring after a tag.

Fortunately Bulk and Walsh's most famous match was too short for any such disasters, though it was by no means a classic for pure sports fans. Rather than World of Sport, it took place in a studio for BBC's Jim'll Fix It with the pair both taking a pinfall loss to a young child who was granted his wish of teaming with Daddy: "It was amazing how many people recognised me from that appearance. For better or worse, it certainly helped establish my name."

Walsh was able to translate his stardom into a string of television appearances. As well as several bit parts, including as a shady character in crime reconstructions for local television, Walsh was a regular on TISWAS alongside Big Daddy. He also had a starring role in the first episode of sitcom Send in the Girls about women working on a sales promotion team. The episode had a wrestling theme and was written by Brian Glover, himself a former grappler as Leon Arras. Walsh also became a regular on BBC drama Gangsters.

Tony Walsh

In later years Walsh turned his hand to writing, working with Giant Haystacks to produce a script for a wrestling-themed sitcom called Back on Top. "It was similar to Auf Wiedersehen Pet but with wrestlers rather than builders," Walsh tells FSM. "We based it on a lot of real characters and events: the promoter was called Max Black, which you can probably figure out! We got good responses to it, but one of the problems was that we were pitching it at a time when TV companies were cutting back budgets and wanted to have no more than five or six characters, which doesn't really work for a wrestling theme. I'm still pitching it though, and if it ever gets picked up we'll pass on Haystacks' share to [his widow] Rita.

In 1985 Walsh was in hospital after a knee operation when he received the heart-breaking news that his sister Sandra had died in a car crash aged just 22. As he grieved at home while laid up "with a plaster cast from ankle to groin," the first call he received from Max Crabtree several weeks later began not with an expression of condolence, but with a demand to know when he would return to work.

An enraged Walsh infamously responded by contacting a friend at a local news agency who helped him arrange a tell-all story to the Sun, revealing (or rather confirming) that Daddy's ring triumphs and persona were a sham. At the time he was resigned to it being an inevitable end to his career, though today Walsh says that "looking back, I should have just got the Crabtrees back by going over to work for Brian Dixon -- in fact I'd already done a couple of jobs for him on the quiet.

"But I've always wished I hadn't done that story. Today I won't slag Daddy off because he's nor around to defend himself."

With bills to pay, Walsh began working as a security guard, reasoning that he wasn't too proud to work an "ordinary job." Eventually this led to him starting his own business, Mayfair Security, which grew into a multi-million pound success. The firm covered a wide range of services from night watchmen for factories and offices to providing security for major sporting and music events.

Walsh himself specialised in acting as a personal "minder" for celebrities including touring regularly with Roy "Chubby" Brown, where his wrestling background proved useful in several ways. "I didn't have any say on what he would do in his act, or when he should pull back from riling up the crowd, so it often got a bit hairy. I'd developed almost an extra-sensory perception in reading the atmosphere and a crowd's mood, so I could tell in advance when things were about to turn nasty. It reminded me of the times when Daddy would leave it too long to make his comeback and the crowd heat turned frightening. Fortunately if that did happen with Chubby's crowds, many of my wrestling moves did prove effective."

Today Walsh has retired from the security business and divides his time between enjoying life in his homes in Kenilworth and Spain, and making a name for himself on the after-dinner celebrity speaking circuit where both his wrestling tales and celebrity stories entertain crowds. In the past couple of years he has taken his show to three of Thomson's transatlantic cruises and hopes to make this a regular gig. "I talk about my life in wrestling and the characters I met like Catweazle and Les Kellett, and I can bring my wife with me to the Caribbean. It's not a bad gig!"

Walsh's son Darren became a wrestler himself and initially came up against lingering resentment over the Sun article. "We knew that would happen, though it wasn't as bad as we feared. Pat Roach took him under his wing, which really helped given how much he was respected." Darren remains active nearly two decades later, working as Thunder and making regular appearances in Germany's European Wrestling Promotion.

Old wounds took a long time to heal however, and it wasn't until around six years ago that Tony Walsh was able to start rebuilding friendships through the various British wrestling reunions. "The first time I went was a very strange feeling, but it worked out OK." Today he is a regular at the events and is back on good terms with virtually all his contemporaries, many of whom now understand that his 'revelations' were meant as an attack on the Crabtree family rather than an intentional attempt to hurt the business itself.

"Doing that story is my only regret in wrestling. but despite how it ended, wrestling was a big part of my life --- and it's been a fantastic life."

Tony Walsh

# WILLIAM REGAL

"I was absolutely diabolical at this when I started" says William Regal of his professional wrestling career. "I didn't have any natural ability for this, I had to learn every little thing I've ever had."

That learning process started early as a pre-teen Darren Matthews accompanied his father to the Wolverhampton Civic Hall which, at this point in the mid-1970s, was still hosting live wrestling every second week. It's here he watched a man who would hugely influence the mix of credibility and comedy that he would eventually adopt himself.

"I absolutely idolised Cyanide Sid Cooper and I still do to this day. He would get in the ring and have me screaming at him one minute and laughing hysterically the next. I never forgot him. He just brought out all these different emotions in me.

"A lot of my act has been doing my version of his stuff, pulling faces to make kids scream, falling on my backside. At the same time, he would switch it round and do some incredible wrestling you wouldn't expect out of him, or start doing physical stuff really whacking people. My dad was wincing, he was a big man, but when Sid was giving people forearm smashes in the chest, you'd see my dad going 'ooh' and even as a little kid I was figuring this stuff out: 'If my dad's wincing, he must be really hitting this fellow.'"

Matthews became obsessed with the idea of becoming a wrestler himself and even had a chosen location: Blackpool, where his family often visited for days out. As well as working regular arena shows at venues including the Tower Ballroom and Winter Gardens, wrestlers were still taking on challengers from the audience for shows at the Horseshoe Bar on the Pleasure Beach.

After spending time in his back garden in a makeshift ring trying to figure out how wrestling worked, a 15-year-old Matthews decided that making a challenge would be his route into the pro ranks. On the fateful day, Colonel Brody (also known as Magnificent Maurice) was the grappler taking on the public.

"I'm watching Colonel Brody in the ring: I don't know if he's in with one of Bobby Barron's fellows or not. I see some fellow jump over the top rope and get a hand on Colonel Brody's shoulder. Brody turns round and chins him and as he's going down he kicks him in the jaw. Still to this day I've never heard a sound like it: it was like a Tom and Jerry cartoon. His jaw whipped off to the side and just shattered. And this fellow's screaming and the crowd's screaming and there's blood spurting out everywhere. And I'm stood there about to go in the ring..."

While terror would have been the logical response, Matthews believed things would be different in his case. "I had been training a little bit in the Midlands with a few local wrestlers, I didn't really know anything, they hadn't really taught me anything. But because I'm 15 I thought 'They'll know. I'll get in and start doing these sort of [pro] wrestling things and they'll realise I'm one of them and take it easy.' This is a 15 year old brain working!

"I started throwing these like [working] punches and stuff. He just slapped me about and put me in a submission. He could have really hurt me, which he didn't. He obviously sees it's just a 15 year old kid."

Undeterred by the experience, Matthews repeatedly returned to the venue until Barron agreed to take him on. Initially he worked as a plant in the audience, posing as a challenger. By this era, and in this setting, many of the challengers were part of the show, and for good reason.

"Real people make dreadful challengers. First of all, there's very few that actually want to do it. Secondly, the ones that do are drunk; you can't have them then. Thirdly, they don't do anything outside: they're either loud and obnoxious, or they come up like quiet little mice. That doesn't draw a crowd: you want somebody who's willing to shout at the crowd. I would say in all the time there was probably five percent of them were ever anyone that you could fight."

Even those who appeared to make suitable challengers didn't pan out. "They wanted to do it outside, [but] when they got inside and were away from their friends and were sat in the dark, waiting, the adrenaline goes and it's going to be another 20 or 30 minutes before they get in the ring. [With] the realisation that they're going to get their head kicked in any minute, a lot of them used to just disappear!"

Using plants also made for a more exciting fight, without the worry of a challenger surviving the contest and winning the prize money. For this reason, once Matthews transferred to the role of the pro, he usually ended most legitimate challenges in a matter of seconds, with a couple of memorable exceptions.

"This little tubby fellow got in and I felt a right idiot, I could not get hold of him. [Normally] you just wait for them to come to you, back yourself in a corner; there's only so much they can do. You can keep them at arm's length, they can't hit you really, and you've got your back to a corner, so they've got to try and get in to get you if they want to try and win any money. They don't want to not do anything because they've got people watching them; their friends are egging them on, and they'll look stupid if they're not doing anything. As soon as you can get them in where you can get a hand on them, that's the end of them: Stick 'em in a grovet or whatever else.

"But this fellow, he wouldn't come near me, and when I did, he was slipping through me. Near the end, I managed to get him near the ropes and push him through. Unfortunately somebody who worked in the crowd, a friend of a friend, took it upon himself to run over and take a liberty and hit this poor fellow. So I felt bad about that.

On the other occasion, Matthews faced a rare challenge from somebody who measured up to his 6'3" frame. "He said 'I always wanted to have a go at this', he was very respectful, so I thought OK, let's give him a shot.

"He got in the ring and I did everything I could to hurt him and I couldn't -- he was just holding on. He got through a round, which threw me a bit. I thought 'I've got to finish him off else I'm going to look daft and cost Bobby Barron some money...'

"Before the match he'd taken off a gold chain which had a pair of boxing Golden Gloves on it, which is usually a sign that they're a boxer. So I thought, I used to box a bit as a kid -- I was useless but I used to go anyway -- so I thought I'd give him a shot, square up to him, and there's a chance I might be able to sneak one on him and then grab hold of him, grab a neck submission or something.

"The bell goes for round two, and he just looked at me and the guy on the microphone and said 'I've had enough. I've always wanted to try it, but it's harder than I thought.' And I'm thinking 'Thank God for that!' because he could have proper chinned me."

While Matthews could handle most challengers in the ring, the real threat came from amped-up audience members who'd try to intervene in a bout. In this situation, any head that made its way through the ropes was fair game for a punch or kick. "It's either you or them. You've got to look after yourself."

While combat skills and showmanship were both skills Matthews learned from the Horseshoe Bar and applied in his pro wrestling career, he also picked up another valuable habit. "When you do that job, you learn to read people's emotion and body language very quickly. You'd be an idiot not to."

The summer season ended, and Matthews completed his final mandatory year at school before returning to work for Barron on the holiday camp circuit. Here he adopted the ring name Steve Regal, taken from a mention of the AWA grappler of the same name in an American wrestling magazine. He spent the next couple of years working almost exclusively with Steve Peacock and Dave Duran. From the former he learned comedy and from the latter he got "a good kicking every day, and I mean proper good hidings. That toughened me up and it taught me respect for the job. I never complain about things and I just get on with my job."

William Regal

Regal's next big step came when he met Marty Jones, who agreed to train him on Sundays at a makeshift gym. Here Jones and Dave Finlay also tested out several largely unskilled newcomers who were being considered as "Daddy fodder", oversized opponents who would be built up on TV before falling to Big Daddy.

This set-up meant promoter Max Crabtree occasionally visited the gym, leading to him offering Regal work for Joint Promotions. Still in his teens and lacking experience, Regal was quickly on television, albeit renamed "Roy" because the promotion already had "too many Steves." (Ironically that's also why he eventually became William Regal in WWE.)

Regal began working main events as Big Daddy's tag partner almost every night, but soon came to realise the position wasn't all it cracked up to be. The star status and public recognition only extended to wrestling viewers, a declining group at this point, and there was little variation in his nightly routine, meaning he wasn't enhancing his skills. As well as appearing in what he and others have called the worst match in televised history (a six man tag with Daddy and Haystacks built around manager Charlie McGee), Regal found himself in a tag bout that was light years away from his preferred style of hard-hitting athleticism.

"It was a tag match with me and Daddy against Drew McDonald and Rex Strong, who was wrestling as the Ninja -- a 28 stone ninja! I'm in there and he was very gentle, picked up gently, and put me upside down in what they call the tree of woe. He's giving me these really open, gentle stomps, really as light as possible, and [Daddy] from the other side of the ring, at the top of his voice, is screaming 'Oh God, this is brutal!" And as I was hanging upside down, I thought 'It's time to go.'"

Regal decided to give up his headline position and make the jump to All Star Promotions, a move that surprised both Max Crabtree and All Star's promoter Brian Dixon. Regal specifically asked to always wrestle opponents better than himself to raise his game. He also benefitted from working a variety of show styles, from daytime holiday camp slots to evening events in both regular and one-off venues.

"I just knew I was learning things. Most of the daytime shows I was working Robbie Brookside. We went on first and we did a six five-minute round wrestling match. So all the stuff that I'd learnt from Marty, and all the little tricks I'd learned from people, Robbie was helping me put it into context. What's the right thing to do at the right time for the right reason. What works, what doesn't? Well let's try this today. [It was all about] ad-libbing and how to learn your craft.

"At night I was either teaming with Robbie or I was on with somebody else. Brian kept to his promise, I was always on with somebody who was better than me. I was constantly learning. You've got to figure out what you do and what you're not good at, and you try to eliminate anything you can't do very well. Let's keep it out of the act."

In the event, the jump didn't mean giving up TV exposure: All Star began receiving occasional slots in 1987, starting the week following the aforementioned McGee match. Regal and Brookside worked as the Golden Boys in a clash with Kendo Nagasaki and Blondie Barratt that was, for better or worse, particularly memorable. The match infamously concluded in Nagasaki "hypnotising" Brookside and forcing him to attack his own partner.

" Oh dear... I will never say anything bad about anybody so... I didn't quite like the idea of it! When we came out they were all shaking their heads. It is what it is.... If you actually look at one point, you get a glimpse of me. Robbie looked over and saw me with my head buried in my arms laughing hysterically in the corner, with tears falling out my eyes, trying to get my composure so I could continue on.

"But I will say this, most of the British fans I meet all over the place, that gets brought up as much as anything else I did in my career, so it obviously worked. Whatever it was at the time, it was different. People believed in Kendo Nagasaki, the aura that he had, he was still on his game. People bought into it, he had ferocious, ferocious heat in all the buildings. It worked at the time and that's all that matters, making a connection with the audience."

1988 also saw Regal achieve another dream by joining the elite crew of British heavyweights working the months-long German tournaments, something he saw as the moment he truly felt comfortable with his in-ring abilities. "There were times before when I thought I [knew what I was doing], then quickly realised I didn't. After I went to the first trip to Hamburg, I was obviously getting some sort of clue, else I wouldn't have been booked there. People like Dave Taylor and Pete Roberts thought that I was good enough there, and at the end of it I was a different wrestler. Six weeks working with those guys, several times each, made me completely pick my game up."

Regal also got the chance to work with Terry Rudge, a pairing that continued in several other overseas bookings. While Regal considered Rudge his favourite opponent, he dismisses the label of 'underrated' despite Rudge's low profile with many fans. "He wasn't underrated with anybody who knows what they are talking about. Finlay will tell you the same as me, that's his favourite wrestler. He's the best wrestler he ever wrestled.

"Terry picked his spots and used the wrestling and didn't let it use him. He owned pubs and antique shops and even did some acting for a bit. He was multi-faceted. He always got trips to Japan or Germany or South Africa.

"You've only got to watch him. Him versus Marty Jones is the best wrestling match you will see. Everything means something, it all looks like it should do, there's nothing anybody could look at and say 'that looks phony.' It's as good as it got. He was somebody you couldn't poke holes in. He looked like a wrestler, he was just brilliant, absolutely brilliant. You came out of the ring and thought 'this is what it's all about, this is as good as it gets.'"

Working in Germany started off a chain reaction of international bookings and recognition, meaning Regal's British appearances became less frequent. However, he did return in 1990 for a Premier Promotions show where he faced Brookside in what he still considers his greatest match. "I can't remember who exactly but there were a lot of old British wrestlers getting honoured or visiting. We did a six five-minute round match with no falls and it was the first time I'd ever seen a standing ovation from everyone in the building. We were the ones setting the standard for wrestling matches at the time. [We thought] we must be getting half decent at this now."

By 1992, Regal had put together a globetrotting schedule that meant he was unaffected by the decline in the British business since the end of television. "I worked for Brian [Dixon in] January, February. On the 1st of March I went to India for a month. I came back from there, went on a tour of American Army bases in Germany. Went back from there, did Easter Sunday in Blackpool, Easter Sunday I flew from Manchester to South Africa for a month, came back from there and went to Egypt for a week, may have worked one or twice in England, then went to Germany for the rest of the year."

Looking back on his career, Regal believes that even if he hadn't made the move to the US, he would still have remained a full-time pro. He notes the Germany and Austria stints continued to provide a viable living to grapplers for most of the 1990s. "I think Germany would have eventually carried me to get to Japan, I was already getting interest. I think my career would have ended up in Japan. The Japanese loved that old British style of wrestling.

"When I went there [for WCW] in 1994 Mr Inoki, on the first day I got there, brought Yuji Nagata, Shinjiro Otani and Tokimistu Ishizawa [the future Kendo Ka Shin] to me and he told me 'Every tour you're on, I want you to teach these guys in the ring every afternoon. Whether they use it or not, I just want them to know it.'"

As things turned out, Regal's career took a different path. He'd had repeated expressions of interest from WWE following a 1991 try-out match before the Battle Royale at the Albert Hall show, but no firm offer had materialised. He'd also worked a UK tour for WCW and continued to keep them informed of his activities. In 1992, following the specific advice of Rip Rogers, he wrote a tailored letter to new WCW boss Bill Watts that led to him getting a job offer to start the following year. Aged just 24, he made the move to Atlanta, which remains his home more than two decades later.

In his early months with WCW, Regal had an opportunity to have another bout with Brookside, who was visiting the US as part of filming for the Video Diaries series on BBC 2. This match has achieved semi-legendary status as it took place not before a paying audience, but rather a group of trainee wrestlers.

"That was at the original Power Plant in Atlanta. We got in there and we started, and after a while everyone stopped and came over. DDP was one of [the trainees] and I think Mark Mero was refereeing. We wrestled a whole hour without any falls. People weren't doing that style of wrestling, a lot of just old British wrestling stuff plus our own spin on stuff. You develop your own way of doing moves, the way you do them, and the aggression you put behind it."

While initially showcasing his technical skills, Regal would go on to develop a partly-comedic, partly-obnoxious character, drawing heavily on Blackpool entertainers and film stars such as Terry Thomas. Regal believes this versatility gave him the ability to read an audience and wrestle appropriately.

"I would look out and I would see 'there's more families out here, a lot of children and ladies, they don't want to see so much strong style wrestling.' Nowadays, I'll figure it out by the time I get halfway down the ramp to the ring: [for example] there's a group of young males out there that are more hardcore wrestling fans, I'll do enough for them. If most of the audience is like that, they want a certain style, they want it more physical, so I can do more of the wrestling stuff. If it's mostly families, I can do enough for that group of people there, I can pull a few faces to make the kids scream to get 'em to boo. Then I can throw a few suplexes in, a few uppercuts that'll keep the hardcore wrestling fans happy.

"Some of those towns in the North [back in the UK days], you'd see a lot of those hard-nosed males, that's no different to having a bunch of hardcore wrestling fans: they want to see something they can believe in."

Regal also believes it's important to appeal to audience members who aren't wrestling fans. "My big thing is to always make sure the man -- it could be the lady -- whoever's paying for the tickets, I'm always going to give him something. Enough physical stuff that if he thinks of me, he's going 'well that looked like it hurt' or something to capture his imagination.

"I know as a parent, I'd take my kids to the movies and I have sat through some of the worst films of all time, and was absolutely happy to do because that's what they want to do. But that's cost me $30, and if it's absolute rubbish, I don't want to spend any more money on that product. If the kids ask me for a video game or an action figure, I'll tell them to rent it or wait until it's in the bargain bucket. So I always think if our audience is spending a lot of money, if you give [the dad] something he can get his teeth into and not feel insulted, there's a good chance he'll buy them the video game, which I get a cut of."

William Regal

Today Regal is best known as an on-screen figure in developmental group NXT, where for many months he provided commentary. He became known for breaking down exactly how particular moves would damage the body, an approach he says was very deliberate.

"If you've got credibility with the audience, which I have, explaining why these moves hurt, that to me is putting over the talent because it shows they know what they're doing, that they're very capable."

However, the commentary was as much for the benefit of the trainee wrestlers as the viewers. "[If they] watch this the show and listen to my commentary and hear me say 'if they'd just done that...' then hopefully they'll pick up on little things that they can better themselves with."

Behind the scenes, Regal now works in the talent development programme, scouting independent and international shows for talent and maintaining a database of prospects who can be called upon for anything from developmental contracts to appearances as extras in television skits. He notes that he's willing to offer advice to any wrestler he encounters: "Even if that person doesn't work out for us, if they go away and pass on that bit of knowledge to somebody else and it comes back to WWE in 15 years, it's paid off."

Regal's last match came against Cesaro on a December 2013 NXT TV show but, despite recently revealing he had undergone neck surgery, he says reports his career is medically over are incorrect. "There's no reason I can't wrestle again: they told me I could, I'm just not in any bother about doing it, if that makes any sense. I've got to do a lot of other things for the company. When you've got 30 solid years, and it's not like I've ever worked an easy style, I think I've done well: my brain's altogether, I'm all in one piece, and I'm alive, so why push it?"

While his time is now spent helping prepare the next generation of wrestlers, Regal freely admits that in today's world, where trainees spend most of their time working with one another, he would have "absolutely no chance whatsoever" of making it. He puts his success down to his height ("Doesn't matter how good I was, I got booked a lot of places because I was tall, and I had a body at the time") and his fortune at coming to wrestling at a time when it was still possible to work 200 days a year against more skilled opponents.

"I'm under no illusions as to why I've had the career I've had. It's because I came along at the right time. In 1983 there were still enough great wrestlers around, in a different world as far as skill level that I could learn from.

"In this day and age, because I had no natural skill for this, no matter how hard I worked I would never have got to where I got to. As far as nuts and bolts and timing and knowing how to really make people react to things and change them on a penny, to have them screaming one minute, loving you the next, booing the next, I was around the best people to do that."

William Regal

# FA CUP FINAL DAY

Today almost every promotion builds to its biggest show of the year but in the television era there was no British equivalent to WrestleMania. As a business built largely around dozens of venues running weekly, the idea of building to a peak made little sense to promoters. The closest thing to the "big show of the year" therefore depended on perspective.

To the live event audience, particularly in the south-east of the country, the night of the biggest matches was arguably the "season-closing" show at the Royal Albert Hall, the last event before the break for Prom season. But to the more casual television viewer, FA Cup Final day was the closest thing to a special occasion.

With wrestling a mainstay on Saturday afternoons for most of the year by 1961, ITV faced a decision on Cup Final day in May when the game aired in the usual wrestling timeslot. They could ditch the wrestling altogether or move it to earlier in the afternoon and make it part of the build-up. Fortunately for grappling fans they chose the former option.

It may be difficult for modern fans to understand just how significant a sporting event the Cup Final was in this era. This was partly because of the prestige of the competition itself. At this time the combination of the strict "league winners only" rule in the European Cup and its knockout format meant far fewer matches between top-flight European competition. As a result, even the leading English teams considered the FA Cup a major prize.

It was just as significant as a television event. Hard as it may be to believe, no league games were broadcast on live TV between 1960 and 1983. The FA Cup Final was thus one of the very rare chances people had to watch live football on the small screen and would attract the interest of people with no allegiance to either team. For most of the 60s and 70s the game aired on both BBC 1 and ITV meaning that in the early years it would literally be the only thing on television.

Joint Promotions took full advantage of its prime position with wrestling airing on ITV as part of the build-up to the game, which would also include footage of the teams arriving at the ground and recaps of their "Road to Wembley" progression through earlier rounds. Indeed, there's a strong argument that wrestling was intended to win over audiences in the hope that they'd then stick around for the big game rather than return to the more popular BBC coverage.

The Cup Final wrestling tradition began in 1961 with a billed line-up of Billy Two Rivers facing Francis Sullivan. Whether this actually aired is unclear, but reports from the day show Mick McManus wrestling Jack Cunningham to a draw and Joe Cornelius defeating Johnny Allen by two falls to one. The special occasion was marked by Kent Walton and Peter Cockburn sharing commentary duties.

As would happen for the first six years, the show came live from Wembley Town Hall (later rebranded Brent Town Hall). While not the largest of venues, it lay less than a mile from Wembley Stadium, regular home of the Cup Final, and could thus capitalise on the buzz, though it might have been a close-run thing for those hoping to attend both events.

1962 put Cup Final Day wrestling on the map with the first televised clash of the infamous Mick McManus vs Jackie Pallo match. Perhaps surprisingly, although the bout had been built up by a rare TV angle with Pallo issuing a grandstand challenge at a previous show from Wembley, it wasn't widely advertised. The listings in the TV Times instead merely mentioned Pallo among the wrestlers who might appear "depending on time."

Other publicity even listed Pallo against Monty Swann, suggesting the McManus match was a case of promoters making a late switch to capitalise on what Pallo always claimed as his own initiative to share in McManus's glory. The prime billing instead went to Bill Howes successfully challenging Jacques Lageott for the European mid-heavyweight title in a bout that still holds up more than fifty years later.

Pallo and McManus were most definitely top of the bill a year later however when they met in a much hyped rematch, won two falls to one by McManus, who took the winning fall by reversing Pallo's trademark piledriver. The match also featured a memorable money with Pallo jumping out of the ring to kiss his wife – an incident considered so outlandish that in the retelling it would often be recast as him kissing McManus's wife. Coming just days after the Duke of Edinburgh attended a Royal Albert Hall show – also broadcast live -- it was arguably the biggest week of the era for British wrestling getting mainstream attention.

The bout was even cited as drawing a bigger viewing audience than the football match, though the hype train was in full effect as this claim was being made in newspapers as a given several days before the broadcast. It's generally accepted that while this may very well have been the most watched British wrestling match, it likely only outdrew the football audience on ITV itself rather than the combined BBC and ITV viewership.

By 1964 the Cup Final wrestling tradition was so established that the main event of Bert Royal and Vic Faulkner vs McManus and Steve Logan (only the sixth ever televised tag match) received prime billing on the TV Times front cover. Whatever the actual numbers McManus and Pallo had drawn was enough to convince ITV to not only fill the pre-football timeslot but air matches – likely on tape delay from earlier in the day – during half-time and after the big game.

Contrary to some accounts, including Pallo's own autobiography, he did not wrestle McManus on the 1965 show. The pair were instead in the midst of several years building up their names individually before a fresh series on the live event circuit. Indeed, on most occasions the Cup Final day broadcast was more about showcasing the top stars than putting on the biggest possible bouts at the possible expense of the live show business.

Instead McManus and Logan defeated Johnny Kwango and Lindsey Caulder in the latest of what became a tradition of tag matches on the big show, while McManus wrestled Bernard Murray. Also on the show was Ricky Starr who would return the following year for a clash with Steve Logan still talked about as a classic today. Another 1966 bout with McManus against Alan Dennison featured an unusual TV Times build-up with Pallo saying he'd beaten both men, didn't care who won, and hoped they'd kill each other!

1967 marked the first time the show moved away from Wembley, instead coming from Rotherham, and it appears McManus didn't fancy the trip North. Instead Pallo took top billing against Bert Royal, with other notable appearances by Billy Robinson and a tag match featuring Roy and Tony St Clair, the latter not only still being in his teens but making his television debut.

McManus was back in prime position on the 1968 show, taking on Alan Miquet from the decidedly unglamorous location of Trowell, a village in Nottinghamshire. Both the venue and the timeslot, now reduced to the usual one hour, suggested Cup Final day wrestling was no longer such a high priority, though it certainly offered a "shop window" for the outlandish team of Bobby Barnes and Adrian Street, the Hells Angels, who wrestled Chic Purvey and Steve Clements.

The show returned to Wembley in 1969 with a main event featuring McManus and Logan against Vassilios Mantopolous and Armand Zarpanalian, a match arguably most notable for one of the worst butcherings of a name in print with the latter partner listed in the TV Times as "Our Man Zorba." The event also featured George Kidd, making a rare appearance both on television and in a Southern England venue. Meanwhile 1970 in Halifax proved something of a showcase with Les Kellett (vs Steve Haggetty), Jackie Pallo (vs Mick McMichael) and the McManus/Logan team (vs the St Clairs) all taking predictable victories.

That's not to say the Cup Final Day show stopped having truly historic moments at this point. 1971's event, from St Albans, featured the televised debut of Kendo Nagasaki, defeating Wayne Bridges. Not only was it the first national sighting of the man who would be one of the biggest stars of the 70s, but it was only the second time a masked wrestler had appeared on television, following a string of appearances in the mid-60s by The Outlaw, better known as American grappler Gordon Nelson.

1972 was the last Cup Final Day at Wembley for several years and the first to be recorded ahead of the big day. (By the end of the year, both the Saturday and midweek timeslots featured pre-recorded shows, possibly because of the switch from film to cheaper and reusable videotape.) It was a familiar story on top with McManus beating Jeff Kaye while Logan lost to Les Kellett, with the tag action provided by the Hells Angels drawing with the Borg Twins from Malta.

The 1973 show, the first of three straight years at Walthamstow, featured a farewell and a welcome when it came to Cup Final shows. Jackie Pallo beat Johnny Kwango in the former's last appearance on the big day broadcast and one of the few complete Pallo bouts that remains widely available to view today.

Meanwhile Johnny Saint made his first Cup Final Day appearance, taking on perennial rival and British lightweight champion Jim Breaks. Those familiar with Saint's smooth sportsmanlike style would be surprised to see the viciousness of the bout. Saint had previously beaten Breaks by two straight falls in a non-title affair that saw Breaks's nose severely damaged and bloodied. The rematch ended with a referee stoppage after a cut to Saint's forehead.

Speaking to FSM, Breaks recalled that "We tried to make it look like a genuine fight although it was showbusiness. For instance, if you did have a nose busted by accident, the other guy would always work on it. If you've got something you might as well use it, and often the audience would see that and think 'Well, this [match] must be straight.'"

In a now familiar pattern, McManus and Logan headlined all three of the Walthamstow shows, taking on the Barons (Ian Gilmour and Jeff Kaye) in 1973, the Saints (Steve Best and Johnny Saint) in 1974 and the New Barons (Mick McMichael and Eddie Capelli) in 1975. That run ended in 1976, though not through a booking decision but rather because wrestling didn't air on Cup Final day. Exactly why this was the case isn't known but ratings for wrestling as a whole had been dropping to the extent that it attracted attention in a TV Times article. It was around this period that McManus was replaced as matchmaker by Mike Marino, a short-lived experiment at freshening up the product that was generally considered unsuccessful.

Wrestling returned to its pre-match slot in 1977 with the main event of Johnny Saint vs Kader Hassouni for the world lightweight title. McManus again featured, taking on Steve Grey, who recalls that with shows taped several weeks beforehand, the participants weren't always aware their match would be shown on Cup Final day. "[When we wrestled] it was just another show. It wasn't until you watched the matches on TV that you thought 'Crikey, this is a big slot

Grey would return in 1978 for the first of two straight matches against Jim Breaks, but it was the other bouts on the broadcast that told the bigger story. Max Crabtree was now in firm control of both the management and booking of Joint Promotions and the show featured new babyface Big Daddy teaming with Tony St Clair against the monster duo of Giant Haystacks and Bruiser Muir, a formula that would become a Cup Final day mainstay.

Meanwhile McManus made his last ever Cup Final day appearance, having appeared on 15 out of 17 shows. For the first time since the Pallo rematch, he failed to take the victory, instead going to a no-contest with Eddie 'Kung Fu' Hamill. The match memorably ended in Kendo Nagasaki making his first TV appearance since voluntarily unmasking, running in to save Hamill from a post-match beatdown and chasing McManus to the back. According to Hamill, it wasn't designed to promote a McManus-Nagasaki feud, but rather to establish a babyface Nagasaki/Kung Fu tag team where both men would wear masks to the ring and then remove them before the bout started. That idea was cut short when Hamill left Joint Promotions for rival group All-Star.

For the most part, Crabtree's Cup Final show booking balanced a Daddy tag match for a more casual audience with a more technical match for the purist, such as 1979's combo of Daddy & Ringo Rigby against Mark Rocco and John Quinn (setting up the Daddy-Quinn singles match at Wembley Arena) and Breaks vs Grey.

1980 was a rare exception however, with Daddy not wrestling on the bill but still very much the focus. After losing to Daddy at Wembley, Quinn had disappeared for several months (working the European tournaments) before returning and cutting a rare promo declaring his desire not only to defeat Daddy but to take the recently-introduced World heavyweight title from Wayne Bridges, leading to a pull-apart brawl.

The match took place on the Cup Final day show, which came from Wembley Town Hall for the final time. Quinn took the decision and the title on a blood stoppage and was in the midst of celebrating with cornerman Yasu Fuji when Daddy came to ringside. Any question that this was an angle was answered not only by Daddy's music playing as he made his entrance, but Kent Walton talking about a tag match as a given before any challenges had been made. The Quinn/Fuji vs Daddy/Bridges match took place at Wembley Arena that summer.

The next two years were both planned to have a Japanese flavour, though the scheduled 1981 appearance of Sammy Lee (Satoru 'Tiger Mask' Sayama) instead had what must surely have been one of most disappointing substitutions of all time with Little Prince taking his place. The following year saw Tony Walsh as a late substitute for Skull Murphy in a team with Crusher Brannigan, with fan speculation and rumour having it that Murphy had second thoughts about the bout. It's hard to tell which half of the unlikely opposition team would have caused such reticence: Big Daddy or 'Kwik-kik Lee', better known as Akira Maeda.

As with 1982, the next two Cup Final shows consisted solely of the Daddy tag. 1983 saw he and a wrestler with the politically incorrect name of Kid Chocolate against the Masked Marauders, part of a long-running feud with Daddy taking on members of a stable led by manager Charlie McGhee. Meanwhile 1984's event had its own unlikely substitution: Honey Boy Zimba was replaced as Daddy's partner against Haystacks and Fit Finlay by Drew McDonald in a rare babyface appearance.

Viewers of a more traditional wrestling persuasion had something to cheer on the 1985 show: while Daddy and Mick McMichael despatched the low-profile duo of Pete LaPaque and Tommy Lorne, rising star Danny Collins – fresh off an intricate storyline that saw him take the British welterweight title from Jim Breaks – took the European crown from Baron von Chenok (also known as Jorg Chenok). It earned him tours of France and Spain, along with a slot teaming with Daddy on Cup Final day 1986 against Finlay and Scrubber Daly.

1987 proved to be not only the first Cup Final day since Joint Promotions lost its exclusivity on ITV (though it did fill that week's slot) but the last such pre-football show. Daddy did not feature but the Crabtree family was represented by his nephew Steve, billed as Greg Valentine. Perhaps surprisingly he lost to Steve Logan (a newcomer rather than McManus's partner.) The feature bout was a 'super heavyweight' battle royale won by Haystacks.

With ratings at an all-time low, due at least in part to wrestling no longer having a consistent timeslot, there were no bouts aired before the 1988 Cup Final, the last to take place before ITV dropped coverage at the end of the year.

# THE HOLIDAY CAMPS

While nobody knows for sure which British venue has hosted the most wrestling shows, there's a good chance it's a Butlins holiday camp. Launched by Billy Butlin, the camps were an evolution of the fairgrounds and amusement parks owned by his ancestors. While Butlin didn't create the idea of an all-inclusive package of budget accommodation and on-site entertainment, he popularised the set-up that still exists today with both Butlins and rival chains.

The Butlin-wrestling connection actually predates the holiday camps. A 1935 advertisement for a carnival event at a Butlin amusement park in Mablethorpe, Lincolnshire includes a promise of wrestling bouts alongside boxing matches and other entertainments. Exactly when Butlin brought wrestling to the camps isn't clear, but it preceded the establishment of both the Mountevans rules and Joint Promotions: a 1946 booking sheet for a wrestling working for George De Relwyskow includes dates at Butlins camps in Ayr, Clacton, Filey, Pwllheli and Skegness.

Wrestling remained a staple at the camps into the TV era and even made a handful of appearances on the small screen with the Prestatyn site playing host for live and taped broadcasts. Fans of the era writing on the Wrestling Heritage website remember some of the top stars of the day making appearances but crowds being disappointing as the Saturday afternoon slot coincided with the changeover between each week's guests.

Despite their TV stranglehold, the contracts to provide wrestling weren't always held by Joint Promotions members. In 1975, Brian Dixon – five years into his run as an independent or "opposition" promoter – secured a lucrative Butlins contract. "I don't remember if I approached them or they approached me," he tells FSM, "but I was offered the northern run which at the time was Ayr, Filey, Pwhelli and Skegness. We did that for one season. Terry Goodrum did the other run but he had… let's say… some problems outside of the job so I was given the chance to take over the rest of the run, which meant Barry Island, Bognor, Clacton, Minehead and Mosney in Ireland." It was a contract that Dixon would go on to hold for four decades.

The advantages to a promoter were multiple and Dixon calls Butlins "the secret to my success." There was of course the guarantee of a fixed income without being at the mercy of drawing a big gate. However, Dixon says this revenue wasn't the biggest benefit of the deal, rather that combining the camp bookings with "town shows" (events held in regular venues before a paying audience) allowed him to attract wrestlers from home and abroad with the prospect of full time work.

There was also another promotional benefit. "In the same way Joint had TV, the camps were our shop window. We'd capture the interest of the holidaymakers and they'd be more likely to come to town shows, which we'd list in the program. For example, we'd have people from Croydon on holiday at a camp show say 'Oh, I never knew there was wrestling at the Fairfield Hall.' You can do all the local promoting you like, but sometimes people are unsure of your presence until they actually see you in action."

It's hard to understate just how much work was available for a successful holiday camp wrestler, both on the Butlins runs and with other promoters at the smaller camp chains. Ricky Knight has previously spoken to FSM about how a rigorous camp circuit meant he once wrestled 11 matches in a single day. Another camp stalwart, Mel Stuart, who worked the Pontins circuit, recalls that "We'd drive up from Kent to Scarborough at the start of the run and do four shows in one day coming down the east coast. You could very easily do 14 shows a week, and I'd say on average it was 10 shows, wrestling twice on each one. And at that time the camp season ran 26 weeks a year."

Such a schedule was possible because the wrestling shows in question would usually run for an hour and could be at any time of the day. For example, on one Monday in 1955 the Pwllheli Butlins had wrestling at both 2.30 and 7.30, the shows fitting into a schedule that included everything from a tea dance to a glamorous grandmother contest to a shaving competition sponsored by Philishave. (In a sign of the times, holidaymakers later in the week could take part in a cigarette rolling contest.)

The fact that many of the audience on hand were not committed grappling fans but instead taking advantage of the free entertainment (or seeking shelter from inclement weather) was both a challenge and an opportunity for wrestlers. Stuart notes that the matches would feature "a lot of the younger generation wrestlers and they'd be more light-hearted. The rule was that there was to be no form of upset for the mums and dads and you had to keep it all nice. It was all very Tom and Jerry." Dixon adds that "The camps have always been the place to learn the trade: as a young wrestler, they'd give you the tools you needed for what the job is about. We'd do a lot matches with a trainee against a more experienced guy." Bob 'Blondie' Barratt explains that "It was a good learning curve because if you can get non-fans shouting at a match, you're halfway there."

Comedy was a big part of the experience, and several wrestlers were able to make a career almost as camp specialists, despite not being big names on the TV and Joint Promotions live scene. Such names brought up by former camp veterans include Johnny Riley, Dave George and Kurt Heinz. Dixon points to Joe Critchley as a great camps wrestler: "It was pure comedy: he'd do a legdrop and his teeth would come out. It was pure vaudeville."

In most cases a show would, while still being aimed at a casual audience, have a mix of styles. A common format was at least one comedy bout and one based more on the hero-villain dynamic or what Stuart calls "the cowboy and Indian stuff." The bout order might depend on the slot: while the comedy was often the opener, 22-year-camp veteran Nigel 'Tommy Stewart' Hanmore notes that "on some camps you'd be on in the evening at around nine when people had had a few drinks and it was a more middle aged audience, so you did the cowboys first and the comedy at the end."

Indeed, Hanmore recalls the mix could even vary depending on the venue. "Somewhere like Exmouth you wouldn't do so much comedy because it was mainly a younger generation of adults. Over in Sand Bay it was what we called the wheelchair and walking stick brigade and they loved the comedy. I can see them now in their chairs laughing and even crying with laughter: that's real job satisfaction and gives you a buzz."

Stuart points out that the mix of styles made the shows more viable for those wrestlers who still needed to draw paying fans at the town venues. "Even while being lighthearted, a few of us kept ourselves strong. You could have the lesser known faces doing the silliness and the comedy stuff and then people like me or Crusher Mason, who were a bit more notable faces, could make our matches more credible."

Another benefit to the mix of styles came in the conclusion of the show. A few of the smaller camp chains would simply have a two match card. Dixon's shows at Butlins, which had a bigger budget to play with, usually had scope for three matches with a six-wrestler crew (or eight in the event of a tag match.) In between, at the likes of Pontins, came the shoestring shows where as few as four wrestlers would have to put on a three match show. Most commonly this would involve some sort of one-night storyline to set up a tag match main event, allowing for some fresh interactions between the wrestlers on either side.

In other cases, creative uses of masks could do the trick. Hanmore explains how this could sometimes be necessary over a wider timeline when he worked for camp specialist promoter Jimmy Hagen. "He'd cycle three teams in from week to week to keep things fresh, which also meant anyone who stayed at a camp for a couple of weeks wouldn't see a repeated show. We'd then meet every Monday morning at Jimmy's house to look through the reports from the venue staff about what shows they did and didn't like.

"One time we had to run the same team twice in a row at Brean Sands, so we had James Mason dress up in a mask and costume to make it different. After the show the entertainments manager came in and said 'Can I have a word? Can you tell that bloke in the mask not to come here anymore?' I said 'Tell him yourself: he's sat right next to me!'"

Keeping on the good side of the camp staff was always an important part of running a successful camp show. Dixon says that the camp's compere, who would act as ring announcer, could "kill a show or make a show. They were almost like Kent Walton where if they said something was good, everyone believed it. Luckily today many of the comperes are actually fans of wrestling and use that background to put it over."

Hanmore points out that many camp entertainers, both staff and performers, have had some involvement in wrestling over the years, with the likes of Shane Richie and Joe Pasquale acting as referees. "We even did a bit where the Chuckle Brothers would be seconds, one in each corner, and end up fighting one another in the ring."

For the wrestlers themselves, the travel meant that having a tolerant nature was as important as in-ring ability. Speak to any wrestler about their camp days and the word "team" is guaranteed to be used in reference to the travelling crew of wrestlers, who'd usually follow a schedule designed for the benefit of the camp chain rather than their own comfort. Barrett recalls that "You'd often get there in the middle of the night and find there was no chalet ready, or it had no bed clothes. It was all a bit ramshackle."

"You could be in a car together 10 hours a day, six days a week, doing 2,000 miles on the road" Dixon explains. "Even the best person in the world will get on your nerves and it takes a certain kind of person to survive. It's also important they can keep fit and supple: if somebody gets injured on a camp show on a Tuesday night, it's a big hassle for a promoter to have to replace them with somebody who can get to the next show in time."

Part of the work outside of the shows was putting the ring up and taking it down multiple times a day, something that could be awkward according to Barrett, "We'd be on a tight schedule because the camps wanted to tidy up. For example, at Great Yarmouth we could set up behind closed doors, the doors opened at 6.30 for a 7pm show, then you'd end at 8 and have to pull the ring down before the evening entertainment started. The crowd just sat there and watched as you worked on the ring together right after they'd seen you battering each other! The worst part was how they'd just sit there and never even move out of your way as you're carrying out these great lumps of steel."

Hanmore remembers that the help of camp staff was particularly important in such circumstances. "It took half an hour to get the ring up, but with the help of the Bluecoats we got to the point where we could take it down and get it in the van in eight minutes."

Some venues had rings kept permanently on site, but Barrett points out that wasn't always a benefit. "In one place, I think it was Ayr, the ring was chucked behind the back of the stage after shows and was rotten. At one stage it only had seven of the eight boards – the other had been nicked or bust. We had to remember to work around one of the corners because otherwise you'd go straight through the canvas!"

Though the basic format remained in place, elements would change as both wrestling and the camps evolved. Dixon explains that "in the 1980s Butlins started doing wrestling as part of a late night cabaret show alongside television stars like Jimmy Tarbuck or Joe Longthorne. We'd have one or two matches with the camp team and then a 'star bout' with main eventers like Les Kellett, Dave Finlay, Mark Rocco or Danny Collins, who'd be introduced as TV stars. The kids were in bed, so the audience was more like a town show.

"Surprisingly the guys in the first couple of matches often got more response than the stars. I think it was because a typical holiday camp wrestler was more used to involving the audience, which the star matches didn't always do. The camp wrestlers have the experience of comparing doing A with doing B on different holiday audiences and seeing which one works."

Moving into the 1990s and new millennium, Butlins in particular underwent revamps to shed its low-rent image. "The old sitcom Hi-Di-Hi was exactly how it used to be," Dixon explains, "but anyone who goes there now with that in mind would be blown away. Honestly, I've learned my trade as a promoter and a presenter from Butlins. They train their staff to excellence and everything has to be 100 percent right. For example, at Minehead and Skegness they turn the room around completely for a wrestling show and put in a walkway and prep the lighting. They'll take two hours to get it ready for a 90-minute show just so the audience can sit there in amazement. It automatically feels like the big time when people walk in."

Indeed, the Skyline Pavilion at Minehead, which can seat more than 5,000 people, now plays host to a WWE event as a regular part of the Autumn tour. Rather than selling show tickets, it's presented as part of a special holiday package that includes both admission and accommodation for a family treat.

For the rest of the year Butlin's wrestling remains British but, as of 2017, is no longer provided by All Star. Dixon says he was fully aware that the contract would not get renewed following what he calls "a silly situation." A match featuring patriotic babyface Tony Spitfire against heel "Arabian Superstar" Hakeem Waqur, complete with compere encouragement to cheer and boo respectively, attracted worldwide media attention after one holidaymaker described the bout as "A horrific race hate-filled ten minutes of everything wrong on racial stereotypes."

Dixon argues that "The compere wasn't encouraging kids to boo the Muslim, he was encouraging the kids to boo the bad guy." However, he says "I hold no grudges against Butlins. Their image is important, and they have holidaymakers from many different nations. When they told me their decision, the [Butlins executive] was very apologetic and said it was one of the hardest decisions he'd ever had to make."

The wrestling is now provided by Hull's New Generation Wrestling, whose Alex Shane tells FSM that "Butlins was always part of the plan right back to when we brought back the FWA for the second run [in 2009], just because we could see it was such a great platform. We wanted to make it less of an end of the pier show, and more contemporary, so we use things like personalised entrances and a massively produced format. When I met the entertainments manager for the initial pitch, I was surprised how well our visions synchronised – we were almost finishing each other's sentences.

"Although the pitch was originally about our product and brand, we have quickly found the experience of working with Butlins has meant we've changed our own brand to fit better with their product and customer base. The overall NGW model has now become far more focused on child-friendly entertainment. That's partly because I've probably done as much in the internet or smart fan side of the business as one man should really do by the age of 37 and find this a massively rewarding new challenge.

"Butlins has taught me something that sounds really obvious but is incredibly important, which is that we're putting on a show totally for the benefit of the customer, as opposed to simply putting on the show that you want to see and just treating the audience as a way to financially facilitate that." While it's still aimed at a family audience, Shane says the NGW offering at Butlins is still a modern product. "Working holiday camps doesn't mean you have to water the in-ring quality down athletically and I don't tell the wrestlers to tone it down at all. Recently we had two wrestlers, very good high-flyers, and if you wrote out a checklist of everything you'd see in a stereotypical camp match, they'd have ticked them all off. I told them next time I wanted them to do the match they'd do on TV and the only difference should be to be mindful of the audience and maybe do a more condensed version of the heel and face dynamic. It's important with very young fans, and I actually think when they watch today's WWE where they see the good guys doing the right thing but being booed, it can be very confusing to somebody whose brain is still developing. We make sure that the lines of good and evil are very clearly defined.

"We're making the Butlins matches more athletic for sure, but it's not about hitting hard or taking massive bumps, it's more about working at a faster, yet smarter pace. Obviously with the family audience we're not having guys doing piledrivers or needless headdrops. As the younger wrestlers adapt to working a busier schedule, it's more about impact modification rather than reducing moves, by minimising big bumps."

Shane notes that with TV acts such as Diversity being regulars at Butlins, audiences have high expectations when it comes to production. "We do a lot of production on the shows and whereas it used to be you'd just turn up before the show with a list of names for the compere, we send a full production runner with a detailed running order with cues for things like on-screen pre match videos and lighting that's synchronised to the ring entrances."

Despite the change of style and presentation, the NGW shows are still produced on the basis that many in the audience won't be wrestling fans, "We also do as much as an hour of pre-show video hyping up the matches and even explaining things like the rules for non-fans, as basic as explaining that you win a match with a count of three. We also make it simple by having yellow and red cards for warnings and we even stock the cards at the merchandise table."

And as has always been the case, some wrestlers who aren't as well known on the more traditional scene have thrived in the new setting. "Kip Sabian is a wrestler who's breaking out and really working well at Butlins. He's wrestled for some smaller companies, but we had him on a couple of shows and now I want him booked on as much as we can. There's also Amir Jordan who does the Bollywood entrance that I originally envisioned for RJ Singh over ten years ago and it adds a different diversity dynamic to the show with two or three thousand people dancing to Bangra during the entrance. And Justin Sysum works so well because he looks just like a larger than life superhero with his cape. Our new company slogan is 'bring out the hero in you' and Justin is the living embodiment of that."

Despite the change, Dixon isn't ruling out a return to Butlins in the future. "I always said that once Butlins was finished, I would finish but here I am! They said the decision was not necessarily permanent and we can put in a tender again in future. In the meantime, we're still doing shows with some of the other camps such as Haven that are owned by the same company but run separately."

Whoever is providing the shows, it seems wrestling is set to stay as a staple of holiday camp entertainment. Indeed, the family-friendly style might even be a possibility for Daniel Bryan were he to see out his WWE contract and seek to wrestle elsewhere in styles that reduced the risk of further head trauma. Bizarre as it might seem for a former WrestleMania headliner to work at Butlins, it would be something of a homecoming for a man who once did the camp circuit for six months and wrote in his autobiography that:

"There was no stress, no pressure, just driving up and down the roads with interesting guys and wrestling... I always get this secret longing in my heart for [those] days gone by when everything was a little more innocent for me.

"It was the most fun I'd ever had wrestling."

# THE PRE-TV ERA

While the ITV era sparked British wrestling's biggest boom, the professional business already had a rich heritage in the country.

While the emergence of professional wrestling as a business in the United State followed a fairly clear path of first betting scams and then match outcomes worked to attract paying crowds, things were a little messier in the UK. One reason for this is the sheer diversity of legitimate grappling styles that developed across the country, both as a participatory sport and a public attraction.

The most relevant to the pro scene was Lancashire's catch-as-catch-can (or simply "Lancashire Catch") a name that didn't just refer to the rules allowing holds to be taken both above and below the waist (as in Olympic "freestyle" wrestling) but also the use of submissions. One theory is that this developed on both sides of the Atlantic as a way for fairground wrestlers accepting challenges from the public to have an extra weapon in their arsenal.

Another regional variation was the Cumberland and Westmoreland style where wrestlers would have to interlock lock arms around one another and maintain this hold, with the winner being the first to throw his opponent onto his back. Perhaps the most painful variant came in Cornwall and Devon where kicking was allowed but only below the knee, usually leading to bloodied or even broken shins.

The first signs of wrestling as we would recognise it today came in the early 20th century when it became part of the well-established tradition of music hall. This was a popular entertainment format where a single venue would offer a range of acts across an evening including circus-like physical performances, stand-up comedy and singing, often with the crowd eating at tables during the show.

For some time a common physical attraction had been muscular men either showing off their physiques or demonstrating their strength. Accounts from the time suggest crowds began to tire of the repetitive and limited nature of such performances, which opened up an opportunity for wrestling exhibitions to satisfy the interest in physiques but with more excitement and variety.

Among the early stars of this genre was Jack Carkeek, an American of Cornish heritage who had turned to the stage in his 40s after a successful run in competitive tournaments in the US. As part of his act he would accept challengers from the audience, most likely plants. This led to a famous incident when a man stood up and removed his suit, revealing a full set of wrestling gear underneath.

Carkeek spotted the would-be challenger was George Hackenschmidt, who had already built up a reputation on the continent by winning several tournaments that at the very least gave the air of being legitimate contests. A quick-thinking Carkeek managed to talk his way out of the challenge by explaining the invitation was for British wrestlers only.

The incident attracted the attention of Charles Cochran, an agent and promoter who would later become best known for his work with Noel Coward and managing the Royal Albert Hall. Cochran took Hackenschmidt on as a client and began promoting him with national press articles before taking him on a theatre run. It took some time for Hackenschmidt to adjust to the theatrical life as he was said to be uncomfortable with carrying an opponent to a crowd-pleasing bout, but eventually settled into a routine with a regular German opponent named Schackmann who may well have been British wrestling's first full-blown heel performer.

The music hall reputation built Hackenschmidt up to the point that his major bouts could be standalone events in themselves. One such match came against Britain's Tom Cannon in Liverpool, where Hackenschmidt's victory was promoted as making him Europe's top claimant to the world heavyweight title.

According to an account in the 1968 book A Pictorial History of Wrestling by Graeme Kent, the match was perhaps more notable for a quite spectacular lack of cooperation in the promotion by the theatre's management, who soured on the sport after taking the booking. The first night of a planned run of shows was delayed after the manager cut off gas supplies, leaving the theatre in darkness, while subsequent attempts to run shows wound up with wrestlers brawling with venue security in an unsuccessful attempt to gain entry.

A more successful bout came in 1904 when Hackenschmidt took on Ahmed Madrali, one of many grapplers of the era to perform in a "Terrible Turk" role. The bout at London's Olympia was hyped as having a purse of £1,000 for the winner and £500 for the loser (£111,000 and £55,000 at today's prices) and was reported in the press as attracting such a crowd that traffic was backed up to Piccadilly, four miles away. The bout ended in a matter of moments with Madrali thrown to the floor and reported as suffering a fractured or broken arm, something that would at least seem unlikely to be a booked finish.

Later in the same year, Hackenschmidt beat American Tom Jenkins at the first show at what would eventually be British wrestling's most prestigious venue, the Royal Albert Hall. Hackenschmidt then made his way to the US where he beat Jenkins again, this time to become the first undisputed world champion of the professional era.

With his top star gone, Cochran brought in Stanislaus Zbyszko from Poland to headline. With Zbyszko apparently not the most charismatic performer, Cochran carried out some creative promotional stunts. One was employed whenever rival shows were in the same city on the same day. A grappler would buy a ticket for the non-Cochran show and make a scene, demanding Zbyszko face him immediately. It was merely a ruse to trick the hall manager to inform the audience that Zbyszko was actually at the other venue. The wrestler would then depart for said hall to wrestle Zbyszko, usually taking curious audience members with him.

Cochran was able to build Zbyszko up for a major match with Russia's Ivan Poddubny at the 2,000-seat London Pavilion Theatre that was said to have drawn a turnaway crowd despite tickets costing one guinea. That would be £117 in today's money so, even allowing for some hyperbolic exaggeration, it was an impressive draw.

The so-called 'Golden Era' of British wrestling went into decline within a few years, with contributing factors said to include the news of Hackenschmidt falling twice to Frank Gotch in the US in 1908 and 1911, along with a particularly lengthy and boring bout at Crystal Palace in 1910. Whatever the reasons, not only was the boom over by the start of the first world war in 1914, but the wrestling business appears to have struggled to revive itself throughout the 1920s.

The story of how wrestling came back in a modern form one is tough to nail down with certainty. The most detailed account is the book Blue Blood on the Mat by Athol Oakeley but the problem is not only that Oakeley is one of the key players (by his own telling) but that several of the objective numbers he quotes are clearly exaggerated to the point that his other recollections come into question.

Either way, it appears clear the key was the adoption of not just American promotional styles with more outlandish finishes, but also American rules with the adoption of submission holds. Given these were already being used for real in the Lancashire catch scene, it led to some confusing terminology in the period between the wars.

An initial revival promoted by Oakeley and American Henri Irslinger (a veteran of the music hall era) among others was billed as a new All-In Wrestling style. While that term was designed to highlight the inclusion of all holds, including submissions, it later became adopted by some to instead emphasize the American influence of matches with virtually no regard for the rules. This form of All-In Wrestling, with use of weapons such as stools and water buckets, appears from accounts of the time to be closer to the modern "hardcore" style.

To add to the confusion for historians, the description of a show as "all-in", "catch-as-catch-can" or "freestyle" appears often to have been less about its actual content and more about finding loopholes when local councils banned or restricted shows that presented a particular form of wrestling by using a given wording.

Whatever the name, the "new" wrestling kicked off in November 1930 with Oakley against Bill Garnon and Georges Modrich against George Boganski as guest matches on a boxing show at the London Sports Club. A planned high-profile wrestling relaunch show at the Royal Albert Hall had to be cancelled over work permit issues, so instead the media's attention was drawn to two more guest matches on boxing shows on 15 December with Irslinger against Modrich at Olympia and Oakeley against Bert Assirati at Manchester's Belle Vue.

Wrestling soon broke away from the boxing connection to appear on shows in its own right, something that no doubt came as a relief to the boxing community given questions over the grappling game's legitimacy and sportsmanship. Indeed, three years later the British Boxing Board of Control banned wrestling bouts from appearing on licensed boxing shows. On the other side of the coin, wrestling promoters such as Oakeley attracted attention by issuing grandstand challenges for boxers to take on grapplers in mixed rules bouts, safe in the knowledge that the proposed rules, which included submissions, would leave the boxer unlikely to prevail in a genuine contest.

The wrestling business certainly boomed in the early 30s: Wrestling Heritage's Alan Bamber cites contemporary articles listing 20 shows a week nationwide in 1931, but a figure of 40 regular venues in London alone just three years later. The Victoria Palace in London held an entire week's run of shows with a round-robin tournament, while other popular venues in the capital included The Ring in Blackfriars and the two-thousand seat Lane's Club. Wrestling even made its TV debut in 1938, on the BBC rather than its later home of ITV, with more than 20 broadcasts of bouts, many featuring Canadian grappler and British Empire champion Earl Macready.

The era also saw what may have been the biggest ever crowd to see a British wrestling match, albeit with no gate receipts. Norman 'the Butcher' Ansell took on Henri Letailler at the Hanworth Air Park as part of the entertainment surrounding a visit by the Graf Zeppelin airship. The crowd for the Zeppelin was reportedly in the tens of thousands (or "four million" if you believe Oakely), though it's unclear how many actually watched the bout.

Oakley was by no means the only promoter of the era. Others included George De Relwyskow in the north, who then began a loose partnership with Leonard 'Jack Dale' Abbey in the south; although De Relwyskow died in 1942, this arrangement sowed the seeds for his son and Abbey to later be key players in Joint Promotions. The decade also saw several female promoters, including Jean Hackenschmidt, wife of George who was now retired but living in the UK again. Another was Kathleen Look, who reportedly made a point of sitting next to the owner of Belle Vue on a train journey and persuading him to bring wrestling back to the venue after a period without shows.

A third female promoter was the wife of Bert Assirati, himself one of the biggest stars of the era. He remains a controversial historical figure, known for an aggressive style, but with historians divided on his legitimate abilities. There's no doubt many wrestlers feared working with him, with plenty of stories of opponents making their excuses when they discovered they were billed against him. In the words of Adrian Street, "Bert's opponent might be good-looking going into the ring, but coming out he'd look like he'd had an argument with a combine harvester." To some this was bullying and taking advantage, while to others it was simply a case that Assirati was perfectly willing to take physical punishment and was going to dish it out regardless.

By other accounts, he was a legitimately skilled competitive grappler, combining a short but powerful stature with submission abilities. Either way he held the most credible claim to a British heavyweight title status in the days before title billing was more unified across the country. (After the war he had a brief run as champion under the Joint Promotions banner before falling out with promoters, moving to the independent circuits, and keeping his name in the news with grandstand challenges to a no less diverse a pair of champions than the future "Big Daddy" Shirley Crabtree and Lou Thesz.)

As well as Assirati, the period between the wars appears to have been driven by the heels, particularly in those venues that preferred a more aggressive style with relaxed rules. Leading stars included Norman the Butcher, Black Butcher Johnson, and Jack Pye, arguably the biggest name of the era and the undisputed king of Belle Vue. Another attraction was Maurice Tillet, also known as the French Angel, a sufferer of the same acromegaly condition that afflicted Andre The Giant, but with greater facial disfigurement. (Indeed, there's even a theory his photograph served as the inspiration for the appearance of the Shrek character.)

The traditional account of British wrestling before the war has it that it fell into disrepute when demand from fans exceeded the supply of skilled grapplers and a descent into a brawling style led it to be banned from venues. While there's certainly some truth to this – leading professionals were on record complaining about unskilled newcomers filling bills and undercutting their payoffs – there also seems to be an element of retro-fitting the story to boost the "legitimate sporting contest" ideal that allowed Joint Promotions to claim respectability in the 1950s.

The ban on wrestling in London did not actually come into force until 1944, although female bouts had been barred six years earlier. Wrestling continued throughout the second world war, albeit on a reduced schedule and with a mixture of veteran wrestlers too old for active service and the occasional visits by younger grapplers on leave. Indeed, arguably the biggest challenge to promoters in the era were tight restrictions on using paper for promotional posters.

Once the conflict was over, the battle began to build the business back up and take advantage of the public's desire to return to enjoying live entertainment. Exposure was helped by a return to broadcasts on the BBC with around one match a month in 1946 and 1947, including the first appearance of a newcomer by the name of Mick McManus.

A report of a 1948 outdoor show at the White Hart Lane football ground headlined by Assirati against the French Angel lists the crowd as 12,000; if that figure is accurate, it remains the biggest paid attendance for a British promotion's show.

If that's not the case, the record may instead have been set at the Harringay Arena, home to Oakeley and company's attempts to take control of the business in the late 40s. Running semi-regular shows, the venue appears to have been attracting crowds in the region of five to six thousand until an event featuring celebrity boxer Jack Doyle against the Estonian "Gorilla" Martin Bucht. Depending on the source it drew between 9,500 fans and a capacity crowd of 10,660 as well as attracting mainstream media attention that had been lacking in recent years. Unfortunately the match itself proved somewhat farcical, amusing rather than enthralling the crowd and providing easy fodder for sportswriters who wanted to knock the business.

Oakeley's crew bemoaned the competition, suggesting that unlike their shows, others were promoting fake contests with unconvincing performances. That was somewhat undermined when his subsequent main events included Doyle against the German wrestler Zehe who was implausibly billed as 8'4" tall, and the wrestling debut of former world boxing champion Primo Carnera, whose involvement in the grappling game was seen as a humiliation that inspired the movie The Harder They Fall.

By the time Harringay Arena closed in 1954, Oakeley had thrown in the towel, leaving the flourishing Joint Promotions set to take full advantage of the opportunities presented by the launch of independent television.

# THE ROYAL ALBERT HALL

"It was the Madison Square Garden of British wrestling" says Marty Jones. "Wrestling there felt like being at a Royal command performance" is how Tony 'Banger' Walsh describes it. Both men are speaking of the most prestigious venue of the ITV wrestling era: the Royal Albert Hall.

"I remember the first time I was booked there," Walsh explained to FSM. "I was down to London a few weeks before the show and got on the Tube. At the station I saw a poster for the event with my name on and I couldn't believe it. I stood there for what felt like an hour just staring at it."

Aside from the few British venues that were purpose built for combat sports, it's hard to imagine a building better designed for a wrestling show. Around 5,500 fans (depending on the use of the permanent private boxes) can sit in comfort with a perfect view of the ring from almost every seat, giving an unusual blend of scale and intimacy.

Opened in 1871, the building is formally titled the Royal Albert Hall of Arts and Sciences. It was built in response to the success of the Great Exhibition in Hyde Park, which led Queen Victoria's husband Albert to propose a permanent venue, part funded by the exhibition's profits.

Despite its suitability for the grapple game it would be three decades before the first wrestling show at the building. On 2 July 1904 George Hackenschmidt, recognised as champion across Europe, took on American contender Tom Jenkins under Greco-Roman rules. Building management insisted there be no gambling and that the bout be "free from anything vulgar or incompatible with the dignity and reputation of the Hall, and that the competitors would be properly clothed so that there would be nothing of the semi-nude in the entertainment"

Reports at the time claimed the match was for a £2,500 purse, equivalent in today's money to around £240,000, though basic economics suggests such a sum is highly implausible. Hackenschmidt took the win in two straight falls, with the bout accompanied by a military band.

Promoter and showbiz impresario CB Cochran staged a rematch in Madison Square Garden the following year that proved even more historic. By this point Jenkins had regained his United States heavyweight championship and

Hackenschmidt's win at MSG saw him crowned the first undisputed world champion. Cochran brought back to the Royal Albert Hall later in 1905, this time with Ahmed Madrali the 2-0 winner.

It seems it would be many years before wrestling returned to the venue. Some reports suggest Irish wrestler and future world champion Danno O'Mahoney's professional debut came against Ed Lewis at the Royal Albert Hall in December 1934, though more reliable accounts put the venue as Holborn's Stadium Club, a popular boxing venue.

What is certain is that wrestling became a permanent fixture at the RAH when Dale Martin (with the assistance of its Joint Promotions partners) began running in the capital after the war. The first show on record took place on October 20, 1954, with Bert Royal vs Charro Montez and Pete Curry against Sandy Orford (who later trained Shirley 'Big Daddy' Crabtree) among the bouts.

Among those making news in these early years was the notorious Bert Assirati who defeated Ernie Baldwin for the British heavyweight title at the Royal Albert Hall in 1955. While officially still the title holder Assirati made an unwelcome appearance at the venue in December 1957. He attempted to interrupt a main event pitting former NWA world champion Lou Thesz against Indian legend Dara Singh to issue a grandstand challenge to Thesz but was held back by either security staff or police officers depending on the telling of the story.

The RAH shows differed from the normal Joint Promotions business model in several ways. Most sizable venues ran weekly, with fortnightly and monthly schedules reserved for smaller towns. However -- due perhaps to the building's busy schedule -- wrestling only took place once a month at the Royal Albert Hall, with a summer layoff during the Proms season.

Whereas most venues were running four-match shows, the Albert Hall regularly presented six, and later seven, bouts in an evening. The shows also featured a more diverse line-up than the usual weekly circuit shows, with wrestlers traveling from around the country, making it a great opportunity for up-and-comers from the Midlands and North to get a chance to work alongside some of the Dale Martin regulars and build their name. Lancashire-based Jones recalls that in his early appearances when he was in the first or second match he could leave the building in time to save accommodation expenses by hopping on the milk train for a 12-hour journey home.

Some stars were even brought in from overseas for a special appearance, a set-up similar to that of the WWWF's booking of Madison Square Garden. Among those who appeared at the venue over the years were Jean Ferre (later Andre the Giant) and Masachiko Kimura, one of the pioneers of Japanese wrestling and the man who gave his name to the armlock often seen in today's UFC.

It wasn't just the wrestlers who journeyed to Kensington, however. Jones explains that whereas most venues were filled only by locals, the RAH "had all the iconic punters from the London scene, and people traveling from Portsmouth, Southampton and even Bristol. You had lots of the well-to-do people as well and we'd always look up to the private boxes to see if we could spot any celebrities. But you didn't get many kids: it was more individuals than families, which spoilt the atmosphere a little in my opinion."

Tony Walsh agrees with this, noting that "You didn't get as many -- not to put it too delicately -- nutters as in places like my regular haunts in Digbeth and Wolverhampton. Up there they'd be ready to lynch me the moment I put my head through the ropes, but the Albert Hall crowd was more reserved."

Both men have less than fond memories of the resident ring at the venue which appeared to be designed primarily for boxing and which Walsh describes as "like concrete... one of the worst I ever worked in." That sometimes meant bad news for fans as well, with Pat Roach admitting to The Wrestling author Simon Garfield that "there was no way I was going to hoist a respected opponent above my head and slam him into that hard mat... you never got the same show out of me [in] a hard ring as in a decent one."

The backstage facilities also proved a disappointment to Jones given the glamour of the venue's public facade, while Walsh had a few Spinal Tap moments: "I must have got lost in those corridors at least three times!" It was in this same rabbit's warren that Giant Haystacks once bumped into Frank Sinatra after a concert and was allegedly told by the singer that "British wrestlers are the best entertainers in the whole world."

The grapple game received another celebrity endorsement on 22 May 1963 when Prince Phillip attended a show at the Royal Albert Hall to raise money for his Duke of Edinburgh award scheme. He returned for another charity show in 1968, while the Queen's cousin, the Duke of Kent, attended a 1977 event with a mouth-watering line-up advertised, including Jim Breaks vs Vic Faulkner, Mark Rocco vs Bert Royal and Dynamite Kid vs Steve Grey.

The royal connection certainly lent prestige to the business, though it has been the source of exaggeration over the years. Former cabinet member Richard Crosman noted in his published diaries that the Queen mentioned having watched the televised broadcast of the 1963 show, a comment that somehow became talked up to Her Majesty being a weekly viewer and, in some more ambitious accounts, a regular visitor to Albert Hall events.

Only two men appeared on both shows before Prince Philip, namely long-time rivals Mick McManus and Jackie Pallo. As detailed in issue 84 of FSM, the pair's feud included several high-profile matches at the Royal Albert Hall. The most impressive from a business perspective came in 1967 when ringside tickets were put up to 63 shillings (£46 in today's money), fully three times the usual price. The final clash between the pair in 1973 also saw prices significantly increased to reflect the drawing power of the feud.

All things considered, however, the biggest Royal Albert Hall show took place on June 8, 1966 with McManus and Pallo in singles action against Ricki Starr and Pancho Zapata respectively, the debut of the masked Doctor Death (aka independent promoter Paul Lincoln who had recently made peace with his rivals at Joint) and a heated tag team bout pitting Steve Veidor and Mike Marino against Togo Tani and Chati Yakouchi, only the second tag match at the venue.

Billed as "THE SUPREME WRESTLING SPECTACULAR", the sold-out show not only left a huge crowd of fans turned away at the door, but was broadcast to 11 cinemas around the country through the Viewsport closed circuit network. Jarvis Astaire, the man behind Viewsport, later owned Joint Promotions for a brief period and promoted SummerSlam 1992 at Wembley Stadium.

Despite their box office success, Pallo and McManus had rivals for the title of wrestling's King of Kensington. One was Tibor Szakacs who was a five-time winner of an annual heavyweight tournament at the venue; other winners included Billy Robinson and Georges Gordienko.) Meanwhile Mike Marino who is believed to be the wrestler who made the most RAH appearances and on one memorable occasion in 1976, beat both Mick McManus and Shirley Crabtree on the same night.

Although the Royal Albert Hall schedule was cut back to around five dates a year in the mid-70s, the venue still played host to several memorable moments including Kendo Nagasaki unmasking Eddie 'Kung Fu' Hamill for the first time (a finish repeated several times around the country before McManus 'officially' took the mask on TV). An all-villain affair pitting McManus and Steve Logan against Nagasaki and manager 'Gorgeous' George Gillette. And Wayne Bridges beating Spiros Arion in 1979 to be the first Brit to claim world heavyweight champion status.

Some other incidents weren't quite so conventional. A 1981 edition of BBC documentary series The Big Time saw schoolteacher Keith Rawlinson trained to be a professional wrestler before embarking on a final challenge of a bout at the Royal Albert Hall. By all accounts Rawlinson was not let in on the secrets of the business while training with Peter 'Tally Ho' Kaye and Sid Cooper and thus went into his bout with John Naylor under the impression he was engaging in a legitimate contest.

Although the match had no planned finish, the outcome was never in doubt. While handpicked by producer Esther Rantzen on the basis of his unimposing appearance in a publicity photograph, Naylor was in fact a product of the Wigan gym scene and highly skilled in legitimate grappling and submission techniques.

Although fending off Rawlinson's attacks, he allowed the outsider just enough offense to create a dramatic contest before putting him away in painful fashion and ensuring nobody watching would question the credibility of the business.

Another controversial match came in November 1980 when Big Daddy and Steve Grey took on the Black Baron and the American Dream, better known as Chris Colt. Accompanied to the ring by singer Joe Cocker, Colt appeared to be under the influence of more than one substance and also appeared to be in no mood to put on the usual performance expected of a Daddy opponent. Having already had a taped match pulled from a scheduled TV airing for his excessive ring style, Colt's Albert Hall antics brought his Joint Promotions career to a swift end, though he soon found work for All Star Promotions as "the man too bad for TV."

As the 80s rolled on and the Big Daddy roadshow became the focus of Dale Martin (based largely around one-off appearances rather than regular feuds and rematches), dates at the RAH became few and far between and crowds declined. In 1985 Daddy and nephew Greg Valentine beat Bull Pratt and Sid Cooper to mark the promotion's swansong at the venue.

The final British show at the Royal Albert Hall came two years later when, after a lengthy campaign that included television appearances and even a musical release, Mitzi Mueller finally succeeded in persuading local officials to overturn a long-running ban on women wrestling. She had been winding down her career and decided the best way to go out was at the city's most famous venue.

Husband and All-Star promoter Brian Dixon booked the Royal Albert Hall for the first time for a show headlined by Mueller and Rusty Blair against Klondyke Kate and Nicky Monroe, known collectively as the Bovver Birds. A strong supporting line-up included Tony St Clair vs Dave Finlay plus appearances by Kendo Nagasaki, John Quinn, Johnny Saint, "Kung Fu" Eddie Hamill and Fuji Yamada (later known as Jushin Liger.) Mueller duly won her match and the timekeeper ceremonially marked the end of her career by ringing the bell for a count of 10.

Unfortunately the night proved bittersweet, with Mueller's send off tempered by a disappointing crowd that may have been as low as a thousand fans. It's not clear in hindsight whether this was because building the show around female grapplers simply didn't draw, the decision to run on a Friday night backfired, or the venue had simply been killed off over the previous few years.

To make things worse, the unexpected discovery that running past a set curfew would incur a financial penalty meant the second half of the show was run at an uncharacteristically fast pace, bringing a low-key end to the days of British wrestling in the building.

Wrestling returned to the Royal Albert Hall in October 1991 when the WWF added a televised date during its latest European tour. With the venue being much smaller than the promotion's usual choices of the Docklands Arena and Wembley Arena, and this being the days before online ticket sales, WWF management decided to avoid the dangers of jammed phonelines by running a postal ballot for the right to buy seats.

The show itself was memorable for the Undertaker's entrance, with his music played live on the hall's spectacular organ, and for Davey Boy Smith winning a battle royale and being presented with what was billed as the Samovar trophy, a Russian metal teapot. The warm-up match before the televised show featured Brian Maxine and Steve Regal, seven years before the latter became a regular for the promotion.

WCW also visited the venue for two shows on the same day in 1993, during a tour in which line-ups had to be rearranged after Arn Anderson and Sid Vicious injured one another with scissors in a hotel room brawl in Blackburn. It proved great news for those attending the evening show which featured the makeshift team of Ric Flair and Ricky Steamboat against the Hollywood Blondes of Steve Austin and Brian Pillman in what Austin later recalled as "a hell of a match."

The WWF returned to the Royal Albert Hall four more times over the next couple of years. A March 29, 1994 show included a notable surprise when Men on a Mission defeated the Quebecers to win the tag titles, losing them back just two days later in Sheffield. It marked the only occasion a WWE title (other than the Hardcore title with its 24/7 rules) has changed hands at a UK house show.

By the time WWF began running regular British tours again at the turn of the millennium, it had outgrown the venue. In 2005 there had been no wrestling shows and only a couple of boxing events in the venue over the previous decade. This may explain an oversight when, following a change in local authority rules, Royal Albert Hall staff failed to renew a specific license required to run boxing and wrestling.

A fresh application in 2010 was blocked by a High Court order on behalf of local residents, one of whom told the Evening Standard that "You learn to put up with a certain amount of disruption living here, but the type of people attending boxing and wrestling matches aren't going to be your average Prom-goer. People could be coming out in the early hours after drinking and making noise and it could lead to more crime and vandalism."

It wasn't until 2011 that the court decided to overturn the verdict and grant a boxing and wrestling license on condition staff informed local residents of upcoming events. But while the sweet science has returned to the Royal Albert Hall it appears that the twin problems of the historic venue being too big for domestic promoters and too small for the WWF means that aside from a possible TNA visit, there's little immediate prospect of grappling fans returning to the mecca of British wrestling.

# THE HOME NATIONS

While both the Joint Promotions set-up and the ITV's broadcasts were somewhat Anglo-centric, pro wrestling has a rich history in the other home nations

## Northern Ireland

Professional wrestling in Northern Ireland appears to have been popularised by Atholl Oakeley, the promoter credited with kickstarting the modern style of wrestling (complete with submissions) in the UK. While his initial shows were in Belfast's Ulster Hall, a 1,000 seat-venue that would later be used by Joint Promotions, Oakeley also ran shows in the city's 10,000-capacity King's Hall. Along with the Harringay Arena and Wembley Arena in London, it was one of the biggest venues run by British wrestling groups.

Long-time Northern Ireland wrestler and promoter Noel 'Darkie' Arnott attended several of these shows and remembers they weren't an unqualified success. "He did decent crowds, usually a few thousand. But he would do mixed shows where you'd have maybe two pro bouts and two or three shooting matches. Once they'd got used to the pro style, people weren't too interested in the shoots. When you've seen people moving around quickly, having two heavyweights go at it and wind up in a headlock for 15 minutes could seem quite boring."

There was more pre-war excitement with visits from Irish-born world heavyweight champion Danno O'Mahoney, but the pro scene didn't really pick up again until after the war with shows put on by wrestler Jack Raymond, who put on shows under his real name of Jack McClelland. As well as the wrestling, he was known as a top-class open water swimmer, taking part in several races across the English Channel. "McClelland really deserves the credit for building up the pro scene," Arnott recalls. "He often ran small shows in small towns and villages, but it established pro wrestling."

The scene caught on, with other promoters including George Connell, who would use stars from the mainland. Soon there were enough people involved that Northern Ireland became one of the rare places where amateur wrestling stemmed from the pro scene rather than vice versa.

"I got involved in a wrestling club at [Belfast aircraft manufacturer] Short Harland," Arnott explained. "Normally it was only open to employees, but a friend got me in. The coaches were all ex-pros, teaching us holds and throws they'd learned. We put together a team for an amateur tournament in Dublin, which was the first time there'd really been a Northern Ireland team.

"The problem was we were trying to beat them with pro holds, which didn't really work! Of the 10 of us, one guy won, I lost on points, and the rest were all pinned. At one stage I was actually ahead on points, but I had no real idea what I was doing!"

The amateur side of the game would get an unexpected boost when Arnott got involved in a Belfast gym nicknamed 'The Pit' thanks to the run-down building having no roof. The gym advertised in the Belfast Telegraph for potential pro wrestling trainees and, while many recruits didn't make the grade, it produced two top pros in Eddie 'Kung Fu' Hamill and David Finlay (father of the WWE performer.) While he had a successful pro career, Finlay also made a concerted effort to build an amateur wrestling community with what Arnott calls "sheer hard work and attention to detail." Today Finlay remains involved in training and is president of the Northern Ireland Wrestling Association; he tells FSM the amateur scene has been boosted by the growth of mixed martial arts, with local fighters wanting to learn grappling skills.

The pro business continued to thrive, with promoters often targeting sold shows where they would be paid a fixed fee to provide a show by community groups and venue owners, meaning they didn't have to worry about publicity. That in turn made it easier to maintain a crew of part-timers who could hold down day jobs. More traditional promoting usually involved tours with TV stars from the mainland headlining and local grapplers filling out the card.

This approach led to some memorable moments as Arnott explains. "There was this guy doing a Big Chief gimmick, so I got him over to do two shows. Our plan was to have him ride a horse around Enniskillen to build up publicity, but after a while the police stopped us and said 'There's bloody traffic jams for miles!' so we had to abandon that and put him on a lorry."

Northern Ireland, and Belfast in particular, was of course an often politically unsettled area from the late-60s on, something that was both a benefit and a drawback to promoters. The main advantage was that people in many forms of entertainment were unwilling to perform in all areas, leaving an opening for wrestling, which happily straddled not just the Northern Ireland/Republic of Ireland border, but also the communities divide in Belfast.

Arnott notes that "There was no difference in the crowds. If they hadn't had flags flying about, you wouldn't have known where you were. We had a mixed crew: we didn't have any apartheid effect and it didn't matter who you were as long as you could put on a good show."

That's not to say promoters didn't harness the situation at times. "We'd get one guy to dress up in green and white and the other went in in red, white and blue and that got everybody's blood up," said Finlay of a tactic that could easily be adapted based on the venue.

The crowd reaction would certainly vary. Arnott recalls that the main effect of the Troubles on wrestlers was the increase in police stops and searches on roads, noting that the scariest moment he ever faced came when a mob put a brick through the window of the ring van, having mistaken it for a police vehicle.

Finlay was involved in a much hairier incident after promoting a show with Adrian Street wrestling local hero Eddie Hamill. The bout had to be cut short after anti-English hostility among the audience (apparently unaware or unconcerned that Street was from Wales) erupted to the point that they began throwing potatoes containing razor blades into the ring, with the final straw coming when Street narrowly avoided being hit by a home-made knife.

"I said to Adrian 'We're going to have to get out of here as quick as we can'. I broke a chair up and took one leg and gave my brother another and we got Adrian out," Finlay recalled. "We were walking up the street and all these guys were yelling and shouting. We ran up the street and got into our car. A couple of guys had followed us, so we smacked them with these chair legs.

"When I got in the car, it wouldn't start. They'd taken the rotor arm from the carburettor out! [Thankfully] a guardian angel came along and ran off and got us a new one and we could escape. And that night, we were driving up the M1 here and saw the Long Kesh prison [also known as The Maze] was on fire because they'd been rioting. I tell you what, it was a scary night!"

Over the years, some of the leading figures on the Northern Ireland scene departed. Eddie Hamill went full time with Joint Promotions on the mainland, as did Finlay's son, who had turned pro as a 14-year old drafted in as a substitute under the Roman Gladiator gimmick of Young Apollo. Finlay Senior also moved away for a brief spell at the height of the Troubles but returned home after deciding against a globetrotting lifestyle.

The scene declined in the 1980s along with that on the mainland and has been relatively slow to revive compared with the rest of the UK. However, the Pro Wrestling Ulster group continues to promote in Belfast, while Republic-based OTT Wrestling is scheduled to make its debut in the city in December.

## Wales

As much as he achieved outside of his homeland, Orig Williams will always be the man most associated with promoting professional wrestling in his homeland. In some senses he filled a void as Joint Promotions' presence in Wales was something of a mixed bag.

Cardiff was most definitely a hotbed, with five promotions running the city at various points in the TV era. Joint ran both the Drill Hall (a building with a large space for military marching practice that was also used for public events) and the 2,500 seat Pavilion in Sophia Gardens. Leading independent Paul Lincoln also ran both buildings, with his move to Sophia Gardens opening up an opportunity for Williams to take over the Drill Hall. Devereaux Promotions, an independent with an arms-length arrangement to use Joint stars when they weren't booked also ran the city. And Cardiff also featured shows from Ringsport, a promotion run by Evan Treharne, the publisher of an independent wrestling magazine of the same name.

The rest of the country appeared to be low on Joint's list priorities however. It did run several shows at seaside holiday destinations and camps in the north of the country, usually through Lancashire-based Wryton promotions, but gave them little attention in their national publicity such as in The Wrestler magazine. The south of the country was particularly under-served, possibly because it would have naturally fallen into the Dale Martin 'territory' and going much further than Cardiff may have been an unappetising prospect for a London-based outfit.

Either way, it left a market for Williams to exploit, something he most certainly did. Whereas Joint was more about running regular shows in areas with a sizable population, Williams was happy to make flying visits to virtually every town no matter its size, building up interest through flyposting and even getting distinctive wrestlers such as Klondyke Bill and Klondyke Jake to walk around town on the afternoon of the show drumming up interest.

Ironically the scene today in Wales somewhat mirrors that of the glory days. Cardiff and Newport remain a hotbed for independent promotions, albeit on a far smaller scale. Nationally the scene is covered by Welsh Wrestling, whose owner Alan Ravenhill learnt his trade from Williams and continues to promote a busy schedule of family-friendly shows.

Meanwhile Rhyl continues to be one of the few non-camp venues (alongside the Blackpool Tower Circus) with enough local interest to support weekly summer shows. They're the work of All Star's Brian Dixon who notes that "Rhyl has had wrestling even back to when I was a kid. It's a lot to do with the Orig connection:

him living there helped give it a great grounding as a wrestling town. It's always had good local support but it's also a place with a lot of people coming on holiday."

## *Scotland*

Small screen viewers in England might have been surprised to learn how busy the Scottish scene was, despite the comparative rarity of televised shows from the country. That was likely due at least in part to the fact that it was ITV rather than promoters who filmed shows, meaning the most convenient TV venues were those within easy distance of other sporting events of the weekend.

According to Aberdeen-based grappler Len Ironside, that created "a little resentment" among Scottish wrestlers who didn't get as much recognition as their counterparts south of the border. He points to the likes of Andy Robin, Bill Ross and Ted Hannan as among the local stars without as much national exposure as they deserved.

As previously covered in FSM, perennial lightweight champion George Kidd was by far the biggest name in Scotland. While he certainly received his fair share of mention from announcer and admirer Kent Walton, he made few TV appearances on the national slot. In his home country though, and in hometown Dundee in particular, he was a genuine mainstream celebrity and even hosted two regular TV chat and entertainment shows.

Scotland's wrestling setup differed a little from England in that it didn't have such a clear-cut geographic split between promoters. Instead the larger distance between towns meant control was more of a venue-by-venue affair. For the most part, Joint venues were run by George De Relwyskow, while Kidd spent time promoting in opposition. Several areas had their own local man such as Aberdeen where boxing promoter Peter Keenan was regularly involved in wrestling (including engaging in an infamous office brawl with Jackie Pallo and son sparked by a dispute over expenses.) And while the strict ban on Joint-contracted wrestlers working independents was enforced as much as anywhere, it appears local grapplers were more willing to move back and forth between the two sides depending on what work was available to them.

Another under-sung element of Scotland's wrestling is that it was running some of the bigger venues on the British circuit. For the most part, the UK lacked large indoor sports facilities, largely because the nation's preferred sports such as cricket, football and rugby are all outdoor affairs requiring large pitches, in contrast to the US where basketball's popularity in pro and college forms necessitated 10,000 seat venues in most major cities. That meant that aside from a few purpose-built boxing and wrestling venues, and places such as the Royal Albert Hall, wrestling was often limited to public halls and cinemas.

The big exception that favoured Scotland was ice rinks built with large capacities for ice hockey crowds. While the biggest such venue to be used for wrestling was in Nottingham, Scottish locations such as Paisley, Air, Kirkcaldy and Falkirk all had wrestling in rinks with a capacity of 4,000 or more, while Paul Lincoln ran a similar-sized rink in Murrayfield, Edinburgh. There was a downside, as noted by Scottish wrestler Dale Storm in his autobiography "And In This Corner": the sheer size of the floor space at an ice rink made for a worryingly long walk back to the safety of the dressing room for a wrestler who had outraged the crowd.

While tastes varied from city to city – Ironside notes that crowds in Aberdeen were more likely to appreciate technical wrestling displays – Scotland certainly seems to have had the most hostile crowds. The Kelvin Hall in Glasgow was unfriendly to villainous wrestlers, particularly those from south of the border, but the Eldorado Stadium in Edinburgh was arguably the closest thing to a bearpit for English visitors.

Promoted for long periods by Max Crabtree (both for Joint Promotions and as an independent), it was a venue where controlling the crowd was a fine art. Mark Rocco has spoken of a bout where he barely made it to safety and, when he angrily enquiring why sent nobody to rescue him, Crabtree pointed to where the crowd sat and explained "Kid, sometimes you've got to feed them."

"He did that [to Mark] more than once," Ironside explained to FSM. "I remember Rocco said to Crabtree 'How do I get out of this if the crowd turn nasty?' because he was on with Andy Robin. So Max says 'There's a door at the bottom there, you go through there, and I'll pull you out.'

"The bout went great but then the crowd turned hostile, so he had to get out. He went down to this door and found it was locked and the crowd was so heated it needed some wrestlers to come out and help get him back to the dressing room. He said to Crabtree 'You promised me that door would be open.' And Crabtree said to him, 'Promoter's luck boy, promoter's luck.'"

Ironside believes Crabtree's success in Scotland helped establish his promoting and matchmaking reputation, paving the way for his eventual takeover of those duties for the entire Joint Promotions empire. "He put on good bills with great matches. He was a real ideas man." One example of this creativity was creating the 'Eldorado All Stars', a group of mainly baby face wrestlers who would act as a 'home team' to take on a revolving crew of visiting challengers.

According to Ironside, like in the rest of the country, Scottish business dropped a little in the 1970s as promoters failed to develop new talent quickly enough to replace big names that disappeared from TV screens when they left Joint Promotions. However, he notes that wrestling being taken off air in 1988 hit the local scene particularly hard with no full-time local groups to pick up the slack. "Scotland became a wrestling desert."

Fortunately, the Scottish wrestling story has a happy ending and, just as it its heyday, the strength of the local scene has arguably been underplayed across the UK as a whole. Several promotions have put on shows before four-figure crowds in recent years, while ICW's Fear & Loathing show at the SSE Hydro was, at press time, on course to not only be the biggest crowd for a British promotion since 1981, but also the biggest show in domestic Scottish wrestling history.

# THE STAMPEDE CONNECTION

It's rare for five brothers to all wrestle in their home territory. It's even rarer for all five to wrestle on another continent. But the Hart family's journeys to the UK helped create some worldwide stars, winding up with the biggest show in British history.

Although several British and Canadian wrestlers had crossed the over the years, the Harts' involvement really began in 1977 when British grappler John Foley was working the family's Stampede territory as the Nazi-esque lead manager JR Foley. He put the two oldest brothers, Smith and Bruce in touch with promoter Max Crabtree who set up a tour of the UK and Germany, in effect a working holiday.

Writing in his autobiography Straight From The Hart, Bruce recalled his memorable debut at Belle Vue in Manchester. Crabtree had explained that Native American star Billy Two Rivers had been among the biggest draws in the UK and that he wanted to continue the cowboys and Indians theme by billing him as Bronco Bruce, riding a stallion to the ring.

Bruce opted not to reveal that that "the only horse I'd ever ridden before was on a merry-ground... When the curtains opened up and the spotlight hit us, there was a big roar from the crowd and that seemed to spook the horse, which went charging down the aisle, full speed, on its way to the ring. I was hanging on for dear life and completely oblivious to the crowd and everything else. As the horse got near the ring, it suddenly put on the brakes and reared up on its hind legs... as nonchalantly as possible -- given that I'd just about crapped my pants en route to the squared circle -- I waved to the audience, who gave me appreciative applause."

In the book Bruce notes that he worked with opponents of all sizes on the tour but, unlike some grappler back home, they all had the ability and despite to make their opponents look good. He also recalls learning a valuable lesson from Jim Breaks who told a story of two bulls, the younger of which of which suggested stampeding into a field to catch and impregnate a cow, only to be told by the wiser elder it would be more productive to walk into the field at a more deliberate pace and impregnate the entire herd. It was of course a metaphor for the important of taking one's time to tell a story in the ring.

That said, it was a young wrestler with a breakneck pace who caught Bruce's eye on a visit to Ted Betley's gym in Warrington. Although he initially believed a recommendation that the scrawny teenager would work well in Stampede was some sort of rib, Bruce was blown away by the ringwork of Tom "Dynamite Kid" Billington and quickly arranged a tour of Stampede which launched his international career.

Several other British wrestlers followed over the next few years including Billington's cousin Davey Boy Smith, Kung Fu and Marty Jones, who tells FSM there were several similarities between the Stampede and British set-ups. "They wrestled in a lot of ice rinks with a few thousand seats, similar to venues like Nottingham Ice Rink. It was a crash bang wallop style, but still more like the British style than the stuff in America. Like us they had lots of live shows each week but only one TV slot, so they had to make their heat and tell a story on the night."

In 1981, Bret Hart made a trip for the German tournaments and then spent a couple of months with Joint Promotions, his first time extended trip away from Calgary. Despite the brevity of his stay, he took on a wide range of opponents, including taking part in a Big Daddy vs Giant Haystacks tag match, as well as working opposite Johnny Saint in a tag bout.

Among his most frequent opponents was a man who'd become a regular rival in Stampede, the Dynamite Kid. Hart tells FSM that the pair had an initially rocky relationship. "We weren't good friends at first -- there were a few potatoes flying about -- but eventually we respected each other. He was the kind of guy who was tough to befriend, but then he was your friend to the end. We were already good friends when I left [for the UK].

"He was a great innovator, so agile and built like a bullet. When he did the diving headbutt it was like watching a missile."

One such Hart-Dynamite clash came in Warrington, around 10 miles from Kid's Wigan birthplace. It's a match Hart recalls fondly as one of the most memorable of his career, partly because after so many bouts as the local hero in Canada, he had to take a different approach in the UK, wrestling as a full-blown villain for the first time in his career.

"It was [almost] his hometown and Dynamite talked Max Crabtree into making me a bad guy. It was such a funny thing to switch the roles, but Dynamite needed me to be a good bad guy to help him be a good good guy.

"It was one of my best matches because he was trying so hard wrestling in front of his friends and family. It was a big break for him to be able to show them he'd made it as a star."

The match also got over well with Crabtree, who booked Hart to appear on what would be the final show at Belle Vue in Manchester, which had been among the largest venues in the country to run weekly (and more often at times). "It was described to me as being like the final show at Madison Square Garden. Former wrestlers in their nineties came along to the show and it was clear there was a lot of history there. I was proud and honoured to be on the card -- a lot of wrestlers were pleading to be on the show."

Hart's opponent that night was Marty Jones, who he also on TV. Jones recalls that Hart picked up the British style quickly. "Top pros could always adapt to the local style anywhere in the world. We came to be very physical in the ring. It sounds odd, but once you've earned somebody's respect in the ring, you can whack them, and they can whack you back."

Hart had hoped to include the Jones bout on "The Dungeon Collection", a DVD set released last year featuring some of his rarer matches.

"I tried my hardest, but [ITV] wanted an outrageous price. It was a million dollars or some outrageous number." With WWE understandably unwilling to make such a deal, Hart remains frustrated at the absence of the bout. "It was a chance for us to keep the footage alive and without it [the British style] is going to fade from memory. British guys like Kendo Nagasaki should be in the WWE Hall of Fame, but that era is dying out. It's not right that these people are not remembered."

Hart also cites Max Crabtree as somebody who should be remembered, and not just as the promoter who pushed his brother as the top star. "Max was ahead of his time and one of the first to have the same genius as Vince McMahon. It's a shame he doesn't get the credit: the business was very special in his heyday and we had so many great times."

It's one particular aspect of Crabtree's booking that Hart recalls. "I learned a lot about endings from him. Max was brilliant for having ways to prolong the storyline. There was always a hook to the match and things moved forward inch by inch. Dynamite brought a lot of Max's ideas with him to Calgary."

Indeed, Hart sees his exposure to the British style as a key part of his development as a wrestler. "I really learned about drama: I thought of British wrestling as like Shakespeare and I learned to be a performer. I learned a lot there that was nothing to do with moves.

"The fans were great for reacting and you could really rile them up with cheating. Guys like Alan Dennison were hilarious: they'd do slapstick, but they'd also do clever things and get a lot of mileage from simple things. It made for easy wrestling."

That said, it wasn't just Dynamite who Hart admired for a fast-paced, action packed style in British rings. "Mark Rocco was great. 'Rollerball' was a perfect name: he was like a pinball. He was a little erratic... no, a lot erratic, but a genius at the same time, and a real pleasure to know."

Several long-term fans have argued that Rocco would have been a perfect fit for the Calgary promotion, and Hart confirms that his family felt the same way. "We tried to get Rocco, but his schedule didn't work as he was doing well in Japan. I feel like it almost could have happened. I think if WWE hadn't changed everything [with the territories dying out] many more British guys would have come in to Calgary."

Hart isn't unqualified in his praise for British wrestlers however. "It was a great crew and some guys were phenomenal, but some were lousy." Among those he recalls less favourably is Colin Bennett, though more for his in-ring character than his technical ability. "He was a hairy-chested guy in a fire helmet and jacket: that was his whole gimmick. He looked like he'd never seen a weight in his life!"

Another aspect of the British scene that Hart struggled to warm to was the rounds system. "The breaks killed all the momentum that you'd built up. It wasn't as if the wrestlers really needed the rest like in boxing." (Jones laughs as he recalls the situation slightly differently. "Bret certainly needed the break once you got into round eight or 10!")

Hart saw both rounds and the boxing-style count administered to grounded opponents as "dated concepts. Fans wanted to see something more updated."

Back in Calgary, Hart continued to see British performers make the trip over. "Calgary was very receptive to British wrestlers. We built up some good contacts and it made for a beautiful chemistry. [Father and promoter] Stu was always keen to promote history: he'd have the program run articles about the history of the titles, or pictures of guys like Lou Thesz, which gave the appearance of a real sport.

"We had a great mixture of old and young wrestlers, and guys not just from Britain, but from Mexico, Puerto Rico, New Zealand, Australia and so on. I was sometimes called a technical genius, but really I just learned lots of little things from the different styles used in Stampede, like the way I did a Russian legsweep."

There was also another reminder of the British influence in Stampede, this time backstage. "I'd picked up the use of rhyming slang in Britain and there'd always be three or four Brits here and they'd use it in the dressing room. It was great because we could talk in private that way in Japan, even when other American wrestlers were there. It became almost a secret way to communicate and the other wrestlers just thought Dynamite was mumbling! Even today I'll still use some rhyming slang when I talk to guys like Fit Finlay or William Regal."

In 1984, the WWF expanded across North America, with Stampede briefly shutting down and Bret, Jim Neidhart, Dynamite Kid and Davey Boy Smith all making the trip to New York. Meanwhile younger Hart brothers Owen and Ross were the latest to wrestle in the UK.

"No disrespect to Ross or Bruce, but they weren't in the same league as Owen and Bret," recalls Marty Jones, who wrestled five of the brothers, three of them on British TV. "It was pretty even stevens between them and they had similar styles, though Bret was already changing to be a bit more American, which was a sign of the times. Owen was more high-flying, but he was still seeking holds and telling stories.

Owen would return to wrestle for British promoters two more times. In 1987 he had a genuine classic on TV against Jones for the vacant world mid-heavyweight titles, described by Kent Walton as one of the finest matches he ever commentated on, while in 1991 he had several memorable matches against Danny Collins.

By that time, however, British wrestling had departed from ITV screens. As well as attracting some attention in guest slots on ITV (including two bouts featuring Bret Hart), WWF was now building up an audience on Sky. Bret appeared on the first WWF tour of the UK in 1989 and could see the writing on the wall.

"I knew WWF going to Britain and Germany would be the death knell. It was like night and day with the slick TV and the polished lights and cameras. The fans loved it. I think of it like the moment The Wizard of Oz turns from black and white into colour.

The WWF's initial boom period in the UK coincided with Bret Hart's rise from tag team specialist to singles star, and it's often been noted that he was disproportionately popular on these shores, something he's quick to acknowledge. "I think the European fans liked the way I wrestled and appreciated it. It wasn't the same guy doing the same things. I had a different slant to babyfaces who were more TV friendly like the Ultimate Warrior who was a crazy real life Bugs Bunny, or Hulk Hogan who looked like he had legs stuck on to his shoulders.

Hart also believes that he benefited in some ways from not being the top star when the WWF broke into the European market. "People there saw me struggle. I had to fight my way to the top and never quite got the job done. I was able to evolve into my character.

That was typified by Hart's televised match at the London Docklands Arena in 1989 when he lost to Dino Bravo and memorably mouthed his frustration in view of the camera, a frustration that affected both the fictional 'Hitman' and the real-life Hart. "I'd lose to people like Bravo who was not as good as me, but fans would still believe in me. [When I moved up] they thought I'd earned it and I'd do shoot-style interviews talking about my struggle."

Hart notes that his size wasn't so much of an issue with British fans as with the "bigger is better" mindset of American fans. "I wasn't a body guy and didn't have a musclebound physique, but I was big enough to be imposing. Today many guys are not that big, but I was about as small as you could get and keep credibility."

Most of all, though, Hart believes his European successes were the result of fortunate timing. "Hogan really didn't like to travel outside of the US and [the European boom] meant Vince didn't need him on the shows. That left a chance for other stars to step up. Fans were chanting our names outside hotels and there was real stampeding and charging. It was really like Beatlemania with fans running three blocks when they saw the bus leave."

When Hogan disappeared from the picture altogether in 1992, Hart was on hand to take full advantage. While only a handful of wrestling shows in Britain had ever attracted crowds of more than 10,000, WWF held SummerSlam at Wembley Stadium and announced an attendance of 80,355, a figure that was at worst only a mild exaggeration. Officially the main event was Randy Savage vs Ultimate Warrior, but the show closed with Hart defending the Intercontinental title against Davey Boy Smith.

Although Hart lost the match, it was a major stepping stone in his career, and something he foresaw as a true victory given the way Brits traditionally support an underdog. He believed that despite their joy at Smith's title win, the fans would also have an important emotional response to Hart's plight after a hard-fought contest.

"I felt I knew the English audience even better than Vince and I told him I knew [losing] would make me. I knew when I lost they'd end up feeling lousy for me, feel bad that I lost." Hart credits that response with his unexpected promotion to WWF champion, taking the title from Ric Flair just six weeks later.

More than 20 years on, Hart still looks back to the Wembley bout as the perfect example of his vision of professional wrestling. "It wouldn't have worked the same way anywhere else. I often tell people to watch that match back and not watch me and Davey, just to watch the fans instead. To see how passionate they are is beautiful to watch: they're focused on every single twist.

"Today's wrestlers can only fantasise about experiencing that."

## The Harts On ITV

5/11/77: Bruce introduced to the crowd at Chester

9/2/80: John Elijah beat Smith Hart by a fall and a submission to one fall

19/12/81: Gil Singh beat Bret Hart two falls to one

9/1/82: Marty Jones beat Bret Hart two falls to one

7/1/84: Owen Hart drew one fall apiece with Steve Logan (the younger wrestler of that name) while Marty Jones beat Ross Hart by knockout

31/3/84: Dave Finlay & Rocky Moran of Northern Ireland beat Owen Hart & Ross Hart of Canada two falls to one in an international tag tournament

17/1/87: Davey Boy Smith and Dynamite Kid beat Bret Hart and Jim Neidhart by pinfall in a bout taped at the Boston Garden

25/4/87: Marty Jones beat Owen Hart by two falls to one to win the vacant World-Mid-Heavyweight title

16/1/88: Bret Hart and Jim Neidhart lost the WWF tag titles to Rick Martel and Tito Santana in a bout from the American show Superstars of Wrestling.

# WEMBLEY ARENA

"When John Quinn walked out, I had goosebumps. It felt like the atmosphere when I wrestled at Arena Mexico or that you get now at WrestleMania." That's how Marty Jones remembers the first Joint Promotions show at Wembley Arena, which to this day is arguably the biggest ever British wrestling event.

The events have become iconic largely because they were so unusual. The Joint Promotions business model was traditionally based on smaller venues seating from a few hundred in Town Halls to several thousand at purpose built arenas. The key was running a steady but busy schedule with as many as 15 shows a night and dozens of venues having weekly shows, rather than building to try to maximise attendances on a single show. Many factors lay behind this model, including the relative lack of large indoor arenas and the way that most fans were not in the habit (nor had the need) to travelling more than a few miles for live entertainment.

Some shows were certainly bigger than others. The Cup Final day show was a big event on television with the biggest names featured, but was not a particularly big live event draw. The monthly Royal Albert Hall shows were certainly the biggest thing on the Dale Martin schedule, with the end of season show (held before the venue was booked solid for the Proms concerts during the summer) usually featuring the biggest rivalries and serving as a gathering for the small community of more dedicated travelling fans. But the idea of trying to fill the biggest available indoor venue with a one-off spectacular promoted far beyond the local area was for many years simply not on the table.

"When Max Crabtree took over at Joint, things completely changed," Brian Dixon tells FSM. Promoter of the leading opposition group at the time, All Star Wrestling, Dixon recalls the sheer scale of the Wembley venture. "To be honest, [even if I had the TV slot], I'd have stuck to the smaller halls. I didn't have the financial backing of Joint and had the memory of suffering bad times in the past. But it was not a great shock that Max gambled on going to Wembley. Daddy and company had become household names and were getting the same level of reaction as McManus and Pallo."

Two years after turning babyface and fleshing out the Big Daddy, Shirley Crabtree was arguably at the peak of his public appeal. But to draw a big crowd, every hero needs a nemesis. Enter John Quinn.

"He definitely created interest with the controversy he caused," Dixon recalls. "Fans had never seen a guy as big as him that could move so well, that didn't hold anything back and was there to really make opponents suffer."

Although hailing from Canada, Quinn was presented as an American loudmouth and made a major impact upon his first televised appearance on 13 January 1979. It wasn't just what he did in the ring, quickly despatching Beau Jack Rowlands by knockout. He also violated a longstanding tradition that wrestlers would rarely speak on the microphone on television. He informed both the live audience and TV viewers that his father was a former air force pilot and had told him the British had been cowards during the second world war. Thirty years on it may have been, but when most viewers had either lived through the war or had fathers who had served in the conflict, it proved an incredibly inciteful speech.

In the coming months, Quinn continued to build his heat. Barry Douglas, Lenny Hurst and Lee Bronson all fell by knockout, while the Canadian continued to work the microphone amid deafening boos of the kind now enjoyed by Zack Gibson at PROGRESS events and prompted the rare appearance of fan-made signs with messages such as "YANKEE GO HOME." While he sometimes elaborated on his claims that the Brits were "stupid and yellow", on other occasions he relied on sarcasm, telling the people of Southend that "I only hope that someday that I'll be in my country when you come to visit there, and I would like to personally be there when you land so I can give you a warm, warm welcome."

The final touches came when Quinn wrestled top-line opponents. He went to a draw with Tony St Clair in a tournament semi-final but angered the crowd by not only advancing on a coin toss, but then refusing to wrestle fellow villain Giant Haystacks in the final. On the Cup Final Day broadcast he and Mark Rocco went down by two falls to one against Daddy and Ringo Rigby – though of course it was Rocco who took the splashes for the loss. For those for whom the booking was still too subtle, commentator Kent Walton made things clear: "But of course the one that everybody's really waiting for is the solo bout that we'll be seeing soon on television between Quinn and Big Daddy."

That match was booked for 27 June at Wembley Arena. Originally built as the swimming venue for the 1934 Empire Games and then used in the 1948 Olympics, it had become a popular concert venue as well as hosting boxing bouts several times a year. With a capacity of around 10,000, filling it would require some significant promotion on Max Crabtree's part.

While a US group would have gone into full hype mode on TV, that wasn't really an option. For one thing, ITV itself produced the show and employed Kent

Walton. For another, broadcasting rules at the time largely forbade direct promotion of commercial products and events within programming itself. In this climate even the few mentions Walton made of the Wembley show, such as during a TV match to build up visitor Chato Pastor for a title shot against Mal Sanders, were notable departures from the norm.

Instead Crabtree relied on two main tactics, as Marty Jones recalls. "He did a deal with the London bus companies and had giant posters all over them, which was the first time I'd ever seen that. Then at all the regular London venues like Lewisham, Walthamstow and Catford, the guys who were on the Wembley show did a lot of gees." That's a British wrestler term somewhat similar to "angle" but more about confrontations and verbal challenges. The key was that such stunts had traditionally always been performed to build up return bouts at the same venue rather than for a larger show elsewhere.

The strategy most certainly worked. While dedicated fans of the time recall that it was possible to get complimentary tickets if you knew where to look, and that many in the audience bought tickets on the night, it was to all practical intents a full house. It's not an absolute certainty it was the biggest ever paid attendance for a British show: the comparably sized Harringay Arena in London hosted wrestling regularly either side of the war, while the White Hart Lane football ground hosted a Bert Assirati vs The Angel bout in 1948 that is sometimes listed as having a crowd in the region of 15,000. At the very least, however, it remains the biggest crowd from a British promotion in the past 60 years.

The crowd was all the more impressive given the ticket pricing of £10, £8, £6, £4 and £2. The top price is the equivalent of £50 at today's prices and while that's roughly the same as a WWE or NXT ticket in the same venue, it was very much out of the ordinary at the time. Even the prestigious Royal Albert Hall shows only had a price structure of £5, £3, £2.50, £2 and £1.25 in 1979, while the cheapest tickets at Wembley were double the cost of ringside seats to see Big Daddy at many small halls.

Marty Jones notes it was a testament to the specific promotion of the event: "They picked all the top feuds for Wembley, but even the same bill on an ordinary show anywhere in the country wouldn't have pulled as many people." He also recalls the riches weren't exactly shared out: "The payday was a little bit more than usual, but I don't remember it as being anything special."

While music fans have often criticised Wembley Arena as being soulless, the wrestling audience on that night was most certainly up for it. Several of those on the show recall the atmosphere compared favourably with the usual Royal Albert Hall experience. "The Albert Hall was more like a Japanese crowd where they'd only applaud for the high spots or at the end of a round," says Jones, while Pete

Roberts says he "found the Albert Hall difficult because you wouldn't get the same reaction and you'd use a lot of the heat in that situation."

Steve Grey notes that "the Albert Hall usually attracted the local residents, while the Wembley show had much more genuine wrestling followers who'd travelled." Jones recalls the show was something of a tourist attraction with a notable number of foreign visitors in the audience.

The atmosphere was also helped by the decision to avoid the temptation of illuminating the entire arena to better show off the crowd to the TV cameras, which recorded the event for broadcast on the first two episodes of World of Sport in July. "It was always better with a single light on the ring," Roberts explained. "It meant the punters didn't feel as self-conscious, so they could scream and shout and lose all their inhibitions."

As much as it was an all-star line-up, it was clear what the main event was, and Jones recalls his show-opening match with Pete Roberts had a particular role. "Max didn't say a word about what we should do in the match: he left it up to us. He just told us we were the best at keeping the crowd quietened down but still entertained."

Following Roberts' win in a hard-hitting affair, European middleweight champion Sanders successfully defended against Pastor. Another all-action bout, an unintended highlight came on the TV broadcast when Sanders was whipped to the ropes and took what appeared to be an over-elaborate bump to the floor. Kent Walton covered it seamlessly, explaining that Sanders had mistakenly assume Pastor would follow up the whip with another attack and had scurried out of his way. It was an example of Walton bringing legitimacy to the product, something he continued in the following Tony St Clair vs Lenny Hurst match in which he openly admitted "the crowd are getting a little impatient for the main event now."

That wait soon ended with the emergence of Quinn for what was not only a rare singles match for Daddy, but a stipulation bout with no pinfalls, no submissions, no rounds and the winner to be decided only by knockout – in effect, what modern fans now know as a Last Man Standing match. The Canadian made his way to the ring accompanied by Haystacks as the public address system played Manfred Mann's "Mighty Quinn.

The audio was, however, difficult to hear thanks to a chorus of boos of a duration and volume far in excess of the catcalling normally seen with ring villains even of the stature of McManus or Jim Breaks. With no ring barriers, the crowd rushed to ringside and one fan even made the mistake of tackling Quinn, soon finding himself kicked away by both Quinn and Haystacks. In another rarity for the period, some fans carried a home-made banner proclaiming that "Big Daddy Rules OK", while another had written a message on a towel only to have it snatched away by Haystacks and used to wipe his backside.

Wembley Arena

Daddy's entrance took things to the other extreme: coming to the ring with a Pearly King and Queen (two button-clad characters representing London's working class culture) he was legitimately mobbed by fans and even received a kiss from a man appearing to be in his 20s. If Daddy appeared emotional, there was an explanation that had less to do with the occasion and more his young daughter Jane, who tells FSM of a special memory of the day.

"Dad was really quite nervous about it; I could tell when he was chatting with Mum about it beforehand. Looking back his nervousness must have been because it was one of the biggest shows of that era and being televised. But at the time, I was hoping he wasn't going to get hurt [by Quinn] -- he'd been hurt before with nose broken and teeth knocked out and things like that.

"I wrote him a little letter saying that he was my hero -- I thought he was actually the strongest man on the planet -- and not to worry and that I loved him very much and he was going to win, and I was dead proud of him. I put it in his wash bag and he didn't know it was there until he came to wrestle on the night and he later told me it brought a tear to his eye."

With what the video clearly shows as one of the more remarkable atmospheres ever seen on a British wrestling show, Walton noted optimistically that "If the bout turns out to be anything like the start, then we're in for quite a session." That proved not to be the case.

The bulk of the brief match consisted of bodychecks (or "belly bumps" to the detractors) and forearms, with the main highlight being Brian Crabtree climbing on to the apron and being knocked to the floor by Quinn. It proved enough distraction for Daddy to hit three bodyslams and then his double elbows finisher (a move loosely similar to a Northern Lights suplex) to not only score the knockout victory, but send Quinn back to the dressing room on a stretcher. The entire bout lasted just 102 seconds.

While some of the more dedicated wrestling purists in the arena were unimpressed, the bulk of the live reaction was undeniably positive. Fans poured into the ring with one appearing on camera taking the opportunity to imply that Quinn enjoyed the pleasure of his own company. It was particularly notable that the mob was more ethnically diverse than the traditional TV wrestling audiences, perhaps reflecting the Wembley neighbourhood. The week's TV broadcast went off the air with the scene of a ring packed full of people literally jumping up and down with the now-traditional chants of "Easy, Easy!"

Where the WWE used to rely on a women's match to give a crowd a chance to catch their breath, Joint opted instead for a clean heavyweight contest with Wayne Bridges overcoming Ray Steele. Jim Breaks then took a stoppage win over Steve Grey for the vacant British welterweight title, with the show closed out by Pat Patton and Chris Adams beating Mark Rocco and Steve Logan in a match that might have held the crowd's interest better were the last opportunity to get public transport not imminent. (Logan's usual partner Mick McManus was a notable absentee from the show, apparently explained by his having arranged a foreign holiday for the period.)

Quinn promptly disappeared from British TV screens, in reality working the European tournament circuit for the rest of the year. He returned the following January in a tag match with Haystacks, then defeated Caswell Martin in a single match before explaining the two reasons he had come back to the UK. "I'm going to take Big Daddy and I'm going to pulverise him and I'm going to beat him once and for all. The second reason is my friend, a congressman in the United States, said 'Quinn, bring back the heavyweight champion of the world to the United States.' As soon as I have accomplished those two things, and I do not intend for it to be a long time, I'm leaving this little island of yours."

After several more knockout victories on TV, Quinn did indeed capture the British version of the world title, beating Bridges on a blood stoppage on the Cup Final day broadcast. Just 22 seconds elapsed between the final bell and the opening notes of Daddy's "We Shall Note Be Moved" playing as the man himself came to the ring and Kent Walton – without waiting for a word to be spoken – somehow surmised he was issuing a challenge for a tag bout with Daddy and Bridges against Quinn and cornerman Yasu Fuji.

That was indeed the main event of a second (untelevised) Wembley Arena show on 11 June 1980. Although not quite as deep an undercard as the original, one notable highlight came with Marty Jones and Mark Rocco renewing their longstanding rivalry in a chain match. "That was Max's idea," Jones recalls. "He'd seen it on an American video or in a magazine and asked us to do it, which happened quite a lot [with gimmick matches]. For this one, we did something where I said we had to be chained together to stop him running away."

The main event had the perhaps predictable finish of the good guys winning two straight falls, but fans who attended the show told FSM the crowd interest by this time was more in the Quinn-Bridges title rivalry rather than the Daddy feud. That may be the explanation for a reduced crowd estimated as 5,000-6,000. The MC on the night mentioned that promoters were working on a Quinn-Bridges match at the arena for a show at the end of the August, but in the event, it never came off. Just a matter of weeks later Quinn took up an offer to work for independent promoter Orig Williams, taking the world title with him. He later wrote in an afterword for Williams' autobiography that he was given a thousand pounds in cash as a down payment against future earnings.

Quinn went on to be a major star for Brian Dixon, who notes that he was easily able to overcome any damage left over from the previous year's decisive loss to Daddy. "He'd still been looking good on TV since coming back, and he had his own charisma. One thing about the Wembley match was that with the size of crowd it drew and the attention, anyone who was in that match would always be recognisable to fans.

"I think also some of the fans were starting to get a little smarter and knew about the Crabtree monopoly so were thinking a bit more about how things operated."

With Quinn out of the picture, the Crabtrees returned to Wembley Arena for a final time on 18 June 1981. The main action on the undercard saw Bridges capture what Joint promoted as the vacant world title (Quinn having been stripped for failing to defend it) by beating Big Jim Harris, later known as Kamala. What would undoubtedly have been the in-ring highlight was lost to history: Satoru 'Sammy Lee' Sayama, who had recently taken on the Tiger Mask character in Japan, pulled out of a scheduled match with Mark Rocco, the future Black Tiger.

The main event pitted Daddy against Haystacks in another knockout-only match which was similarly short on both time (running 2 minutes 50 seconds) and traditional wrestling holds as the Quinn bout. Given those constraints, it holds up as being about as well booked as possible. The referee was flattened early on by a collision between the two giants, calling back to a similar incident in the pair's only other televised singles match four years earlier. That distraction allowed Haystacks to take control of the match and even get Daddy in a compromising position on the mat, only to miss a potentially match-ending splash. Daddy then hit a series of forearms and bodychecks to send Haystacks over the top rope where he was counted out (which was classed as a KO under British rules), though 'Stacks had an out by claiming he'd slipped on water that had been spilt by a second between rounds in an earlier match.

The match is often cited as the biggest in British wrestling, with claims of a TV audience of 18 million. At best that's inaccurate (the show doesn't appear in a BARB list of the top ten rated TV shows of the year, the lowest of which attracted 17.6 million views) and at worst it's likely a gross exaggeration given the verifiable wrestling audience figures over the years and the Saturday afternoon slot. The match is also often listed as another sellout, but the video clearly shows large banks of empty seats at the back of the floor section, while fans who were in attendance estimate the crowd at around seven thousand.

Hyperbole notwithstanding, it was still likely the second biggest British show in the TV era. The subsequent decline in British wrestling's fortunes has sparked much debate about whether both the style of the bouts and the failure of any villain to sustain an advantage over Daddy hurt business, but Pete Roberts perhaps best describes the brief Wembley Arena era.

"You can definitely say it was hotshotting: they were living for the moment and it was never going to have much longevity. But much as I often disagreed with the approach the Crabtrees took to wrestling, they really built those shows up. It was a great period, the last of the good periods, and I was lucky to be involved."

Wembley Arena

# JOINT PROMOTIONS

Joint Promotions was an alliance of many of the leading wrestling figures of its day, but one man above all other was key to the creation of British wrestling's most glorious era. Norman Morrell began life as a skilled amateur wrestler, winning the national featherweight (139lbs) championship four straight years from 1933 to 1936 -- a reign bookended by Joe Taylor, grandfather of future WWE performer Dave Taylor.

In 1936 Morell visited Germany for the Berlin Olympics and claimed to have met Adolf Hitler, prompting Adrian Street to later write that "Many wrestlers who knew Norman best claimed that much of Der Fuhrer's most endearing qualities may well have rubbed off!" What is certain is that Morrell competed as a featherweight in both the freestyle and Greco-Roman disciplines, finishing eighth in the former but failing to rank in the latter.

Following a short professional career during the war years, he turned his hand to promoting where he earned respect, if not always warm feeling. Johnny Kincaid tells FSM his abiding memory of Morrell is "his funny little ways. He'd pay you in old shilling pieces or tanners and keep handing over the coins and then stop and look at you and ask 'Is that enough?'"

Beyond his amateur background, promoting and training achievements (including breaking the likes of George Kidd and Les Kellett into the business), Morell took the opportunity in 1946 to quite literally rewrite the rules of the game.

While the adoption of an "all-in" style in the 1930s, complete with more aggression and the use of submissions, had led to a mini-boom, British wrestling had been left with a sullied reputation come the outbreak of war. For all the talent and excitement of the era, it was excessive violence and an overuse of outlandish gimmicks such as mud wrestling that had stuck in the minds of the public and media.

To help reshape wrestling's image, Morrell recruited Antarctic explorer and naval commander Admiral Lord Mountevans, MP Maurice Webb and radio broadcaster Archibald Campbell to form a committee, dubbed "The British Wrestling Board of Control", to examine and draw up more formal and respectable rules. This has often been described as a Parliamentary committee, though it appears more likely that Morrell and company simply hired a room in the Palace of Westminster on a commercial basis for their deliberations.

While many modern uses of the term "Mountevans rules" have involved best of three falls matches held over a number of rounds, neither of these points were mandated in the resulting rules. They state that a match can be over either one or three falls, and although they note that a fall automatically ends any round in which it occurs, they do not specifically say a match must be under the round system, let alone stipulate the length of a round. Indeed, while five minute rounds were commonplace, things varied between Joint Promotions members, with both three and 10-minute rounds used at some venues.

The rules did lay down that a knockout or disqualification would automatically end the contest regardless of the score, something that led to some intriguing situations where a wrestler trailing by a fall with a round to go would have to choose whether to play safe by attempting a fall for a draw or to go all-out for the KO victory. One inconsistency was that the Mountevans rules defined a fall as being either a pin or a submission, meaning the common MC reference to "two falls, two submissions or a knockout" was technically redundant.

Perhaps most importantly the rules laid down the allowable holds. Whereas "All In" rules had been focused on the very few things that were barred (principally a closed fist to the head, eye gouging, biting and low blows), Mountevans stressed what was allowed, namely grips with the hand for throws or submissions, plus strikes with the forearms, soles and sides of the feet, and shoulder-barges.

Many of the leading promoters of the day signed up to the new rules and were thus plausibly able to promote professional wrestling as effectively a jazzed-up version of freestyle amateur wrestling (with three counts and submissions) rather than the All-In style, which was promoted as something closer to modern mixed martial arts.

The changes appeared to leave 1930s kingpin promoter Athol Oakeley behind the times. He continued to promote events at the 10,000 capacity Harringay Arena -- at the time the premier wrestling venue in the country -- but struggled to maintain public relations. A much-hyped bout featuring former boxing champion Jack Doyle against the Estonian "Bucth" proved too implausible for the media representatives who had attended to cover it as a legitimate sporting event.

Oakeley's controversy and promotional demise left a void for rivals to establish themselves as a credible governing body of sorts. That came on 13 March 1952 with the formal creation of Joint Promotions, made up initially of four directors: Morrell, Ted Beresford, George De Relwyskow and Arthur Wright, all of whom were firmly established in their respective regions.

Beresford ran his own group, Globe Promotions, but worked closely with Morrell with the pair running shows in Yorkshire, the Midlands and Scotland. His son later wrestled as Steve Clements and, while not a huge star in the UK, later claimed a world welterweight title after reportedly beating Karloff Lagarde in Mexico.

De Relwyskow, who also promoted across Northern England, came from a rich wrestling heritage. His father, also named George, was one of Britain's finest ever amateurs. He took both the national lightweight and middleweight titles in 1907 and 1908 then went to the London Olympics of 1908 and took a silver medal at middleweight and the gold at lightweight, making him the only Brit to win two wrestling medals at a single games.

De Relwyskow Jr also wrestled as an amateur and a pro before being injured during the war on a parachuting mission for the SAS. After turning to promoting, he was one of several men who used the goodwill and credibility of the Mountevans rules to overturn bans on wrestling. In his case this involved successful appeals to the watch committees of Leeds and Sheffield. These agencies were forerunners to police authorities and were responsible for overseeing local law enforcement.

In the case of Sheffield, the acceptance of wrestling came with strings: officials demanded a strict ban on the headbutt (which was already technically illegal under Mountevans), back elbow and "the arm leveller over the top of the shoulder joint" (in effect the Jim Breaks special.) Kincaid recalls that this ban was only really enforced when watch committee members were on hand at shows and even then, wrestlers could usually get away with them so long as the referee instantly handed out a public warning. "It did help build up some of the moves, so you got more heat when you used them. But sometimes you just had to ignore it: there was no way Johnny Kwango was doing a match without a headbutt!"

The family connection continued with brother Douglas, best known as a referee. His son Barry later wrestled but, like many second- or third-generation performers in the UK, used an alias. He worked most commonly as Barry Douglas, but also donned a mask as Battle Star and Bull Blitzer.

Arthur Wright ran Wryton Promotions, based in Bolton but putting on shows across Lancashire and the surrounding area. Like the Lutteroths in Mexico City and Don Owen in Portland, he had the foresight to run his own arena, a converted cinema dubbed Wryton Stadium. The premises also included a gym where wrestlers trained or had try-outs, overseen by stars including Francis St Clair Gregory. (The stadium also played host to the 1969 World Snooker Championships.) Wright worked in cooperation with Billy Best, who ran wrestling at the prestigious Liverpool Stadium and Blackpool Tower Circus.

Conspicuous by its absence from the original shareholding was Dale Martin, a London-based collaboration of the Abbey brothers Billy, Jack and Johnny (each using Jack's wrestling surname of Dale) and businessman Les Martin. The group was already on good terms with the rest of the Joint crew, having been named alongside them a few years earlier as part of the less formal "British Promoters Association", but didn't formally sign up to Joint until 1953. Running across southern England, they proved to be a dominant member, putting on around half of all Joint's shows.

Officially the role of Joint was to be, in its own words "the authoritative wrestling control" and guardian of the Mountevans rules. It quickly declared itself responsible for recognising a single British champion in each of seven weight divisions, something that wasn't addressed in the rules itself but was a stated desire of the committee's report. With no formal independent body regulating the titles, the Mountevans championships remained exclusively on Joint-contracted wrestlers into the 1980s.

In the first couple of decades at least, the belts were mainly held by Northern-based grapplers, often with at least a credible background in legitimate wrestling. This appears partly to be for the sake of authenticity and partly because the belts were a draw in themselves, with ticket prices raised for title matches, so they may have been promotionally wasted on those box office stars who leaned more towards showmanship.

Less officially, Joint was about control of the wrestlers. Speaking to Simon Garfield, Max Crabtree argued the alliance had been necessary to combat unscrupulous grapplers who would accept multiple bookings on the same night and then simply turn up to whichever show provided the best combination of payday and easy travel.

Joint also worked as a more formalised territory system. While there were a few quirks such as Morrell promoting at Lime Grove in London and Wryton Promotions running shows in Cornwall (which perhaps not coincidentally was top star St Clair Gregory's family base), each promoter generally stuck to his own geographic area, minimising the risk of conflict.

There were exceptions to the usual cooperation. The infamous 1967 incident in which Peter Preston stopped cooperating with Mick McManus appears to have been instigated by Morrell, with the most logical explanation being disgruntlement that McManus's fame benefitted Dale Martin more than the northern promoters. On the flipside, Adrian Street believed he was ordered by Dale Martin to lose to the unknown Idra Musa on TV solely to harm his drawing power before heading north for an extended tour for Morrell. (In the event Street informed Musa that the finish had been changed, then claimed to have misheard the promoter's instructions.)

Despite its dominance in the public eye, Joint was by no means the only wrestling around. Indeed, rough estimates have it that as many independently promoted shows took place each year as those under the Joint banner. The relationship between Joint and the independents was more nuanced than the all-out rivalry of its US counterpart the NWA and America's "outlaw" promotions.

For example, Lancashire promoter Jack Atherton was on good terms with Joint Promotions and, while not a formal member, was at one stage listed as an "Associate." Meanwhile Ken Joyce's Deveraux Promotions was technically an independent, but had an arrangement allowing him to book Joint wrestlers if they had any spare dates on their schedule for the month.

With totally unaligned promoters it was a more mixed story. As a general principle it appeared Joint did not interfere with those who "knew their place" and stuck to venues and towns where Joint did not already have a presence (and showed no signs of doing so.) Those who tried to explicitly compete head-to-head with Joint found life more difficult, by fair means and foul.

The combination of promotional skill, the benefits of the Joint set-up and some positive breaks meant that those involved were thriving a decade into the project. An initial ITV airing in 1955 (just weeks after the channel launched) led to several runs before picking up a weekly slot in 1960. This morphed into twice-weekly shows year round from 1964, with a Saturday airing becoming a cornerstone of the World of Sport magazine program when it launched the following year.

Expansion was also aided by a government decision in 1957 to drop an entertainment tax which had previously levied 25% on ticket prices. By January 1963, business was so brisk that Joint ran 335 shows during the month. The schedule included 36 venues around the country which had a regular weekly show. In 1965, Dale Martin alone reported pre-tax profits of £100,000, equivalent to £1.8 million at today's prices.

While plenty of Joint's shows were at swimming baths and town halls, in many cities it ran the largest indoor facility, with large capacities including the Royal Albert Hall in London (5,500 capacity), Belle Vue's King's Hall in Manchester (5,000), Paisley Ice Rink (5,000), Liverpool Stadium (4,000), Nottingham Ice Stadium (approx. 3,000), Glasgow's Kelvin Hall (2,500) and the Colston Hall in Bristol (2,000).

With plenty of work to go about, the sheer administration of getting the right wrestlers in the right place was a significant task, particularly in an era before mobile telephones and e-mail. This responsibility fell to Joint's secretary Arthur Green, the business partner of George De Relwyskow. Green came into wrestling from the boxing world where his father Ben was a leading referee before being suspended after giving a particularly controversial decision.

Wrestlers generally fell into three categories. Many were part-timers who had a regular job during the day and worked only on shows near their home, known as a "tea-time job" because it was usually possible to eat before heading to the show. Some were full-timers who would work a wider circuit for a particular promoter.

Then there were the headliners who would work across the country, often on almost unbelievable schedules. Their bookings would be determined at a monthly Joint Promotions management meeting. Johnny Saint tells FSM that each wrestler would be made available for a fixed number of dates per promoter and that at each meeting "the promoters would rotate who got first pick. Whoever went first could choose a wrestler and have first choice on his dates and then the second promoter picked another wrestler and so on."

Once the dates had been assigned, wrestlers would receive a monthly date sheet in the post which listed their bookings and assigned promoter. In most cases they would be required to sign and return the sheet within a week to confirm the dates and would then get a second sheet through later which told them where they would actually be performing.

Eddie Hamill recalls that "You'd get a pink slip in the post if a date was cancelled. You could give notice if you had to miss a show and they were generally OK. If your car broke down on the night or something you had to phone in either to head office or the promoter. It was a pretty easy going setup: you just had to come, do your stuff and they'd give you the money."

To Marty Jones, the sheet was all important. "I'd get a date sheet from [Wryton office worker] Martin Conroy and then a separate one from Dale Martin. To be honest, I didn't worry about the politics and organisation: the monthly date sheet was all I cared about. If it was full, everything was good!"

Copies of the sheets which have been made available by wrestlers do serve as a reminder of the control Joint's promoters had over the performers. A 1946 sheet from Morrell notes that a wrestler was under an exclusive six month contract barring him from appearing for any other promoters in Yorkshire, the Northeast and Scotland, but that he was only guaranteed 24 dates during that period. By 1966, the Joint sheet informed wrestlers that by accepting the dates, they agreed not to wrestle for any non-Joint promoters without permission during the month in question and that they would need to give 14 days' notice to cancel any booking.

Johnny Kincaid recalls that the reality was a little stricter: "You had no control over the date sheets. If somebody knocked a few back, the promoters would slap his wrists and he wouldn't work for a month." That said, wrestler leverage would vary depending on the health of the independent circuit: Tony St Clair recalled he and his brother Roy successfully demanding a pay rise by threatening to give the 14 days' notice and then move over to work for Orig Williams.

Pay was certainly a controversial issue on both sides. Unlike in the US, British wrestlers generally received a fixed payoff per match regardless of the venue or the box office takings. While Kincaid notes wrestlers got an unexplained £2 bonus for working Colston Hall, generally the only exceptions to the usual wage were higher amounts paid for televised bouts and appearances at the Royal Albert Hall.

While Joint Promotion wrestlers had the security of a guaranteed payoff, many remained unhappy with the amount on offer, particularly when considering Joint's blooming business and the lack of leverage to play its members off against one another. On several occasions that led to attempts to unionise. In 1959 the "Professional Wrestlers Welfare Association" spearheaded by Jim Lewis managed to get all 10 wrestlers on a show at Seymour Hall in London to refuse to perform, only for promoters to quickly put together an entire replacement bill.

In 1962 the Wrestler's Alliance began negotiations for its members to join theatre union Variety. Joint's Johnny Dale publicly argued that this was farcical given that wrestling was sport rather than theatre, though in reality his objection seemed to be that Variety laid down a minimum fee of £30 for a television appearance, well in excess of what many wrestlers received at the time. While it appears some wrestlers joined the group, it doesn't appear they were able to get the increased TV payoffs and, according to Jackie Pallo, their membership was quickly terminated when Variety merged with the Equity union.

And in 1970 several Dale Martin wrestlers went on strike and picketed a show at Fairfield Halls. While promoters were again able to put together a replacement bill, the publicity did its job and, Adrian Street recalls, the wrestlers negotiated a £2 a match pay rise (having asked for £5) and a new minimum TV payment of £40 regardless of experience. Perhaps unsurprisingly this "minimum" also became a maximum in virtually every case.

Despite all the disgruntlement, the fixed pay and date sheet system made life a lot easier for wrestlers than negotiating the less predictable independent circuit. Dale Martin in particular earned praise for its organisation, with accommodation available near its Brixton head office (albeit at a price) and minibus transport laid on to shows rather than wrestlers having to drive. The promotion even set up its own printing business, producing all its promotional posters in house, along with a reported 21,000 programs each week, then taking on outside commissions with any spare capacity.

Pete Roberts tells FSM that "Dale Martin was the best set-up as far as I was concerned. With the other promoters you were somewhat on your own and really had to promote yourself. Aside from Paul Lincoln, it didn't seem that promoters actually promoted anything!

"But the first time I went to the Dale Martin office, Joe D'Orazio introduced himself as the head of publicity and took me straight off to get promotional pictures taken. That was all new to me."

Eddie Hamill recalls that the Dale Martin headquarters seemed to be a revolving door of former grapplers. "Everybody in the office was an ex-wrestler. You never knew who was in charge as it was different every week, but you'd never actually see the big boss."

Joint's original promoter line-up was largely made up of former wrestlers, with Les Martin and Arthur Green the most notable exceptions. Johnny Kincaid believes this was a benefit, noting that "It's like when a pub manager gets promoted to area manager. He's more sympathetic because he understands the problems of the job, but at the same time he's wise to all the little tricks."

Contrastingly Roberts notes that "ex-wrestlers didn't always make good promoters. They're all good when business is good! But in the 60s and early 70s you could just put eight Joe Schmoes on the bill and draw, it was that big. You really found out who the good promoters were when business went down."

The success of wrestling in the TV era inevitably drew the attention of outside interests and in 1964 Dale Martin agreed to a takeover offer from the Hurst Park Syndicate. The total purchase price was £225,000 (equivalent to £4.2 million today) made up of £165,000 in cash and the rest in Hurst shares.

Hurst was an organisation that had originally been based around operating a racecourse in Surrey. The previous year it had switched tack as betting began to move into the high street; it closed the course and bought 16 bookmaker shops owned by former boxing middleweight champion Terry Downes, making him a Hurst shareholder as part of the deal. With both the bookies and the wrestling groups, Hurst took a hands-off approach and left the existing management in day-to-day control.

The next big business move came at the end of 1965 when, after many years of battling as the leading independent, Paul Lincoln conceded defeat and agreed to sell out to Dale Martin. The two sides put their differences behind them to stage a promotional stunt on a live wrestling broadcast as stars such as Mike Marino stormed the Joint ring with mouthpiece Al Hayes asking why his crew had been kept off television. Although some venues ran Joint vs Independent themed shows, it didn't develop into a major TV storyline and instead Lincoln continued running pseudo-independent shows as a subsidiary of Hurst until the early 1970s.

As the decade rolled on, Hurst consolidated its involvement, buying out the Best/Wryton promotions and then Morrell & Beresford. This left only De Relwyskow & Green as Joint Promotions members still independently owned and operated, a situation that continued for the rest of the group's history.

Most accounts of the period relate that high-profile sports figure Jarvis Astaire bought Dale Martin and the other promotions from Hurst and then sold them to William Hill. However, media reports from the time suggest this may not have precisely the case.

Astaire had made his name behind the scenes in the boxing world, managing several boxers, bringing over Cassius Clay to fight Henry Cooper, and pioneering closed circuit television in British cinemas for big fights. He was also a business partner of manager and promoter Mickey Duff who, in one of wrestling's stranger trivia notes, was once listed in a WWF program as the federation's vice-president.

It appears Astaire's involvement in wrestling may have dated back to the original Hurst takeover: he was Terry Downe's manager at the time and was likely involved in the negotiations. A few months later Hurst launched closed circuit company Viewsport, which was very much Astaire's baby, suggesting he was likely a shareholder in Hurst at this point. (Several reports later simply referred to Hurst Park as his company.)

Indeed, newspaper coverage at the time specifically mentioned wrestling alongside boxing as the likely focus for Viewsport, and one theory has it that he masterminded the Dale Martin takeover with the hope of using wrestling as source of content in plans for early attempts at pay television on cable in London and Sheffield.

Among the Viewsport directors was Bill Abbey, the younger brother of Johnny & Jackie Dale. While he didn't have a wrestling background before Dale Martin's launch, having instead worked for insurers Prudential, it appears that his power within the wrestling group was greatly increased during the Hurst years at the expense of his brothers, something that went down poorly with some wrestlers.

Curiously, just a year after the takeover, Astaire worked with independent promoter Don Robinson to run the second of two 1965 wrestling shows aired on BBC 1. They were the first wrestling shows on the channel since a brief run either side of the war and proved to be the last.

However, the following year Astaire was working with rather than against Joint Promotions when Viewsport put together a closed circuit broadcast beaming a Royal Albert Hall show headlined by Ricki Starr vs Mick McManus live to 11 cinemas, some of which charged the equivalent of £25 at today's prices.

In February 1971, William Hill bought the entire Hurst Park Syndicate for £1.78 million (£24 million today). The purchase was primarily for the bookmaker shops (with the deal kickstarting its growth into a high street chain) but included golf centres and the wrestling promotions. Later that year William Hill itself was bought out by the Sears retail group, creating the somewhat unlikely situation that Dale Martin was technically a sister company of department store Selfridges and shoe chain Freeman, Hardy and Willis.

Joint Promotions

As part of the deal, Bill Abbey became a director in William Hill, while Jarvis Astaire was the overall manager of the wrestling operations, albeit in a very behind-the-scenes manner. Eddie Hamill recalls being invited to visit Astaire at his office, a rare meeting he assumed would involve some sort of promotion or news of an enhanced push. In fact he was there for the mother of all dressing downs with Astaire revealing he was aware of Hamill having worked an independent date without permission. "He informed me that should he hear I was working for them again, he would have no hesitation in sacking me for Joint Promotions and then I would be free to work for whomever I pleased."

Between retirement and the details of the various takeovers, the involvement of the original Joint Promoters appears to have declined heavily in the early 1970s, which coincides with the business itself taking a slide. Dale Martin's profits for the 1970 financial year were £61,668, down nearly 40 percent compared with five years earlier.

A 1975 TV Times report noted that average Saturday afternoon wrestling viewing figures had declined from 8.5 million to 7.5 million at a time when audiences for other World of Sport segments was on the rise. The article specifically addressed the problem of the likes of Mick McManus, Les Kellett, Bert Royal and Jackie Pallo continuing to headline after many years on top, along with an overemphasis on gimmicks.

Meanwhile fans of the era recall falling attendances may have been linked to the loss of the veteran promoters' attention to detail, such as making sure to always have a full and logical card to announce for the return to a venue, then making sure to deliver it. Behind the scenes the increased business operations role of MC and non-wrestler Mike Judd caused further unrest and was cited by Jackie Pallo as one of the reasons he quit Joint Promotions. (Judd later left his position amid controversial circumstances.)

Pallo started his own promotion and soon found himself at the sharp end of Joint's desire for control. He claims he almost wound up with help from two unlikely sources: long-time opposition promoter Max Crabtree and an out-in-the-cold Johnny Dale. In the event, Dale was unable to proceed thanks to ill health, while Crabtree accepted a job with Joint Promotions.

Publicly acknowledged as Joint's managing director in 1975, Crabtree's initial role was to take over operations in the northern venues. Down at Dale Martin, long-time booker Mick McManus was replaced with Mike Marino, who was charged with addressing the problems of stale talent. The problem was that he went too far in the opposite direction: while he pushed some highly skilled fresh faces such as Mal Sanders (given a rare high-profile win over McManus) and Steve Grey, bills quickly became filled with inexperienced and largely unknown wrestlers.

With that experiment over, in 1977 Crabtree took control of both day to day operations and matchmaking across the country, with the Dale Martin and Joint Promotions brand names often being treated as interchangeable. (De Relwyskow and Green venues remained the exception.) It began the final era in the Joint Promotions story and arguably its most controversial.

In the ring, most of the next decade was built around two main in-ring themes. Firstly the increasing push of Crabtree's brother Shirley as Big Daddy, including lengthy feuds with John Quinn and Giant Haystacks and then a parade of outlandish villains managed by Charlie McGee. Secondly, Crabtree created a world heavyweight title battled over by Quinn and Wayne Bridges among others.

There's little dispute that what Max Crabtree did, he did very well, and that initially he revived a slumping business. According to Johnny Saint, when it came to matchmaking he was "a shrewd, astute fellow. He had the ability to know that Tom whoever vs Dick whoever would be an electric match."

On the other hand, wrestlers were not impressed by the change in the business model. While shows featuring Daddy consistently drew well (to the point that independent bookers who hired out Daddy on a Saturday would have to hand over 50 percent of their profits), the combination of putting all the promotional eggs in one basket and an economic recession meant there was less work to go round. While Joint ran three successful supershows at the 10,000 seat Wembley Arena, it stopped running regular venues such as the Royal Albert Hall and Belle Vue during Daddy's peak.

In 1983, an independently produced Sportsviewers Guide to Wrestling reported around 1,200 shows took place each year, noting it was "considerably less than five or ten years ago"; indeed, it was down around two-thirds from the 1960s peak. This trend likely didn't come as a surprise to Crabtree. Johnny Kincaid recalls returning from a foreign tour to find that under the new regime "If your face didn't fit, you didn't get booked. You had to be up his arse to get work. I only had about five jobs for the whole month and he told me he can't guarantee work and that 'There's no such thing as full time wrestlers now.'"

Pete Roberts believes that the decision of who felt the brunt of the contraction wasn't necessarily based on business. "Look at Steve Veidor: all of a sudden no one used him. He was one of the biggest babyface names in the south and you can't say he didn't draw big houses, but he was pushed by the wayside."

The lack of job security, and the breakdown of the unspoken pact that if you committed yourself to Joint, you could make a full-time living, proved a benefit to rival promoters such as Brian Dixon's All Star Wrestling. At the start of the 80s he was able to recruit several key performers based simply on offering hefty pay increases. By the middle of the decade, other Joint wrestlers were able to work for both sides without issue as Crabtree could no longer credibly enforce the exclusivity rules.

Between the deliberate shift to a more child-focused product in the ring and the ongoing unease of a bookmaker being involved in a "bent" business, William Hill decided it was time to sell up and Crabtree bought the promotion in the mid-80s. It proved a poorly timed purchase as a succession of minor scandals hit the business: Jackie Pallo and Tony 'Banger' Walsh both went public with revelations about how matches operated, while the tragic death of Mal Kirk in a match with Big Daddy prompted a negative response when Daddy insisted to newspapers that "Nothing is fixed in wrestling and this move had not been arranged beforehand".

Joint even lost its prize jewel: the exclusive rights to air on ITV. From the start of 1987, several slots were instead assigned to All Star Wrestling, which had a more action-packed and attention-grabbing content, and tapes of WWF programming, which had a production quality and big-time feel light years ahead of the British product. At the end of 1988 British wrestling departed ITV, axed by boss Greg Dyke who believed it represented an outdated working class audience that didn't appeal to advertisers. By the time the axe fell -- and admittedly with a little help from some bafflingly inconsistent scheduling -- viewing figures had fallen to an average of four million, half the figure in 1970s.

Even with the introduction of multi-channel satellite television, Crabtree was unable to find a new television outlet: having come from a world where ITV paid thousands of pounds in rights fees and took care of the production, Joint simply couldn't compete in the new world where stations could buy in tapes of already-produced US shows at rock bottom prices.

Joint responding by switching almost its entire focus to what was dubbed by some as the "Daddy roadshow": a series of one-off dates in every town on the map built entirely around the opportunity to see the former TV superstar, with little effort put into building up return visits. Inevitably that had a limited shelf life and Dale Martin was formally dissolved on 22 October 1991, with Joint Promotions Ltd following on 3 November 1992, just over 40 years after its creation.

Crabtree rebranded as Ring Wrestling Stars and got one more year out of Daddy before he was forced into retirement through ill health. He then repeated the strategy using Davey Boy Smith who found himself out of work in the US just 18 months after headlining at Wembley Stadium (whose board of directors included one Jarvis Astaire.) When Smith signed with WWE, the game was up, and Crabtree pulled out of the business within a few months.

That wasn't technically the end of the Joint Promotions legacy however. Following George De Relwyskow's death, his daughter Anne took over the promotion and continued running shows in Yorkshire until dissolving Relwyskow

Promotions in 1992. She then operated Wrestling Superstars Limited until 30 April 1996.

In 2003, she moved out of the long-time Relwyskow family home and decided to clear out the cellar and dispose of three generations of wrestling paperwork, photos and memorabilia. Wrestler Darren Ward, a keen historian, bought the entire collection, which made up several carloads of material. It now forms a major part of Darren's collection which serves as the primary picture archive for FSM's Greetings Grapple Fans series.

# By The Same Author

## Turning The Tables: The Story of Extreme Championship Wrestling

ECW was the upstart promotion that revolutionised the wrestling industry. Turning The Tables is the first published history of the company that grew from a run-down bingo hall to become a national pay-per-view competitor... then crashed in a sea of debt.

John Lister gives an independent, objective and informative account that reveals hidden secrets and shatters common myths. From a little-known truth about ECW's most famous feud to a blow-by-blow account of what really happened in Revere, this book will give you the true story behind America's most controversial wrestling group.

(www.turningthetables.co.uk)

## Slamthology: Collected Wrestling Writings 1991-2004

John Lister is one of Britain's most respected wrestling journalists. Mixing travelogue, humour, fiction, history and opinion, this collection brings together the best of his work from the past fourteen years.

The first section of this book features three epic accounts of voyages to see wrestling in the United States, from the ECW Arena to the Dallas Sportatorium by way of WWF pay-per-views and Memphis television.

The second section comprises more than 40 articles, some previously unpublished, including histories of British and American wrestling, the statistics behind WCW's collapse, and a disgraceful allegation about Tommy Rich.

(www.slamthology.co.uk)

**Purodyssey: A Tokyo Wrestling Diary**

Twenty years after his first voyages to watch wrestling abroad, writer John Lister finally made it to Tokyo. Purodyssey shares the experience of seeing 14 shows from 11 promotions in just eight days, visiting venues from the Tokyo Dome to a converted pharmacy. It also details encountering Japanese culture in person for the first time.

The book also includes a comprehensive yet concise guide to the practicalities of visiting Tokyo for wrestling, including ticket buying, transport and key Japanese phrases.

If you're a fan of wrestling books, you may also enjoy my blog www.prowrestlingbooks.com which has reviews of more than 150 books as well as regular updates on forthcoming releases.

Made in the USA
Lexington, KY
04 September 2018